ACTUARIAL SCIENCE

Theory and Methodology

ACTUARIAL SCIENCE

Theory and Methodology

editor

Hanji Shang

Fudan University, China

高等教育出版社
HIGHER EDUCATION PRESS

World Scientific

NEW JERSEY · LONDON · SINGAPORE · BEIJING · SHANGHAI · HONG KONG · TAIPEI · CHENNAI

图书在版编目 (CIP) 数据

精算学：理论与方法 = *Actuarial Science: Theory and Methodology* / 尚汉冀 (Shang, Hanji) 主编.
— 北京：高等教育出版社, 2006.4
ISBN 7-04-019232-2

I. 精… II. 尚… III. 精算学—英文 IV. F224.0

中国版本图书馆 CIP 数据核字 (2006) 第022967号

World Scientific Publishing Co. Pte. Ltd.
5 Toh Tuck Link, Singapore 596224
USA office: 27 Warren Street, Suite 401-402, Hackensack, NJ 07601
UK office: 57 Shelton Street, Covent Garden, London WC2H 9HE

ISBN-13 978-981-256-505-1
ISBN-10 981-256-505-1

Preface

Since actuarial education was introduced into China in 1980s, more and more attention have been paid to the theoretical and practical research of actuarial science in China.

In 1998, the National Natural Science Foundation of China approved a 1 million Yuan RMB financial support to a key project ≪Insurance Information Processing and Actuarial Mathematics Theory & Methodology≫ (project 19831020), which is the first key project on actuarial science supported by the government of China. From 1999 to 2003, professors and experts from Fudan University, Peking University, Institute of Software of Academia Sinica, East China Normal University, Shanghai University of Finance and Economics, Shanghai University and Jinan University worked together for this project, and achieved important successes in their research work. In a sense, this book is a summation of what they had achieved.

The book consists of seven chapters. Chapter 1 mainly presents the major results about ruin probabilities, the distribution of surplus before and after ruin for a compound Poisson model with a constant premium rate and a constant interest rate. This chapter also gives asymptotic formulas of the low and upper bounds for the distribution of the surplus immediately after ruin under subexponential claims. Chapter 2 introduces some recent results on compound risk models and copula decomposition. For the compound risk models, it includes the recursive evaluation of compound risk models on mixed type severity distribution in one-dimensional case, the bivariate recursive equation on excess-of-loss reinsurance, and the approximation to total loss of homogeneous individual risk model by a compound Poisson random variable. On the copula decomposition, the uniqueness of bivariate copula convex decomposition is proved, while the coefficient of the terms in the decomposition equation is given.

Chapter 3 is concerned with distortion premium principles and some related topics. Apart from the characterization of a distortion premium principle, this chapter also examines the additivities involved in premium pricing and reveals the relationship among the three types of additivities. Furthermore, reduction of distortion premium to standard deviation principle for certain distribution families is investigated. In addition, ordering problem for real-valued risks (beyond the nonnegative risks) is addressed, which suggests that it is more reasonable to order risks in the dual theory than the original theory.

Chapter 4 illustrates the application of fuzzy mathematics in evaluating and analyzing risks for insurance industry. As an example, fuzzy comprehensive evaluation is used to evaluate the risk of suffering from diseases related to better living conditions. Fuzzy information processing (including information distribution and information diffusion) is introduced in this chapter and plays an important role in dealing with the small sample problem. Chapter 5 presents some basic definitions and principles of Fuzzy Set Theory and the fuzzy tools and techniques applied to actuarial science and insurance practice. The fields of application involve insurance game, insurance decision, etc. Chapter 6 is concerned with some applications of financial economics to actuarial mathematics, especially to life insurance and pension. Combining financial economics, actuarial mathematics with partial differential equation, a general framework has been established to study the mathematical model of the fair valuation of life insurance policy or pension. In particular, analytic solutions and numerical results have been obtained for various life insurance policies and pension plans. Chapter 7 provides a working framework for exploring the risk profile and risk assessment of China insurance. It is for the regulatory objective of building a risk-oriented supervision system based on China insurance market profile and consistent to the international development of solvency supervision.

The authors of various chapters of this book are: Professor Rongming Wang of East China Normal University (Chapter 1), Dr. Jingping Yang of Peking University (Chapter 2), Dr. Xianyi Wu of East China Normal University, Dr. Xian Zhou of Hong Kong University and Professor Jinglong Wang of East China Normal University (Chapter 3), Professor Hanji Shang of Fudan University (Chapter 4), Professor Yuchu Lu of Shanghai University (Chapter 5), Professor Weixi Shen of Fudan University (Chapter 6) and Professor Zhigang Xie of Shanghai University of Finance & Economics (Chapter 7). As the editor, I am most grateful to all authors for their cooperation. I would like to thank Professor Tatsien Li, Professor Zhongqin

Xu and Professor Wenling Zhang. Their support is very important to our research work and to the publication of this book. I also thank Mr. Hao Wang for his effective work in editing the book.

Hanji Shang
Fudan University, China

Contents

Chapter 1

Risk Models and Ruin Theory

Three particular questions of interest in classical ruin theory are (a) *the time of ruin*, (b) *the deficit at ruin*, and (c) *the surplus immediately before ruin*. From a mathematical point of view, a crucial role is played by the amounts of surplus before and after ruin. In this chapter we mainly present the major results about ruin probabilities, the distribution of surplus before and after ruin for a compound Poisson model with a constant premium rate and a constant interest rate. The compound Poisson risk process with a constant interest force is an interesting stochastic model in risk theory and it provides a basic understanding about how investments will affect the ruin probability and related ruin functions. At first, we provide some results on the severity of ruin for a compound Poisson model with a constant interest rate. Then, we investigate the distribution of surplus process immediately before ruin in particular. Equations satisfied by the distributions of surplus immediately before ruin and their Laplace transform are given. Some special cases are also discussed and Lundberg type bounds are presented. Next, by using the techniques of [Kalashnikov and Konstantinides(2000)] and a formula obtained by [Yang and Zhang (2001a)], we give asymptotic formulas of the low and upper bounds for the distribution of the surplus immediately after ruin under subexponential claims. Finally, a class of risk processes in which claims occur as a renewal process is studied. A clear expression for Laplace transform of the finite time ruin probability time is well given when the claim amount distribution is a mixed exponential. As its consequence, a well-known result about ultimate ruin probability in the classical risk model is obtained. All results in Sections 1 and 2 of this chapter are from [Yang and Zhang (2001a)] and [Yang and Zhang (2001b)]. The main results in Sections 3 and 4 are from [Wang *et. al.* (2004)] and [Wang and Liu(2002)].

1.1 On the Distribution of Surplus Immediately after Ruin under Interest Force

In this section, we consider the problem of the severity of ruin for a compound Poisson model with a constant interest rate. By using the techniques of [Sundt and Teugels (1995)], equations satisfied by the distributions of surplus immediately after ruin have been obtained. Some special cases are also discussed. Some results on the severity of ruin given in this section are similar to those in [Sundt and Teugels (1995)] on ruin probability.

1.1.1 *The Risk Model*

We use the same model as in [Sundt and Teugels (1995)]. Let $U_\delta(t)$ denote the value of the reserve at time t. $U_\delta(t)$ is given by

$$dU_\delta(t) = p\,dt + U_\delta(t)\;\delta\,dt - dX(t),$$

where p is a constant which denotes the premium rate that the insurance company receives and δ is the interest force,

$$X(t) = \sum_{j=1}^{N(t)} Y_j\;,$$

where $N(t)$ denotes the number of claims occurring in an insurance portfolio in the time interval $(0, t]$ and Y_i denotes the amount of the ith claim. We assume that $\{N(t), t \geqslant 0\}$ is a homogeneous Poisson process with intensity λ, and $N(t)$ and Y_j are two independent processes. We further assume that Y_j (j = 1, 2, ...) are positive and mutually independent and $\{Y_j\}$ is an identically distributed random sequence with common distribution F. We also assume that $F(0) = 0$ and $\mu_k = \int_0^\infty x^k dF(x)$. When $k = 1$, we denote $\mu = \mu_1$.

It follows from [Sundt and Teugels (1995)] that

$$U_\delta(t) = u\,e^{\delta t} + p\bar{s}_{\overline{t}|}^{(\delta)} - \int_0^t e^{\delta(t-v)} dX(v)\;,$$

where $u = U(0) \geqslant 0$ and

$$\bar{s}_{\overline{t}|}^{(\delta)} = \int_0^t e^{\delta v} dv = \begin{cases} t, & \text{if } \delta = 0, \\ \frac{e^{\delta t}-1}{\delta}, & \text{if } \delta > 0. \end{cases}$$

For convenience, we will drop the index δ when the force of interest is zero.

Let $\psi_\delta(u)$ denote the ultimate ruin probability with initial reserve u. That is

$$\psi_\delta(u) = P\left\{ \bigcup_{t\geqslant 0}(U_\delta(t) < 0) \,\Big|\, U_\delta(0) = u \right\}.$$

We use $\bar{\psi}_\delta(u) = 1 - \psi_\delta(u)$ to denote the non-ruin probability (i.e. the probability that ruin never occurs).

It follows immediately from [Sundt and Teugels (1995)] that the integral equation is satisfied

$$\bar{\psi}_\delta(u) = \frac{p}{p+\delta u}\bar{\psi}_\delta(0) + \frac{1}{p+\delta u}\int_0^u \bar{\psi}_\delta(u-y)\{\delta + \lambda(1-F(y))\}dy. \quad (1.1)$$

Next, we are interested in the function $G_\delta(u,y)$, representing the probability of ruin beginning with initial reserve u and that the deficit at the time of ruin is less than $y > 0$.

$$G_\delta(u,y) = \Pr\left(T < \infty, -y < U_\delta(T) < 0 \,\Big|\, U_\delta(0) = u\right),$$

where T is the ruin time defined by

$$T = \inf\{t \geqslant 0 : U_\delta(t) < 0\}.$$

It is easy to see that $\psi_\delta(u) = \lim\limits_{y\to+\infty} G_\delta(u,y)$.

For notational convenience, we define

$$\begin{aligned} \bar{G}_\delta(u,y) &= \psi_\delta(u) - G_\delta(u,y) \\ &= P\left(T < \infty, U_\delta(T) \leqslant -y \,\Big|\, U_\delta(0) = u\right), \\ \bar{\bar{G}}_\delta(u,y) &= 1 - \bar{G}_\delta(u,y). \end{aligned}$$

1.1.2 *Equations for $\bar{\bar{G}}_\delta(u,y)$*

1.1.2.1 *Integral Equations for $\bar{\bar{G}}_\delta(u,y)$, $\bar{G}_\delta(u,y)$ and $G_\delta(u,y)$*

In this subsection, we will try to obtain integral equations for $\bar{\bar{G}}_\delta(u,y)$, $\bar{G}_\delta(u,y)$ and $G_\delta(u,y)$. Using the renewal property of the surplus process, an integral equation, satisfied by the function which we are interested in, can be obtained. This is a commonly used technique in risk theory. Although we cannot, in general, solve the integral equation, some asymptotic results can often be obtained by using the integral equation. The main result of this subsection is given in the following theorem.

Theorem 1.1

$$\bar{\bar{G}}_\delta(u,y) = \frac{p}{p+\delta u}\bar{\bar{G}}_\delta(0,y) + \frac{1}{p+\delta u}\int_0^u \bar{\bar{G}}_\delta(u-z,y)[\delta+\lambda(1-F(z))]dz$$
$$+\frac{\lambda}{p+\delta u}\int_0^y (F(z)-F(u+z))dz, \tag{1.2}$$

$$\bar{G}_\delta(u,y) = \frac{p}{p+\delta u}\bar{G}_\delta(0,y) + \frac{1}{p+\delta u}\int_0^u \bar{G}_\delta(u-z,y)[\delta+\lambda(1-F(z))]dz$$
$$-\frac{\lambda}{p+\delta u}\int_0^u (1-F(z))dz - \frac{\lambda}{p+\delta u}\int_0^y (F(z)-F(u+z))dz, \tag{1.3}$$

$$G_\delta(u,y) = \frac{p}{p+\delta u}G_\delta(0,y) + \frac{1}{p+\delta u}\int_0^u G_\delta(u-z,y)[\delta+\lambda(1-F(z))]dz$$
$$+\frac{\lambda}{p+\delta u}\int_0^y (F(z)-F(u+z))dz. \tag{1.4}$$

Proof. The proof goes along the lines of page 10 of [Sundt and Teugels (1995)]. We only present the main steps of the proof. Notice that, given the first claim time $T_1 = t$ and the first claim amount $Y_1 = z$, the reserve just after the first claim is $ue^{\delta t} + p\cdot\frac{e^{\delta t}-1}{\delta} - z$. Therefore

$$\bar{\bar{G}}_\delta(u,y) = E[\bar{\bar{G}}_\delta(ue^{\delta T_1} + p\frac{e^{\delta T_1}-1}{\delta} - Y_1, y)]$$
$$= \int_0^{+\infty} \lambda e^{-\lambda t}\int_{(0,ue^{\delta t}+p\frac{e^{\delta t}-1}{\delta}+y)} \bar{\bar{G}}_\delta(ue^{\delta t}+p\frac{e^{\delta t}-1}{\delta} - z, y)$$
$$dF(z)dt$$
$$= \lambda(p+\delta u)^{\frac{\lambda}{\delta}}\int_u^{+\infty}(p+\delta s)^{-\frac{\lambda}{\delta}-1}\int_0^{s+y}\bar{\bar{G}}_\delta(s-z,y)dF(z)ds,$$

where the last equality is obtained by using the substitution

$$s = ue^{\delta t} + p\frac{e^{\delta t}-1}{\delta}.$$

By taking partial derivative of the above expression with respect to u, and rearrange the terms, we have

$$(p+\delta u)\frac{\partial}{\partial u}\bar{\bar{G}}_\delta(u,y) = \lambda\bar{\bar{G}}_\delta(u,y) - \lambda\int_0^{u+y}\bar{\bar{G}}_\delta(u-z,y)dF(z). \tag{1.5}$$

By integrating both sides of (1.5) from 0 to u, we have that the left hand side of (1.5) equals

$$(p+\delta u)\overline{\overline{G}}_\delta(u,y) - p\,\overline{\overline{G}}_\delta(0,y) - \delta\int_0^u \overline{\overline{G}}_\delta(v,y)dv$$

and the right hand side of (1.5) equals

$$\lambda\int_0^u \overline{\overline{G}}_\delta(v,y)dv + \lambda\int_0^u\int_0^{v+y} \overline{\overline{G}}_\delta(v-z,y)d(1-F(z))dv. \quad (1.6)$$

After some calculation and rearrangement of the terms, the second term of the right hand side of (1.6) equals

$$\begin{aligned}&-\lambda\int_0^u \overline{\overline{G}}_\delta(v,y)dv + \lambda\int_0^u (1-F(z))\overline{\overline{G}}_\delta(u-z,y)dz\\&+\lambda\int_0^y \overline{\overline{G}}_\delta(-z,y)(F(z)-F(u+z))dz.\end{aligned}$$

So we have

$$\begin{aligned}&(p+\delta u)\overline{\overline{G}}_\delta(u,y) - p\,\overline{\overline{G}}_\delta(0,y) - \delta\int_0^u \overline{\overline{G}}_\delta(v,y)dv\\&=\lambda\int_0^u \overline{\overline{G}}_\delta(v,y)dv - \lambda\int_0^u \overline{\overline{G}}_\delta(v,y)dv\\&\quad+\lambda\int_0^u (1-F(z))\overline{\overline{G}}_\delta(u-z,y)dz\\&\quad+\lambda\int_0^y \overline{\overline{G}}_\delta(-z,y)(F(z)-F(u+z))dz.\end{aligned}$$

Therefore,

$$\begin{aligned}\overline{\overline{G}}_\delta(u,y) &= \frac{p}{p+\delta u}\overline{\overline{G}}_\delta(0,y)\\&\quad+\frac{1}{p+\delta u}\int_0^u \overline{\overline{G}}_\delta(u-z,y)\big(\delta+\lambda(1-F(z))\big)dz\\&\quad+\frac{\lambda}{p+\delta u}\int_0^y \overline{\overline{G}}_\delta(-z,y)(F(z)-F(u+z))dz.\end{aligned}$$

By the definition of $\overline{\overline{G}}_\delta(u,y)$, we know that

$$\overline{\overline{G}}_\delta(-z,y) = 1 \quad \text{for all} \quad z\in(0,y).$$

Based on this, we obtain Equation (1.2). Equations (1.3) and (1.4) can be obtained from Equations (1.1) and (1.2). □

1.1.2.2 *The Case $\delta = 0$*

Denote the equilibrium distribution of F by F_1, which is defined by

$$F_1(x) = \frac{1}{\mu}\int_0^x (1 - F(v))dv.$$

Let $\nu_k = \int_0^\infty x^k dF_1(x)$ be the moments of the equilibrium distribution. From [Sundt and Teugels (1995)], we know that

$$\nu_k = \frac{1}{k+1} \cdot \frac{\mu_{k+1}}{\mu}.$$

Suppose the Laplace transforms of F_1 are given by

$$\phi(s) = \int_0^{+\infty} e^{-su} dF_1(u) = \phi_0(s),$$

$$\phi_y(s) = \int_y^{+\infty} e^{-su} dF_1(u).$$

The following result generalizes the asymptotic result for the probability of ruin, as given in [Grandell (1991)], to the case where the severity of ruin is taken into account.

Theorem 1.2 *Assume that the net profit condition $\lambda\mu < p$ is true and that there exists a positive constant R, called adjustment coefficient, such that*

$$\frac{\lambda}{p}\int_0^{+\infty} e^{Rz}(1 - F(z))dz = 1. \tag{1.7}$$

Then, for $u \to +\infty$ we have that

$$G(u, y) \sim \frac{1 - e^{-Ry}\int_y^{+\infty} \frac{\lambda}{p} e^{Rz}(1 - F(z))dz - \frac{\lambda\mu}{p} F_1(y)}{\frac{\lambda}{p}(-\phi'(-R) - \frac{p}{\lambda})} e^{-Ru}. \tag{1.8}$$

Proof. The proof here is similar to that in [Grandell (1991)] for the ruin probability case. When $\delta = 0$, (1.4) becomes

$$G(u, y) = G(0, y) + \frac{\lambda}{p}\int_0^u G(u - z, y)(1 - F(z))dz$$
$$+\frac{\lambda}{p}\int_0^y (F(z) - F(u + z))dz. \tag{1.9}$$

Since $\int_0^{+\infty} \frac{\lambda}{p}(1 - F(z))dz = \frac{\lambda\mu}{p} = m < 1$, equation (1.9) is a defective renewal equation. From equation (1.7), we know that $\frac{\lambda}{p} e^{Rz}(1 - F(z))$ is the density of a proper probability distribution. Multiplication of (1.9) by e^{Ru} yields

$$e^{Ru}G(u,y) = e^{Ru}G(0,y) + \int_0^u G(u-z,y)e^{R(u-z)}\frac{\lambda e^{Rz}}{p}(1-F(z))dz$$
$$+\frac{\lambda}{p}e^{Ru}\int_0^y (F(z)-F(u+z))dz,$$

which is a proper renewal equation. From the key renewal theorem, it follows that

$$\lim_{u\to\infty} e^{Ru}G(u,y) = \frac{c_1(y)}{c_2(y)},$$

where

$$c_1(y) = \int_0^{+\infty}\Big(e^{Ru}G(0,y) + \frac{\lambda}{p}e^{Ru}\int_0^y (F(z)-F(u+z))dz\Big)du, \tag{1.10}$$

$$\begin{aligned} c_2(y) &= \frac{\lambda}{p}\int_0^{+\infty} z\, e^{Rz}(1-F(z))dz \\ &= \frac{\lambda}{p}\cdot\frac{1}{R}(-\phi'(-R)-p/\lambda). \end{aligned} \tag{1.11}$$

From [Willmot and Lin (1998)], we know that

$$G(0,y) = \frac{\lambda\mu}{p}F_1(y) = \frac{\lambda}{p}\int_0^y (1-F(z))dz.$$

Plugging this expression of $G(0,y)$ into (1.10), we have

$$\begin{aligned} c_1(y) &= \int_0^{+\infty}\frac{\lambda}{p}e^{Ru}\Big(\int_0^y (1-F(u+z))dz\Big)du \\ &= \int_y^{+\infty}\frac{\lambda}{p}\int_{z-y}^{z} e^{Ru}(1-F(z))du\,dz + \int_0^y\frac{\lambda}{p}\int_0^z e^{Ru}(1-F(z))du\,dz \\ &= \frac{1}{R}[1-e^{-Ry}\int_y^{+\infty}\frac{\lambda}{p}(1-F(z))\cdot e^{Rz}dz] - \frac{\lambda\mu}{pR}F_1(y). \end{aligned}$$

From this and (1.11), we obtain (1.8). □

Remark 1.1 *Theorem 1.2 shows that $G(u,y)$ converges to zero at an exponential rate when the initial surplus becomes large. This is the same* *as in the case for ruin probability. If we let $y \to +\infty$, we have, for u sufficiently large,*

$$\lim_{y\to\infty} G(u,y) = \psi(u) \sim \frac{1-\frac{\lambda\mu}{p}}{\frac{\lambda}{p}(-\phi'(-R)-\frac{p}{\lambda})}\, e^{-Ru}.$$

This gives the same result as in [Grandell (1991)].

Remark 1.2 *Following [Sundt and Teugels (1995)], if we introduce the auxiliary distribution*

$$B_\delta(u,y) = \frac{\bar{\bar{G}}_\delta\,(u,y) - \bar{\bar{G}}_\delta\,(0,y)}{1 - \bar{\bar{G}}_\delta\,(0,y)},$$

the integral equation satisfied by B_δ can be obtained from (1.2). Following the exact same steps as those in [Sundt and Teugels (1995)], we can obtain a solution for the Laplace transform of B_δ.

Remark 1.3 *Similar to [Sundt and Teugels (1995)], we can also obtain the following expression for $\bar{\bar{G}}_\delta\,(0,y)$:*

$$\bar{\bar{G}}_\delta\,(0,y) = 1 - \lambda\mu\Big(p\int_0^{+\infty} e^{-\int_0^z (p-\lambda\mu\phi(\delta w))dw}dz\Big)^{-1} \cdot\Big(\int_0^{+\infty} e^{\delta z y}\phi_y(\delta z)e^{-\int_0^z (p-\lambda\mu\phi(\delta w))dw}dz\Big). \qquad (1.12)$$

1.1.3 *Upper and Lower Bounds for $\bar{G}_\delta(0,y)$*

Equation (1.12) provides an expression for $\bar{\bar{G}}_\delta\,(0,y)$. However, the expression is complex and difficult to compute. Similar to the case of ruin probability, in many situations, we do not need the exact value of $\bar{\bar{G}}_\delta\,(0,y)$. An upper or lower (or both) bound will be sufficient. In this subsection, we provide both upper and lower bounds for $\bar{G}_\delta(0,y)$. The main result of this subsection is the following theorem.

Theorem 1.3

$$p^{-1}(p-\lambda\mu)\Big[\sqrt{\frac{\lambda\mu}{\nu_1\delta}}\Big(1-F_1(y)+\sqrt{\frac{\nu_1^2\delta}{\lambda\mu\nu_1}}\beta\Big)R(\beta) - \frac{\nu_1}{\nu_1}e^{\frac{\beta^2}{2}}\Big]$$
$$\leqslant \bar{G}_\delta(0,y) \leqslant \frac{(1-F_1(y))\lambda\mu}{(p-\lambda\mu)\Big[R(\alpha)\cdot p\sqrt{\frac{1}{\lambda\mu\delta\nu_1}}\Big]}, \qquad (1.13)$$

where $R(\alpha)$ is the well known Mills' ratio, that is

$$R(\alpha) = e^{\frac{\alpha^2}{2}} \int_{\alpha}^{+\infty} e^{-\frac{x^2}{2}} dx$$

and $\alpha = \frac{\lambda\mu - p}{\sqrt{\lambda\mu\delta\nu_1}}$, $\phi_y'(0) = \int_y^{+\infty} x\, dF_1(x) = \underline{\nu_1}$.

Proof. Put

$$\begin{aligned} A_1 &= 1 + \int_0^{+\infty} \lambda\mu\phi(\delta z) e^{\int_0^z (\lambda\mu\phi(\delta w) - p) dw} dz \\ &\leqslant 1 + \int_0^{+\infty} \lambda\mu e^{\int_0^z (\lambda\mu - p) dw} dz = \frac{p}{p - \lambda\mu}, \end{aligned}$$

where the inequality holds because $\phi(s)$ is a strictly decreasing convex function. On the other hand,

$$\begin{aligned} A_1 &= p \int_0^{+\infty} e^{-\int_0^z (p - \lambda\mu\phi(\delta w)) dw} dz \\ &\geqslant p \int_0^{+\infty} e^{\int_0^z (\lambda\mu(1 - \nu_1 \delta w) - p) dw} dz = p \int_0^{+\infty} e^{-\frac{(z - \frac{p - \lambda\mu}{\lambda\mu\delta\nu_1})^2}{2\frac{1}{\lambda\mu\delta\nu_1}}} \cdot e^{\frac{(p-\lambda\mu)^2}{2\lambda\mu\delta\nu_1}} dz. \end{aligned}$$

Using the substitution

$$x = \frac{z - \frac{p - \lambda\mu}{\nu_1 \delta\lambda\mu}}{\sqrt{\frac{1}{\nu_1\delta\lambda\mu}}} = \frac{z}{\sqrt{\frac{1}{\lambda\mu\delta\nu_1}}} + \alpha,$$

we have

$$\begin{aligned} A_1 &\geqslant p \int_{\alpha}^{+\infty} e^{-\frac{x^2}{2}} \cdot e^{\frac{\alpha}{2}} \cdot \sqrt{\frac{1}{\lambda\mu\delta\nu_1}} dx = p\sqrt{\frac{1}{\lambda\mu\delta\nu_1}} e^{\frac{\alpha^2}{2}} \int_{\alpha}^{+\infty} e^{-\frac{x^2}{2}} dx \\ &= p\sqrt{\frac{1}{\lambda\mu\delta\nu_1}} R(\alpha). \end{aligned}$$

Therefore,

$$p\sqrt{\frac{1}{\lambda\mu\delta\nu_1}} \cdot R(\alpha) \leqslant A_1 \leqslant \frac{p}{p - \lambda\mu}.$$

Put

$$\begin{aligned} A_2 &= \int_0^{+\infty} e^{\delta z y} \phi_y(z\delta) e^{\int_0^z (\lambda\mu\phi(\delta w) - p) dw} dz \\ &\leqslant \int_0^{+\infty} \Big(\int_0^{+\infty} dF_1(y + s) \Big) e^{(\lambda\mu - p) z} dz = \frac{1 - F_1(y)}{p - \lambda\mu}, \end{aligned}$$

where the inequality holds because $\phi_y(s)$ is a strictly decreasing convex function. On the other hand,

$$\begin{aligned}
A_2 &= \int_0^{+\infty} e^{\delta zy}\phi_y(z\delta)e^{\int_0^z(\lambda\mu\phi(\delta w)-p)dw}dz \\
&\geqslant \int_0^{+\infty} e^{\delta yz}(1-F_1(y)-\underline{\nu_1}z\delta)e^{-\nu_1\delta\lambda\mu\frac{z^2}{2}-pz+\lambda\mu z}dz \\
&= \int_0^{+\infty}(1-F_1(y)-\underline{\nu_1}z\delta)e^{-\frac{(z-\frac{p-\lambda\mu-\delta y}{\nu_1\delta\lambda\mu})^2}{\frac{1}{2}\frac{1}{\nu_1\delta\lambda\mu}}}\cdot e^{\frac{(p-\lambda\mu-\delta y)^2}{2\nu_1\delta\lambda\mu}}dz.
\end{aligned}$$

Using the substitution

$$x = \frac{z-\frac{p-\lambda\mu-\delta y}{2\nu_1\delta\lambda\mu}}{\sqrt{\frac{1}{\nu_1\delta\lambda\mu}}}, \quad \beta = -\frac{p-\lambda\mu-\delta y}{\sqrt{\nu_1\delta\lambda\mu}},$$

we have

$$\begin{aligned}
A_2 &\geqslant \int_\beta^{+\infty}\left[(1-F_1(y))-x\cdot\sqrt{\frac{\underline{\nu_1^2\delta}}{\lambda\mu\nu_1}}-\frac{(p-\lambda\mu-\delta y)\underline{\nu_1}}{\lambda\mu\nu_1}\right]e^{-\frac{x^2}{2}} \\
&\quad\cdot e^{\frac{\beta^2}{2}}\cdot\sqrt{\frac{1}{\nu_1\delta\lambda\mu}}dx \\
&\geqslant \sqrt{\frac{1}{\nu_1\delta\lambda\mu}}\left(1-F_1(y)+\beta\sqrt{\frac{\underline{\nu_1^2\delta}}{\lambda\mu\nu_1}}\right)R(\beta)-\frac{\underline{\nu_1}}{\lambda\mu\nu_1}e^{\frac{\beta^2}{2}}.
\end{aligned}$$

Note that

$$\int_\beta^{+\infty} x e^{-\frac{x^2}{2}}dx \leqslant \int_0^{+\infty} x e^{-\frac{x^2}{2}}dx = 1$$

holds for all real β. Therefore, we have

$$\sqrt{\frac{1}{\nu_1\delta\lambda\mu}}\left(1-F_1(y)+\beta\sqrt{\frac{\underline{\nu_1^2\delta}}{\lambda\mu\nu_1}}\right)R(\beta)-\frac{\underline{\nu_1^2}}{\lambda\mu\nu_1}e^{\frac{\beta^2}{2}} \leqslant A_2 \leqslant \frac{1-F_1(y)}{p-\lambda\mu}.$$

From these inequalities and (1.12), we can obtain an inequality for $\bar{\bar{G}}_\delta(0,y)$. Using $\bar{G}_\delta(0,y) = 1-\bar{\bar{G}}_\delta(0,y)$, (1.13) can be obtained. □

Remark 1.4 *Same as in [Sundt and Teugels (1995)], we can expand* $\bar{G}_\delta(0,y)$ *as a McLaurin series with respect to variable* δ*. We have*

$$\bar{G}_\delta(0,y) = \frac{\lambda\mu}{p}(1-F_1(y)) + \frac{\lambda\mu}{p}\cdot\frac{y(1-F_1(y)) - \int_y^{+\infty} s dF_1(s)}{(p-\lambda\mu)^2}\delta + o(\delta). \tag{1.14}$$

Remark 1.5 *Similar to [Sundt and Teugels (1995)], we can obtain a Lundberg type upper bound for* $1 - B_\delta(u,y)$*, where* $B_\delta(u,y)$ *is given in Remark 1.2 of Subsection 1.1.2.*

Remark 1.6 *As remarked in Subsection 1.1.2 (Remark 1.2), we can obtain an expression for the Laplace transform of* $B_\delta(u,y)$*. If we assume that the claim random variables are exponentially distributed, similar to [Sundt and Teugels (1995)], we can obtain an expression for* $B_\delta(u,y)$ *by inverting its Laplace transform.*

1.2 On the Distribution of Surplus Immediately before Ruin under Interest Force

In last section, the distribution of surplus immediately after ruin, denoted by $G_\delta(u,x)$, was studied. In this section, we consider another interesting function, $B_\delta(u,y)$, which denotes the probability that ruin occurs beginning with the initial reserve u and that the surplus immediately prior to ruin is less than y, i.e.

$$\begin{aligned} B_\delta(u,y) &= P\big(T < +\infty, 0 < U(T-) \leqslant y | U(0) = u\big) \\ &= \psi_\delta(u) - P\big(T < +\infty, U(T-) > y | U(0) = u\big), \end{aligned} \tag{1.15}$$

where T is the ruin time. Clearly,

$$\lim_{y\to+\infty} B_\delta(u,y) = \psi_\delta(u).$$

Equations satisfied by the distributions of surplus immediately before ruin and their Laplace transform have been obtained. Some special cases are also discussed and Lundberg type bounds are presented in this section.

1.2.1 *Equations for $B_\delta(u,y)$*

1.2.1.1 *Integral Equations for $B_\delta(u,y)$*

Theorem 1.4

$$B_\delta(u,y)=\frac{p}{p+\delta u}B_\delta(0,y)+\frac{1}{p+\delta u}\int_0^u B_\delta(u-z,y)\big[\delta+\lambda(1-F(z))\big]\,dz$$
$$-\frac{\lambda}{p+\delta u}\left[I_{(u\leqslant y)}\int_0^u(1-F(v))\,dv+(1-I_{(u\leqslant y)})\int_0^y(1-F(v))\,dv\right],\ (1.16)$$

where

$$I_{\{u\geqslant y\}}=\begin{cases}1, & \text{if } u\geqslant y,\\ 0, & \text{otherwise}\end{cases}$$

is an indicator function.

Proof. We condition on the first claim time T_1 and the amount of the first claim Y_1. Given that $T_1=t$ and $Y_1=z$, the reserve just before the occurrence of the claim is $ue^{\delta t}+p\cdot\frac{e^{\delta t}-1}{\delta}$. Then,

$$B_\delta(u,y)=E\left[B_\delta\Big(ue^{\delta T_1}+p\cdot\frac{e^{\delta T_1}-1}{\delta}-Y_1,y\Big)\right]I_{(ue^{\delta T_1}+p\cdot\frac{e^{\delta T_1}-1}{\delta}\leqslant y)}$$
$$=E\left[B_\delta\Big(ue^{\delta T_1}+p\cdot\frac{e^{\delta T_1}-1}{\delta}-Y_1,y\Big)\,\middle|\,Y_1\leqslant ue^{\delta T_1}+p\cdot\frac{e^{\delta T_1}-1}{\delta}\right]$$
$$\cdot P\left[Y_1\leqslant ue^{\delta T_1}+p\cdot\frac{e^{\delta T_1}-1}{\delta}\right]I_{(ue^{\delta T_1}+p\cdot\frac{e^{\delta T_1}-1}{\delta}\leqslant y)}$$
$$+E\left[B_\delta\Big(ue^{\delta T_1}+p\cdot\frac{e^{\delta T_1}-1}{\delta}-Y_1,y\Big)\,\middle|\,Y_1>ue^{\delta T_1}+p\cdot\frac{e^{\delta T_1}-1}{\delta}\right]$$
$$\cdot P\left[Y_1>ue^{\delta T_1}+p\cdot\frac{e^{\delta T_1}-1}{\delta}\right]I_{(ue^{\delta T_1}+p\cdot\frac{e^{\delta T_1}-1}{\delta}\leqslant y)}$$
$$=\int_0^{+\infty}\lambda e^{-\lambda t}\int_0^{ue^{\delta t}+p\cdot\frac{e^{\delta t}-1}{\delta}}B_\delta\Big(ue^{\delta t}+p\cdot\frac{e^{\delta t}-1}{\delta}-z,y\Big)\,dF(z)\,dt$$
$$+I_{(u\leqslant y)}\int_0^{\frac{\ln(\frac{\delta y+p}{\delta u+p})}{\delta}}\lambda e^{-\lambda t}\int_{ue^{\delta t}+p\cdot\frac{e^{\delta t}-1}{\delta}}^{+\infty}dF(z)\,dt.$$

By using the substitution $s = ue^{\delta t} + p \cdot \frac{e^{\delta t}-1}{\delta}$, we obtain

$$\begin{aligned}B_\delta(u,y) &= \lambda(p+\delta u)^{\frac{\lambda}{\delta}} \int_u^{+\infty} (p+\delta s)^{-\frac{\lambda}{\delta}-1} \int_0^s B_\delta(s-z,y)\,dF(z)\,ds \\ &\quad + \lambda(p+\delta u)^{\frac{\lambda}{\delta}} I_{(u\leqslant y)} \int_u^y (\delta s+p)^{-\frac{\lambda}{\delta}-1}(1-F(s))\,ds.\end{aligned}$$

Assume that F is continuous, differentiation of the above expression gives

$$\begin{aligned}\frac{\partial B_\delta(u,y)}{\partial u} &= \frac{\lambda}{p+\delta u} B_\delta(u,y) - \frac{\lambda}{p+\delta u}\int_0^u B_\delta(u-z,y)dF(z) \\ &\quad - \frac{\lambda}{p+\delta u} I_{(u\leqslant y)}(1-F(u)).\end{aligned} \tag{1.17}$$

For $u \leqslant y$, integrating both sides of (1.17) from 0 to u, we have

$$\begin{aligned}B_\delta(u,y) &= \frac{p}{p+\delta u} B_\delta(0,y) + \frac{1}{p+\delta u}\int_0^u B_\delta(u-z,y)\big[\delta + \lambda(1-F(z))\big]\,dz \\ &\quad - \frac{\lambda}{p+\delta u}\int_0^u (1-F(v))\,dv.\end{aligned} \tag{1.18}$$

From (1.18), we obtain (1.16) in the case where $u \leqslant y$.

For $u \geqslant y$, integrating both sides of (1.17) from y to u, we have

$$\begin{aligned}&(p+\delta u)B_\delta(u,y) - (p+\delta y)B_\delta(y,y) - \delta\int_y^u B_\delta(v,y)\,dv \\ &= \lambda\int_y^u B_\delta(v,y)dv - \lambda\int_y^u\int_0^v B_\delta(v-z,y)\,dF(z)\,dv,\end{aligned}$$

the second term on the right hand side of the above equation equals

$$\begin{aligned}&\lambda\int_y^u\int_0^v B_\delta(v-z,y)\,dF(z)\,dv \\ &= \lambda\int_y^u B_\delta(v-z,y)\,F(z)\Big|_{z=0}^{v} dv + \lambda\int_y^u\int_0^v \frac{\partial B_\delta(v-z,y)}{\partial v}F(z)\,dz\,dv \\ &= \lambda\int_0^u B_\delta(u-z,y)\,F(z)\,dz + \lambda\int_0^y \big[-B_\delta(y-z,y)\big]F(z)\,dz,\end{aligned}$$

so we have

$$
\begin{aligned}
&(p+\delta u)B_\delta(u,y) - (p+\delta y)B_\delta(y,y) - \delta\int_y^u B_\delta(v,y)\,dv \\
&= \lambda\int_y^u B_\delta(v,y)\,dv - \lambda\int_0^u B_\delta(u-z,y)\,F(z)\,dz \\
&\quad +\lambda\int_0^y B_\delta(y-z,y)\,F(z)\,dz \\
&= \lambda\int_0^u \big(B_\delta(u-z,y)(1-F(z))\big)\,dz - \lambda\int_0^y B_\delta(y-z,y)(1-F(z))\,dz.
\end{aligned}
$$

Hence

$$
\begin{aligned}
B_\delta(u,y) &= \frac{p+\delta y}{p+\delta u}B_\delta(y,y) + \frac{1}{p+\delta u}\int_0^u B_\delta(u-z,y)[\delta+\lambda(1-F(z))]\,dz \\
&\quad -\frac{1}{p+\delta u}\int_0^y B_\delta(y-z,y)[\delta+\lambda(1-F(z))]\,dz. \qquad (1.19)
\end{aligned}
$$

From the definition of $B_\delta(u,y)$, it follows that $B_\delta(u,y)$ is a continuous function of $u \geqslant 0$ for a given value of y. Let $u = y$ in (1.18), we then have

$$
\begin{aligned}
B_\delta(y,y) &= \frac{p}{p+\delta y}B_\delta(0,y) + \frac{1}{p+\delta y}\int_0^y B_\delta(y-z,y)\big(\delta+\lambda(1-F(z))\big)\,dz \\
&\quad -\frac{\lambda}{p+\delta y}\int_0^y (1-F(v))\,dv.
\end{aligned}
$$

Plugging $B_\delta(y,y)$ into (1.19),

$$
\begin{aligned}
B_\delta(u,y) &= \frac{p}{p+\delta u}B_\delta(0,y) + \frac{1}{p+\delta u}\int_0^u B_\delta(u-z,y)\big(\delta+\lambda(1-F(z))\big)\,dz \\
&\quad -\frac{\lambda}{p+\delta u}\int_0^y (1-F(v))\,dv. \qquad (1.20)
\end{aligned}
$$

This is (1.16) for $u \geqslant y$. □

1.2.1.2 *The Case $\delta = 0$*

When $\delta = 0$, denote $B_0(u,y)$ by $F(u,y)$, we have the following theorem.

Theorem 1.5 *When the adjustment coefficient R exists(see Theorem 1.2), we have when $u \leqslant y$ (in this case, when $u \to \infty$, $y \to \infty$)*

$$
\lim_{u\to\infty} e^{Ru}F(u,y) = \frac{(1-\frac{\lambda\mu}{p})}{\frac{\lambda}{p}(-\phi'(-R)-\frac{p}{\lambda})}, \qquad (1.21)
$$

and when $u \geqslant y$

$$\lim_{u\to\infty} e^{Ru}F(u,y) = \frac{F^*(y) - \frac{\lambda\mu}{p}F_1(y)}{\frac{\lambda}{p}\left(-\phi'(-R) - \frac{p}{\lambda}\right)}, \tag{1.22}$$

where

$$F^*(x) = \int_o^x \frac{\lambda}{p} e^{Rz}(1 - F(z))\,dz.$$

Proof. In the case of $u \leqslant y$, $\lim_{u\to\infty} e^{Ru}F(u,y) = \lim_{u\to\infty} e^{Ru}\psi(u)$. From [Grandell (1991)], we have $\psi(u) \sim \frac{1-\frac{\lambda\mu}{p}}{\frac{\lambda}{p}\left(-\phi'(-R)-\frac{p}{\lambda}\right)} e^{-Ru}$. This proves that (1.21) is true. For $u \geqslant y$, it comes from [Dickson(1992)] that

$$F(u,y) = G(u-y,y) - \frac{1-G(0,y)}{1-\psi(0)}(\psi(u-y) - \psi(u)) \quad \text{for } u \geqslant y,$$

where $G(u,y)$ denotes the distribution of the surplus at ruin. So

$$\begin{aligned} &\lim_{u\to\infty} e^{Ru}F(u,y) \\ &= \lim_{u\to\infty}\left[G(u-y,y) - \frac{1-G(0,y)}{1-\psi(0)}(\psi(u-y)-\psi(u))\right]e^{Ru}. \end{aligned} \tag{1.23}$$

Using the asymptotic result for $G(u,y)$ obtained in last section, and the asymptotic result of $\psi(u)$ in [Grandell (1991)], we obtain (1.22).

1.2.1.3 *Solution of the Integral Equation*

Following [Sundt and Teugels (1995)], we introduce the following auxiliary function

$$A_\delta(u,y) = \frac{B_\delta(u,y) - B_\delta(0,y)}{1 - B_\delta(0,y)}.$$

Equation (1.16), in terms of $A_\delta(u,y)$ and $F_1(x)$, the equilibrium distribution of F, can be rewritten as

$$\begin{aligned} pA_\delta(u,y) + \delta\, u\, A_\delta(u,y) &= \delta \int_0^u A_\delta(v,y)\,dv + \lambda\mu\, A_\delta * F_1(u,y) \\ &\quad - \lambda \int_0^u (1-F(z))\,dz \\ &\quad + \frac{\lambda}{B_\delta(0,y)}\Big[I_{\{u\geqslant y\}} \int_0^y (1-F(v))\,dv \\ &\quad + (1-I_{\{u\geqslant y\}})\cdot \int_0^u (1-F(v))\,dv\Big]. \qquad (1.24) \end{aligned}$$

Let

$$\gamma_{\delta 1}(s,y) = \int_0^{+\infty} e^{-sv} d\,A_\delta(v,y),$$

where y is regarded as a parameter.

The first order differential equation for the function, $\gamma_{\delta 1}(s,y)$, can be obtained by taking the Laplace transform of (1.24) with respect to u

$$\begin{aligned} &-\delta\, \gamma_{\delta 1}'(s,y) + (p - \lambda\mu\phi(s))\gamma_{\delta 1}(s,y) \\ &= \frac{\lambda\mu}{B_\delta(0,y)}(\phi(s) - \phi_y(s)) - \lambda\mu\phi(s), \qquad (1.25) \end{aligned}$$

and the initial condition of the above equation is given by $\lim_{s\to\infty} \gamma_{\delta 1}(s,y) = 0$.

Similar to [Sundt and Teugels (1995)], the solution of Equation (1.25) is given by

$$\begin{aligned} \gamma_{\delta 1}(s,y) &= \delta^{-1} \int_s^{+\infty} e^{-\{\chi(v)-\chi(s)\}/\delta} \Big[\frac{\lambda\mu(\phi(v)-\phi_y(v))}{B_\delta(0,y)} - \lambda\mu\phi(v)\Big]\,dv \\ &= \lambda\mu \int_0^{+\infty} e^{-\int_0^w [p-\lambda\mu\phi(s+\delta z)]dz} \Big[\frac{\phi(s+\delta w) - \phi_y(s+\delta w)}{B_\delta(0,y)} \\ &\quad -\phi(s+\delta w)\Big]\,dw, \qquad (1.26) \end{aligned}$$

where

$$\chi(s) := \int_0^s (p - \lambda\mu\phi(v))\,dv.$$

By letting $s = 0$ we have

$$B_\delta(0,y) = \Big(\frac{\delta}{\lambda\mu} + \int_0^{+\infty} e^{-\chi(v)/\delta}\phi(v)dv\Big)^{-1}\Big(\int_0^{+\infty} e^{-\chi(v)/\delta}(\phi(v)-\phi_y(v))dv\Big)$$
$$= \Big[\frac{1}{\lambda\mu} + \int_0^{+\infty} e^{-\int_0^w [p-\lambda\mu\phi(\delta z)]dz}\phi(\delta w)dw\Big]^{-1}\cdot$$
$$\Big[\int_0^{+\infty} e^{-\int_0^w [p-\lambda\mu\phi(\delta z)]dz}(\phi(\delta w)-\phi_y(\delta w))dw\Big]. \tag{1.27}$$

From [Sundt and Teugels (1995)], we know

$$\psi_\delta(0) = 1 - \Big(p\int_0^{+\infty} e^{-\int_0^z (p-\lambda\mu\phi(\delta w))dw}dz\Big)^{-1}.$$

Also by last section, we have

$$G_\delta(0,y) = \Big(p\int_0^{+\infty} e^{-\int_0^z (p-\lambda\mu\phi(\delta w))dw}dz\Big)^{-1}$$
$$\Big(\int_0^{+\infty} e^{\int_0^z (p-\lambda\mu\phi(\delta w))dw}\cdot(\lambda\mu\phi(\delta z) - \lambda\mu e^{\delta z y}\phi_y(\delta z))\,dz\Big),$$

so, when $\delta = 0$, $F(0,y) = G(0,y)$, but for $\delta > 0$, $G_\delta(0,y) \neq B_\delta(0,y)$. Hence, the reflection principle is not valid when $\delta \neq 0$. In addition, the relationships among $G(u,y)$, $F(u,y)$ and $\psi(u)$ in [Dickson(1992)], [Willmot and Lin (1998)] are not valid when $\delta \neq 0$.

1.2.2 $B_\delta(u,y)$ *with Zero Initial Reserve*

The main result of this subsection is the following theorem.

Theorem 1.6

$$\Big(\frac{1}{p-\lambda\mu} + \frac{1}{\lambda\mu}\Big)^{-1}\cdot$$
$$\Big[\Big(F_1(y) + \delta\alpha\nu_{11}(y)\sqrt{\frac{1}{\lambda\mu\delta\nu_1}}\Big)\cdot\sqrt{\frac{1}{\lambda\mu\delta\nu_1}}R(\alpha) - e^{\frac{\alpha^2}{2}}\frac{\nu_{11}(y)}{\lambda\mu\nu_1}\Big]$$
$$\leqslant B_\delta(0,y)$$
$$\leqslant \Big[\Big(\sqrt{\frac{1}{\lambda\mu\delta\nu_1}} + \frac{\alpha}{\lambda\mu}\Big)R(\alpha) - \frac{e^{\frac{\alpha^2}{2}}}{\lambda\mu} + \frac{1}{\lambda\mu}\Big]^{-1}\cdot\frac{F_1(y)}{p-\lambda\mu}, \tag{1.28}$$

where $R(\alpha)$ *is the well known Mills' ratio given by* $R(\alpha) = e^{\frac{\alpha^2}{2}}\int_\alpha^{+\infty} e^{-\frac{x^2}{2}}dx$, *and* $\alpha = \frac{\lambda\mu - p}{\sqrt{\nu_1\delta\lambda\mu}}$ *and* $\nu_{11}(y) = \int_0^y z\,dF_1(z)$.

Proof. Let

$$\begin{aligned} A_1 := & \int_0^{+\infty} e^{-\int_0^w (p-\lambda\mu\phi(\delta z))dz}\phi(\delta w)\,dw \\ = & \int_0^{+\infty} e^{\int_0^w (\lambda\mu\phi(\delta z)-p)dz}\phi(\delta w)\,dw. \end{aligned} \tag{1.29}$$

Using the property that $\phi(s)$ is a strictly decreasing convex function, we have

$$\begin{aligned} & \int_0^{+\infty} e^{\int_0^w ((1-\nu_1\delta z)\lambda\mu-p)dz}(1-\nu_1\delta w)\,dw \\ & \leqslant A_1 \\ & \leqslant \int_0^{+\infty} e^{\int_0^w (\lambda\mu-p)dz}dw = \frac{1}{p-\lambda\mu}. \end{aligned}$$

Using a similar method given by [Sundt and Teugels (1995)], we have the following inequality for A_1:

$$\left(\sqrt{\frac{1}{\lambda\mu\delta\nu_1}}+\frac{\alpha}{\lambda\mu}\right)R(\alpha)-\frac{e^{\frac{\alpha^2}{2}}}{\lambda\mu}\leqslant A_1\leqslant\frac{1}{p-\lambda\mu}. \tag{1.30}$$

Put

$$A_2 := \int_0^{+\infty} e^{-\int_0^w (p-\lambda\mu\phi(\delta z))dz}(\phi(\delta w)-\phi_y(\delta w))\,dw. \tag{1.31}$$

Since $\phi(s)$, $\phi_y(s)$ and $\phi(s)-\phi_y(s)$ are strictly decreasing convex functions, we get

$$\begin{aligned} A_2 \geqslant & \int_0^{+\infty} e^{\int_0^w (\lambda\mu-\nu_1\delta z\lambda\mu-p)dz}\left(F_1(y)-\delta w\int_0^y u\,dF_1(u)\right)dw \\ = & \int_0^{+\infty} e^{-\frac{(w-\frac{p-\lambda\mu}{\lambda\delta\mu\nu_1})^2}{2\cdot\frac{1}{\lambda\mu\delta\nu_1}}+\frac{(p-\lambda\mu)^2}{2\lambda\mu\delta\nu_1}}(F_1(y)-\delta w\nu_{11})\,dw \end{aligned}$$

and

$$A_2 \leqslant \int_0^{+\infty} e^{\int_0^2 (\lambda\mu-p)dz}F_1(y)dw = \frac{F_1(y)}{p-\lambda\mu}.$$

Therefore, we have the following inequality for A_2:

$$\left(F_1(y) + \delta\alpha\nu_{11}(y)\sqrt{\frac{1}{\lambda\mu\delta\nu_1}}\right) \cdot \sqrt{\frac{1}{\lambda\mu\delta\nu_1}} R(\alpha) - e^{\frac{\alpha^2}{2}} \frac{\delta\nu_{11}(y)}{\lambda\mu\delta\nu_1}$$
$$\leqslant A_2 \leqslant \frac{F_1(y)}{p - \lambda\mu}. \tag{1.32}$$

Notice that (1.27) can be rearranged as

$$B_\delta(0, y) = \left(A_1 + \frac{1}{\lambda\mu}\right)^{-1} A_2.$$

So Theorem 1.6 is proved. □

Similar to [Sundt and Teugels (1995)], we can expand $B_\delta(0, y)$ as a McLaurin series with respect to the variable δ, and we have

$$B_\delta(0, y) = \frac{\lambda\mu}{p} F_1(y) + \frac{-\lambda\mu\nu_1}{p(p - \lambda\mu)} \cdot \delta + o(\delta). \tag{1.33}$$

1.2.3 *Exponential Claim Size*

In this subsection, we will try to evaluate expression (1.27) in the case of an exponential claim size. First, we have

$$\begin{aligned} B_\delta(0, y) = & \left[\frac{\delta}{\lambda\mu} + \int_0^{+\infty} e^{-(pv - \lambda\log(1+\mu v))/\delta}(1 + \mu v)^{-1} dv\right]^{-1} \\ & \cdot \left[\int_0^{+\infty} e^{-(pv - \lambda\log(1+\mu v))/\delta}(1 + \mu v)^{-1}(1 - e^{-(v + \frac{1}{\mu})y})\, dv\right] \\ = & \left[\frac{\delta}{\lambda\mu} + \int_0^{+\infty} e^{-\frac{p}{\delta}v}(1 + \mu v)^{\frac{\lambda}{\delta} - 1} dv\right]^{-1} \\ & \cdot \left[\int_0^{+\infty} e^{-\frac{p}{\delta}v}(1 + \mu v)^{\frac{\lambda}{\delta} - 1}(1 - e^{-(v + \frac{1}{\mu})y})\, dv\right], \end{aligned} \tag{1.34}$$

then

$$\begin{aligned}
&\gamma_{\delta 1}(s,y) \\
&= \delta^{-1}\int_s^{+\infty} e^{-[p(v-s)-\lambda\log\frac{1+\mu v}{1+\mu s}]/\delta}\lambda\mu(1+\mu v)^{-1}\Big[\frac{1-e^{-(v+\frac{1}{\mu})y}}{B_\delta(0,y)}-1\Big]\,dv \\
&= \delta^{-1}\lambda\mu\Big[\int_s^{+\infty} e^{-\frac{p}{\delta}(v-s)}(1+\mu v)^{-1}\Big(\frac{1+\mu v}{1+\mu s}\Big)^{\frac{\lambda}{\delta}}\Big[\frac{1}{B_\delta(0,y)}-1\Big]\,dv \\
&\quad -\frac{1}{B_\delta(0,y)}\int_s^{+\infty} e^{-\frac{p}{s}(v-s)}(1+\mu v)^{-1}\Big(\frac{1+\mu v}{1+\mu s}\Big)^{\frac{\lambda}{\delta}}e^{-vy}\cdot e^{-\frac{y}{\mu}}dv\Big] \\
&= \int_0^{+\infty} e^{-sx}\cdot e^{-\frac{x}{\mu}}(1+\frac{\delta}{p}x)^{\frac{\lambda}{\delta}-1}\frac{\lambda}{p}\cdot\Big(\frac{1}{B_\delta(0,y)}-1\Big)dx \\
&+\frac{\lambda}{p}\int_0^{+\infty} e^{-s(x+\frac{\delta y}{p}x+y)}\cdot e^{-(\frac{x+y}{\mu}+\frac{\delta y}{p\mu}x)}\Big(1+\frac{\delta}{p}x\Big)^{\frac{\lambda}{\delta}-1}dx\cdot\frac{1}{B_\delta(0,y)}. \qquad (1.35)
\end{aligned}$$

Using the substitution

$$x+\frac{\delta y}{p}x+y=t,$$

we have

$$\begin{aligned}
\gamma_{\delta 1}(s,y) &= \int_0^{+\infty} e^{-st}e^{-\frac{t}{\mu}}(1+\frac{\delta}{p}x)^{\frac{\lambda}{\delta}-1}\frac{\lambda}{p}\Big(\frac{1}{B_\delta(0,y)}-1\Big)\,dt \\
&-\int_y^{+\infty} e^{-st}e^{-\frac{t}{\mu}}\Big(1+\frac{\delta(t-y)}{p+\delta y}\Big)^{\frac{\lambda}{\delta}-1}\cdot\frac{\lambda}{p+\delta y}\cdot\frac{1}{B_\delta(0,y)}\,dt. \qquad (1.36)
\end{aligned}$$

Remember that $\gamma_{\delta 1}(s,y)$ was introduced as a Laplace transformation of $A_\delta(u,y)$ with respect to u. Hence, by inverting, we find that

$$\begin{aligned}
A_\delta(u,y) &= \int_0^u e^{-\frac{t}{\mu}}(1+\frac{\delta}{p}x)^{\frac{\lambda}{\delta}-1}\frac{\lambda}{p}\Big(\frac{1}{B_\delta(0,y)}-1\Big)\,dt \\
&-\int_y^u e^{-\frac{t}{\mu}}\Big(1+\frac{\delta(t-y)}{p+\delta y}\Big)^{\frac{\lambda}{\delta}-1}\cdot\frac{\lambda}{p+\delta y}\cdot\frac{1}{B_\delta(0,y)}\cdot I_{\{u\geqslant y\}}dt, \qquad (1.37)
\end{aligned}$$

where $I_{\{u\geqslant y\}}$ is the indicator function.

1.2.4 *Lundberg Bound*

Following the arguments in [Sundt and Teugels (1995)], we are also able to obtain the Lundberg type inequality. Same as in [Sundt and Teugels (1995)], we assume that $\phi(s)$ has $-\sigma$ as an abscissa of convergence. So for any $u > 0$ and for $s \in I := (-\sigma, 0)$, we have

$$\gamma_{\delta 1}(s,y) \geqslant \int_u^{+\infty} e^{-sx} d\,A_\delta(x,y) \geqslant e^{-su}\{1 - A_\delta(u,y)\},$$

so we obtain the Chernoff type estimate

$$1 - A_\delta(u,y) \leqslant \exp\Big\{\inf_{s\in I}\{su + \log\gamma_{\delta 1}(s,y)\}\Big\}. \tag{1.38}$$

Let $s_\delta(u,y)$ denote the solution of the following equation:

$$u\,\gamma_{\delta 1}(s,y) = -\gamma'_{\delta 1}(s,y)\ , \tag{1.39}$$

and we call $|s_\delta(u,y)|$ the adjustment function.

Similar to [Sundt and Teugels (1995)], put

$$\underline{u}_\delta = \frac{\left(\frac{\lambda\mu}{B_\delta(u,y)}F_1(y) - p\right)}{\delta}\ , \tag{1.40}$$

we have the following result.

Theorem 1.7 *When the initial surplus u satisfies $u \geqslant \underline{u}_\delta$, then $1 - A_\delta(u,y)$ satisfies a Lundberg type inequality:*

$$1 - A_\delta(u,y) \leqslant \frac{\frac{\lambda\mu}{B_\delta(0,y)}[\phi(s_\delta(u,y)) - \phi_y(s_\delta(u,y))] - \lambda\mu\phi(s_\delta(u,y))}{u\delta + p - \lambda\mu\phi(s_\delta(u,y))} \cdot e^{us_\delta(u,y)}.$$

1.3 Asymptotic Estimates of the Low and Upper Bounds for the Distribution of the Surplus Immediately after Ruin under Subexponential Claims

The asymptotic estimates of ruin probability is one of the most important topics in risk theory. A lot of results have been obtained since the establishment of Cramér-Lundberg model. These results range from the exponential type estimates as given by Cramér, till the estimates when exponential moment of the claim size distribution does not exist. The purpose of this section is to show that the techniques of [Kalashnikov and Konstantinides(2000)] can be used to deal with the distribution of surplus immediately after ruin. In this section, we give asymptotic formulas of the low and upper bounds for the distribution of the surplus immediately after ruin under subexponential claims. The result is similar to that in [Kalashnikov and Konstantinides(2000)] on ruin probability.

1.3.1 *Preliminaries and Auxiliary Relations*

We also consider the same model as in [Sundt and Teugels (1995)]. We are interested in the function $G_\delta(u,y)$, which is a special form of the Gerber-Shiu penalty function. A detailed study of the Gerber-Shiu penalty function under the model can be found in [Cai and Dickson(2002)]. This is interesting in theory and application to discuss the function $G_\delta(u,y)$. From (1.4), we know that

$$G_\delta(u,y) = \frac{p}{p+\delta u}G_\delta(0,y) + \frac{1}{p+\delta u}\int_0^u G_\delta(u-z,y)[\delta+\lambda(1-F(z))]dz \\ -\frac{\lambda}{p+\delta u}\int_0^y [F(u+z)-F(z)]dz. \tag{1.41}$$

This result is often referred to as the *integral equation* satisfied by $G_\delta(u,y)$. Following [Kalashnikov and Konstantinides(2000)], if we introduce the auxiliary distribution

$$E_\delta(u,y) = \frac{G_\delta(0,y)-G_\delta(u,y)}{G_\delta(0,y)},$$

then we have

$$G_\delta(u,y) = G_\delta(0,y) - G_\delta(0,y)E_\delta(u,y). \tag{1.42}$$

Replacing $G_\delta(u,y)$ in (1.41) by the expression of (1.42) and making some calculations, we get

$$(p+\delta u)E_\delta(u,y) = \delta\int_0^u E_\delta(z,y)dz - \lambda\mu F_1(u) + \lambda\mu E_\delta(\cdot,y)*F_1(u) \\ +\frac{\lambda\mu}{G_\delta(0,y)}(F_1(u)-F_1(u+y)+F_1(y)), \tag{1.43}$$

where $*$ stands for the Stieltjes convolution. Put

$$k_\delta(u,y) = \int_u^\infty v\frac{\partial E_\delta(v,y)}{\partial v}dv.$$

Then, using integral by parts, we have

$$\int_0^u E_\delta(v,y)dv = uE_\delta(u,y) - (k_\delta(0,y)-k_\delta(u,y)).$$

Plugging this expression of $\int_0^u E_\delta(v,y)dv$ into (1.43), we have that

$$\begin{aligned} E_\delta(u,y) &= -\frac{\delta}{p}(k_\delta(0,y)-k_\delta(u,y)) + \frac{k_\delta}{p}F_1(u) \\ &+ \frac{k_\delta+\rho}{p}(F_1(y)-F_1(u+y)) + \frac{\rho}{p}E_\delta(\cdot,y)*F_1(u), \end{aligned}$$

where

$$\rho = \lambda\mu, \quad k_\delta = \frac{\rho(1-G_\delta(0,y))}{G_\delta(0,y)}.$$

With the abbreviations

$$\begin{aligned} m &= \frac{\rho}{p}, \\ C_\delta(u,y) &= -\frac{\delta}{p}(k_\delta(0,y)-k_\delta(u,y)) + \frac{k_\delta}{p}F_1(u) \\ &+ \frac{k_\delta+\rho}{p}(F_1(y)-F_1(u+y)) \end{aligned}$$

then we obtain

$$E_\delta(u,y) = C_\delta(u,y) + mE_\delta(\cdot,y)*F_1(u). \tag{1.44}$$

Let us assume that the positive safety loading condition $\rho < p$ takes place, which yields $m < 1$. So, the solution of (1.44) is

$$E_\delta(u,y) = C_\delta(\cdot,y)*H(u), H(u) = \sum_{n=0}^{\infty} m^n F_1^{n*}(u).$$

Thus we can rewrite (1.44) in the form

$$\begin{aligned} E_\delta(u,y) = &-\frac{\delta}{p}(\sum_{n=0}^{\infty} m^n F_1^{n*}) * (k_\delta(0,y)-k_\delta(\cdot,y))(u) + \frac{k_\delta}{p}\sum_{n=0}^{\infty} m^n F_1^{(n+1)*}(u) \\ &+ \frac{(k_\delta+\rho)F_1(y)}{p}\sum_{n=0}^{\infty} m^n F_1^{n*}(u) \\ &- \frac{k_\delta+\rho}{p}F_1(\cdot+y)*(\sum_{n=0}^{\infty} m^n F_1^{n*})(u). \end{aligned} \tag{1.45}$$

Letting $\delta = 0$ in (1.41) yields

$$\begin{aligned}
G_0(u,y) &= G_0(0,y) + \frac{\lambda}{p}\int_0^u G_0(u-z,y)(1-F(z))dz \\
&\quad -\frac{\lambda}{p}\int_0^y (F(u+z)-F(z))dz \\
&= D_0(u,y) + mG_0(\cdot,y) * F_1(u), \qquad (1.46)
\end{aligned}$$

here $D_0(u,y)$ is defined by

$$D_0(u,y) = G_0(0,y) - \frac{\lambda}{p}\int_0^y (F(u+z)-F(z))dz.$$

Noting that

$$\begin{aligned}
D_0(u,y) &= G_0(0,y) - \frac{\lambda}{p}\int_0^y (F(u+z)-F(z))dz \\
&= G_0(0,y) - \frac{\lambda\mu}{p}\int_0^y \frac{F(u+z)-F(z)}{\mu}dz \\
&= G_0(0,y) - m\int_0^y \left[\frac{1-F(z)}{\mu} - \frac{1-F(u+z)}{\mu}\right] dz \\
&= G_0(0,y) - mF_1(y) + m\int_0^y \frac{1-F(u+z)}{\mu}dz \\
&= G_0(0,y) - mF_1(y) + m\int_u^{u+y} \frac{1-F(z)}{\mu}dz \\
&= G_0(0,y) - mF_1(y) + m[F_1(u+y)-F_1(u)],
\end{aligned}$$

the solution of (1.46) is then

$$\begin{aligned}
G_0(u,y) &= D_0(\cdot,y) * H(u) \\
&= D_0(\cdot,y) * (\sum_{n=0}^{\infty} m^n F_1^{n*})(u) \\
&= (G_0(0,y) - mF_1(y)) \sum_{n=0}^{\infty} m^n F_1^{n*}(u) - \sum_{n=0}^{\infty} m^{n+1} F_1^{(n+1)*}(u) \\
&\quad + \sum_{n=0}^{\infty} m^{n+1} F_1(\cdot + y) * F_1^{n*}(u).
\end{aligned}$$

From [Willmot and Lin(2001)], $G_0(0,y) = mF_1(y)$. Thus

$$G_0(u,y) = \sum_{n=0}^{\infty} m^{n+1} F_1(\cdot + y) * F_1^{n*}(u) - \sum_{n=0}^{\infty} m^{n+1} F_1^{(n+1)*}(u). \qquad (1.47)$$

It immediately follows from the above expression of $G_0(u,y)$ that

$$\sum_{n=0}^{\infty} m^n F_1(\cdot+y) * F_1^{n*}(u) = \frac{1}{m} G_0(u,y) + \sum_{n=0}^{\infty} m^n F_1^{(n+1)*}(u). \qquad (1.48)$$

On the other hand, by the Pollaczek-Khinchine formula (or, which is the same, by the Beckman convolution formula, see [Rolski *et. al.* (1999)] , we have

$$\sum_{n=0}^{\infty} m^n F_1^{n*}(u) = \frac{1-\psi_0(u)}{1-m}. \qquad (1.49)$$

In terms of (1.45), (1.48) and (1.49) we arrive at

$$\begin{aligned} E_\delta(u,y) = & -\frac{\delta}{p}\left(\frac{1-\psi_0(\cdot)}{1-m} * (k_\delta(0,y) - k_\delta(\cdot,y))(u) + 1 - \frac{1-\psi_0(u)}{1-m}\right. \\ & + \frac{k_\delta+\rho}{p} F_1(y)\left(\frac{1-\psi_0(u)}{1-m}\right) - \frac{k_\delta+\rho}{p}\frac{G_0(u,y)}{m}. \end{aligned}$$

Further,

$$\begin{aligned} 1 - E_\delta(u,y) = & \frac{\delta}{p-\rho}\phi_0 * (k_\delta(0,y) - k_\delta(\cdot,y))(u) + \frac{p\phi_0(u)}{p-\rho} \\ & - \frac{k_\delta+\rho}{p-\rho} F_1(y)\phi_0(u) + \frac{k_\delta+\rho}{\rho} G_0(u,y), \end{aligned} \qquad (1.50)$$

where $\phi_0(u) = 1 - \psi_0(u)$ is the survival probability (without interest rate).

Now we are in a position to take Laplace-Stieltjes transform (see, [Rolski *et. al.* (1999)] on both sides of (1.50). The Laplace-Stieltjes transform will be denoted by equipping the corresponding original function with hat and using s as its argument. It is easy to see from (1.50) that

$$\begin{aligned} 1 - \hat{E}_\delta(s,y) = & \frac{\delta}{p-\rho}(k_\delta(0,y)\hat{\phi}_0(s) - \hat{k}_\delta(s,y)\hat{\phi}_0(s)) + \frac{p}{p-\rho}\hat{\phi}_0(s) \\ & - \frac{k_\delta+\rho}{p-\rho} F_1(y)\hat{\phi}_0(s) + \frac{k_\delta+\rho}{\rho}\hat{G}_0(s,y), \end{aligned} \qquad (1.51)$$

where $\hat{k}_\delta(s,y) = \int_0^\infty e^{-su} dk_\delta(u,y), \hat{G}_0(s,y) = \int_0^\infty e^{-su} dG_0(u,y)$, and by the Pollaczek-Khinchine formula (see [Rolski *et. al.* (1999)], or [Kalashnikov and Konstantinides(2000)]),

$$\hat{\phi}_0(s) = \int_0^\infty e^{-su} d\phi_0(u) = \frac{p-\rho}{p-\rho\hat{F}_1(s)}. \qquad (1.52)$$

Because of (1.47), in order to get the Laplace-Stieltjes transform of $G_0(u,y)$, it suffices to compute that of $F_1(u+y)$. In fact,

$$\begin{aligned}\int_0^\infty e^{-su}dF_1(u+y) &= e^{sy}\int_0^\infty e^{-s(u+y)}dF_1(u+y)\\ &= e^{sy}\int_y^\infty e^{-su}dF_1(u)\\ &= e^{sy}\int_0^\infty e^{-su}dF_1(u) - e^{sy}\int_0^y e^{-su}dF_1(u)\\ &= e^{sy}\hat{F}_1(s) - e^{sy}\int_0^y e^{-su}dF_1(u). \qquad (1.53)\end{aligned}$$

Thus we can obtain from (1.47) the Laplace-Stieltjes transform of $G_0(u,y)$ that

$$\begin{aligned}\hat{G}_0(s,y) &= \sum_{n=0}^\infty m^{n+1}\hat{F}_1^n(s)(e^{sy}\hat{F}_1(s) - e^{sy}\int_0^y e^{-su}dF_1(u))\\ &\quad -\sum_{n=0}^\infty m^{n+1}\hat{F}_1^{n+1}(s)\\ &= e^{sy}\sum_{n=0}^\infty m^{n+1}\hat{F}_1^{n+1}(s) - e^{sy}\int_0^y e^{-su}dF_1(u)\sum_{n=0}^\infty m^{n+1}\hat{F}_1^n(s)\\ &\quad -\sum_{n=0}^\infty m^{n+1}\hat{F}_1^{n+1}(s)\\ &= (e^{sy}-1)\frac{m\hat{F}_1(s)}{1-m\hat{F}_1(s)} - e^{sy}\int_0^y e^{-su}dF_1(u)\frac{m}{1-m\hat{F}_1(s)}\\ &= (e^{sy}-1)\frac{\rho\hat{F}_1(s)}{p-\rho\hat{F}_1(s)} - e^{sy}\int_0^y e^{-su}dF_1(u)\frac{\rho}{p-\rho\hat{F}_1(s)}. \qquad (1.54)\end{aligned}$$

By virtue of (1.51), (1.52) and (1.54) we have that

$$\begin{aligned}(p-\rho\hat{F}_1(s))(1-\hat{E}_\delta(s,y)) &= \delta(k_\delta(0,y) - \hat{k}_\delta(s,y)) + p\\ &\quad -(k_\delta+\rho)F_1(y) + (k_\delta+\rho)(e^{sy}-1)\hat{F}_1(s)\\ &\quad -(k_\delta+\rho)e^{sy}\int_0^y e^{-su}dF_1(u). \qquad (1.55)\end{aligned}$$

Now, we need find the value of $k_\delta(0,y)$. Letting $u \to \infty$ in the expression of (1.44) leads to $1 = C_\delta(\infty,y) + m$, which means that $C_\delta(\infty,y) = 1-m$.

Since

$$C_\delta(u,y) = -\frac{\delta}{p}(k_\delta(0,y) - k_\delta(u,y)) + \frac{k_\delta}{p}F_1(u) + \frac{k_\delta+\rho}{p}(F_1(y) - F_1(u+y)),$$

and letting $u \to \infty$ on both sides of above equation yields

$$1 - m = -\frac{\delta}{p}k_\delta(0,y) + \frac{k_\delta}{p} + \frac{k_\delta+\rho}{p}(F_1(y) - 1).$$

Hence

$$k_\delta(0,y) = \frac{(k_\delta+\rho)F_1(y) - p}{\delta}. \tag{1.56}$$

By making use of (1.55) and (1.56) and making some calculation we get

$$\begin{aligned}\hat{k}_\delta(s,y) = {} & \frac{k_\delta+\rho}{\delta}(1 - \hat{F}_1(s)) - \frac{k_\delta+\rho}{\delta}[1 - (e^{sy}\hat{F}_1(s) - e^{sy}\int_0^y e^{-su}dF_1(u))] \\ & -\frac{p}{\delta}(1 - \hat{E}_\delta(s,y)) + \frac{\rho}{\delta}(1 - \hat{E}_\delta(s,y))\hat{F}_1(s). \end{aligned} \tag{1.57}$$

Upon inverting Laplace-Stieltjes transform, and applying (1.53), the above relation yields

$$\begin{aligned} k_\delta(u,y) = {} & \frac{k_\delta+\rho}{\delta}(1 - F_1(u)) - \frac{k_\delta+\rho}{\delta}(1 - F_1(u+y)) \\ & -\frac{p}{\delta}(1 - E_\delta(u,y)) + \frac{\rho}{\delta}F_1 * (1 - E_\delta(\cdot,y))(u). \end{aligned} \tag{1.58}$$

1.3.2 *Asymptotic Estimates of the Low and Upper Bounds*

Proposition 1.1 *If $\rho < p$, then*

$$k_*(u,y) \leqslant k_\delta(u,y) \leqslant k^*(u,y), \tag{1.59}$$

where

$$\begin{aligned} k_*(u,y) = {} & (1 + \frac{p}{\delta u})^{-1}\frac{k_\delta+\rho}{\delta}(1 - F_1(u)) \\ & -(1 + \frac{p}{\delta u})^{-1}\frac{k_\delta+\rho}{\delta}(1 - F_1(u+y)), \end{aligned} \tag{1.60}$$

$$k^*(u,y) = \frac{p-\rho}{\rho}\frac{(k_\delta+\rho)G_0(u,y)}{\delta\phi_0(u)}. \tag{1.61}$$

Proof. It is obvious that

$$k_\delta(u,y) = \int_u^\infty z\frac{\partial(E_\delta(z,y))}{\partial z}dz \geqslant u(1 - E_\delta(u,y)).$$

So

$$1 - E_\delta(u,y) \leqslant \frac{k_\delta(u,y)}{u}.$$

According to the last inequality and (1.58) we have

$$k_\delta(u,y) \geqslant \frac{k_\delta+\rho}{\delta}(1-F_1(u)) - \frac{p}{\delta}\frac{k_\delta(u,y)}{u} - \frac{k_\delta+\rho}{\delta}(1-F_1(u+y)).$$

Hence

$$\begin{aligned} k_\delta(u,y) &\geqslant (1+\frac{p}{\delta u})^{-1}\frac{k_\delta+\rho}{\delta}(1-F_1(u)) \\ &\quad -(1+\frac{p}{\delta u})^{-1}\frac{k_\delta+\rho}{\delta}(1-F_1(u+y)) \\ &= k_*(u,y). \end{aligned}$$

In addition, it is easy to see that

$$\phi_0 * k_\delta(\cdot,y)(u) \geqslant \phi_0(u)k_\delta(u,y).$$

In view of (1.50), (1.56) and last inequality we get

$$\begin{aligned} 1 - E_\delta(u,y) &\leqslant \frac{\delta}{p-\rho}\phi_0(u)k_\delta(0,y) - \frac{\delta}{p-\rho}\phi_0(u)k_\delta(u,y) \\ &\quad + \frac{p\phi_0(u)}{p-\rho} - \frac{k_\delta+\rho}{p-\rho}F_1(y)\phi_0(u) + \frac{k_\delta+\rho}{\rho}G_0(u,y) \\ &= \frac{k_\delta+\rho}{\rho}G_0(u,y) - \frac{\delta}{p-\rho}\phi_0(u)k_\delta(u,y). \end{aligned}$$

Consequently,

$$\begin{aligned} \phi_0(u)\frac{\delta}{p-\rho}k_\delta(u,y) &\leqslant \frac{k_\delta+\rho}{\rho}G_0(u,y) - (1-E_\delta(u,y)) \\ &\leqslant \frac{k_\delta+\rho}{\rho}G_0(u,y). \end{aligned}$$

Thus

$$k_\delta(u,y) \leqslant \frac{k_\delta+\rho}{\delta}\frac{(p-\rho)G_0(u,y)}{\rho\phi_0(u)} = k^*(u,y).$$

This completes the proof of Proposition 1.1.

Proposition 1.2 *If $\rho < p$, for subexponential F_1,*

$$k_*(u,y) \sim \frac{k_\delta+\rho}{\delta}(1-F_1(u)) - \frac{k_\delta+\rho}{\delta}(1-F_1(u+y)), \quad u\to\infty, \tag{1.62}$$

$$k^*(u,y) \sim \frac{k_\delta+\rho}{\delta}(1-F_1(u)) - \frac{k_\delta+\rho}{\delta}(1-F_1(u+y)) + \frac{k_\delta+\rho}{\delta}\frac{\rho F_1(y)}{p-\rho}(1-F_1(u)), \quad u\to\infty. \tag{1.63}$$

Proof. Clearly, by the definition of $k_*(u,y)$,

$$\begin{aligned} k_*(u,y) &= (1+\frac{p}{\delta u})^{-1}\frac{k_\delta+\rho}{\delta}(1-F_1(u)) \\ &\quad -(1+\frac{p}{\delta u})^{-1}\frac{k_\delta+\rho}{\delta}(1-F_1(u+y)) \\ &\sim \frac{k_\delta+\rho}{\delta}(1-F_1(u)) - \frac{k_\delta+\rho}{\delta}(1-F_1(u+y)),\ u\to\infty. \end{aligned}$$

Because

$$\begin{aligned} G_0(u,y) &= \sum_{n=0}^{\infty} m^{n+1}F_1^{n*}*F_1(\cdot+y)(u) - \sum_{n=0}^{\infty} m^{n+1}F_1^{(n+1)*}(u) \\ &= \sum_{n=0}^{\infty} m^{n+1}(1-\overline{F_1^{n*}})*F_1(\cdot+y)(u) - \sum_{n=0}^{\infty} m^{n+1}(1-\overline{F_1^{(n+1)*}}(u)) \\ &= \sum_{n=0}^{\infty} m^{n+1}F_1(u+y) - \sum_{n=0}^{\infty} m^{n+1} + \sum_{n=0}^{\infty} m^{n+1}\overline{F_1^{(n+1)*}}(u) \\ &\quad - \sum_{n=0}^{\infty} m^{n+1}\overline{F_1^{n*}}*F_1(\cdot+y)(u) \\ &= \frac{-\rho}{p-\rho}(1-F_1(u+y)) + \sum_{n=0}^{\infty} m^{n+1}\overline{F_1^{(n+1)*}}(u) \\ &\quad - \sum_{n=0}^{\infty} m^{n+1}\overline{F_1^{n*}}*F_1(\cdot+y)(u). \end{aligned}$$

Noting that

$$
\begin{aligned}
&\overline{F_1^{n*}} * F_1(\cdot + y)(u) \\
&= \int_0^u \overline{F_1^{n*}}(u-z)dF_1(z+y) = \int_y^{y+u} \overline{F_1^{n*}}(u+y-z)dF_1(z) \\
&= \int_0^{y+u} \overline{F_1^{n*}}(u+y-z)dF_1(z) - \int_0^y \overline{F_1^{n*}}(u+y-z)dF_1(z) \\
&= \int_0^{y+u} (1 - F_1^{n*}(u+y-z))dF_1(z) - \int_0^y \overline{F_1^{n*}}(u+y-z)dF_1(z) \\
&= F_1(y+u) - \int_0^{y+u} F_1^{n*}(u+y-z)dF_1(z) - \int_0^y \overline{F_1^{n*}}(u+y-z)dF_1(z) \\
&= F_1(y+u) - F_1^{(n+1)*}(y+u) - \int_0^y \overline{F_1^{n*}}(u+y-z)dF_1(z),
\end{aligned}
$$

and making use of Lemma 2.5.1, Lemma 2.5.3 and Theorem 2.5.3 in [Rolski *et al.* (1999)] and the dominated convergence theorem we obtain

$$
\begin{aligned}
&\lim_{u\to\infty} \frac{\sum_{n=0}^{\infty} m^{n+1}\overline{F_1^{(n+1)*}}(u) - \sum_{n=0}^{\infty} m^{n+1}\overline{F_1^{n*}} * F_1(\cdot + y)(u)}{\frac{\rho}{p-\rho}\overline{F_1}(u)} \\
&= \frac{p-\rho}{\rho}\sum_{n=0}^{\infty} m^{n+1} \lim_{u\to\infty} \frac{\overline{F_1^{(n+1)*}}(u)}{\overline{F_1}(u)} - \frac{p-\rho}{\rho}\sum_{n=0}^{\infty} m^{n+1} \cdot \\
&\quad \lim_{u\to\infty} \left[\frac{F_1(y+u) - F_1^{(n+1)*}(y+u) - \int_0^y \overline{F_1^{n*}}(u+y-z)dF_1(z)}{\overline{F_1}(u)} \right] \\
&= \frac{p-\rho}{\rho}\sum_{n=0}^{\infty} m^{n+1}(n+1) - \frac{p-\rho}{\rho}\sum_{n=0}^{\infty} m^{n+1} \cdot \\
&\quad \lim_{u\to\infty} \left[\frac{\overline{F_1^{(n+1)*}}(y+u) - \overline{F_1}(y+u) - \int_0^y \overline{F_1^{n*}}(u+y-z)dF_1(z)}{\overline{F_1}(u)} \right] \\
&= \frac{p-\rho}{\rho}\sum_{n=0}^{\infty} m^{n+1}(n+1) - \frac{p-\rho}{\rho}\sum_{n=0}^{\infty} m^{n+1}(n - nF_1(y)) \\
&= \frac{p-\rho\overline{F_1}(y)}{p-\rho}.
\end{aligned}
$$

The above limit is due to the subexponentiality of F_1. Hence,

$$\sum_{n=0}^{\infty} m^{n+1}\overline{F_1^{(n+1)*}}(u) - \sum_{n=0}^{\infty} m^{n+1}\overline{F_1^{n*}} * F_1(\cdot + y)(u)$$
$$\sim \frac{\rho\overline{F_1}(u)(p-\rho\overline{F_1}(y))}{(p-\rho)^2}, \quad u\to\infty.$$

So we have that

$$G_0(u,y) \sim \frac{-\rho}{p-\rho}(1-F_1(u+y)) + \frac{\rho\overline{F_1}(u)(p-\rho\overline{F_1}(y))}{(p-\rho)^2}, \quad u\to\infty.$$

Thus

$$\begin{aligned}
k^*(u,y) &\sim \frac{k_\delta+\rho}{\delta}\cdot\frac{p-\rho}{\rho}\cdot\frac{\rho\overline{F_1}(u)(p-\rho\overline{F_1}(y))}{(p-\rho)^2} \\
&\quad -\frac{k_\delta+\rho}{\delta}\cdot\frac{p-\rho}{\rho}\cdot\frac{\rho}{p-\rho}(1-F_1(u+y)) \\
&= \frac{k_\delta+\rho}{\delta}\left[\frac{\overline{F}_1(u)(p-\rho+\rho F_1(y))}{p-\rho} - (1-F_1(u+y))\right] \\
&= \frac{k_\delta+\rho}{\delta}(1-F_1(u)) - \frac{k_\delta+\rho}{\delta}(1-F_1(u+y)) \\
&\quad +\frac{k_\delta+\rho}{\delta}\cdot\frac{\rho F_1(y)}{p-\rho}(1-F_1(u)).
\end{aligned}$$

Therefore, (1.62) and (1.63) are all true, and this completes the proof of Proposition 1.2.

From (1.42) and the definition of $k_\delta(u,y)$ it follows that

$$\begin{aligned}
\frac{G_\delta(u,y)}{G_\delta(0,y)} &= 1-E_\delta(u,y) = E_\delta(\infty,y)-E_\delta(u,y) = \int_u^\infty \frac{\partial E_\delta(v,y)}{\partial v}dv \\
&= -\int_u^\infty \frac{1}{v}\frac{\partial k_\delta(v,y)}{\partial v}dv = \frac{k_\delta(u,y)}{u} - \int_u^\infty \frac{k_\delta(v,y)}{v^2}dv. \qquad (1.64)
\end{aligned}$$

Evidently, $k_*(z,y) \leqslant k_\delta(z,y) \leqslant k^*(z,y)$, it is easy to verify that

$$\frac{k_*(u,y)}{u} - \int_u^\infty \frac{k^*(v,y)}{v^2}dv \leqslant \frac{G_\delta(u,y)}{G_\delta(0,y)} \leqslant \frac{k^*(u,y)}{u} - \int_u^\infty \frac{k_*(v,y)}{v^2}dv. \quad (1.65)$$

Put

$$G^*(u,y) = G_\delta(0,y)\left[\tfrac{k^*(u,y)}{u} - \int_u^\infty \tfrac{k_*(v,y)}{v^2}dv\right],$$
$$G_*(u,y) = G_\delta(0,y)\left[\tfrac{k_*(u,y)}{u} - \int_u^\infty \tfrac{k^*(v,y)}{v^2}dv\right].$$

Then (1.65) implies

$$G_*(u,y) \leqslant G_\delta(u,y) \leqslant G^*(u,y). \tag{1.66}$$

Next, we are going to estimate $G_*(u,y)$ and $G^*(u,y)$, the lower and upper bounds of $G_\delta(u,y)$. Before we give our main result of this section, we need one lemma, which is used in the proof of following Theorem 1.8.

Lemma 1.1 *Suppose that $f_1(u) \sim g_1(u)$ and $f_2(u) \sim g_2(u), u \to \infty$. If $\lim\limits_{u\to\infty} \frac{f_2(u)}{f_1(u)} \neq 1$, then $f_1(u) - f_2(u) \sim g_1(u) - g_2(u), u \to \infty$.*

Proof. By the assumptions of Lemma we have that

$$\begin{aligned}
\lim_{u\to\infty} \frac{f_1(u) - f_2(u)}{g_1(u) - g_2(u)} &= \lim_{u\to\infty} \frac{1 - \frac{f_2(u)}{f_1(u)}}{\frac{g_1(u)}{f_1(u)} - \frac{g_2(u)}{f_1(u)}} \\
&= \frac{1 - \lim\limits_{u\to\infty} \frac{f_2(u)}{f_1(u)}}{\lim\limits_{u\to\infty} \frac{g_1(u)}{f_1(u)} - \lim\limits_{u\to\infty} \frac{g_2(u)}{f_2(u)} \cdot \frac{f_2(u)}{f_1(u)}} \\
&= \frac{1 - \lim\limits_{u\to\infty} \frac{f_2(u)}{f_1(u)}}{1 - \lim\limits_{u\to\infty} \frac{f_2(u)}{f_1(u)}} = 1.
\end{aligned}$$

Hence, we obtain immediately the required assertion.

Theorem 1.8 *If $\rho < p$, F_1 is subexponential. Then for $u \to \infty$,*

$$G_*(u,y) \sim \frac{\lambda}{\delta} \int_u^{u+y} \frac{1-F(z)}{z} dz - \frac{\rho^2 F_1(y)}{(p-\rho)\delta} \int_u^\infty \frac{1-F(z)}{z^2} dz, \tag{1.67}$$

$$G^*(u,y) \sim \frac{\lambda}{\delta} \int_u^{u+y} \frac{1-F(z)}{z} dz + \frac{\rho^2 F_1(y)}{(p-\rho)\delta} \cdot \frac{1-F(u)}{u}. \tag{1.68}$$

Proof. Firstly, it is easy to see from (1.60), (1.61) and (1.47) that

$$\lim_{u\to\infty} \frac{\int_u^\infty \frac{k^*(v,y)}{v^2} dv}{\frac{k_*(u,y)}{u}} \neq 1.$$

So, according to (1.62) and (1.63) and Lemma 1.1, a straightforward computation gives

$$\begin{aligned}
\frac{G_*(u,y)}{G_\delta(0,y)} &= \frac{k_*(u,y)}{u} - \int_u^\infty \frac{k^*(v,y)}{v^2}dv \\
&\sim \frac{k_\delta+\rho}{\delta}\left[\frac{1-F_1(u)}{u} - \frac{1-F_1(u+y)}{u}\right] \\
&\quad -\frac{k_\delta+\rho}{\delta}\int_u^\infty \left(\frac{1-F_1(z)}{z^2} - \frac{1-F_1(z+y)}{z^2}\right. \\
&\quad \left. + \frac{\rho F_1(y)}{p-\rho}\cdot\frac{1-F_1(z)}{z^2}\right)dz \\
&\sim \frac{k_\delta+\rho}{\delta}\left[\frac{F_1(u+y)}{u+y} - \frac{F_1(u)}{u}\right] \\
&\quad -\frac{k_\delta+\rho}{\delta}\int_u^\infty \left(\frac{F_1(z+y)}{(z+y)^2} - \frac{F_1(z)}{z^2}\right)dz \\
&\quad -\frac{k_\delta+\rho}{\delta}\cdot\frac{\rho F_1(y)}{p-\rho}\int_u^\infty \frac{1-F_1(z)}{z^2}dz \\
&= \frac{k_\delta+\rho}{\delta}\left[\frac{F_1(u+y)}{u+y} - \frac{F_1(u)}{u}\right] + \frac{k_\delta+\rho}{\delta}\int_u^\infty \frac{F_1(z)}{z^2}dz \\
&\quad -\frac{k_\delta+\rho}{\delta}\int_u^\infty \frac{F_1(z+y)}{(z+y)^2}dz - \frac{k_\delta+\rho}{\delta}\cdot\frac{\rho F_1(y)}{p-\rho}\int_u^\infty \frac{1-F_1(z)}{z^2}dz \\
&= \frac{k_\delta+\rho}{\delta}\int_u^{u+y}\frac{1}{z}dF_1(z) - \frac{k_\delta+\rho}{\delta}\cdot\frac{\rho F_1(y)}{p-\rho}\int_u^\infty \frac{1-F_1(z)}{z^2}dz \\
&= \frac{\lambda}{\delta}\int_u^{u+y}\frac{1-F(z)}{z}dz\cdot\frac{1}{G_\delta(0,y)} \\
&\quad -\frac{\rho^2 F_1(y)}{\delta(p-\rho)}\int_u^\infty \frac{1-F_1(z)}{z^2}dz\cdot\frac{1}{G_\delta(0,y)},
\end{aligned}$$

and this yields (1.67). (1.68) is proven similarly by using (1.62) and (1.63) and making some calculations.

Remark 1.7 *Although Theorem 1.8 gives asymptotic formulas of the low and upper bounds for the distribution of the surplus immediately after ruin under subexponential claims, unfortunately, the asymptotic formulas for $G_*(u,y)$ and $G^*(u,y)$ given in Theorem 1.8 are not equal. Thus, we still do not know what the asymptotic formula for $G_\delta(u,y)$ is.*

1.4 On the Ruin Probability under a Class of Risk Processes

In this section a class of collective risk model with non-Poissonian claims' arrival processes is considered. A clear expression for Laplace transform of the finite time ruin probability is well given when the claim amount distribution is the mixture of two exponentials. As its consequence, one result by [Malinovskii(1998)] about the expression for Laplace transform of the ruin probability within finite time is obtained when the claim amount distribution is a exponential. Finally, a well-known result in [Gerber(1979)] about ultimate ruin probability in the classical risk model is proved again.

1.4.1 *The Risk Model*

In this section we consider a Sparre Andersen risk process

$$R(t) = u + ct - \sum_{i=1}^{N(t)} Y_i,$$

defined in terms of the following values: $u = R(0) \geqslant 0$ is the initial risk reserve, $c > 0$ is the premium received continuously per unit time, $\{T_i, i \geqslant 1\}$ are the (iid) interclaim time, $N(t)$ denotes number of claims having occurred up to time t, i.e., $N(t) = \max\{n : T_1 + T_2 + \cdots + T_n \leqslant t\}$, and $\{Y_i, i \geqslant 1\}$ are the (iid) amounts of claims. Throughout this section, we suppose that $\{T_i, i \geqslant 1\}$ and $\{Y_j, j \geqslant 1\}$ are independent, and the relative security loading $\Lambda = \frac{c \cdot ET_1}{EY_1} - 1 > 0$, which means that the premium received per unit time exceed the expected claim payments per unit time. Denote by $\psi(t,u), \psi(u)$ and $\phi(t,u)$ the probability of ruin within finite time, the probability of ultimate ruin and the probability of survival to time t, respectively. Clearly, $\psi(t,u) = 1 - \phi(t,u)$.

1.4.2 *The Laplace Transform of the Ruin Probability with Finite Time*

Our main result in this subsection is the following theorem.

Theorem 1.9 *Let the claim sizes $\{Y_i, i \geqslant 1\}$ and interoccurrence times $\{T_i, i \geqslant 1\}$ be mutually independent and i.i.d. Let Y_1 be a mixed exponential and its p.d.f. be $p\lambda_1 e^{-\lambda_1 y} + q\lambda_2 e^{-\lambda_2 y}, y > 0, 0 < \lambda_1 < \lambda_2, p + q = 1, 0 \leqslant p, q \leqslant 1$. Assume that $\gamma(\alpha) = \int_0^\infty e^{-\alpha u} P_T(du)$ is the Laplace transform of*

T_1, where $P_T(u)$ is the distribution function of T_1. Then for $\alpha > 0$,

$$\begin{aligned}&\alpha\int_0^\infty e^{-\alpha t}\psi(t,u)dt\\&=\frac{(\lambda_1-\lambda_2)[y_1(\alpha)\beta_2(\alpha)e^{-\beta_1(\alpha)u}-y_2(\alpha)\beta_1(\alpha)e^{-\beta_2(\alpha)u}]}{(\lambda_1-\beta_2(\alpha))(\lambda_2-\beta_1(\alpha))-(\lambda_1-\beta_1(\alpha))(\lambda_2-\beta_2(\alpha))},\end{aligned} \tag{1.69}$$

where $y_1(\alpha) = (1-\frac{\beta_1(\alpha)}{\lambda_1})(1-\frac{\beta_1(\alpha)}{\lambda_2})$, $y_2(\alpha) = (1-\frac{\beta_2(\alpha)}{\lambda_1})(1-\frac{\beta_2(\alpha)}{\lambda_2})$, $\beta_1(\alpha), \beta_2(\alpha)$ *are, respectively, the unique solutions of the equation*

$$(\lambda_1-\beta)(\lambda_2-\beta)-[\lambda_1\lambda_2-(p\lambda_1+q\lambda_2)\beta]\gamma(\alpha+c\beta)=0 \tag{1.70}$$

in $(0,\lambda_1]$ *and* $[\beta_0,\lambda_2]$, *and* $\beta_0=\frac{\lambda_1\lambda_2}{p\lambda_1+q\lambda_2}$.

Remark 1.8 *Equation (1.70) has the unique root, respectively, in* $(0,\lambda_1]$ *and* $[\beta_0,\lambda_2]$. *In fact, Let*

$$f(\beta)=(\lambda_1-\beta)(\lambda_2-\beta)-[\lambda_1\lambda_2-(p\lambda_1+q\lambda_2)\beta]\gamma(\alpha+c\beta),$$

then $f(0)>0, f(\lambda_1)\leqslant 0, f(\beta_0)\leqslant 0, f(\lambda_2)\geqslant 0$. *By the existence theorem of root we know that Equation (1.70) has the roots in* $(0,\lambda_1]$ *and* $[\beta_0,\lambda_2]$. *On the other hand, it is very easy to prove the uniqueness of roots by the positiveness of relative security loading and the convexity of* $\gamma(\alpha+c\beta)$ *with respect to* β.

Proof. Let $\tau=\inf\{t>0: R(t)<0\}$ be the *first time of ruin* with the understanding that $\tau=\infty$ if $R(t)\geqslant 0$ for all t. Let $U_n=\sum_{i=1}^n T_i, U_0=0, \nu=\inf\{n\geqslant 1: R(U_n)<0\}$, and ν is the index of that claim which causes the first ruin. If for each n, $R(U_n)\geqslant 0$, then $\nu=\infty$. Clearly, $\tau=U_\nu$. For $t,x\geqslant 0$, denote $Q^n(t,x)=P\{U_n\leqslant t, R(U_n)\leqslant x, n<\nu\}, H(t,x)=\sum_{n\geqslant 0}Q^n(t,x)$, and Laplace transform of $H(t,x)$ denoted by $\hat{H}(\alpha,\beta)$. Then for $\alpha,\beta>0$,

$$\begin{aligned}&\hat{H}(\alpha,\beta)\\&=\int_0^\infty\int_0^\infty e^{-\alpha t-\beta x}H(dt,dx)=\sum_{n\geqslant 0}E[e^{-\alpha U_n-\beta R(U_n)}I_{\{\nu>n\}}].\end{aligned} \tag{1.71}$$

Obviously, (1.71) is *analytical*. Since

$$\begin{aligned}\phi(t,u) &= P(\tau > t)\\ &= \sum_{n\geqslant 0} P(\tau > t, U_n \leqslant t < U_{n+1})\\ &= \sum_{n\geqslant 0} P(\nu > n, U_n \leqslant t, T_{n+1} > t - U_n)\\ &= \sum_{n\geqslant 0}\int_0^t\int_0^\infty Q^n(d\mu, dz)(1 - P_T(t-\mu))\\ &= \int_0^t H(d\mu,\infty)(1 - P_T(t-\mu)),\end{aligned} \tag{1.72}$$

then we get

$$d\phi(t,u) = -\int_0^t P_T'(t-\mu)H(d\mu,\infty)dt + H(dt,\infty). \tag{1.73}$$

Consequently,

$$\begin{aligned}\alpha\int_0^\infty e^{-\alpha t}\phi(t,u)dt &= -\int_0^\infty \phi(t,u)de^{-\alpha t}\\ &= \int_0^\infty e^{-\alpha t}d\phi(t,u)\\ &= \int_0^\infty\int_0^t e^{-\alpha t}(-P_T'(t-\mu))H(d\mu,\infty)dt\\ &\quad + \int_0^\infty e^{-\alpha t}H(dt,\infty)\\ &= \int_0^\infty\int_0^t e^{-\alpha\mu}e^{-\alpha(t-\mu)}(-P_T'(t-\mu))H(d\mu,\infty)dt\\ &\quad + \hat{H}(\alpha,0)\\ &= \int_0^\infty e^{-\alpha\mu}(\int_\mu^\infty e^{-\alpha(t-\mu)}(-P_T'(t-\mu))dt)H(d\mu,\infty)\\ &\quad + \hat{H}(\alpha,0)\\ &= \int_0^\infty e^{-\alpha\mu}\int_0^\infty e^{-\alpha y}(-P_T'(y))dyH(d\mu,\infty) + \hat{H}(\alpha,0)\\ &= -\int_0^\infty \gamma(\alpha)e^{-\alpha\mu}H(d\mu,\infty) + \hat{H}(\alpha,0)\\ &= \hat{H}(\alpha,0)(1-\gamma(\alpha)).\end{aligned} \tag{1.74}$$

Now we turn our attention to computation of $\hat{H}(\alpha, 0)$. To this end, denote $\Omega_n = \sigma\{Y_1, T_1, Y_2, T_2, \cdots, Y_n, T_n\}$. Noting that

$$
\begin{aligned}
& E[e^{-\beta R(U_n)} I_{\{R(U_n)\geqslant 0\}} | \Omega_{n-1}, T_n] \\
= & \int_0^{R(U_{n-1})+cT_n} \exp\{-\beta(R(U_{n-1}) + cT_n - y)\}(p\lambda_1 e^{-\lambda_1 y} + q\lambda_2 e^{-\lambda_2 y}) dy \\
= & \frac{p\lambda_1}{\lambda_1 - \beta}[e^{-\beta(R(U_{n-1})+cT_n)} - e^{-\lambda_1(R(U_{n-1})+cT_n)}] \\
& + \frac{q\lambda_2}{\lambda_2 - \beta}[e^{-\beta(R(U_{n-1})+cT_n)} - e^{-\lambda_2(R(U_{n-1})+cT_n)}],
\end{aligned}
$$

we get

$$
\begin{aligned}
& E[e^{-\alpha U_n - \beta R(U_n)} I_{\{R(U_n)\geqslant 0\}} | \Omega_{n-1}] \\
= & E[E(e^{-\alpha U_n - \beta R(U_n)} I_{\{R(U_n)\geqslant 0\}} | \Omega_{n-1}, T_n) | \Omega_{n-1}] \\
= & E[e^{-\alpha U_n} (\frac{p\lambda_1}{\lambda_1 - \beta}[e^{-\beta(R(U_{n-1})+cT_n)} - e^{-\lambda_1(R(U_{n-1})+cT_n)}] \\
& + \frac{q\lambda_2}{\lambda_2 - \beta}[e^{-\beta(R(U_{n-1})+cT_n)} - e^{-\lambda_2(R(U_{n-1})+cT_n)}]) | \Omega_{n-1}] \\
= & \frac{p\lambda_1}{\lambda_1 - \beta} e^{-\alpha U_{n-1}} [e^{-\beta R(U_{n-1})}\gamma(\alpha + c\beta) - e^{-\lambda_1 R(U_{n-1})}\gamma(\alpha + c\lambda_1)] \\
& + \frac{q\lambda_2}{\lambda_2 - \beta} e^{-\alpha U_{n-1}} [e^{-\beta R(U_{n-1})}\gamma(\alpha + c\beta) - e^{-\lambda_2 R(U_{n-1})}\gamma(\alpha + c\lambda_2)].
\end{aligned}
\tag{1.75}
$$

Therefore, by using (1.75) we get

$$
\begin{aligned}
& \hat{H}(\alpha, \beta) - e^{-\beta u} = \sum_{n\geqslant 1} E[e^{-\alpha U_n - \beta R(U_n)} I_{\{\nu > n\}}] \\
= & \sum_{n\geqslant 1} E[E(e^{-\alpha U_n - \beta R(U_n)} I_{\{\nu > n\}} | \Omega_{n-1})] \\
= & \sum_{n\geqslant 1} E[I_{\{\nu > n-1\}} E(e^{-\alpha U_n - \beta R(U_n)} I_{\{R(U_n)\geqslant 0\}} | \Omega_{n-1})] \\
= & \frac{p\lambda_1}{\lambda_1 - \beta}[\gamma(\alpha + c\beta)\hat{H}(\alpha, \beta) - \gamma(\alpha + c\lambda_1)\hat{H}(\alpha, \lambda_1)] \\
& + \frac{q\lambda_2}{\lambda_2 - \beta}[\gamma(\alpha + c\beta)\hat{H}(\alpha, \beta) - \gamma(\alpha + c\lambda_2)\hat{H}(\alpha, \lambda_2)].
\end{aligned}
\tag{1.76}
$$

It is easy from (1.76) to get that

$$\hat{H}(\alpha,\beta)=\frac{e^{-\beta u}-\frac{p\lambda_1}{\lambda_1-\beta}\gamma(\alpha+c\lambda_1)\hat{H}(\alpha,\lambda_1)-\frac{q\lambda_2}{\lambda_2-\beta}\gamma(\alpha+c\lambda_2)\hat{H}(\alpha,\lambda_2)}{1-(\frac{p\lambda_1}{\lambda_1-\beta}+\frac{q\lambda_2}{\lambda_2-\beta})\gamma(\alpha+c\beta)}$$

$$=\frac{A-B-C}{(\lambda_1-\beta)(\lambda_2-\beta)-[\lambda_1\lambda_2-(p\lambda_1+q\lambda_2)\beta]\gamma(\alpha+c\beta)}, \quad (1.77)$$

where

$$A=(\lambda_1-\beta)(\lambda_2-\beta)e^{-\beta u},$$

$$B=p\lambda_1(\lambda_2-\beta)\gamma(\alpha+c\lambda_1)\hat{H}(\alpha,\lambda_1),$$

$$C=q\lambda_2(\lambda_1-\beta)\gamma(\alpha+c\lambda_2)\hat{H}(\alpha,\lambda_2).$$

Since $\beta_1(\alpha)$ and $\beta_2(\alpha)$ are two roots of Equation (1.70), and $\hat{H}(\alpha,\beta)$ is *analytical*, thus $\beta_1(\alpha),\beta_2(\alpha)$ satisfy the following equations:

$$(\lambda_1-\beta_1(\alpha))(\lambda_2-\beta_1(\alpha))e^{-\beta_1(\alpha)u}-p\lambda_1(\lambda_2-\beta_1(\alpha))\gamma(\alpha+c\lambda_1)\hat{H}(\alpha,\lambda_1)$$
$$=q\lambda_2(\lambda_1-\beta_1(\alpha))\gamma(\alpha+c\lambda_2)\hat{H}(\alpha,\lambda_2),$$

$$(\lambda_1-\beta_2(\alpha))(\lambda_2-\beta_2(\alpha))e^{-\beta_2(\alpha)u}-p\lambda_1(\lambda_2-\beta_2(\alpha))\gamma(\alpha+c\lambda_1)\hat{H}(\alpha,\lambda_1)$$
$$=q\lambda_2(\lambda_1-\beta_2(\alpha))\gamma(\alpha+c\lambda_2)\hat{H}(\alpha,\lambda_2).$$

Solving the above equations we obtain

$$\gamma(\alpha+c\lambda_1)\hat{H}(\alpha,\lambda_1)$$
$$=\frac{(\lambda_1-\beta_1(\alpha))(\lambda_1-\beta_2(\alpha))[(\lambda_2-\beta_1(\alpha))e^{-\beta_1(\alpha)u}-(\lambda_2-\beta_2(\alpha))e^{-\beta_2(\alpha)u}]}{p\lambda_1[(\lambda_1-\beta_2(\alpha))(\lambda_2-\beta_1(\alpha))-(\lambda_1-\beta_1(\alpha))(\lambda_2-\beta_2(\alpha))]},$$

$$\gamma(\alpha+c\lambda_2)\hat{H}(\alpha,\lambda_2)$$
$$=\frac{(\lambda_2-\beta_1(\alpha))(\lambda_2-\beta_2(\alpha))[(\lambda_1-\beta_2(\alpha))e^{-\beta_2(\alpha)u}-(\lambda_1-\beta_1(\alpha))e^{-\beta_1(\alpha)u}]}{q\lambda_2[(\lambda_1-\beta_2(\alpha))(\lambda_2-\beta_1(\alpha))-(\lambda_1-\beta_1(\alpha))(\lambda_2-\beta_2(\alpha))]}.$$

Thus

$$
\begin{aligned}
&\hat{H}(\alpha,\beta)\\
&= \left[(\lambda_1-\beta)(\lambda_2-\beta)-[\lambda_1\lambda_2-(p\lambda_1+q\lambda_2)\beta]\gamma(\alpha+c\beta)\right]^{-1}\\
&\quad\times\big\{(\lambda_1-\beta)(\lambda_2-\beta)e^{-\beta u}\\
&\quad-[(\lambda_1-\beta_2(\alpha))(\lambda_2-\beta_1(\alpha))-(\lambda_1-\beta_1(\alpha))(\lambda_2-\beta_2(\alpha))]^{-1}\\
&\quad\times\big[(\lambda_2-\beta)(\lambda_1-\beta_1(\alpha))(\lambda_1-\beta_2(\alpha))[(\lambda_2-\beta_1(\alpha))e^{-\beta_1(\alpha)u}\\
&\quad-(\lambda_2-\beta_2(\alpha))e^{-\beta_2(\alpha)u}]\\
&\quad+(\lambda_1-\beta)(\lambda_2-\beta_1(\alpha))(\lambda_2-\beta_2(\alpha))[(\lambda_1-\beta_2(\alpha))e^{-\beta_2(\alpha)u}\\
&\quad-(\lambda_1-\beta_1(\alpha))e^{-\beta_1(\alpha)u}]\big]\big\}.
\end{aligned}
$$

Let $\beta = 0$, then

$$
\begin{aligned}
&\hat{H}(\alpha,0)\\
&= \frac{1}{1-\gamma(\alpha)}\cdot\left\{1-\frac{(\lambda_1-\lambda_2)D}{(\lambda_1-\beta_2(\alpha))(\lambda_2-\beta_1(\alpha))-(\lambda_1-\beta_1(\alpha))(\lambda_2-\beta_2(\alpha))}\right\},
\end{aligned}
\tag{1.78}
$$

where

$$
\begin{aligned}
D = [(1-\frac{\beta_1(\alpha)}{\lambda_1})(1-\frac{\beta_1(\alpha)}{\lambda_2})\beta_2(\alpha)e^{-\beta_1(\alpha)u}\\
-(1-\frac{\beta_2(\alpha)}{\lambda_1})(1-\frac{\beta_2(\alpha)}{\lambda_2})\beta_1(\alpha)e^{-\beta_2(\alpha)u}].
\end{aligned}
$$

By (1.74) and (1.78) we have

$$
\begin{aligned}
&\alpha\int_0^\infty e^{-\alpha t}\phi(t,u)dt = \hat{H}(\alpha,0)(1-\gamma(\alpha))\\
&= 1-(\lambda_1-\lambda_2)\frac{y_1(\alpha)\beta_2(\alpha)e^{-\beta_1(\alpha)u}-y_2(\alpha)\beta_1(\alpha)e^{-\beta_2(\alpha)u}}{(\lambda_1-\beta_2(\alpha))(\lambda_2-\beta_1(\alpha))-(\lambda_1-\beta_1(\alpha))(\lambda_2-\beta_2(\alpha))},
\end{aligned}
\tag{1.79}
$$

where $y_1(\alpha) = (1-\frac{\beta_1(\alpha)}{\lambda_1})(1-\frac{\beta_1(\alpha)}{\lambda_2})$, $y_2(\alpha) = (1-\frac{\beta_2(\alpha)}{\lambda_1})(1-\frac{\beta_2(\alpha)}{\lambda_2})$. Since $\psi(t,u) = 1-\phi(t,u)$, (1.69) follows immediately from (1.79).

Remark 1.9 *Theorem 1.9 shows an exact numerical technique which requires merely numerical inversion of the Laplace transform of the ruin probability within finite time. Numerical methods of such an inversion could be found in [Abate and Whitt(1992)], and we don't discuss it here. On the other hand, it is well known that the probabilities of ruin $\psi(t,u)$ and $\psi(u)$*

can be identified with the virtual and limiting waiting time distributions, respectively, in a single server queue fed by a renewal process and having the service time distribution B. So, it is possible to prove Theorem 1.9 by virtue of related results from the theory of queues (see, for example, [Prabhu(1965)] and [Prabhu(1980)]).

1.4.3 *Two Corollaries*

As one application of Theorem 1.9, we can get the following two corollaries. The first corollary is about the expression for Laplace transform of the ruin probability within finite time when the claim amount distribution is a exponential, which was obtained by [Malinovskii(1998)]. The second corollary is concerned with a result about ultimate ruin probability in the classical risk model which was proved by [Gerber(1979)].

Corollary 1.1 *Let the sizes of claims $\{Y_i, i \geqslant 1\}$ and the inter-claims $\{T_i, i \geqslant 1\}$ be iid and mutually independent. Assume that $Y_1 \sim$ Exponential$(\lambda), \lambda > 0$, and $\gamma(\alpha) = \int_0^\infty e^{-\alpha u} P_T(du)$ is the Laplace transform of T_1. Then*

$$\alpha \int_0^\infty e^{-\alpha t}\phi(t,u)dt = 1 - y(\alpha)\exp\{-u\lambda(1-y(\alpha))\}, \alpha > 0, \quad (1.80)$$

where $y(\alpha)$ is the unique root in $(0,1)$ of Equation

$$y = \gamma(\alpha + c\lambda(1-y)), \alpha > 0. \quad (1.81)$$

Proof. Taking $p = 1, \lambda_1 = \lambda$ in (1.70) of Theorem 1.9 yields

$$(\lambda_2 - \beta)(\lambda - \beta - \lambda\gamma(\alpha + c\beta)) = 0, \alpha > 0. \quad (1.82)$$

Therefore we get that $\beta_2(\alpha) = \lambda_2$, and $\beta_1(\alpha)$ is the unique root of Equation

$$\lambda - \beta - \lambda\gamma(\alpha + c\beta) = 0, \alpha > 0. \quad (1.83)$$

Moreover, $y_1(\alpha) = (1 - \frac{\beta_1(\alpha)}{\lambda})(1 - \frac{\beta_1(\alpha)}{\lambda_2}), y_2(\alpha) = 0$, and the right side of (1.69) is $(1 - \frac{\beta_1(\alpha)}{\lambda})e^{-\beta_1(\alpha)u}$. Put $y(\alpha) = 1 - \frac{\beta_1(\alpha)}{\lambda}$. Then

$$(1 - \frac{\beta_1(\alpha)}{\lambda})e^{-\beta_1(\alpha)u} = y(\alpha)\exp\{-u\lambda(1-y(\alpha))\}.$$

Again by (1.83) we see that $y(\alpha)$ is the unique root of the Equation (1.81) in $(0,1)$. Finally, (1.80) follows immediately from (1.69) by $\psi(t,u) = 1 - \phi(t,u)$.

Corollary 1.2 *For the classical risk model, in the case of exponential claim amounts, the ultimate ruin probability is an exponential function of the initial surplus measured in mean claim amounts. In other words, if the interclaims* $\{T_i, i \geqslant 1\} \sim$ *Exponential*$(\mu), \mu > 0$, *the sizes of claims* $\{Y_i, i \geqslant 1\} \sim$ *Exponential*$(\lambda), \lambda > 0$. *Then* $\psi(u) = \frac{1}{1+\Lambda} \exp\{-\frac{\Lambda}{1+\Lambda} \frac{u}{E(Y_1)}\}$, *where* $\Lambda = \frac{c}{\mu E Y_1} - 1 = \frac{c\lambda}{\mu} - 1$.

Before we give the proof of this Corollary, we need the following Lemma, whose proof is very easy by induction, and so is omitted.

Lemma 1.2 *When* $0 < x \leqslant \frac{1}{4}$, *for any nonnegative integer* n, *the following equality always holds:*

$$\sum_{k=0}^{\infty} \frac{(n+2k)!}{k!(n+k+1)!} x^k = \frac{1}{(n+1)} \left(\frac{1+\sqrt{1-4x}}{2}\right)^{-(n+1)}. \tag{1.84}$$

Remark 1.10 *When* $0 < p < 1, 0 < q < 1, p+q = 1$, *for any nonnegative interger* n,

$$\sum_{k=0}^{\infty} \frac{(n+1)(n+2k)!}{k!(n+k+1)!} p^k q^{n+k+1} = \begin{cases} 1, & 0 < p \leqslant \frac{1}{2}, \\ (\frac{q}{p})^{n+1}, & \frac{1}{2} < p < 1. \end{cases} \tag{1.85}$$

Proof. Evidently, $0 < pq \leqslant \frac{1}{4}$. Therefore by Lemma 1.2 we see that

$$\sum_{k=0}^{\infty} \frac{(n+2k)!}{k!(n+k+1)!} (pq)^k = \frac{1}{n+1} \left(\frac{1+\sqrt{1-4pq}}{2}\right)^{-(n+1)}.$$

Consequently,

$$\begin{aligned} \sum_{k=0}^{\infty} \frac{(n+1)(n+2k)!}{k!(n+k+1)!} p^k q^{n+k+1} &= q^{n+1} \left(\frac{1+|1-2p|}{2}\right)^{-(n+1)} \\ &= \begin{cases} 1, & 0 < p \leqslant \frac{1}{2}, \\ (\frac{q}{p})^{n+1}, & \frac{1}{2} < p < 1. \end{cases} \end{aligned}$$

The following (1.86) comes immediately from the above (1.85).

Remark 1.11 *Let* $p = \frac{1}{2+\Lambda}, q = \frac{1+\Lambda}{2+\Lambda}$, *where* Λ *is the relative safety loading,* $\Lambda > 0$. *Then for any nonnegative integer* n *we have*

$$\sum_{k=0}^{\infty} \frac{(n+1)(n+2k)!}{k!(n+k+1)!} \left(\frac{1}{2+\Lambda}\right)^k \left(\frac{1+\Lambda}{2+\Lambda}\right)^{n+k+1} = 1. \tag{1.86}$$

The Proof of Corollary 1.2 Since $\{T_i, i \geqslant 1\} \sim E(\mu), \mu > 0, \gamma(\alpha) = \frac{\mu}{\alpha+\mu}$, by Corollary 1.1 we have $y(\alpha) = \gamma(\alpha + c\lambda(1-y(\alpha))) = \frac{\mu}{\alpha+c\lambda(1-y(\alpha))+\mu}$, i.e.,

$$c\lambda y^2(\alpha) - (\alpha + \mu + c\lambda)y(\alpha) + \mu = 0.$$

Again by Corollary 1.1 we get

$$y(\alpha) = 4\mu\left(\sqrt{\alpha + (\sqrt{\mu} + \sqrt{c\lambda})^2} + \sqrt{\alpha + (\sqrt{\mu} - \sqrt{c\lambda})^2}\right)^{-2}. \quad (1.87)$$

Put $x = (\sqrt{\mu} + \sqrt{c\lambda})^2, y = (\sqrt{\mu} - \sqrt{c\lambda})^2$, then

$$y(\alpha) = \sqrt{\frac{\mu}{c\lambda}}(x - y)(\sqrt{\alpha + x} + \sqrt{\alpha + y})^{-2}. \quad (1.88)$$

Thus $y(\alpha)$ is the Laplace transform of $\sqrt{\frac{\mu}{c\lambda}}e^{-(\mu+c\lambda)t}t^{-1}\mathrm{I}_1(2\sqrt{\mu c\lambda}t)$, where $\mathrm{I}_1(z) = \sum_{k=0}^{\infty}\frac{1}{k!\Gamma(k+2)}(\frac{z}{2})^{2k+1}$ is the first kind of Bessel function (see [Feller(1971)]). On the other hand, $\alpha\int_0^\infty e^{-\alpha t}\phi(t,u)dt = 1 - y(\alpha)\exp\{-u\lambda(1-y(\alpha)\}, \alpha > 0$, and $\alpha\int_0^\infty e^{-\alpha t}\phi(t,u)dt = 1 - E(e^{-\alpha\tau})$. Hence

$$\begin{aligned} E(e^{-\alpha\tau}) &= e^{-u\lambda}\sum_{n=0}^{\infty}\frac{(u\lambda)^n}{n!}y^{n+1}(\alpha) \\ &= e^{-u\lambda}\sum_{n=0}^{\infty}\frac{(u\lambda)^n}{n!}(\sqrt{\frac{\mu}{c\lambda}})^{n+1}((x-y)(\sqrt{\alpha+x}+\sqrt{\alpha+y})^{-2})^{n+1}. \end{aligned} \quad (1.89)$$

The (1.89) is the Laplace transform of $e^{-u\lambda}\sum_{n=0}^{\infty}\frac{(u\lambda\sqrt{\frac{\mu}{c\lambda}})^n}{n!t}\sqrt{\frac{\mu}{c\lambda}}(n+1)e^{-(\mu+c\lambda)t}\mathrm{I}_{n+1}(2\sqrt{\mu c\lambda}t)$, where $\mathrm{I}_n(z) = \sum_{k=0}^{\infty}\frac{1}{k!\Gamma(n+k+1)}(\frac{z}{2})^{n+2k}$ (see Feller(1971)). Hence

$$\begin{aligned} \psi(t,u) &= P(\tau \leqslant t) \\ &= \int_0^t e^{-u\lambda}\sum_{n=0}^{\infty}\frac{(u\lambda\sqrt{\mu/c\lambda})^n}{n!s}\sqrt{\frac{\mu}{c\lambda}}(n+1)e^{-(\mu+c\lambda)s}\mathrm{I}_{n+1}(2\sqrt{\mu c\lambda}s)ds \\ &= \frac{\mu}{c\lambda}e^{-u\lambda}\sum_{n=0}^{\infty}\frac{(\frac{u\mu}{c})^n}{n!}(\frac{\mu}{c\lambda})^{-\frac{n+1}{2}}\int_0^t e^{-(\mu+c\lambda)s}\frac{n+1}{s}\mathrm{I}_{n+1}(2\sqrt{\mu c\lambda}s)ds. \end{aligned}$$

Thus, letting $t \to \infty$ and using Remark 1.11 gives

$$\begin{aligned}
&\psi(u) = P(\tau < \infty) \\
&= \frac{\mu}{c\lambda} e^{-u\lambda} \sum_{n=0}^{\infty} \frac{(\frac{u\mu}{c})^n}{n!} (\frac{\mu}{c\lambda})^{-\frac{n+1}{2}} \int_0^{\infty} e^{-(\mu+c\lambda)s} \frac{n+1}{s} I_{n+1}(2\sqrt{\mu c\lambda}s) ds \\
&= \frac{\mu}{c\lambda} e^{-u\lambda} \sum_{n=0}^{\infty} \frac{(\frac{u\mu}{c})^n}{n!} (\frac{\mu}{c\lambda})^{-\frac{n+1}{2}} \cdot \\
&\quad \int_0^{\infty} e^{-(\mu+c\lambda)s} \frac{n+1}{s} \sum_{k=0}^{\infty} \frac{1}{k!\Gamma(n+k+2)} (\sqrt{\mu c\lambda}s)^{n+2k+1} ds \\
&= \frac{\mu}{c\lambda} e^{-u\lambda} \sum_{n=0}^{\infty} \frac{(\frac{u\mu}{c})^n}{n!} (\frac{\mu}{c\lambda})^{-\frac{n+1}{2}} (n+1) \cdot \\
&\quad \sum_{k=0}^{\infty} \frac{\Gamma(n+2k+1)}{k!\Gamma(n+k+2)} \frac{(\sqrt{\mu c\lambda})^{n+2k+1}}{(\mu+c\lambda)^{n+2k+1}} \\
&= \frac{\mu}{c\lambda} e^{-u\lambda} \sum_{n=0}^{\infty} \frac{n+1}{n!} (\frac{u\mu}{c})^n \cdot \\
&\quad \sum_{k=0}^{\infty} \frac{\Gamma(n+2k+1)}{k!\Gamma(n+k+2)} (\frac{c\lambda}{\mu})^{n+k+1} (1+\frac{c\lambda}{\mu})^{-(n+2k+1)} \\
&= \frac{1}{1+\Lambda} e^{-u\lambda} \sum_{n=0}^{\infty} \frac{1}{n!} (\frac{u\lambda}{1+\Lambda})^n (n+1) \cdot \\
&\quad \sum_{k=0}^{\infty} \frac{(n+2k)!}{k!(n+k+1)!} (\frac{1+\Lambda}{2+\Lambda})^{n+k+1} (\frac{1}{2+\Lambda})^k \\
&= \frac{1}{1+\Lambda} e^{-u\lambda} e^{\frac{\lambda u}{1+\Lambda}} \\
&= \frac{1}{1+\Lambda} \exp\{-\frac{\Lambda}{1+\Lambda}\lambda u\} \\
&= \frac{1}{1+\Lambda} \exp\{-\frac{\Lambda}{1+\Lambda} \frac{u}{E(Y_1)}\}.
\end{aligned}$$

References

Abate J, Whitt W. (1992). Fourier series method for inverting transforms of probability distributions, *Queuing Systems*, **10**, 5-88.

Asmussen S. (1998). Subexponential asymptotics for stochastic processes:

extremal behavior, stationary distribution and first passage probabilities, *The Annals of Applied Probability*, **8**, 354-374.

Boogaert P, Crijns V. (1987). Upper bound on ruin probabilities in case of negative loadings and positive interest rates, *Insurance: Mathematics and Economics*, **6**, 221-232.

Cai J, Dickson D C M. (2002). On the expected discounted penalty function at ruin of a surplus process with interest, *Insurance:Mathematics and Economics*, **30**, 389-404.

Di Lorenzo E, Tessitore G. (1996). Approximation solutions of severity of ruin, *Blatter Deutsche Gesellschaft fur Versicherungsmathematik*, **XXII**, 705-709.

Dickson D C M. (1992). On the distribution of the surplus prior to ruin, *Insurance: Mathematics and Economics*, **11**, 191-207.

Dickson D C M. (1998). On a clas of renewal risk processes, *North American Actuarial Journal*, **2**, 60-73.

Dufresne F, Gerber H U. (1988a). The surpluses immediately before and at ruin,and the amount of the claim causing ruin, *Insurance: Mathematics and Economics*, **7**, 193-199.

Dufresne F, Gerber H U. (1988b). The probability and severity of ruin for combinations of exponential claim amount distributions and their translations, *Insurance: Mathematics and Economics*, **7**, 75-80.

Feller W. (1971). *An Introduction to Probability Theory and its Applications*, 2Ed ed., **2**, Wiley, New York.

Gerber H V, Goovaerts M J, Kaas R. (1987). On the probability and severity of ruin, *Astin Bulletin*, **17**, 2, 151-163.

Gerber H V, Shiu E S W. (1997). The joint distribution of the time of ruin, the surplus immediately before ruin, and the deficit at ruin, *Insurance: Mathematics and Economics*, **21**, 129-137.

Gerber H U. (1979). *An Introduction to Mathematical Risk Theory*, S. S. Huebner Foundation Monograph Series, Philadelphia, **8**, 114-116.

Gerber H V, Shiu E S W. (1998). On the time value of ruin, *North American Actuarial Journal*, **2**, 1, 48-78.

Grandell J. (1991). *Aspects of Risk Theory*, Springer-Verlag.

Kalashnikov V, Konstantinides D. (2000). Ruin under interest force and subexponential claims: a simple treatment, *Insurance: Mathematics and Economics*, **27**, 145-149.

Klüppelberg C, Stadtmüller U. (1998). Ruin probabilities in the presence of heavy-tails and interest rates, *Scandinavian Actuarial Journal*, 49-58.

Konstantinides D, Tang Q H, Tsitsiashvili G. (2002). Estimates for the ruin probability in the classical risk model with constant interest force in the presence of heavy tails, *Insurance: Mathematics and Economics*, **31**, 447-460.

Malinovskii V K. (1998). Non-Poissonian claims' arrivals and calculation of the probability of ruin, *Insurance: Mathematics and Economics*, **22**, 123-138.

Paulsen J. (1998). Ruin theory with compounding assets - a survey, *Insurance: Mathematics and Economics*, **22**, 3-16.

Paulsen J, Gjessing H K. (1997). Ruin Theory with Stochastic Return on Investments, *Advances in Applied Probability*, **29**, 965-985.

Prabhu N U. (1965). *Queues and Inventories,* J. Wiley& Sons, New York.

Prabhu N U. (1980). *Stochastic Storage Processes. Queues, Insurance Risk, and Dams,* New York: Springer-Verlag.

Rolski T, Schmidli H, Schmidt V, Teugels J. (1999). *Stochastic Processes for Insurance and Finance,* John Wiley & Sons Ltd.

Sparre Andersen E. (1957). On the Collective Theory of Risk in the Case of Contagion between the Claims, *Transactions of the XV International Congress of Actuaries*, **2**, 212-219.

Sundt B, Teugels J L. (1995). Ruin estimates under interest force, *Insurance: Mathematics and Economics*, **16**, 7-22.

Sundt B, Teugels J L. (1997). The adjustment function in ruin estimates under interest force, *Insurance: Mathematics and Economics*, **19**, 85-94.

Wang R M, Yang H L, Wang H X. (2004). On the distribution of surplus immediately after ruin unde interest force and subexponential claims, *Insurance: Mathematics and Economics*, **35**, 703-714.

Wang R M, Liu H F. (2002). On the ruin probability under a class of risk processes, *Astin Bulletin*, **32**, 81-90.

Willmot G E, Lin X S. (1998). Exact and approximate properties of the distribution of surplus before and after ruin, *Insurance: Mathematics and Economics*, **23**, 91-110.

Willmot G E, Lin X S. (2001). Lundberg Approximations for Compound Distributions with Insurance Applications, *Lecture Notes in Statistics*, **156**, New York: Springer-Verlag.

Yang H. (1999). Non-exponential Bounds for Ruin Probability with Interest Effect Included, *Scandinavian Actuarial Journal*, 66-79.

Yang H L, Zhang L H. (2001a). On the distribution of surplus immediately after ruin under interest force, *Insurance: Mathematics and*

Economics, **29**, 2, 247-255.

Yang H L, Zhang L H. (2001b). On the distribution of surplus immediately before ruin under interest force, *Statistics and Probability Letters*, **55**, 3, 329-338.

Chapter 2

Compound Risk Models and Copula Decomposition

2.1 Introduction

This chapter intends to introduce our recent works (Yang, Zhou and Zhang (2005), Yang, Cheng and Wu (2005), Yang, Cheng and Wang (2004), Yang, Cheng and Zhang(2004)). We will concentrate on recursive evaluation of compound risk models, the approximation of individual risk models by a compound poisson model, and bivariate copula convex decomposition .

It is organized as follows: The second section is mainly a basic introduction on the risk models in risk theory, and it is the preparation for our further introduction. The section introduces two basic models normally discussed in our papers, the individual risk models and the compound risk models, and the method to link the individual risk model to the compound binomial model is also introduced; One theorem on excess-of-loss reinsurance is also proved (Yang, Cheng and Wang (2004)).

The third section concentrates on the recursive equations of the compound poisson model. First, the one-dimensional recursive equations on mixed type severity distribution is derived (Yang, Cheng and Wu (2005)). Secondly, we present bivariate recursive methods by focusing on excess-of-loss reinsurance (Yang, Cheng and Wang(2004)) .

The fourth section presents a new idea to approximate the individual risk models (Yang, Zhou and Zhang (2005)). The total loss of the individual risk models is approximated by a compound Poisson random variable. The optimal property of the approximation is also discussed.

The last section introduces the bivariate copula decomposition (Yang, Cheng and Zhang (2004)). The methods to determine the coefficients of the decomposition are also given.

2.2 Individual Risk Model and Compound Risk Model

For a portfolio of policies, let N denote the number of claims during a fixed time period and $X_1, X_2, \cdots$ denote the amounts of successive claims. The total loss of the portfolio during the period can be expressed as

$$S = \sum_{i=1}^{N} X_i. \tag{2.1}$$

Here N is a random variable. This model is called compound risk model. When N is a Poisson random variable, it is called compound Poisson model and S is called compound Poisson random variable; When N is a Binomial random variable, S is called compound Binomial random variable. The distribution function of S in (2.1) is denoted by F_S.

In the compound risk model, we assume that $X, X_1, X_2, \cdots$ are independent identically distributed with common severity distribution function (sdf), denoted as F_X. The sequence $X, X_1, X_2, \cdots$ are also independent of the number of claims N.

The individual risk model illustrates the total loss of a portfolio from another viewpoint. Consider a portfolio consisting of n policies, where Z_i denotes the loss associated with the i-th policy, $i = 1, 2, \cdots, n$. Then the total loss for the portfolio $\{Z_1, Z_2, \cdots, Z_n\}$ can be written as

$$S_n = \sum_{i=1}^{n} Z_i. \tag{2.2}$$

Assume that $Z, Z_1, Z_2, \cdots, Z_n$ are independent identically distributed with common distribution F_Z.

The individual risk model and the compound risk model describe the total loss of one portfolio from the different viewpoints. The compound risk model focuses only on the loss amounts of the claim policies, and the individual risk model considers each policy in the portfolio. For the detailed introduction about the two models, see Panjer and Willmot (1993) or Kass, et al (2001).

2.2.1 *The Link between the Compound Risk Model and the Individual Risk Model*

Denote the number of claims in the individual portfolio $Z_1, Z_2, \cdots, Z_n$ by N_n, i.e.,

$$N_n = \#\{i : Z_i > 0, i \leqslant n\}.$$

We also introduce an auxiliary risk sequence $\{Z_{n+1}, Z_{n+2}, \cdots\}$ with common distribution as Z_i's. Write

$$M_1 = \inf\{i \geqslant 1 : Z_i > 0\};$$
$$M_n = \inf\{i > M_{n-1} : Z_i > 0\}, \quad n \geqslant 2.$$

It can be proved that $P(M_i < \infty) = 1$. Thus we can define a claim sequence

$$Y_i = Z_{M_i}, \quad i \geqslant 1,$$

which is a subsequence of $\{Z_i, i \geqslant 1\}$.

One interesting result is that $Y_i, i \geqslant 1$ are independent with common distribution function

$$F_Y(x) = \frac{F_Z(x) - F_Z(0)}{1 - F_Z(0)}, \quad x \geqslant 0.$$

The counting number N_n is Binomial(n, q) with $q = 1 - F_Z(0)$, independent of the sequence $Y_i, i \geqslant 1$. That is,

$$P(N_n = m) = C_n^m q^m (1-q)^{n-m}, \quad m = 0, 1, \cdots, n.$$

Here C_n^m denotes $\binom{n}{m}$. See Li and Yang (2001).

Based on the above method, the link between the individual risk model and the compound binomial model can be established. By the definition of $\{Y_i\}$, we know that S_n in (2.2) can be expressed as another form:

$$S_n = \sum_{i=1}^{N_n} Y_i. \tag{2.3}$$

Note that the individual claims Y_i, $i \geqslant 1$ are independent and identically distributed, N_n is the number of claims in the portfolio $\{Z_1, Z_2, \cdots, Z_n\}$, and the independence between N_n and Y_i is fulfilled. Summing over the first N_n claims of the sequence $Y_i, i \geqslant 1$, we thus obtain the total loss S_n associated with the portfolio $\{Z_1, Z_2, \cdots, Z_n\}$.

2.2.2 *One Theorem on Excess-of-loss Reinsurance*

Consider the excess-of-loss reinsurance treaty for the compound model $X_1, X_2, \cdots, X_N$ with retention d, here N is an integer-valued random variable. The reinsurer pays the amount in excess of some retention limit d for each claim. For the claim amount X_i, the reinsurer and the cedent pay the shares $(X_i - d)_+ = \max\{X_i - d, 0\}$ and $X_i \wedge d = \min\{X_i, d\}$, respectively. Then the total payment of the reinsurer can be written

$$S_R = \sum_{i=1}^{N} (X_i - d)_+,$$

and the total payment of the cedent equals

$$S_C = \sum_{i=1}^{N} X_i \wedge d.$$

Let $N_R(d)$ be the number of claims in excess of the retention limit d,$N_C(d)$ be the number of claims less than or equal to the retention limit d. Then the two numbers can be expressed as

$$N_R(d) = \sum_{i=1}^{N} I_{\{X_i > d\}}, \qquad N_C(d) = \sum_{i=1}^{N} I_{\{X_i \leqslant d\}}.$$

Note that

$$N_R(d) + N_C(d) = N.$$

The distribution of $(N_R(d), N_C(d))$ is denoted by $p(j,n)$, and the marginal pf's are denoted as $p^{(1)}(j)$ and $p^{(2)}(n)$, respectively. Then

$$\begin{aligned} p(j,n) &= P(N_R(d) = j, N_C(d) = n) \\ &= p_{n+j}\, C_{n+j}^{j}\, F_X(d)^n\, (1 - F_X(d))^j, j, n \in Z =: \{0, 1, \cdots\} \end{aligned}$$

and

$$p^{(1)}(j) = P(N_R(d) = j) = \sum_{n=0}^{\infty} p(j,n),$$
$$p^{(2)}(n) = P(N_C(d) = n) = \sum_{j=0}^{\infty} p(j,n).$$

We also introduce two independent identically distributed sequences $\{Y(d), Y_i(d), i \geqslant 1\}$ and $\{Z(d), Z_i(d), i \geqslant 1\}$. It is assumed that the two sequences are independent of $N_R(d)$ and $N_C(d)$, and that the two sequences are also independent each other. $Y(d)$ has distribution function

$$P(Y(d) \leqslant y) = \frac{F(d+y) - F(d)}{1 - F(d)}, \quad y \geqslant 0$$

and $Z(d)$ has distribution function

$$P(Z(d) \leqslant z) = \frac{F(d \wedge z)}{F(d)}, \quad z \geqslant 0.$$

Theorem 2.1 *For the excess-of-loss reinsurance with the limit $d > 0$,*

$$\begin{aligned}&(S_R, S_C, N_R(d), N_C(d)) \\ &=^d \left(\sum_{i=1}^{N_R(d)} Y_i(d), \sum_{i=1}^{N_C(d)} Z_i(d) + dN_R(d), N_R(d), N_C(d) \right)\end{aligned}$$

holds. Here $=^d$ denotes "equal in distribution".

Proof. For non-negative integers j, n, let

$$\mathcal{A}_{n,j} = \{X_1 > d, X_2 > d, \cdots, X_j > d, X_{j+1} \leqslant d, \cdots, X_{j+n} \leqslant d\}.$$

For $y \geqslant 0, z \geqslant 0, j \geqslant 1, n \geqslant 1$, we have

$$\begin{aligned}&P\left(S_R \leqslant y, S_C \leqslant z, N_R(d) = j, N_C(d) = n\right) \\ &= P\left(\sum_{i=1}^{N} (X_i - d)_+ \leqslant y, \sum_{i=1}^{N} X_i \wedge d \leqslant z, N = n + j, \right. \\ &\qquad \left. N_R(d) = j, N_C(d) = n \right) \\ &= P\left(\sum_{i=1}^{n+j} (X_i - d)_+ \leqslant y, \sum_{i=1}^{n+j} X_i \wedge d \leqslant z, \right. \\ &\qquad \left. N = n + j, \sum_{i=1}^{n+j} I_{\{X_i > d\}} = j, \sum_{i=1}^{n+j} I_{\{X_i \leqslant d\}} = n \right) \\ &= p_{n+j} P\left(\sum_{i=1}^{n+j} (X_i - d)_+ \leqslant y, \sum_{i=1}^{n+j} X_i \wedge d \leqslant z, \right. \\ &\qquad \left. \sum_{i=1}^{n+j} I_{\{X_i > d\}} = j, \sum_{i=1}^{n+j} I_{\{X_i \leqslant d\}} = n \right)\end{aligned}$$

$$= p_{n+j}C_{n+j}^{j}P\left(\sum_{i=1}^{n+j}(X_i-d)_+ \leqslant y, \sum_{i=1}^{n+j}X_i \wedge d \leqslant z, \mathcal{A}_{n,j}\right)$$

$$= p_{n+j}C_{n+j}^{j}P\left(\sum_{i=1}^{j}(X_i-d)_+ \leqslant y, \sum_{i=j+1}^{n+j}X_i \leqslant z-jd, \mathcal{A}_{n,j}\right)$$

$$= p_{n+j}C_{n+j}^{j}P\left(\sum_{i=1}^{j}(X_i-d)_+ \leqslant y|X_1>d,\cdots,X_j>d\right)$$

$$\times P\left(\sum_{i=j+1}^{n+j}X_i \leqslant z-jd|X_{j+1}\leqslant d,\cdots,X_{n+j}\leqslant d\right)\times P(\mathcal{A}_{n,j})$$

$$= p_{n+j}C_{n+j}^{j}F^n(d)(1-F(d))^jP\left(\sum_{i=1}^{j}Y_i(d)\leqslant y\right)P\left(\sum_{i=1}^{n}Z_i(d)\leqslant z-jd\right)$$

$$= p(j,n)P\left(\sum_{i=1}^{j}Y_i(d)\leqslant y\right)P\left(\sum_{i=1}^{n}Z_i(d)\leqslant z-jd\right)$$

$$= P\left(N_R(d)=j, N_C(d)=n, \sum_{i=1}^{N_R(d)}Y_i(d)\leqslant y, \sum_{i=1}^{N_C(d)}Z_i(d)+dN_R(d)\leqslant z\right).$$

Similarly, we can prove that the above equation also holds for the cases $j=0$ or $n=0$. Now we complete the proof of Theorem 2.1. □

Theorem 2.1 gives the correlation structure between S_R and S_C. Note that $Y_i(d), i \geqslant 1$ and $Z_i(d), i \geqslant 1$ are independent, thus the correlation relationship between S_R and S_C is determined through the correlation between $N_R(d)$ and $N_C(d)$.

2.3 Recursive Calculation of Compound Distributions

One interesting topic in risk theory is how to compute the values of compound distribution function F_S of S in (2.1). Panjer (1981) presented a recursive method to calculate F_S.

For the compound risk model S introduced before, the number of claims N is said to belong to (a,b)-*family*, if there are constants $a, b \in R$ such that

$$p_n = p_{n-1}(a+\frac{b}{n}) \tag{2.4}$$

holds for all $n=1,2,\cdots$ with $p_n = P(N=n)$. It was shown in Sundt and Jewell (1981) that apart from the degenerate case, the members of the (a, b)-*family* have to be Poisson, Binomial or Negative Binomial.

Under the assumption as above, Panjer (1981) presented a recursive algorithm for the calculation of F_S. His results can be summarized as follows:

(a) Suppose that the sdf F_X is of the discrete type on the non-negative integers, then the compound distribution F_S is also of the discrete type on the non-negative integers. The compound distribution F_S has probability function (pf) $f_S(x) := P(S = x)$ satisfying

$$(1 - af_X(0))f_S(x) = \sum_{y=1}^{x}(a + \frac{by}{x})f_X(y)f_S(x - y), \quad x = 1, 2, 3, \cdots, \tag{2.5}$$

where $f_X(y) = P(X = y), \quad y = 0, 1, 2, \cdots;$

(b) Suppose that the sdf F_X is of the continuous type on the positive axis with probability density function (pdf) f_X, then F_S is of the continuous type on the positive axis with a possible atom at 0. The probability density function (pdf) f_S of F_S satisfies that

$$f_S(x) = p_1 f_X(x) + \int_0^x (a + \frac{by}{x})f_X(y)f_S(x - y)dy, \quad x > 0. \tag{2.6}$$

Since then, there are many papers on this topic. In the following, we will focus on one-dimensional case and two-dimensional case separately.

2.3.1 *One-dimensional Recursive Equations*

Panjer(1981) investigated the case that the severity distribution function is continuous or discrete. Sometimes the severity distribution contains both continuous portions and point masses. It is interesting to get the recursive equation on the mixed type. Yang, Cheng and Wu (2005) discussed the case of mixed-type severity distribution.

We introduce the following two assumptions:

B1: *There exist a discrete distribution function (df) H_X taking on non-negative integers, a continuous df G_X with bounded density function which is continuous on $(n, n + 1), n \in Z =: \{0, 1, 2, \cdots\}$ and a constant $c \in [0, 1]$ such that*

$$F_X(x) = cH_X(x) + (1 - c)G_X(x), \quad x \geqslant 0 \tag{2.7}$$

holds. Note that if $0 < c < 1$, H_X, G_X *and* c *are uniquely determined by* F_X, *see Loève (1978).*

B2: *The number of claims* N *belongs to* (a, b)*-family.*

We have the following Theorem.

Theorem 2.2 *Suppose the assumption **B1** holds. Then there exist a df* H_S *on* $Z = \{0, 1, 2, \cdots\}$, *a df* G_S *with bounded density function which is continuous on* $(n, n+1), n \in Z$, *and a constant* $w \in [0, 1]$ *such that*

$$F_S(x) = wH_S(x) + (1-w)G_S(x), \quad x \geqslant 0 \tag{2.8}$$

holds. Here w, wH_S *and* $(1-w)G_S$ *are uniquely determined by* F_S.

For F_X satisfying (2.7), write

$$q_X(n) = P(X = n), \quad n \in Z,$$

and let

$$p_X(x) = (1-c)g_X(x), \quad x \notin Z,$$

where $g_X(x)$ is the pdf of G_X. Then

$$p_X(x) = \frac{dF_X(x)}{dx}, \quad x \notin Z.$$

Assuming $p_X(n) = 0, n \in Z$, (2.7) is equivalent to

$$F_X(x) = \int_0^x p_X(t)dt + \sum_{n=0}^{[x]} q_X(n), \quad x \geqslant 0, \tag{2.9}$$

here $[x]$ denote the integer part of x. By the continuity of $g_X(x), x \notin Z$, we know that $p_X(x), x \notin Z$ and $q_X(n), n \in Z$ are uniquely determined by F_X.

By Theorem 2.2, there exists two functions $q_S(n)$ and $p_S(t)$ such that

$$F_S(x) = \int_0^x p_S(t)dt + \sum_{n=0}^{[x]} q_S(n), \quad x \geqslant 0, \tag{2.10}$$

where $p_S(t)$ is continuous for $t \notin Z$ and $q_S(n)$ is discrete on Z. $p_S(t), t \notin Z$ and $q_S(n), n \in Z$ are uniquely determined by F_S.

The next theorem gives the recursive equations on p_S and q_S, respectively.

Theorem 2.3 *Suppose the assumptions **B1** and **B2** hold. Then the following recursive equations hold for* q_S *and* p_S *in (2.10):*

(A) For positive integer n,

$$(1 - aq_X(0))nq_S(n) = \sum_{j=1}^{n} q_X(j)q_S(n-j)(an+bj) \tag{2.11}$$

holds with the starting value $q_S(0) = \sum_{n=0}^{\infty} p_n\{P(X=0)\}^n$;

(B) For positive $x \notin Z$,

$$\begin{aligned}(1 - aq_X(0))xp_S(x) = &\int_0^x p_X(t)p_S(x-t)(ax+bt)dt \\ &+ \sum_{n=1}^{[x]} q_X(n)p_S(x-n)(ax+bn) \\ &+ \sum_{n=0}^{[x]} p_X(x-n)q_S(n)\left((a+b)x - bn\right). \end{aligned} \tag{2.12}$$

Remark 2.1 *Theorem 2.3 generalizes Panjer (1981)'s result. When* F_X *is of the discrete type on* Z, *(2.11) is the same as (2.5). When* F_X *is of the continuous type with density function, from* $q_X(n) = 0, n \in Z$ *and (2.11) we get* $q_S(n) = 0, n \geqslant 1$, *thus (2.12) can be simplified to*

$$\begin{aligned} xp_S(x) &= \int_0^x p_X(t)p_S(x-t)(ax+bt)dt + p_X(x)q_S(0)(a+b)x \\ &= \int_0^x p_X(t)p_S(x-t)(ax+bt)dt + p_1xp_X(x), \end{aligned}$$

which is the same as (2.6).

Note that p_S may be discontinuous at integer points. Its right and left limits are given by the following Theorem.

Theorem 2.4 *Suppose the assumptions* ***B1*** *and* ***B2*** *hold. Further, it is also assumed that for* $m \in Z$, $p_X(m+) = \lim_{s \searrow m} p_X(s)$ *and* $p_X(m-) = \lim_{s \nearrow m} p_X(s)$ *exist. Then it holds that*

$$p_S(0+) = \frac{(a+b)p_X(0+)q_S(0)}{1 - aq_X(0)},$$

and for $m = 1, 2, \cdots$, *we have*

$$\begin{aligned} p_S(m+) = \Bigg(&\int_0^m p_X(t)p_S(m-t)(a+bt/m)dt \\ &+ \sum_{n=1}^{m} q_X(n)p_S((m-n)+)(a+bn/m) \end{aligned}$$

$$
\begin{aligned}
&\quad + \sum_{n=0}^{m} p_X((m-n)+) q_S(n)(a+b-bn/m) \Bigg) /(1-aq_X(0)), \\
p_S(m-) &= \Bigg(\int_0^m p_X(t) p_S(m-t)(a+bt/m)dt \\
&\quad + \sum_{n=1}^{m-1} q_X(n) p_S((m-n)-)(a+bn/m) \\
&\quad + \sum_{n=0}^{m-1} p_X((m-n)-) q_S(n)(a+b-bn/m) \Bigg) /(1-aq_X(0)), \\
p_S(m+) &= p_S(m-) \\
&\quad + \Bigg(\sum_{n=1}^{m-1} q_X(n)(p_S((m-n)+) - p_S((m-n)-))(a+bn/m) \\
&\quad + \sum_{n=0}^{m-1} \{p_X((m-n)+) - p_X((m-n)-)\} q_S(n)(a+b-bn/m) \\
&\quad + q_X(m) p_S(0+)(a+b) + a p_X(0+) q_S(m) \Bigg) /(1-aq_X(0)).
\end{aligned}
$$

Consider the excess-of-loss reinsurance treaty in which the reinsurer pays the part of each claim in excess of the limit d, where d is an integer. For S_R and S_C defined before, the related recursive equations are given in the followings.

Corollary 2.1 *Suppose that F_X has bounded continuous density function $f(x)$ over $[0, \infty)$ and N belongs to (a, b)-family. Then*

(1) There exist functions p_{S_R}, p_{S_C} on $[0, \infty)$ and q_{S_R}, q_{S_C} on Z such that

$$P(S_R \leqslant x) = \int_0^x p_{S_R}(t)dt + \sum_{n=0}^{[x]} q_{S_R}(n), \quad x \in [0, \infty), \tag{2.13}$$

$$P(S_C \leqslant x) = \int_0^x p_{S_C}(t)dt + \sum_{n=0}^{[x]} q_{S_C}(n), \quad x \in [0, \infty), \tag{2.14}$$

here the functions $p_{S_R}(t)$ and $p_{S_C}(t)$ are continuous and uniformly bounded for $t \notin Z$;

(2) For the functions q_{S_R}, p_{S_R} defined in (2.13), we have

$$q_{S_R}(0) = \sum_{i=0}^{\infty} p_i F_X(d)^i; \quad q_{S_R}(n) = 0, \quad n = 1, 2, \cdots,$$

and

$$\begin{aligned}(1 - aF_X(d))xp_{S_R}(x) &= \int_0^x f(t+d)p_{S_R}(x-t)(ax+bt)dt \\ &+(a+b)xq_{S_R}(0)f(x+d), \quad x \notin Z; \quad (2.15)\end{aligned}$$

(3) For the functions q_{S_C} and p_{S_C} defined in (2.14), we have

$$q_{S_C}(k) = 0, \quad k \neq nd, \quad n \in Z; \quad q_{S_C}(nd) = (1 - F_X(d))^n p_n, \quad n \in Z \quad (2.16)$$

and for $x \notin Z$,

$$\begin{aligned}xp_{S_C}(x) = &\int_0^{x \wedge d} f(t)p_{S_C}(x-t)(ax+bt)dt \\ &+(1-F_X(d))p_{S_C}(x-d)(ax+bd) \\ &+f(x-[\frac{x}{d}]d)q_{S_C}([\frac{x}{d}]d)\left\{(a+b)x - b[\frac{x}{d}]d\right\} \quad (2.17)\end{aligned}$$

holds, where $[\frac{x}{d}]$ is the integer part of $\frac{x}{d}$.

Remark 2.2 *Equation (2.15) was obtained in Chapter 6 of Panjer and Willmot (1993), while a discretization method was also introduced in the chapter to approximate the distribution of S_C.*

Here we give some numerical results of p_{S_C} and q_{S_C}. (See Yang, Cheng and Wu (2005) for the numerical methods.)

Let the retention $d = 1$ and the span $h = 0.0002$. Suppose X is Pareto with density function

$$f(x) = \frac{\alpha\theta^\alpha}{(x+\theta)^{\alpha+1}}, \quad x > 0,$$

here $\theta = 1, \alpha = 2$. And N is Geometric,

$$P(N = k) = \frac{\beta^k}{(1+\beta)^{k+1}}, \quad k = 0, 1, 2, \cdots,$$

where $\beta = 1$. The upper and lower bounds for F_{S_C} are obtained by applying Method of Rounding (Panjer and Willmot (1993)). The numerical results are listed in Tables 2.1-2.2.

Table 2.1 Numerical values of q_{S_C}.

n	0	1	2	3	4	5
$q_{S_C}(n)$	0.5	0.0625	0.007813	0.000977	0.000122	0.0000105
$\sum_{j=0}^{n} q_{S_C}(j)$	0.5	0.5625	0.570313	0.57129	0.571412	0.571427

Table 2.2 Numerical values of $\hat{p}_{S_C}$ and $\hat{F}_{S_C}$.

x	$\hat{p}_{S_C}(x+)$	$\hat{F}_{S_C}(x)$	Upper Bound $h = 0.05$	Lower Bound $h = 0.05$	Upper Bound $h = 0.001$	Lower Bound $h = 0.001$
0	0.500000	0.50000	0.524376	0.5	0.5005	0.5
1.0	0.204587	0.823845	0.836727	0.820837	0.824175	0.82385
2.0	0.067486	0.943415	0.948858	0.941248	0.943633	0.943477
3.0	0.021008	0.982349	0.984511	0.981317	0.982517	0.982451

2.3.2 *Proofs of Theorems 2.2-2.3*

We only give the proofs of Theorems 2.2-2.3 here.

In the following expression, the symbol $\int_0^x$ means integration over compact interval $[0, x]$.

Lemma 2.1 *Suppose the assumption **B1** holds. Then the distribution function $F_{\sum_{j=1}^n X_j}$ of $\sum_{j=1}^n X_j$ can be decomposed into follows:*

$$P(\sum_{j=1}^{n} X_j \leqslant x) = c_n V_n(x) + (1 - c_n) W_n(x).$$

Where $V_n(x)$ is a discrete distribution function over Z with pf v_n, $W_n(x)$ is a continuous distribution function with pdf $w_n(x)$ which is continuous except integer points, and $0 \leqslant c_n \leqslant 1$. Furthermore, there exists some constant $M > 0$ such that for $n = 1, 2, \cdots,$

$$\sup_{t>0,\ t \notin Z} |(1 - c_n) w_n(t)| \leqslant M.$$

Proof. First we prove that the lemma holds for $n = 2$. For $F_X(t)$ satisfying (2.7), the pf of $H_X(t)$ is denoted by $h(t)$, and the pdf of G_X is denoted by g. Then for $x \geqslant 0$,

$$\begin{aligned}
&P(X_1 + X_2 \leqslant x)\\
&= \int_0^x F_X(x-t)dF_X(t)\\
&= \int_0^x \{cH_X(x-t) + (1-c)G_X(x-t)\}\, d\{cH_X(t) + (1-c)G_X(t)\}\\
&= \int_0^x \left\{ \int_0^t (1-c)^2 g(t-s)g(s)ds + 2\sum_{j=0}^{\infty} c(1-c)h(j)g(t-j) \right\} dt\\
&\quad + \sum_{j=0}^{[x]} c^2 \sum_{m=0}^{j} h(m)h(j-m).
\end{aligned}$$

So, $P(X_1 + X_2 \leqslant x)$ can be decomposed into the continuous part

$$\int_0^x \left\{ \int_0^t (1-c)^2 g(t-s)g(s)ds + 2\sum_{j=0}^{\infty} c(1-c)h(j)g(t-j) \right\} dt$$

and the discrete part

$$\sum_{j=0}^{[x]} c^2 \sum_{m=0}^{j} h(m)h(j-m).$$

Denote $c_2 = c^2$. If $1 - c_2 \neq 0$, let

$$w_2(t) = \frac{\int_0^t (1-c)^2 g(t-s)g(s)ds + 2\sum_{j=0}^{\infty} c(1-c)h(j)g(t-j)}{1-c_2},$$

and

$$w_2(t) = I_{\{0<t\leqslant 1\}}, \quad \textit{if} \quad 1 - c_2 = 0,$$

and

$$v_2(j) = \sum_{m=0}^{j} h(m)h(j-m), \quad j \in Z.$$

Then we have

$$P(X_1 + X_2 \leqslant x) = c_2 \sum_{j=0}^{[x]} v_2(j) + (1-c_2)\int_0^x w_2(t)dt.$$

It is easy to show that $w_2(t)$ is a density function and is continuous for $t \notin Z$. Define

$$M = \max\{\sup_{t>0,\ t\notin Z} \{g(t)\}, 1\}.$$

Then for $t \notin Z$,

$$\begin{aligned}
&\sup_{t>0,\ t\notin Z} |(1-c_2)w_2(t)| \\
&= \max\left\{\sup_{t>0,\ t\notin Z}\{\int_0^t (1-c)^2 g(t-s)g(s)ds + 2\sum_{j=0}^{\infty}(1-c)ch(j)g(t-j)\}, 1\right\} \\
&\leqslant \max\{\sup_{t>0,\ t\notin Z} g(t), 1\}\left((1-c)^2 + 2(1-c)c\right) \\
&\leqslant M.
\end{aligned}$$

The lemma is proved for $n = 2$. Then by induction we can prove the lemma holds for $n > 2$. □

Proof of Theorem 2.2: Using the notations defined in Lemma 2.1, let $w = \sum_{n=0}^{\infty} p_n c_n$ and

$$p_S(t) = \sum_{n=0}^{\infty} p_n(1-c_n)w_n(t), \quad q_S(t) = \sum_{n=0}^{\infty} p_n c_n v_n(t).$$

By the fact that $(1-c_n)w_n(t) \leqslant M$ proved in Lemma 2.1, $p_S(t)$ is well-defined for $t \notin Z$, and it is continuous for $t \notin Z$. Thus for $x \geqslant 0$, by Lemma 2.1 we have

$$\begin{aligned}
P(S \leqslant x) &= \sum_{n=0}^{\infty} p_n\, P(\sum_{j=1}^{n} X_j \leqslant x) \\
&= \sum_{n=0}^{\infty} p_n\, c_n V_n(x) + \sum_{n=0}^{\infty} p_n(1-c_n)W_n(x) \\
&= \sum_{n=0}^{[x]} q_S(n) + \int_0^x p_S(t)dt,
\end{aligned}$$

hence (2.8) holds. It is easy to prove that $p_S(t), t \notin Z$ and $q_S(n), n \in Z$ are uniquely determined by F_S. Theorem 2.2 is proved. □

Let $L_W(z)$ denote the Laplace transform of random variable W,

$$L_W(z) = E(e^{-zW}), \quad z \geqslant 0.$$

Lemma 2.2 *Suppose the assumption **B2** holds. Then for $x \geqslant 0$,*

$$\int_0^x s\,dF_S(s)$$
$$= a\int_0^x F_X(x-s)s dF_S(s) + (a+b)\int_0^x F_S(x-s)s\,dF_X(s). \quad (2.18)$$

Proof. (a)First we assume that $E(X_i)$ is finite. Under the assumption **B2**, Theorem 6.6.1 of Panjer and Willmot (1993) states that

$$L'_S(z) = aL_X(z)L'_S(z) + (a+b)L'_X(z)L_S(z), \quad z \geqslant 0. \quad (2.19)$$

On the other hand, one can verify that for $z \geqslant 0$,

$$L'_S(z) = -\int_0^\infty e^{-zt} d\left\{\int_0^t s dF_S(s)\right\},$$
$$L_X(z)L'_S(z) = -\int_0^\infty e^{-zt} d\left\{\int_0^t F_X(t-s) s dF_S(s)\right\},$$
$$L'_X(z) = -\int_0^\infty e^{-zt} d\left\{\int_0^t s dF_X(s)\right\},$$
$$L_S(z)L'_X(z) = -\int_0^\infty e^{-zt} d\left\{\int_0^t F_S(t-s) s dF_X(s)\right\}.$$

Substituting the above equations into (2.19) yields

$$\int_0^\infty e^{-zt} d\left\{\int_0^t s dF_S(s)\right\} = a\int_0^\infty e^{-zt} d\left\{\int_0^t F_X(t-s) s dF_S(s)\right\}$$
$$+(a+b)\int_0^\infty e^{-zt} d\left\{\int_0^t F_S(t-s) s dF_X(s)\right\}.$$

Inversion of this equation yields (2.18).

(b)In the case $E(X_i)$ is infinite, for $d > 0$ we define

$$S(d) = \sum_{i=1}^N \min\{X_i, d\}.$$

Then $E(\min\{X_i, d\})$ is finite and

$$P(\min\{X_i, d\} \leqslant x) = F_X(x), \quad P(S(d) \leqslant x) = P(S \leqslant x), \quad x < d.$$

Then using the result of (a), we obtain that for $x < d$, (2.18) holds. Letting $d \to \infty$, we have that (2.18) holds for all $x \geqslant 0$. The lemma is proved. □

Proof of Theorem 2.3 Suppose $x \geqslant 0$. Under the condition of Theorem 2.3, there exist functions q_S and p_S satisfying (2.10). Then

$$\int_0^x s dF_S(s) = \int_0^x s p_S(s) ds + \sum_{n=0}^{[x]} n q_S(n) \tag{2.20}$$

holds. On the other hand, using (2.9) and (2.10), (2.18) can be decomposed as follows:

$$\begin{aligned}
&\int_0^x s dF_S(s) \\
&= a\int_0^x F_X(x-s) s dF_S(s) + (a+b)\int_0^x F_S(x-s) s\, dF_X(s) \\
&= \int_0^x \int_0^x I_{\{s+t\leqslant x\}}\{as+(a+b)t\} dF_X(t) dF_S(s) \\
&= \int_0^x \Bigg\{ \int_0^s p_X(t) p_S(s-t)(as+bt) ds + \sum_{n=0}^{\infty} q_X(n) p_S(s-n)(as+bn) \\
&\quad + \sum_{n=0}^{\infty} p_X(s-n) q_S(n)\{(a+b)s - bn\} \Bigg\} ds \\
&\quad + \sum_{n=0}^{[x]} \sum_{j=0}^{n} q_X(j) q_S(n-j)(an+bj).
\end{aligned} \tag{2.21}$$

The corresponding continuous parts of (2.20) and (2.21) should be equal, thus for $x \notin Z$,

$$\begin{aligned}
\int_0^x s p_S(s) ds = \int_0^x \Bigg\{ &\int_0^s p_X(t) p_S(s-t)(as+bt) dt \\
&+ \sum_{n=0}^{\infty} q_X(n) p_S(s-n)(as+bn) \\
&+ \sum_{n=0}^{\infty} p_X(s-n) q_S(n)\{(a+b)s - bn\} \Bigg\} ds
\end{aligned}$$

holds. By the continuity of p_S and p_X, the above equation is equivalent to

$$\begin{aligned}
x p_S(x) &= \int_0^x p_X(t) p_S(x-t)(ax+bt) dt + \sum_{n=0}^{\infty} q_X(n) p_S(x-n)(ax+bn) \\
&\quad + \sum_{n=0}^{\infty} p_X(x-n) q_S(n)\{(a+b)x - bn\}
\end{aligned}$$

$$= \int_0^x p_X(t)p_S(x-t)(ax+bt)dt + \sum_{n=0}^{[x]} q_X(n)p_S(x-n)(ax+bn)$$
$$+ \sum_{n=0}^{[x]} p_X(x-n)q_S(n)\{(a+b)x - bn\}, \quad x > 0, \quad x \notin Z,$$

(2.12) is proved. Similarly, for the corresponding discrete parts of (2.20) and (2.21),

$$\sum_{n=0}^{[x]} nq_S(n) = \sum_{n=0}^{[x]} \sum_{j=0}^{n} q_X(j)q_S(n-j)(an+bj), \quad x \in (0,\infty)$$

holds, which is equivalent to

$$nq_S(n) = \sum_{j=0}^{n} q_X(j)q_S(n-j)(an+bj),$$

(2.11) holds. Now we finish the proof of Theorem 2.3. □

2.3.3 *Bivariate Recursive Equations*

Sundt (1999) obtained the bivariate recursive equations on (S_R, S_C) when the severity distribution function F_X is discrete. Yang, Cheng and Wang (2004) investigated the case that the severity distribution is continuous with density function. In the following, we will only introduce the main results of Yang, Cheng and Wang (2004).

It is assumed that

(1)The sdf F_X has bounded continuous pdf f.

(2)The number of claims belongs to (a, b) family.

Under the above assumptions, $Y(d)$ has pdf

$$f_{Y(d)}(x) = \frac{f(x+d)}{1-F(d)}, \quad x \geqslant 0,$$

and $Z(d)$ has pdf

$$f_{Z(d)}(x) = \frac{f(x)I_{\{x \leqslant d\}}}{F(d)}, \quad x \geqslant 0.$$

One can also show that $N_R(d)$ belongs to $(\frac{a(1-F(d))}{1-aF(d)}, \frac{b(1-F(d))}{1-aF(d)})$-family.

Then applying (2.6), the pdf $f_{S_R}(y)$ of S_R exists for $y > 0$ and satisfies

$$\begin{aligned} &f_{S_R}(y) \\ &= \frac{1-F(d)}{1-aF(d)} \int_0^y \left(a + \frac{bu}{y}\right) f_{Y(d)}(u) f_{S_R}(y-u)du + p^{(1)}(1) f_{Y(d)}(y), y > 0. \end{aligned}$$

In addition, $P(S_R = 0) = P(N_R(d) = 0) = p^{(1)}(0)$.

For notational convenience, denote the k-th convolution of $f_{Y(d)}$ by $f^{*(k)}_{Y(d)}$, here we define $f^{*(0)}_{Y(d)} = 1$. Similarly for the notations $f^{*(k)}_{Z(d)}$ and $f^{*(k)}$.

Theorem 2.5 *(1) For integer $k \in Z = \{0, 1, 2, \cdots\}$, we have*

$$\begin{aligned} q^{c,d}_{S_R,S_C}(y, kd) &=: \frac{d}{dy}(P\{S_R \leqslant y, S_C = kd\}) \\ &= p_k\,(1-F(d))^k f^{*(k)}_{Y(d)}(y) I_{\{k \neq 0\}}. \end{aligned}$$

Moreover, $q^{c,d}_{S_R,S_C}(y, kd)$ is continuous for $y > 0$, and it satisfies the following recursive equation

$$q^{c,d}_{S_R,S_C}(y, kd) = \left(a + \frac{b}{k}\right) \int_0^y q^{c,d}_{S_R,S_C}(y-s, (k-1)d) f(s+d)ds, \quad k \geqslant 2$$

with the starting function

$$q^{c,d}_{S_R,S_C}(y, d) = p_1 f(y+d), \quad y \geqslant 0;$$

(2) For positive $z > 0, z \neq 0, d, 2d, \cdots$,

$$q^{d,c}_{S_R,S_C}(0, z) =: \frac{d}{dz}(P\{S_R = 0, S_C \leqslant z\})$$

exists and is continuous, and it satisfies

$$q^{d,c}_{S_R,S_C}(0, z) = p_1 f(z) I_{\{z<d\}} + \int_0^{z \wedge d} \left(a + \frac{bs}{z}\right) q^{d,c}_{S_R,S_C}(0, z-s) f(s)ds.$$

Specially,

$$q^{d,c}_{S_R,S_C}(0, z) = f_S(z) = \sum_{n=1}^{\infty} p_n f^{*(n)}(z), \quad z < d;$$

(3) For $y > 0, z > 0$ and $z \neq d, 2d, 3d, \cdots$,

$$p_{S_R,S_C}(y, z) =: \frac{\partial^2}{\partial y \partial z}(P\{S_R \leqslant y, S_C \leqslant z\})$$

exists and is continuous, and it satisfies

$$\begin{aligned}
&p_{S_R,S_C}(y,z)\\
&=(a+b)f(y+d)q^{d,c}_{S_R,S_C}(0,z-d)\\
&+aq^{c,d}_{S_R,S_C}(y,j_0d)f(z-j_0d)+a\int_0^{z\wedge d}p_{S_R,S_C}(y,z-s)f(s)ds\\
&+\int_0^y\left(a+\frac{bs}{y}\right)p_{S_R,S_C}(y-s,z-d)f(s+d)ds
\end{aligned}$$

and

$$p_{S_R,S_C}(y,z)=0,\quad z<d,$$

where $j_0=[\frac{z}{d}]$*;*

(4) The distribution of (S_R,S_C) *can be expressed as the following form:*

$$\begin{aligned}
&P(S_R\leqslant y,S_C\leqslant z)\\
&=\int_0^y\int_0^z p_{S_R,S_C}(u,v)dvdu+\sum_{k=0}^{[z/d]}\int_0^y q^{c,d}_{S_R,S_C}(u,kd)du\\
&+\int_0^z q^{d,c}_{S_R,S_C}(0,v)dv+p_0,\quad y\geqslant 0,\quad z\geqslant 0.
\end{aligned}$$

2.4 The Compound Poisson Random Variable's Approximation to the Individual Risk Model

This section will introduce Yang, Zhou and Zhang(2005)'s method to approximate the total loss of the homogeneous individual risk model S_n in (2.2) by a compound Poisson random variable. Here the homogeneous means that $Z, Z_i, i\geqslant 1$ have common distribution.

It is assumed that the variance $Var(Z_1)$ is finite and $0<F_Z(0)<1$, here F_Z is the distribution function of Z_i.

For the approximation, suppose that the compound Poisson model has the same claim sequence as the individual risk model $Z_1, Z_2, \cdots, Z_n$. The Poisson number $N(\theta)$ with mean θ, is to be estimated based on the individual risk models. Naturally, it is required that $N(\theta)$ and $Y_i, i\geqslant 1$ are independent. Then S_n can be approximated by a compound Poisson random variable

$$S^* = \sum_{i=1}^{N(\theta)} Y_i. \tag{2.22}$$

Let $F_{poi(\theta)}$ denote Poisson distribution function with mean θ, and $F_{bin(n,q)}$ denote binomial distribution function with parameters (n, q) , where $q = 1 - F_Z(0)$. The family of all Poisson r.v.'s with common mean θ and being independent of the claim sequence $Y_i, i \geqslant 1$, is denoted as $R(F_{poi(\theta)})$. Optimal Poisson r.v. $N_n^0(\theta) \in R(F_{poi(\theta)})$ is chosen by the following minimizing principle:

$$H_n(\theta) =: E|S_n - \sum_{i=1}^{N_n^0(\theta)} Y_i| = \inf_{N(\theta)\in R(F_{poi(\theta)})} E|S_n - S^*|, \tag{2.23}$$

here $H_n(\theta)$ represents the expectation of the absolute approximation error.

2.4.1 *The Existence of the Optimal Poisson r.v.*

A r.v. U can be defined as below. Define r.v.'s $U_m, m = 0, 1, \cdots, n$ such that $U_m, m = 0, 1, \cdots, n$ and $Z_i, i \geqslant 1$ are independent, where U_m is uniformly distributed over $(F_{bin(n,q)}(m-1)), F_{bin(n,q)}(m)]$ with probability density function

$$\frac{1}{F_{bin(n,q)}(m) - F_{bin(n,q)}(m-1)}.$$

Write

$$U = \sum_{m=0}^{n} U_m I_{\{N_n=m\}}.$$

Note that $U_m, m = 0, 1, 2, \cdots, n$ are independent of N_n and $Y_i, i = 1, 2, \cdots$. Followed the independence between N_n and Y_i, U is also independent of Y_i. Moreover, the conditional distribution

$$P(U \leqslant x | N_n = m) \tag{2.24}$$

$$= \begin{cases} 1, & x \geqslant F_{bin(n,q)}(m), \\ \frac{x - F_{bin(n,q)}(m-1)}{F_{bin(n,q)}(m) - F_{bin(n,q)}(m-1)}, & F_{bin(n,q)}(m-1) \leqslant x < F_{bin(n,q)}(m), \\ 0, & x < F_{bin(n,q)}(m-1). \end{cases}$$

The inverse function $F^{-1}_{bin(n,q)}$ of $F_{bin(n,q)}$ is defined as

$$F^{-1}_{bin(n,q)}(y) = \inf\{x : F_{bin(n,q)}(x) \geqslant y\}, \quad y \in [0,1].$$

Similarly, the inverse function $F^{-1}_{poi(\theta)}$ of $F_{poi(\theta)}$ is defined as

$$F^{-1}_{poi(\theta)}(y) = \inf\{x : F_{poi(\theta)}(x) \geqslant y\}.$$

Lemma 2.3 *The r.v. U is uniformly distributed over $[0,1]$, and*

$$N_n = F^{-1}_{bin(n,q)}(U).$$

Proof For fixed $s \in (0,1)$, denote $M = \sup\{k : F_{bin(n,q)}(k) \leqslant s, k = 0,1,\cdots\}$. It follows from (2.24) that

$$P(U \leqslant s | N_n = M+1) = \frac{s - F_{bin(n,q)}(M)}{F_{bin(n,q)}(M+1) - F_{bin(n,q)}(M)}$$

and

$$P(U \leqslant s|N_n = m) = 0, \quad m > M+1; \quad P(U \leqslant s|N_n = m) = 1, \quad m \leqslant M.$$

Thus

$$\begin{aligned}
&P(U \leqslant s) \\
&= \sum_{m=0}^{n} P(U \leqslant s|N_n = m)P(N_n = m) \\
&= \sum_{m=M+1}^{n} P(U \leqslant s|N_n = m)P(N_n = m) \\
&\quad + \sum_{m=0}^{M} P(U \leqslant s|N_n = m)P(N_n = m) \\
&= P(U \leqslant s|N_n = M+1)P(N_n = M+1) + \sum_{m=0}^{M} P(N_n = m) \\
&= \frac{s - F_{bin(n,q)}(M)}{F_{bin(n,q)}(M+1) - F_{bin(n,q)}(M)} \times \{F_{bin(n,q)}(M+1) - F_{bin(n,q)}(M)\} \\
&\quad + F_{bin(n,q)}(M) \\
&= s.
\end{aligned}$$

That is, the r.v. U is uniformly distributed over $[0,1]$.

Next we prove that $N_n = F^{-1}_{bin(n,q)}(U)$ holds. Fix nonnegative integer $m, 0 \leqslant m \leqslant n$. Suppose that $N_n = m$. Thus $F_{bin(n,q)}(m-1) <$

$U \leqslant F_{bin(n,q)}(m)$ follows. Equivalently, $F^{-1}_{bin(n,q)}(U) = m$. Hence $N_n = F^{-1}_{bin(n,q)}(U) = m$. The lemma is proved. □

In the following we will prove the existence of the optimal Poisson r.v. $N_n^0(\theta)$, while a mathematical expression for the corresponding approximation error is given.

Theorem 2.6 *The Poisson r.v. $N_n^0(\theta)$ defined by $N_n^0(\theta) = F^{-1}_{poi(\theta)}(U)$ satisfies (2.23), i.e., $F^{-1}_{poi(\theta)}(U)$ is a possible choice for the optimal Poisson r.v. with mean θ. Moreover, the approximation error $H_n(\theta)$ satisfies*

$$\begin{aligned} H_n(\theta) &= E(Y_1)E|F^{-1}_{bin(n,q)}(U) - F^{-1}_{poi(\theta)}(U)| \\ &= E(Y_1)\int_0^\infty |F_{bin(n,q)}(x) - F_{poi(\theta)}(x)|dx. \end{aligned} \tag{2.25}$$

Proof. Let $R(F_{bin(n,q)}, F_{poi(\theta)})$ denote the family consisting of all random vector (W, V)'s, where W has distribution $F_{bin(n,q)}$ and V has distribution $F_{poi(\theta)}$, and the vector (W, V) is independent of the claim sequence $Y_i, i \geqslant 1$. Followed the independence relation between $Y_i, i \geqslant 1$ and $R(F_{bin(n,q)}, F_{poi(\theta)})$, we find that

$$\begin{aligned} &\inf_{(W,V)\in R(F_{bin(n,q)},F_{poi(\theta)})} E|\sum_{i=1}^{W} Y_i - \sum_{i=1}^{V} Y_i| \\ &= \inf_{(W,V)\in R(F_{bin(n,q)},F_{poi(\theta)})} E|I_{\{V<W\}} \sum_{i=V+1}^{W} Y_i + I_{\{V>W\}} \sum_{i=W+1}^{V} Y_i| \\ &= E(Y_1) \inf_{(W,V)\in R(F_{bin(n,q)},F_{poi(\theta)})} E|W - V|. \end{aligned} \tag{2.26}$$

From the result of L_1- Wassertein distance (Barrio, Gine and Matran (1999), or Shorack and Wellner (1986)), it holds that

$$\begin{aligned} &\inf_{(W,V)\in R(F_{bin(n,q)},F_{poi(\theta)})} E|W - V| \\ &= E|F^{-1}_{bin(n,q)}(U) - F^{-1}_{poi(\theta)}(U)| \\ &= \int_0^\infty |F_{bin(n,q)}(x) - F_{poi(\theta)}(x)|dx. \end{aligned} \tag{2.27}$$

Obviously,

$$H_n(\theta) = \inf_{N \in R(F_{poi(\theta)})} E|\sum_{i=1}^{N_n} Y_i - \sum_{i=1}^{N} Y_i|$$
$$= \inf_{(W,V) \in R(F_{bin(n,q)}, F_{poi(\theta)})} E|\sum_{i=1}^{W} Y_i - \sum_{i=1}^{V} Y_i|. \quad (2.28)$$

Combining equations (2.26)–(2.28), we obtain (2.25) and complete the proof. □

In this paper, we choose the optimal Poisson r.v. as

$$N_n^0(\theta) = F_{poi(\theta)}^{-1}(U). \quad (2.29)$$

Comonotonicity is an important concept in modern risk theory. The two risks P and Q are comonotonic if there exist two nondecreasing real-valued functions f, g and a risk Z such that

$$P =^d f(Z), \quad Q =^d g(Z).$$

The two random variables $N_n^0(\theta)$ and N_n are both nondecreasing functions of the r.v. U, thus they are comonotonic.

2.4.2 *The Joint Distribution of* $(N_n^0(\theta), N_n)$

The joint distribution $F_{N_n,N(\theta)}$ of $(N_n, N(\theta))$ satisfies

$$\max\{F_{bin(n,q)}(x) + F_{poi(\theta)}(y) - 1, 0\}$$
$$\leqslant F_{N_n,N(\theta)}(x,y) \leqslant \min\{F_{bin(n,q)}(x), F_{poi(\theta)}(y)\}. \quad (2.30)$$

See Joe (1997) for its related discussion. Note that the distribution function of $(N_n, N_n^0(\theta))$ equals the upper bound $\min\{F_{bin(n,q)}(x), F_{poi(\theta)}(y)\}$.

Given $N_n = m, m = 0, 1, \cdots, n$, the conditional probability

$$P(N_n^0(\theta) = k|N_n = m)$$
$$= P(F_{poi(\theta)}^{-1}(U) = k|U \in (F_{bin(n,q)}(m-1), F_{bin(n,q)}(m)])$$
$$= P(U \in (F_{poi(\theta)}(k-1), F_{poi(\theta)}(k))|U \in (F_{bin(n,q)}(m-1), F_{bin(n,q)}(m)])$$
$$= \max\{\frac{\min\{F_{poi(\theta)}(k), F_{bin(n,q)}(m)\}}{F_{bin(n,q)}(m) - F_{bin(n,q)}(m-1)}$$
$$- \frac{\max\{F_{poi(\theta)}(k-1), F_{bin(n,q)}(m-1)\}}{F_{bin(n,q)}(m) - F_{bin(n,q)}(m-1)}, 0\}.$$

Then the joint probability

$$\begin{aligned}
&P(N_n = m, N_n^0(\theta) = k) \\
&= P(N_n^0(\theta) = k | N_n = m) P(N_n = m) \\
&= \max\left\{\min\{F_{poi(\theta)}(k), F_{bin(n,q)}(m)\}\right. \\
&\qquad \left. - \max\{F_{poi(\theta)}(k-1), F_{bin(n,q)}(m-1)\}, 0\right\}. \qquad (2.31)
\end{aligned}$$

Furthermore, the probability $P(N_n^0(\theta) = N_n)$ can be evaluated by

$$\begin{aligned}
P(N_n^0(\theta) = N_n) &= \sum_{i=1}^{n} P(N_n^0(\theta) = N_n = i) \\
&= \sum_{i=0}^{n} \max\left\{\min\{F_{poi(\theta)}(i), F_{bin(n,q)}(i)\}\right. \\
&\qquad \left. - \max\{F_{poi(\theta)}(i-1), F_{bin(n,q)}(i-1)\}, 0\right\}.
\end{aligned}$$

Table 2.3 gives some values of the joint probabilities of $(N_n, N_n^0(\theta))$ in the case $n = 1000, \theta = 1, p = 0.001, EY_1 = 1$, calculated by using (2.31). Table 2.4 gives some results in the case $n = 10, \theta = 0.01, p = 0.001, EY_1 = 1$. The values in the two tables show the comonotonic trend between N_n and $N_n^0(\theta)$.

Table 2.3 The probability $P(N_n = i, N_n^0(\theta) = j)$ when $n = 1000, \theta = 1, p = 0.001$ and $EY_1 = 1$.

	$j=0$	$j=1$	$j=2$	$j=3$	$j=4$	$j=5$
$i=0$	0.3677	0	0	0	0	0
$i=1$	0.0002	0.3679	3.0687E-08	0	0	0
$i=2$	0	0	0.1840	9.2054E-05	0	0
$i=3$	0	0	0	0.0612	6.1323E-05	0
$i=4$	0	0	0	0	0.0153	2.2969E-05
$i=5$	0	0	0	0	0	0.0030

2.4.3 *Evaluating the Approximation Error*

$H_n(\theta)$ measures the expectation of the absolute approximation error. In this section we will show how to compute the error.

At the beginning we will list a useful lemma.

Lemma 2.4 *If $\theta \geqslant -n\log(1-q)$, then $F_{bin(n,q)}(t) \geqslant F_{poi(\theta)}(t)$ for all t. Conversely, if $F_{bin(n,q)}(0) \geqslant F_{poi(\theta)}(0)$, then $\theta \geqslant -n\log(1-q)$.*

Table 2.4 The probability $P(N_n = i, N_n^0(\theta) = j)$ when $n = 10, \theta = 0.01, p = 0.001$ and $EY_1 = 1$.

	$j=0$	$j=1$	$j=2$	$j=3$	$j=4$	$j=5$
$i=0$	0.9900	0	0	0	0	0
$i=1$	4.9535E-06	0.0099	4.9072E-06	0	0	0
$i=2$	0	0	4.4595E-05	4.6050E-08	0	0
$i=3$	0	0	0	1.1896E-07	2.0435E-10	0
$i=4$	0	0	0	0	2.0817E-10	5.7532E-13
$i=5$	0	0	0	0	0	2.498E-13

Lemma 2.4 can be obtained directly by Theorem 1 of De Pril and Dhaene (1992).

Theorem 2.7

(a) If $\theta \geqslant -n\log(1-q)$, *then*

$$H_n(\theta) = (\theta - nq)EY_1. \tag{2.32}$$

(b) If $0 \leqslant \theta < -n\log(1-q)$, *then*

$$H_n(\theta) = \{2\sum_{i=0}^{n}\sum_{j=0}^{i}(i-j)P(N_n = i, N_n^0(\theta) = j) + \theta - nq\}EY_1. \tag{2.33}$$

Proof. (a) In the case $\theta \geqslant -n\log(1-q)$, by Lemma 2.4 we have

$$P(N_n > t) \leqslant P(N_n^0(\theta) > t), \quad t \in [0, \infty].$$

Then using (2.25), we obtain

$$\begin{aligned} H_n(\theta) &= EY_1 \int_0^{\infty} |P(N_n \leqslant t) - P(N_n^0(\theta) \leqslant t)|dt \\ &= EY_1 \int_0^{\infty} \{P(N_n^0(\theta) > t) - P(N_n > t)\}dt \\ &= EY_1(EN_n^0(\theta) - EN_n) = EY_1(\theta - nq). \end{aligned}$$

(b) In the case $0 \leqslant \theta < -n\log(1-q)$, by Theorem 2.6 we have

$$\begin{aligned} H_n(\theta) &= EY_1 \times E|N_n - N_n^0(\theta)| \\ &= EY_1 \times \{2E(N_n - N_n^0(\theta))_+ - E(N_n - N_n^0(\theta)\} \\ &= EY_1 \times \{2E(N_n - N_n^0(\theta))_+ + \theta - nq\} \\ &= \{2\sum_{i=0}^{n}\sum_{j=0}^{i}(i-j)P(N_n = i, N_n^0(\theta) = j) + \theta - nq\}EY_1. \end{aligned}$$

□

The Poisson parameter θ is often chosen as $\theta = nq$ or $\theta = -n\log(1-q)$ (Gerber (1979, Chapter 4)). Tables 2.5–2.7 list some numerical values of $H_n(nq)$ and $H_n(-n\log(1-q))$ when $EY_1 = 1$. By comparing $H_n(nq)$ with $H_n(-n\log(1-q))$, one can analyze the accuracy of the approximation. For instance, in the case $nq = 0.05$, $H_{10}(nq) > H_{10}(-n\log(1-q))$,$H_{100}(nq) < H_{100}(-n\log(1-q))$ and $H_{1000}(nq) < H_{1000}(-n\log(1-q))$. Generally speaking, one can not assert that the parameter nq is optimal than the parameter $-n\log(1-q)$.

Table 2.5 The expected errors when $n = 10$.

q	nq	$n\log(1-q)$	$H_n(nq)$	$H_n(-n\log(1-q))$
0.001	0.01	0.010005	0.000010	0.000005
0.005	0.05	0.050125	0.000239	0.000125
0.01	0.1	0.100503	0.000911	0.000503
0.05	0.5	0.512933	0.015587	0.012933
0.1	1	1.053605	0.038402	0.053605
0.5	5	6.931472	0.524205	1.931472

Table 2.6 The expected errors when $n = 100$.

q	nq	$n\log(1-q)$	$H_n(nq)$	$H_n(-n\log(1-q))$
0.0001	0.01	0.010001	9.90116E-07	5.00033E-07
0.001	0.1	0.100050	0.000091	0.000050
0.005	0.5	0.501254	0.001520	0.001254
0.01	1	1.005034	0.003694	0.005034
0.05	5	5.129329	0.044504	0.129329
0.1	10	10.536051	0.128624	0.536051
0.5	50	69.314718	1.653039	19.314718

Table 2.7 The expected errors when $n = 1000$.

q	nq	$n\log(1-q)$	$H_n(nq)$	$H_n(-n\log(1-q))$
0.0001	0.1	0.100005	0.000009	0.000005
0.001	1	1.000500	0.000368	0.000500
0.005	0.5	5.012542	0.004393	0.012542
0.01	10	10.050336	0.012545	0.050336
0.05	50	51.293294	0.142642	1.293294

2.4.4 *The Approximation to Functions of the Total Loss*

Given the values $\{N_n, Y_1, Y_2, \cdots, Y_{N_n}\}$ obtained from the portfolio $\{Z_1, Z_2, \cdots, Z_n\}$, the optimal Poisson r.v. is determined as follows: First simulate the r.v. U by (2.24). Then calculate the Poisson counting number $N_n^0(\theta) = F_{poi(\theta)}^{-1}(U)$. In the case $N_n \geqslant N_n^0(\theta)$, $Y_1, Y_2, \cdots, Y_{N_n^0(\theta)}$ are available from the data set $\{Y_1, Y_2, \cdots, Y_{N_n}\}$. Otherwise, one can obain the additional values $\{Y_{N_n+1}, \cdots, Y_{N_n^0(\theta)}\}$ through simulation.

Consider the total amount $\sum_{i=1}^n g(Z_i)$, where g is a non-negative measurable function and $g(0) = 0$. Then an approximation for the amount $\sum_{i=1}^n g(Z_i)$ is

$$\sum_{i=1}^{N_n^0(\theta)} g(Y_i),$$

with the approximation error

$$h_n(\theta, g) =: \sum_{i=1}^{n} g(Z_i) - \sum_{i=1}^{N_n^0(\theta)} g(Z_i).$$

Note that when $g(x) = x$,

$$S_n = \sum_{i=1}^{N_n^0(\theta)} Y_i + h_n(\theta, g).$$

Theorem 2.8 *For the non-negative function g with $g(0) = 0$,*

$$Eh_n(\theta, g) = (nq - \theta)Eg(Y_1) \tag{2.34}$$

and

$$E|h_n(\theta, g)| = \frac{Eg(Y_1)}{EY_1} H_n(\theta). \tag{2.35}$$

Proof. It is easy to prove (2.34). Here we only prove (2.35) in details.

Since $g(0) = 0$, we have

$$\sum_{i=1}^{n} g(Z_i) = \sum_{i=1}^{N_n} g(Y_i).$$

Thus

$$E|h_n(\theta, g)| = E|\sum_{i=1}^{N_n} g(Y_i) - \sum_{i=1}^{N_n^0(\theta)} g(Y_i)| = \frac{Eg(Y_1)}{EY_1} H_n(\theta).$$

Therefore, the theorem is proved. □

Now we illustrate an interesting fact when $\theta = -nlog(1-q)$, the approximation shows special property. In this case, by Lemma 2.4 we have

$$F^{-1}_{poi(\theta)}(s) \geqslant F^{-1}_{bin(n,q)}(s), \quad s \in (0,1).$$

Then

$$N_n = F^{-1}_{bin(n,q)}(U) \leqslant F^{-1}_{poi(\theta)}(U) = N^0_n(\theta),$$

and it leads to

$$\sum_{i=1}^{n} g(X_i) = \sum_{i=1}^{N_n} g(Y_i) \leqslant \sum_{i=1}^{N^0_n(\theta)} g(Y_i).$$

The approximated total amount is always greater than the actual aggregate claims.

2.4.5 *The Uniqueness of the Poisson Parameter to Minimizing* $H_n(\theta)$

This section investigates the uniqueness of θ^0_n for

$$H_n(\theta^0_n) = \min_{\theta \geqslant 0} H_n(\theta). \tag{2.36}$$

The answer to this problem is affirmative.

For $k = 0, 1, 2, \cdots, n-1$, denote $\theta^{(k)}$ to be the solution of equation

$$F_{bin(n,q)}(k) = F_{poi(\theta^{(k)})}(k).$$

Then we have the following result.

Theorem 2.9 *It holds that*

$$\theta^{(n-1)} > \theta^{(n-2)} > \cdots > \theta^{(1)} > \theta^{(0)}.$$

Denote

$$sign\left(F_{bin(n,q)}(x) - F_{poi(\theta)}(x)\right) = \begin{cases} 1, & \textit{if } F_{bin(n,q)}(x) > F_{poi(\theta)}(x), \\ 0, & \textit{if } F_{bin(n,q)}(x) = F_{poi(\theta)}(x), \\ -1, & \textit{if } F_{bin(n,q)}(x) < F_{poi(\theta)}(x). \end{cases}$$

In the following we give a theorem on the uniqueness of θ^0_n and present an approach to solve θ^0_n. For simplicity it is assumed that $EY_1 = 1$.

Theorem 2.10 *There exists a unique θ_n^0 with $0 \leqslant \theta_n^0 \leqslant -n\log(1-q)$, such that (2.36) holds. Further, for $\theta \in (\theta^{(k+1)}, \theta^{(k)}), k = 0, 1, 2, \cdots, n-1$, the derivative function of H_n with respect to θ satisfies*

$$H_n'(\theta) = \sum_{k=0}^{n-1} \left(\text{sign}(F_{bin(n,q)}(k) - F_{poi(\theta)}(k)) - 1\right) \frac{e^{-\theta}\theta^k}{k!} + 1. \tag{2.37}$$

$H_n'(\theta)$ is strictly increasing for $\theta \neq \theta^{(k)}, k = 0, 1, 2, \cdots, n-1$, and

$$H_n'(\theta_n^0-) \leqslant 0, \quad H_n'(\theta_n^0+) \geqslant 0, \tag{2.38}$$

where $H_n'(\theta_n^0-)$ and $H_n'(\theta_n^0+)$ denote respectively the left and right limits of H_n' at point θ_n^0.

In the case $n = 1$, (2.37) can be used to find θ_1^0. For $\theta < -\log(1-q)$, $F_{bin(1,q)}(0) < F_{poi(\theta)}(0)$. Then by (2.37) we have

$$H_1'(\theta) = -2e^{-\theta} + 1.$$

Solving $H_1'(\theta) = 0$, we have $\theta = \log 2$. Moreover, $H_1'(\theta) < 0$ for $\theta < \log 2$. Then we can conclude that in the case $q > 0.5$, $H_n(\theta)$ achieves its minimum $\log 2 + q - 1$ at point $\theta_1^0 = \log 2$; when $q \leqslant 0.5$, $H_n(\theta)$ achieves its minimum $-q - \log(1-q)$ at point $\theta_1^0 = -\log(1-q)$.

In general, θ_n^0 can be solved numerically. By Theorem 2.10, θ_n^0 is the solution of $H_n'(\theta) = 0$ if the solution exits. Otherwise, it satisfies $H_n'(\theta-) \geqslant 0$ and $H_n'(\theta+) \leqslant 0$. Thus by Theorem 2.10 we can focus on the strictly increasing function $h(\theta)$ defined as

$$h(\theta) = \sum_{k=0}^{n-1} \left(sign(F_{bin(n,q)}(k) - F_{poi(\theta)}(k)) - 1\right) \frac{e^{-\theta}\theta^k}{k!} + 1, \quad \theta \in [0, \infty),$$

and use the Newtonian method to locate θ_n^0.

Tables 2.8-2.9 list some numerical results. It can be seen that when n is large, the difference between θ_n^0 and nq is very small. Thus nq is a good approximation for θ_n^0 when nq is large while $-n\log(1-q)$ is a good approximation when nq is small.

2.4.6 *Proofs*

In what follows, we will prove Theorems 2.9-2.10. First we introduce several lemmas.

Table 2.8 nq, $n\log(1-q)$ and θ_n^0.

n	q	nq	$-n\log(1-q)$	θ_n^0
2	0.001	0.002	0.002001	0.002001
2	0.01	0.02	0.020101	0.020101
2	0.10	0.2	0.210721	0.210721
2	0.5	1	1.386294	0.961278
10	0.001	0.01	0.010005	0.010005
10	0.01	0.1	0.100503	0.100503
10	0.10	1	1.053605	0.99907
10	0.5	5	6.931472	4.95961
100	0.001	0.1	0.100050	0.100050
100	0.01	1	1.005034	1.000
100	0.1	10	10.536051	9.9991
100	0.5	50	69.314718	49.959
1000	0.001	1	1.0005	1.000
1000	0.01	10	10.050336	10.00

Table 2.9 The corresponding error $H_n(\theta_n^0)$.

n	q	$H_n(nq)$	$H_n(-n\log(1-q))$	$H_n(\theta_n^0)$
2	0.001	1.997E-06	1.001E-06	1.001E-06
2	0.01	0.000197	0.000101	0.000101
2	0.10	0.017462	0.010721	0.010721
2	0.5	0.235797	0.386294	0.226086
10	0.001	0.00001	0.000005	0.000005
10	0.01	0.000911	0.000503	0.000503
10	0.10	0.038402	0.053605	0.038161
10	0.5	0.524205	1.931472	0.519686
100	0.001	0.000091	0.000050	0.000050
100	0.01	0.003694	0.005034	0.003694
100	0.1	0.128624	0.536051	0.128548
100	0.5	1.653039	19.314718	1.651654
1000	0.001	0.000368	0.000500	0.000368
1000	0.01	0.012545	0.050336	0.012545

Lemma 2.5 *There exists a non-negative integer $C \leqslant n-1$ such that*

$$\frac{P(N_n = k+1)}{P(N_n = k)} = \begin{cases} > \frac{P(N(\theta)=k+1)}{P(N(\theta)=k)}, & k < C, \\ < \frac{P(N(\theta)=k+1)}{P(N(\theta)=k)}, & n > k > C, \\ \geqslant \frac{P(N(\theta)=k+1)}{P(N(\theta)=k)}, & k = C. \end{cases}$$

Proof. It is easy to verify that for $k+1 \leqslant n$,

$$\frac{P(N_n = k+1)}{P(N_n = k)} = \frac{C_n^{k+1} q^{k+1}(1-q)^{n-k-1}}{C_n^k q^k (1-q)^{n-k}} = \frac{n-k}{k+1}\frac{q}{1-q}, \tag{2.39}$$

and

$$\frac{P(N(\theta) = k+1)}{P(N(\theta) = k)} = \frac{\theta}{k+1}. \tag{2.40}$$

Comparing (2.39) with (2.40), we observe that

$$\frac{P(N_n = k+1)}{P(N_n = k)} \geqslant \frac{P(N(\theta) = k+1)}{P(N(\theta) = k)},$$

if and only if $(n-k)\frac{q}{1-q} \geqslant \theta$, i.e.,

$$k \leqslant n - \frac{\theta(1-q)}{q}.$$

Denote

$$C = \max\{\min\{n-1, [n - \frac{\theta(1-q)}{q}]\}, 0\}.$$

Thus if $C < n-1$, for the integer $n > k > C$ it holds that

$$\frac{P(N_n = k+1)}{P(N_n = k)} < \frac{P(N(\theta) = k+1)}{P(N(\theta) = k)}.$$

And if $k < C$,

$$\frac{P(N_n = k+1)}{P(N_n = k)} > \frac{P(N(\theta) = k+1)}{P(N(\theta) = k)}$$

holds. In the case $k = C$, it holds that

$$\frac{P(N_n = k+1)}{P(N_n = k)} \geqslant \frac{P(N(\theta) = k+1)}{P(N(\theta) = k)}.$$

Hence the lemma is proved. □

It is easy to verify the following Lemma. We omit its proof here.

Lemma 2.6 *Suppose $a_n > 0, b_n > 0$ and $\frac{a_{n+1}}{a_n} \geqslant \frac{b_{n+1}}{b_n}, n \geqslant 0$. Then for $n \geqslant 1$,*

$$\frac{a_n + a_{n-1} + \cdots + a_0}{a_{n-1} + \cdots + a_0} \geqslant \frac{b_n + b_{n-1} + \cdots + b_0}{b_{n-1} + \cdots + b_0}.$$

Lemma 2.7 *Suppose that for non-negative integer M, $F_{bin(n,q)}(M) \geqslant F_{poi(\theta)}(M)$. Then*

$$F_{bin(n,q)}(M+1) > F_{poi(\theta)}(M+1). \tag{2.41}$$

Proof. It is trivial for the case $M \geqslant n$. Now we consider the case $M < n$. In the case $\theta \geqslant -n\log(1-q)$, by Lemma 2.4 we see that $F_{bin(n,q)}(k) \geqslant F_{poi(\theta)}(k), k = 0, 1, 2, \cdots$, thus (2.41) holds. Next we assume that $\theta < -n\log(1-q)$. We will divide our proof into the two cases $M \leqslant C$ and $M > C$, where C is the integer defined in Lemma 2.5.

Case 1. $M \leqslant C$.

Since $\theta < -n\log(1-q)$, it leads to $P(N_n = 0) < P(N(\theta) = 0)$. Then according to the definition of C and $F_{bin(n,q)}(M) \geqslant F_{poi(\theta)}(M)$, by Lemma 2.5 and Lemma 2.6 we conclude that

$$P(N_n = M) > P(N(\theta) = M).$$

Also by Lemma 2.5 we have

$$\frac{P(N_n = M+1)}{P(N_n = M)} \geqslant \frac{P(N(\theta) = M+1)}{P(N(\theta) = M)}.$$

Then it follows that

$$P(N_n = M+1) > P(N(\theta) = M+1).$$

Thus

$$\begin{aligned} F_{bin(n,q)}(M+1) &= F_{bin(n,q)}(M) + P(N_n = M+1) \\ &> F_{poi(\theta)}(M) + P(N(\theta) = M+1) \\ &= F_{poi(\theta)}(M+1), \end{aligned}$$

which implies (2.41).

Case 2. $M > C$.

If $P(N_n = M+1) \geqslant P(N(\theta) = M+1)$, then it is obvious that (2.41) holds. Next we consider the case $P(N_n = M+1) < P(N(\theta) = M+1)$.

Since $P(N_n = M+1) < P(N(\theta) = M+1)$ and $M > C$, by Lemma 2.5 we have

$$P(N_n = k) < P(N(\theta) = k), \quad k \geqslant M+1.$$

Then

$$\begin{aligned}
P(N_n \leqslant M+1) &= 1 - \sum_{k=M+2}^{n} P(N_n = k) \\
&> 1 - \sum_{k=M+2}^{n} P(N(\theta = k) \\
&> 1 - \sum_{k=M+2}^{\infty} P(N(\theta) = k) = P(N(\theta) \leqslant M+1).
\end{aligned}$$

Thus the lemma is proved. □

Proof of Theorem 2.9 Fix $k < n$. From the definition $F_{bin(n,q)}(k) = F_{poi(\theta^{(k)})}(k)$ and Lemma 2.7, we have

$$F_{bin(n,q)}(k+1) > F_{poi(\theta^{(k)})}(k+1).$$

Since for fixed k the function $F_{poi(\theta)}(k+1)$ is strictly decreasing about θ, we have

$$\theta^{(k+1)} < \theta^{(k)}.$$

Now we complete the proof of the theorem. □

Lemma 2.8 *For $\theta \neq \theta^{(i)}, i = 0, 1, \cdots, n-1$, the derivative $H_n'(\theta)$ of $H_n(\theta)$ exists and (2.37) holds.*

Proof. Fix $\theta_0 > 0$ and $\theta_0 \neq \theta^{(i)}, i = 0, 1, \cdots, n-1$. Denote

$$g(\theta, x) = F_{bin(n,q)}(x) - F_{poi(\theta)}(x).$$

First consider the case $\theta > \theta_0$. From (2.25) we have

$$\begin{aligned}
&\frac{H_n(\theta) - H_n(\theta_0)}{\theta - \theta_0} \\
&= \frac{1}{\theta - \theta_0} \int_0^\infty (|g(\theta, x)| - |g(\theta_0, x)|) dx \\
&= \frac{1}{\theta - \theta_0} \int_0^\infty \big(g(\theta, x) I_{\{g(\theta,x)>0\}} - g(\theta_0, x) I_{\{g(\theta_0,x)>0\}}\big) dx \\
&\quad + \frac{1}{\theta - \theta_0} \int_0^\infty \big(-g(\theta, x) I_{\{g(\theta,x)<0\}} + g(\theta_0, x) I_{\{g(\theta_0,x)<0\}}\big) dx \\
&=: A + B. \qquad (2.42)
\end{aligned}$$

By using the fact that $g(\theta, x) > g(\theta_0, x)$ for $\theta > \theta_0$ and $g(\theta_0, x) \neq 0$, we have

$$\begin{aligned}
A &= \frac{1}{\theta - \theta_0} \int_0^\infty \big(g(\theta, x) I_{\{g(\theta,x)>0\}} - g(\theta_0, x) I_{\{g(\theta,x)>0\}}\big) dx \\
&\quad + \frac{1}{\theta - \theta_0} \int_0^\infty \big(g(\theta_0, x)(I_{\{g(\theta,x)>0\}} - I_{\{g(\theta_0,x)>0\}}\big) dx \\
&= \frac{\int_0^\infty \big(F_{poi(\theta_0)}(x) - F_{poi(\theta)}(x)\big) I_{\{g(\theta,x)>0\}} dx}{\theta - \theta_0} \\
&\quad + \frac{\int_0^\infty \big(F_{bin(n,q)}(x) - F_{poi(\theta_0)}(x)\big) I_{\{g(\theta,x)>0,\ g(\theta_0,x)<0\}} dx}{\theta - \theta_0}. \qquad (2.43)
\end{aligned}$$

For the case $g(\theta, x) > 0$ and $g(\theta_0, x) < 0$, it holds that $F_{bin(n,q)}(x) > F_{poi(\theta)}(x)$ and $F_{bin(n,q)}(x) < F_{poi(\theta_0)}(x)$. Thus in this case it follows that

$$\begin{aligned}
0 &\leqslant \int_0^\infty \left|\frac{F_{bin(n,q)}(x) - F_{poi(\theta_0)}(x)}{\theta - \theta_0}\right| I_{\{g(\theta,x)>0, g(\theta_0,x)<0\}} |dx \\
&\leqslant \int_0^\infty \frac{F_{poi(\theta_0)}(x) - F_{poi(\theta)}(x)}{\theta - \theta_0} I_{\{g(\theta,x)>0, g(\theta_0,x)<0\}} dx. \qquad (2.44)
\end{aligned}$$

For $x \in [0, \infty)$,

$$\frac{\partial}{\partial \theta} F_{poi(\theta)}(x) = \frac{e^{-\theta} \theta^{[x]}}{[x]!} \leqslant \frac{(2\theta_0)^{[x]}}{[x]!}, \qquad \theta < 2\theta_0,$$

where $[x]$ is the integral part of x. Then by the dominated convergence theorem and $g(\theta, x) \to g(\theta_0, x)$ we have

$$\begin{aligned}
&\frac{1}{\theta - \theta_0} \int_0^\infty \big(F_{poi(\theta_0)}(x) - F_{poi(\theta)}(x)\big) I_{\{g(\theta,x)>0\}} dx \\
&\to \int_0^\infty \frac{e^{-\theta_0} \theta_0^{[x]}}{[x]!} I_{\{g(\theta_0,x)>0\}} dx, \qquad (2.45)
\end{aligned}$$

and by (2.44) we obtain

$$\begin{aligned}
&\left| \int_0^\infty \frac{F_{bin(n,q)}(x) - F_{poi(\theta)}(x)}{\theta - \theta_0} I_{\{g(\theta,x)>0, g(\theta_0,x)<0\}} dx \right| \\
&\leqslant \int_0^\infty \frac{F_{poi(\theta_0)}(x) - F_{poi(\theta)}(x)}{\theta - \theta_0} I_{\{g(\theta,x)>0, g(\theta_0,x)<0\}} dx \to 0. \qquad (2.46)
\end{aligned}$$

Combining (2.45) and (2.46), from (2.43) we conclude that

$$\lim_{\theta \searrow \theta_0} A = \int_0^\infty \frac{e^{-\theta_0} \theta_0^{[x]}}{[x]!} I_{\{g(\theta_0,x)>0\}} dx.$$

Similarly,

$$\lim_{\theta \searrow \theta_0} B = -\int_0^\infty \frac{e^{-\theta_0}\theta_0^{[x]}}{[x]!} I_{\{g(\theta_0,x)<0\}} dx.$$

Summarizing the above two equations and (2.42), we deduce that

$$\lim_{\theta \searrow \theta_0} \frac{H_n(\theta) - H_n(\theta_0)}{\theta - \theta_0} = \int_0^\infty \frac{e^{-\theta_0}\theta_0^{[x]}}{[x]!} sign(F_{bin(n,q)}(x) - F_{poi(\theta_0)}(x))dx. \tag{2.47}$$

Similarly,

$$\lim_{\theta \nearrow \theta_0} \frac{H_n(\theta) - H_n(\theta_0)}{\theta - \theta_0} = \int_0^\infty \frac{e^{-\theta_0}\theta_0^{[x]}}{[x]!} sign(F_{bin(n,q)}(x) - F_{poi(\theta_0)}(x))dx \tag{2.48}$$

holds. Thus combining (2.47) and (2.48), we obtain

$$\begin{aligned} H_n'(\theta_0) &= \int_0^\infty \frac{e^{-\theta}\theta_0^{[x]}}{[x]!} sign(F_{bin(n,q)}(x) - F_{poi(\theta_0)}(x))dx \\ &= \sum_{k=0}^{n-1} sign(F_{bin(n,q)}(k) - F_{poi(\theta_0)}(k))\frac{e^{-\theta_0}\theta_0^k}{k!} + \sum_{k=n}^{\infty} \frac{e^{-\theta_0}\theta_0^k}{k!} \\ &= \sum_{k=0}^{n-1} \left(sign(F_{bin(n,q)}(k) - F_{poi(\theta_0)}(k)) - 1\right)\frac{e^{-\theta_0}\theta_0^k}{k!} + 1. \end{aligned}$$

□

Proof of Theorem 2.10 Fix $\theta \in (\theta^{(i+1)}, \theta^{(i)})$. Since

$$F_{bin(n,q)}(i) = F_{poi(\theta^{(i)})}(i), \quad F_{bin(n,q)}(i+1) = F_{poi(\theta^{(i+1)})}(i+1),$$

we have

$$F_{bin(n,q)}(i) < F_{poi(\theta)}(i), \ F_{bin(n,q)}(i+1) > F_{poi(\theta)}(i+1).$$

Thus by Lemma 2.7 we assert that

$$F_{bin(n,q)}(k) < F_{poi(\theta)}(k), \quad k \leqslant i$$

and

$$F_{bin(n,q)}(k) > F_{poi(\theta)}(k), \quad k \geqslant i+1.$$

Then by Lemma 2.8 we have

$$H'(\theta) = -2\sum_{k=0}^{i} \frac{e^{-\theta}\theta^k}{k!} + 1,$$

which is strictly increasing with respect to $\theta \in (\theta^{(i+1)}, \theta^{(i)})$.

From the above equation it is easy to verify

$$H'(\theta^{(i)}-) < H'(\theta^{(i)}+), \quad i = 0, 1, \cdots, n-1.$$

Thus we conclude that $H'(\theta)$ is strictly increasing with respect to $\theta \neq \theta^{(i)}$.

Since $H_n(\theta)$ is continuous, from Theorem 2.7 we assert that the minimum point θ_n^0 exists and $\theta_n^0 \leqslant n\log(1-q)$. By the monotonicity of $H_n'(\theta)$ with respect to θ, we assert that $H_n'(\theta_n^0+) \geqslant 0$ and $H_n'(\theta_n^0-) \leqslant 0$. Since $H_n'(\theta)$ is strictly increasing, thus θ_n^0 is unique. Hence the uniqueness is proved.

As (2.37) has been proved in Lemma 2.8, we now complete the proof of Theorem 2.10. □

2.5 Bivariate Copula Decomposition

A bivariate copula is a two dimensional distribution with uniform marginal distributions. A copula $C(u,v), u, v \in [0,1]$ satisfies the following properties:

(1) $C(u,1) = u, C(1,v) = v, u, v \in [0,1]$;

(2) $C(u,0) = 0, C(0,v) = 0, u, v \in [0,1]$;

(3) For every $u_1 \leqslant u_2, v_1 \leqslant u_2$ and $u_1, u_2, v_1, v_2 \in [0,1]$,

$$C(u_2, v_2) + C(u_1, v_1) - C(u_2, v_1) - C(u_1, v_2) \geqslant 0;$$

See Nelsen (1999), Mari and Kotz (2001) or Joe (1997).

The three important bivariate copulas are C^-, C^+ and $C^\perp$, defined respectively as follows:

$$\begin{aligned} C^+(u,v) &= \min\{u,v\}; \\ C^-(u,v) &= \max\{u+v-1, 0\}; \\ C^\perp(u,v) &= uv. \end{aligned}$$

Of these three copulas, M. Frêchet established what have come to known as the Frêchet upper bound C^+ and the Frêchet lower bound C^-, namely that for any copula C and real numbers u and v,

$$C^-(u,v) \leqslant C(u,v) \leqslant C^+(u,v)$$

holds. The copula $C^\perp$ is named as product copula, it is important because X and Y are independent if and only if the copula of (X,Y) equals $C^\perp$.

Consider two random variables X and Y with marginal distributions F_1 and F_2. Their joint distribution function is denoted as $F(x,y)$. Then

Theorem 2.11 (Sklar's Theorem (Nelsen(1999)) *There exists a copula C such that for all $x, y \in R$,*

$$F(x,y) = C(F_1(x), F_2(x)).$$

We have introduced the definition of Comonotonicity before. Two risks X and Y are said to be comonotonic, if there exist a random variable Z and non-decreasing functions f and g such that

$$(X,Y) =^d (f(Z), g(Z)).$$

Two risks X, Y are called countermonotonic , if $X, -Y$ are comonotonic.

Theorem 2.12 (Dhaene, et al (2002a, 2002b))

(1) Two risks X, Y are comonotonic if and only if

$$F(x,y) = \min\{F_1(x), F_2(y)\}.$$

(2) Two risks X, Y are countermonotonic if and only if

$$F(x,y) = \max\{F_1(x) + F_2(y) - 1, 0\}.$$

From copula's viewpoint, the above theorem states that X, Y are comonotonic if and only if the copula of (X,Y) equals $C^+(u,v)$. X, Y are countermonotonic if and only if the copula of (X,Y) equals $C^+(u,v)$.

2.5.1 *Copula Decomposition*

For convenience, for bivariate function g we denote

$$\triangle_{(x_1,y_1)}^{(x_2,y_2)}(g) = g(x_1,y_1) + g(x_2,y_2) - g(x_1,y_2) - g(x_2,y_1).$$

If g is a distribution function and V_g is the measure generated by g, then for $x_1 \leqslant x_2, y_1 \leqslant y_2$,

$$\triangle_{(x_1,y_1)}^{(x_2,y_2)}(g) = V_g((x_1,y_1] \times (x_2,y_2]).$$

In measure theory, a standard result is that V_g is unique.

For one copula $C(u,v)$, its comonotonic factor is defined as

$$\alpha_C \qquad (2.49)$$
$$= \sup\{a : \Delta_{(x_1,y_1)}^{(x_2,y_2)}(C) \geqslant a\Delta_{(x_1,y_1)}^{(x_2,y_2)}(C^+) \quad for \quad all\ x_2 \geqslant x_1, y_2 \geqslant y_1\}.$$

We can explain α_C as follows. Consider the convex decomposition

$$C(u,v) = \alpha C^+(u,v) + (1-\alpha)G(u,v),$$

where $G(u,v)$ is an unknown copula and α is some constant to be determined. Note that the above decomposition holds with $\alpha = \alpha_C$. Further, α_C is the largest number of α's satisfying the above equation. Hence, (2.49) presents a reasonable description about $C(u,v)$'s comonotonitic characteristic.

Similarly, the independent factor of $C(u,v)$ is defined as

$$\beta_C \qquad (2.50)$$
$$= \sup\{b : \Delta_{(x_1,y_1)}^{(x_2,y_2)}(C) \geqslant b\Delta_{(x_1,y_1)}^{(x_2,y_2)}(C^\perp) \quad for \quad all\ x_2 \geqslant x_1, y_2 \geqslant y_1\},$$

and the countermonotonic factor of $C(u,v)$ is defined as

$$\gamma_C \qquad (2.51)$$
$$= \sup\{c : \Delta_{(x_1,y_1)}^{(x_2,y_2)}(C) \geqslant c\Delta_{(x_1,y_1)}^{(x_2,y_2)}(C^-) \quad for \quad all\ x_2 \geqslant x_1, y_2 \geqslant y_1\}.$$

It is easy to see that $\alpha_C, \beta_C, \gamma_C \in [0,1]$. Sometimes it is difficult to compute α_C,β_C and γ_C from their definitions. In the following, one theorem is introduced for calculating the three factors by the partial derivatives of $C(u,v)$.

First we need some notations. Let $\mathcal{D}_C$ be the set of all points $(u,v) \in [0,1]^2$ such that $\frac{\partial^2}{\partial u \partial v}C(u,v)$ exists, $\mathcal{D}_{C,1}$ be the set of all points $(u,v) \in [0,1]^2$ such that $\frac{\partial}{\partial u}C(u,v)$ exists, and $\mathcal{D}_{C,2}$ be the set of all points $(u,v) \in [0,1]^2$ such that $\frac{\partial}{\partial v}C(u,v)$ exists. Then

$$\mathcal{D}_C = \{(u,v) \in [0,1]^2 : \frac{\partial^2}{\partial u \partial v}C(u,v)\ \ exists\},$$

$$\mathcal{D}_{C,1} = \{(u,v) \in [0,1]^2 : \frac{\partial}{\partial u}C(u,v)\ \ exists\}$$

and

$$\mathcal{D}_{C,2} = \{(u,v) \in [0,1]^2 : \frac{\partial}{\partial v}C(u,v)\ \ exists\}.$$

With respect to Lebesgue measure, $\frac{\partial}{\partial u}C(u,v)$, $\frac{\partial}{\partial v}C(u,v)$ and $\frac{\partial^2}{\partial u \partial v}C(u,v)$ exist for almost all $(u,v) \in [0,1]^2$. See Theorem 7.1.8 of Lojasiewicz (1988) and Theorem 2.2.7 of Nelsen (1991).

For simplicity, we denote

$$\begin{aligned}
M_1(u) &= \lim_{v\downarrow u,(u,v)\in\mathcal{D}_{C,1}} \frac{\partial C(u,v)}{\partial u} - \lim_{v\uparrow u,\,(u,v)\in\mathcal{D}_{C,1}} \frac{\partial C(u,v)}{\partial u},\\
M_2(v) &= \lim_{u\downarrow v,\,(u,v)\in\mathcal{D}_{C,2}} \frac{\partial C(u,v)}{\partial v} - \lim_{u\uparrow v,\,(u,v)\in\mathcal{D}_{C,2}} \frac{\partial C(u,v)}{\partial v},\\
M_3(u) &= \lim_{v\uparrow u,(u,1-v)\in\mathcal{D}_{C,1}} \frac{\partial C(u,1-v)}{\partial u} - \lim_{v\downarrow u,(u,1-v)\in\mathcal{D}_{C,1}} \frac{\partial C(u,1-v)}{\partial u},\\
M_4(v) &= \lim_{u\uparrow v,(1-u,v)\in\mathcal{D}_{C,2}} \frac{\partial C(1-u,v)}{\partial v} - \lim_{u\downarrow v,(1-u,v)\in\mathcal{D}_{C,2}} \frac{\partial C(1-u,v)}{\partial v},\\
M_5(u,v) &= \frac{\partial^2 C(u,v)}{\partial u \partial v}.
\end{aligned}$$

It is easy to verify that if M_i exists, then $M_i \geqslant 0$.

Another notation is needed. For one measurable function $h(x), x \in R^2$, its essential infimum in measurable set $A \in R^2$, denoted as $g = essinf_{x\in A}h(x)$, is defined by the properties:

(1) For almost all $x \in A$, $h(x) \geqslant g$;

(2) For every $\epsilon > 0$, the lebesgue measure of the set $\{x \in A : h(x) < g + \epsilon\}$ is greater than zero.

Then the following theorem gives one way to determine the factors α_C, β_C and γ_C by $M_i, i = 1, \cdots, 5$.

Theorem 2.13 *The functions $M_i, i = 1, \cdots, 4$ exist almost everywhere on $[0,1]$. And the factors α_C, β_C and γ_C can be determined by the following equations:*

$$\begin{aligned}
\beta_C &= \text{essinf}_{(u,v)\in[0,1]^2} M_5(u,v),\\
\alpha_C &= \text{essinf}_{u\in[0,1]} M_1(u) = \text{essinf}_{v\in[0,1]} M_2(v),\\
\gamma_C &= \text{essinf}_{u\in[0,1]} M_3(u) = \text{essinf}_{v\in[0,1]} M_4(v).
\end{aligned}$$

Although the factors α_C, β_C and γ_C play different roles on measuring the structure of correlation, they are correlated each other and their relationship can be stated as one convex decomposition of $C(u,v)$.

Theorem 2.14 *$C(u,v)$ has the following convex decomposition*

$$C(u,v) = \alpha_C C^+(u,v) + \beta_C C^\perp(u,v) + \gamma_C C^-(u,v) + l_C G_C(u,v), \quad (2.52)$$

where $l_C = 1 - \alpha_C - \beta_C - \gamma_C \geqslant 0$. When $l_C \neq 0$,

$$G_C(u,v) = \frac{C(u,v) - \alpha_C C^+(u,v) - \beta_C C^\perp(u,v) - \gamma_C C^-(u,v)}{l_C},$$

and G_C is indecomposable. Conversely, if

$$C(u,v) = \alpha C^+(u,v) + \beta C^\perp(u,v) + \gamma C^-(u,v) + lG(u,v),$$

holds and either $l \neq 0$ and G is indecomposable or $l = 0$, then $\alpha = \alpha_C, \beta = \beta_C, \gamma = \gamma_C, l = 1 - \alpha_C - \beta_C - \gamma_C$, and

$$G(u,v) = \frac{C(u,v) - \alpha_C C^+(u,v) - \beta_C C^\perp(u,v) - \gamma_C C^-(u,v)}{l},$$

if $l \neq 0$.

Note that $C(u,v)$ can be decompensated as the four terms concerning its different components. The first term is its comonotonic part, the second term is its independent part, the third is its countermonotonic part. If $l_C \neq 0$, the fourth term is the indecomposable part of $C(u,v)$. The coefficients of the first three terms are the factors α_C,β_C and γ_C defined before. Thus, equation (2.52) accounts for the rationality of the definitions (2.49)-(2.51) from another viewpoint. Further, (2.52) also provides a new way to analyze the correlation structure of a copula.

The following two corollaries can be derived from the above theorems.

Corollary 2.2 *Copula $C(u,v)$ is indecomposable if and only if the following conditions hold:*

$$\text{essinf}_{(u,v)\in[0,1]^2} M_5(u,v) = \text{essinf}_{u\in[0,1]} M_1(u) = \text{essinf}_{u\in[0,1]} M_3(u) = 0.$$

Corollary 2.3 *Suppose the density function of $C(u,v)$ exists. Then $\alpha_C = \gamma_C = 0$. Furthermore, $C(u,v)$ is indecomposable if and only if*

$$\text{essinf}_{(u,v)\in[0,1]^2} M_5(u,v) = 0.$$

Example 2.1 Normal copula is given by

$$C(u,v) = \Phi(\Phi^{-1}(u), \Phi^{-1}(v); \rho),$$

where $\Phi(x, y; \rho)$ is bivariate normal distribution with standard normal margins and correlation coefficient $-1 < \rho < 1$, and Φ^{-1} is the inverse function of standard normal distribution. We can get $\alpha_C = \gamma_C = 0$. When $\rho \neq 0$, we can verify that

$$\beta_C = essinf_{(u,v)\in[0,1]^2} \frac{\partial^2}{\partial u \partial v} C(u, v) = 0.$$

Hence, normal copula is indecomposable when $\rho \neq 0$.

Example 2.2 Frank copula is defined as

$$C(u, v) = \frac{1}{-\theta} \ln(1 + \frac{(e^{-\theta u} - 1)(e^{-\theta v} - 1)}{e^{-\theta} - 1}),$$

where the parameter $\theta \neq 0$. Obviously $\alpha_C = \gamma_C = 0$. By the detailed calculation one can prove that for $\theta > 0$,

$$\beta_C = \frac{\theta}{e^{\theta} - 1}.$$

In Mikusinski, Sherwood and Taylor (1991), the probability interpretation of a finite convex sum of copulas is presented. As a consequence of their result, the probabilistic model on (2.52) can be obtained. We state it in the following Theorem.

Theorem 2.15 *Let U, V and W be uniform $[0, 1]$ random variables in probability space $(\Omega, \mathcal{F}, P)$, and the disjoint sets $A^+, A^\perp, A^-, A^I \in \mathcal{F}$ satisfy that*

$$A^+ \cup A^\perp \cup A^- \cup A^I = \Omega.$$

Suppose

$$P(A^+) = \alpha_C, \quad P(A^\perp) = \beta_C, \quad P(A^-) = \gamma_C, \quad P(A^I) = l_C,$$

U and V are independent, and (U, W) has joint distribution $G_C(u, v)$. Further, $A^+, A^\perp, A^-, A^I$ are independent of U, V and W. Then the random vector (ζ, η) defined by

$$(\zeta, \eta) = (U, UI_{A^+} + VI_{A^\perp} + (1 - U)I_{A^-} + WI_{A^I})$$

has distribution $C(u,v)$. *Moreover,*

$$P(\zeta \leqslant u, \eta \leqslant v|A^+) = C^+(u,v), \quad P(\zeta \leqslant u, \eta \leqslant v|A^\perp) = C^\perp(u,v);$$
$$P(\zeta \leqslant u, \eta \leqslant v|A^-) = C^-(u,v), \quad P(\zeta \leqslant u, \eta \leqslant v|A^I) = G_C(u,v).$$

2.5.2 *Application of the Copula Decomposition*

Suppose that the two variables X and Y have continuous margins F_1, F_2 and copula $C(u,v)$. As mentioned before, the joint distribution $F(x,y)$ of (X,Y) can be expressed as

$$F(x,y) = C(F_1(x), F_2(y)).$$

Thus according to (2.52), it yields that

$$\begin{aligned} F(x,y) = {} & \alpha_C C^+(F_1(x), F_2(y)) + \beta_C C^\perp(F_1(x), F_2(y)) \\ & + \gamma_C C^-(F_1(x), F_2(y)) + l_C G_C(F_1(x), F_2(y)). \end{aligned} \tag{2.53}$$

Note that for different marginal distributions, the four coefficients of the right-hand side of (2.53) are invariant. In the following, we will show some invariant properties when applying (2.53).

Define the inverse functions of F_1 and F_2 respectively by

$$F_1^{\leftarrow}(x) = \inf\{s : F_1(s) \geqslant x\}, \quad F_2^{\leftarrow}(x) = \inf\{s : F_2(s) \geqslant x\}.$$

A well-known result is that for any uniform [0,1] random variable Z, $F_1^{\leftarrow}(Z)$ has common distribution with X and $F_2^{\leftarrow}(Z)$ has common distribution with Y.

Given the variables U, V and W introduced in Theorem 2.15, we denote

$$(X^+, Y^+) = (F_1^{\leftarrow}(U), F_2^{\leftarrow}(U)), \quad (X^\perp, Y^\perp) = (F_1^{\leftarrow}(U), F_2^{\leftarrow}(V))$$

and

$$(X^-, Y^-) = (F_1^{\leftarrow}(U), F_2^{\leftarrow}(1-U)), \quad (X^I, Y^I) = (F_1^{\leftarrow}(U), F_2^{\leftarrow}(W)).$$

Note that the four pairs $(X^+, Y^+), (X^\perp, Y^\perp), (X^-, Y^-)$ and (X^I, Y^I) all have marginal distributions F_1 and F_2, and (X^+, Y^+) is a comonotonic pair, $(X^\perp, Y^\perp)$ is an independent pair, (X^-, Y^-) is an countermonotonic pair. If $l_C \neq 0$, (X^I, Y^I) is a indecomposable pair.

Theorem 2.16 *Given the notations introduced as above, we have*

$$(X,Y) =^d (X^+, Y^+) I_{A^+} + (X^\perp, Y^\perp) I_{A^\perp} + (X^-, Y^-) I_{A^-} + (X^I, Y^I) I_{A^I},$$

where '$=^d$' denotes 'equal in distribution'. Further, for any no-negative measurable function f on R^2, the following equation holds:

$$Ef(X,Y) = \alpha_C Ef(X^+,Y^+) + \beta_C Ef(X^\perp,Y^\perp) + \gamma_C Ef(X^-,Y^-) + l_C Ef(X^I,Y^I). \tag{2.54}$$

Theorem 2.16 can be used to deal with the correlation of risks in finance and insurance. Note that the coefficients of the right-hand side of (2.54) are invariant with the marginal distributions. We will illustrate its applications briefly in the following.

Case 1: On variance decomposition.

From Theorem 2.16 one can prove that for every $a, b \in R$, it holds that

$$Var(aX + bY) = \alpha_C Var(aX^+ + bY^+) + \beta_C Var(aX^\perp + bY^\perp) + \gamma_C Var(aX^- + bY^-) + l_C Var(aX^I + bY^I).$$

In investment, the above equation can be used to find the optimal investment portfolio.

Case 2: On stop-loss premium $E(X+Y-t)_+$. Here $(X+Y-t)_+ = \max\{X+Y-t, 0\}$.

It can also be verified that

$$E(X+Y-t)_+ = \alpha_C E(X^+ + Y^+ - t)_+ + \beta_C E(X^\perp + Y^\perp - t)_+ + \gamma_C E(X^- + Y^- - t)_+ + l_C E(X^I + Y^I - t)_+.$$

Using the above equation, an upper and lower bounds for $E(X+Y-t)_+$ can be obtained. By the well-known fact

$$E(X^- + Y^- - t)_+ \leqslant E(X^I + Y^I - t)_+ \leqslant E(X^+ + Y^+ - t)_+,$$

we get that

$$E(X+Y-t)_+ \leqslant (\alpha_C + l_C)E(X^+ + Y^+ - t)_+ + \beta_C E(X^\perp + Y^\perp - t)_+ + \gamma_C E(X^- + Y^- - t)_+,$$

and

$$E(X+Y-t)_+ \geqslant \alpha_C E(X^+ + Y^+ - t)_+ + \beta_C E(X^\perp + Y^\perp - t)_+ + (\gamma_C + l_C)E(X^- + Y^- - t)_+.$$

When l_C is small, the above inequalities provide good approximations. The background on stop-loss premium can be found in Dhaene et al (2002a, 2002b).

For the proofs of the theorems, see Yang, Cheng and Zhang(2004).

References

Barrio E D, Gine E, Matran C. (1999). Central limit theorems for the Wasserstein distance between the empirical and the true distributions, *The Annals of Probability*, **27**(2), 1009-1071.

Bühlmann H, Gagliardi B, Gerber H U, Straub E. (1977). Some inequalities for stop-loss premiums, *ASTIN BULLETIN*, **9**, 75-83.

De Pril N, Dhaene J. (1992). Error bounds for the compound Poisson approximations of the individual risk model, *ASTIN BULLETIN*, **22**(2), 135-148.

Dhaene J, Sundt B. (1997). On error bounds for approximations to aggregate claims distributions, *ASTIN BULLETIN*, **27**(2), 243-262.

Dhaene J, Denuit M, Goovaerts M J, Kaas R, Vynche D. (2002a). The concept of comonotonicity in Actuarial Science and Finance: Theory, *Insurance: Mathematics and Economics*, **31**(1), 3-33.

Dhaene J, Denuit M, Goovaerts M J, Kaas R, Vynche D. (2002b). The concept of comonotonicity in Actuarial Science and Finance: Application. *Insurance: Mathematics and Economics*, **31**(2), 133-161.

Gerber H U. (1979). An introduction to Mathematical Risk Theory. S. S. Hueber Foundation Monograph No.8, Illinois: Richard D. Irwin, Inc., Homewood.

Gerber H U. (1984). Error bounds for the compound Poisson Approximation, *Insurance: Mathematics and Economics*, **31**(3), 191-194.

Hesselager O. (1995). Order relations for some distributions, *Insurance: Mathematics and Economics*, **16**, 129-134.

Hesselager O. (1996). Recursions for certain bivariate counting distributions and their compound distributions, *ASTIN BULLETIN*, *26*(1), 35-52.

Hipp C. (1985). Approximation of aggregate claims distributions by compound Poisson approximation, *Insurance: Mathematics and Economics*, **4**, 227-232.

Hipp C. (1986). Improved approximations for the aggregate claims distribution in the individual model, *ASTIN BULLETIN*, **16**(2), 89-100.

Joe H. (1997). Multivariate Models and Dependence Concepts. New York, Chapman & Hall, 35-52.

Kaas R, Van Heerwaarden, Goovaerts M J. (1988). On stop-loss premiums for the individual risk model, *ASTIN BULLETIN*, **18**, 91-98.

Kaas R, Goovaerts M, Dhaene J, Denuit M. (2001). Modern Actuarial Risk Theory. Kluwer Academic Publishers, London.

Kuon S, Radtke M, Reich A. (1993). An approximate way to switch from the individual risk model to the collective one, *ASTIN BULLETIN*, **23**(1), 23-32.

Lojasiewicz S. (1988). An Introduction to the Theory of Real Functions. John Wiley & Sons, New York.

Loéve M. (1978). Probability Theory I. 4th Edition. New York: Springer-Verlag, 178-179.

Li X D, Yang J P. (2001). Compound Poisson approximation to individual risk models. *Acta Scientiarum Naturalium, Universitatis Pekinensis*, **37**(5), 609-617. (in Chinese)

Mari D D, Kotz S. (2001). Correlation and Dependence. Imperial College Press, Singapore.

Michel R. (1987). An improved error bound for the compound Poisson approximation of a family of a nearly homogeneous portfolio, *ASTIN BULLETIN*, **17**(2), 165-169.

Mikusinski P, Sherwood H, Taylor M D. (1991). Probabilistic interpretations of copulas and their convex sums. In Advances in Probability Distributions with Given Marginals, edited by G. Dall'Aglio, S. Kotz and G. Salinetti, 95-112.

Nelsen R B. (1991). Copulas and associations. Edited by G. Dall'Aglio, So. Kotz and G. Salinetti, 51-74.

Nelsen R B. (1999). An Introduction to Copulas. New York: Springer-Verlag.

Panjer H H. (1981). Recursive evaluation of a family of compound distributions, *ASTIN BULLETIN*, **12**(1), 22-26.

Panjer H H, Willmot G E. (1993). Insurance Risk Models. Schaumburg, Society of Actuaries.

Shorack G R, Welllner J A. (1986). Empirical Processes with Applications to Statistics. New York: Jone Wiley & Sons, 64.

Sundt B. (1993). Improved error bounds for BERTRAM's method, *ASTIN BULLETIN*, **23**(2), 301-303.

Sundt B. (1999). On multivariate panjer recursions, *ASTIN BULLETIN*, **29**(1), 29-45.

Sundt B, Dhaene J. (1991). On approximating claims distributions and stop-loss premiums by truncation. *Insurance: Mathematics and Economics*, **10**, 133-136.

Sundt B, Dhaene J. (1996). On bounds for the difference between the stop-loss transforms of the two compound distributions, *ASTIN BULLETIN*, **26**(2), 225-231.

Yang J P, Cheng S H, Wu Q. (2005). Recursive equations for compound distributions with severity distributions of the mixed type, *Science in China (Series A: Mathematics)*, **48**(5), 594-609.

Yang J P, Zhou S L, Zhang Z Y. (2005). The compound Poisson random variable's approximation to the individual risk model, *Insurance: Mathematics and Economics*, **36**, 57-77.

Cheng S H, Wang X Q, Yang J P. (2003). On a kind of integrals of empirical processes concerning insurance risk, *Science in China (Series A)*, **46**(2), 262-270.

Yang J P, Cheng S H, Wang X Q. (2004). Bivariate recursive equations on excess-of-loss reinsurance. Accepted by *Acta Mathematica Sinica*.

Yang J P, Cheng S H, Zhang L H. (2004). Bivariate copula decomposition in terms of comonotonicity, countermonotonicity and independence.

Chapter 3

Comonotonically Additive Premium Principles and Some Related Topics

3.1 Introduction

The notion of distortion function was introduced into risk theory by, at the latest, Yaari (1987) and Schmeidler (1989). It was then used to produce distortion premium principles that are designed to be additive for comonotonic risks by Wang and his collaborators in a series of works; see, for example, Wang (1995), Wang (1996), Wang et al (1997), Wang (1998), Wang and Dhaene (1998). The comonotonic is a coined term that means "common monotonic". "It is, in fact, an analogue of perfect correlation. When two random variables are comonotonic, then it can be said that neither of them is hedge against the other. The variability of one is never tempered by counter-variability of the other." (See Yaari, 1987, p.104). Comonotonic risks arise, at least approximately, when the risks in a portfolio are subject to the same external mechanism such as earthquake for the earthquake risk portfolio which are located in the same geographic area. Due to the consideration that no hedging effects exist between comonotonic risks, the additivity on comonotonic risks are required as a principle of premium calculation.

In this chapter, we first address the representation of comonotonically additive premium principles. Based on the fact that non-additive measure integrals can be represented as integrals with respected to some correspondingly defined additive measure, it is shown that any comonotonically additive premium principle can be represented as an integral of a distorted decumulative distribution function of the insurance risk, where the distortion may be dependent on the distribution function of the risk. By means of this representation, we establish the sufficient and necessary conditions under which a premium principle is an integral of the distorted decumulative distribution of the risk with the distortions independent of the individual distributions. Such a premium principle is referred to as a distortion premium principle.

Furthermore, the additivity in premium pricing is investigated. By means of the results obtained for comonotonically additive premiums, the representations for strictly additive principle are derived and a relationship among comonotonic, strict and independent additivity is presented. It states that a premium principle is strictly additive if and only if it is additive for not only comonotonic risks but also independently distributed risks.

Thirdly, we investigate some properties regarding a distortion premium principle. For a single (or a class of) distortion premium principle, there is a distribution family in which it actually reduces to a standard deviation principle. This family is called a natural set of the distortion principle. We present some results on natural sets. One shows that a natural set of a single distortion is the union of some location-scale families and the others indicate that it can only be a location-scale family for some special classes of distortions.

At last discussed are the high-ordered stochastic and dual stochastic orders of real-valued random variables. We address the high-ordered orders of real-valued random variables in parallel to derive some specifications of the orders by means of expected utility theory and the dual theory, respectively, which make clear that, compared with nonnegative risks, for real-valued random variables, the high-ordered dual ordering is more reasonable.

Most of this chapter is mainly based on the works of Wang (2001), Wu (2001b), Wu (2003) and Wu and Wang (2003).

3.2 Characterization of Distortion Premium Principles

Distortion premium principles are derived mainly to fulfil the comonotonic additivity. Due to their having many good properties, considerable attention has been given to the distortion premium principle, for example, Wang (1995), Wang (1996), Wang et al (1997), Wang (1998), Wang and Dhaene (1998) and Young (1999), to name just a few. Some sufficient conditions under which a premium principle is a distortion premium principle were given by Wang et al (1997), which requires the condition that the collection of risks contains all Bernoulli variables taking values 0 and 1 only. In this section, we will further discuss the issue of characterizing distortion premium principles. By means of the additive measure integral representation of a non-additive measure integral, we show that any comonotonically additive premium principle can be represented as an integral of the distorted decumulative function of the insurance risk with the distortion function being related to the risk involved. This result is then used to establish the characterization of the distortion premium principles. At last, three types of additivity (independent, comonotonic and strict) are discussed together and a relationship among them is presented.

3.2.1 *Preliminaries*

Let (Ω, F, P) be a probability space where Ω represents the outcomes of the world and F is a σ-algebra of some subsets of Ω, P is a probability measure defined in measurable space (Ω, F). The following concepts of the comonotonicity and the comonotonic additivity can be found in Yaari (1987), Denneberg (1994), Wang et al (1997) and Wang (1998), among others.

Definition 3.1 (Comonotonicity). Let $X(\omega)$ and $Y(\omega)$ be two random variables defined on (Ω, F, P). They are said to be comonotonic if

$$[X(\omega_1) - X(\omega_2)][Y(\omega_1) - Y(\omega_2)] \geqslant 0, \quad a.s.$$

The following lemma describes the comonotonicity in an intuitive way.

Lemma 3.1 *Two random variables X and Y, defined in (Ω, F, P), are comonotonic if and only if there exist a random variable Z defined on (Ω, F, P) and two non-decreasing functions f and g such that $X = f(Z)$ and $Y = g(Z)$ almost surely.*

Definition 3.2 Let L be a collection of insurance risks. We say that H is

(1) comonotonically additive in L if a premium principle H satisfies $H[X+Y] = H[X] + H[Y]$ for all couples of comonotonic risks X and Y in L;

(2) monotonic or preserves order if $H[X] \leqslant H[Y]$ for all X and Y satisfying $X \leqslant Y$ a.s.;

(3) continuous if $\lim_{a\to+\infty} H[X \wedge a] = H[X]$ and $\lim_{a\to-\infty} H[X \vee a] = H[X]$, where $X \wedge a$ and $X \vee a$ are the minimum and the maximum of (X, a) respectively;

(4) continuous in distributions if, for two arbitrary sequences of risks $\{X_n\}$ and $\{Y_n\}$ in L with cumulative functions sequences $\{F_n\}$ and $\{G_n\}$ respectively, $\lim_{n\to+\infty} H[X_n] = \lim_{n\to+\infty} H[Y_n]$ provided $\lim_{n\to+\infty} F_n = \lim_{n\to+\infty} G_n$;
(5) finite if $|H[X]| < \infty$ for all bounded risk $X \in L$, i.e., there exists a constant C such that $|X| \leqslant C$ a.s. ;
(6) conditional state independent if for given market conditions, the premium of an insurance risk depends only on its distribution.

For a collection of risks, say L, let $F_L = \{F_X | X \in L\}$ be the set of all distributions of X in L. Obviously, when conditional state independence is satisfied, H can be treated as a functional on F_L. Moreover, we note that continuity in distributions implies conditional state independence.

We use 2^Ω to represent the class of all subsets of Ω, and let γ be a set function from 2^Ω onto the extended nonnegative space $\mathbb{R}^+ = [0, \infty)$. If $\gamma(A) \geqslant \gamma(B)$ for all $A \subseteq B$, γ is called a *nonnegative monotonic set function* or a *non-additive measure* on Ω.

Definition 3.3 (Choquet Integral). Let X be a random variable defined in measurable space (Ω, F). The Choquet integral of X with respect to nonadditive measure γ is defined as

$$\int_\Omega X d\gamma = \int_{-\infty}^{0} [\gamma\{\omega : X(\omega) > t\} - \gamma(\Omega)]dt + \int_0^\infty \gamma\{\omega : X(\omega) > t\}dt. \quad (3.1)$$

If X is nonnegative, (3.1) reduces to

$$\int_\Omega X d\gamma = \int_0^\infty \gamma\{\omega : X(\omega) > t\}dt. \quad (3.2)$$

The Choquet integral is different from the traditional additive measure integral, but the following proposition shows that a non-additive measure integral can be represented as an additive measure integral.

Lemma 3.2 *Let X be a random variable defined in (Ω, F). For any non-additive measure γ in (Ω, F), there exists an additive measure γ^* in (Ω, F) such that*

$$\int_\Omega X d\gamma = \int_\Omega X d\gamma^*.$$

Proof. For simplicity, we only prove the lemma in the case where X is nonnegative. Obviously, by the definition of a Choquet integral in (3.1) and (3.2), it suffices to prove that for any non-increasing function $g(t)$ there exists a non-increasing and right-continuous function $g^*(t)$ such that

$$\int_0^{\infty} g(t)dt = \int_0^{\infty} g^*(t)dt. \tag{3.3}$$

Let $g^*(t) = g(t+)$ be the right-side limit of $g(t)$. Since $g^*(t) = g(t)$ almost everywhere, equation (3.3) holds. It remains to prove that $g^*(t)$ is right continuous.

Firstly, we note that, since $g(t)$ is non-increasing, $g^*(t) = \lim_{\varepsilon\to 0+} g(t+\varepsilon) \leqslant g(t)$. Therefore

$$\lim_{\varepsilon\to 0+} g^*(t+\varepsilon) \leqslant \lim_{\varepsilon\to 0+} g(t+\varepsilon) = g^*(t). \tag{3.4}$$

On the other hand, for any fixed $\varepsilon > 0$, we take δ and η such that $0 < \delta$, $\eta < \varepsilon/2$. Then $g^*(t+\delta) = \lim_{\eta\to 0+} g(t+\delta+\eta) \geqslant g(t+\varepsilon)$. Let $\varepsilon \to 0+$, and then $\delta \to 0+$, we have

$$\lim_{\delta\to 0+} g^*(t+\delta) \geqslant g^*(t). \tag{3.5}$$

It follows from (3.4) and (3.5) that $g^*(t)$ is right-continuous. The lemma is thus proved. □

Lemma 3.3 *Let L be a set of some risks satisfying that for any $X \in L$ and $a \geqslant 0$, $aX \in L$, and let H be a comonotonically additive premium principle in L. Then H is positively homogeneous, that is, for any $a \geqslant 0$, we have*

$$H[aX] = aH[X]. \tag{3.6}$$

Proof. The result is trivial for $a = 0$. When a is a positive integer, (3.6) follows from the comonotonicity of H. When a is a positive rational number, say $a = m/n$ where m and n are positive integers, then $nH[(m/n)X] = H[n(m/n)X] = H[mX] = mH[X]$. Thus (3.6) holds.

When a be a positive number. In the case $H[X] < \infty$, there exists a strictly decreasing series of positive rational numbers, $\{a_n\}$, such that $a_n \to a$. Then $\varepsilon_n = a_n - a$ converges to 0 decreasingly. Therefore

$$\begin{aligned} aH[X] &= \lim_{n\to\infty} a_n H[X] = \lim_{n\to\infty} H[a_n X] = \lim_{n\to\infty} H[(a+\varepsilon_n)X] \\ &= H[aX] + \lim_{n\to\infty} H[\varepsilon_n X]. \end{aligned} \tag{3.7}$$

Let $\{b_n\}$ be a series of positive rational numbers such that $0 \leqslant \varepsilon_n \leqslant b_n$ and $b_n \to 0$. It follows from the comonotonic additivity of H that $0 \leqslant H[\varepsilon_n X] \leqslant H[b_n X] = b_n H[X]$, which implies $H[\varepsilon_n X] \to 0$. Hence, (3.6) follows from (3.7).

In the case $H[X] = \infty$, there exists a positive rational number, say b, such that $b \leqslant a$. The comonotonic additivity of H then implies $H[aX] \geqslant H[bX] = bH[X] = \infty = aH[X]$. □

We now state the concept of the distortion premium principle (see e.g. Want et al (1997)). A distortion function g is a non-decreasing function on $[0, 1]$ with $g(0) = 0$ and $g(1) = 1$. A distortion premium principle H of a real-valued risk X is defined as

$$H[X] = \int_{-\infty}^{0} (g[S_X(t)] - 1)\, dt + \int_{0}^{\infty} g[S_X(t)] dt, \tag{3.8}$$

where $S_X(t) = P(X > t)$ is the decumulative distribution function of X.

The positive homogeneity of a distortion premium principle was first presented by Wang (1996). Since while the distortion premium principle is comonotonically additive, a comonotonically additive premium principle may not be a distortion premium principle (see below), the above lemma presents a deeper insight for the positive homogeneity of a distortion premium principle, showing that the positive homogeneity comes from the comonotonic additivity.

3.2.2 *Greco Theorem*

Greco theorem (see, for example, Denneberg, 1994) plays a key role in establishing the distortion premium principle. The traditional version of Greco theorem is concerned with the non-random phenomena. When applying it to a probability space, it should be revised somewhat. The following theorem presents the stochastic version of Greco theorem and a new and simple proof is also provided.

Theorem 3.1 *(Modified Greco Theorem). Let L be a nonempty collection of some nonnegative risks in Ω. For any given $X \in L$ and any nonnegative numbers a, a_1 and a_2, $a_1 \leqslant a_2$, both aX and $X \wedge a_2 - X \wedge a_1$ also belong to L. Suppose that a premium principle H: $L \to \bar{R}^+$ satisfies monotonicity, comonotonic additivity, continuity and finiteness. Then* *there exists a monotone set function $\gamma : 2^\Omega \to \mathbb{R}^+$ such that for all $X \in L$,*

$$H[X] = \int_\Omega X d\gamma = \int_{-\infty}^0 [\gamma\{\omega : X > x\} - \gamma(\Omega)]dx + \int_0^\infty \gamma\{\omega : X(\omega) > x\}dx. \tag{3.9}$$

Proof. We first prove the theorem for L of nonnegative variables.

Two set functions on 2^Ω are defined as follows:

$$\alpha(A) = \sup\{H[X] | X \in L, X \leqslant I_A\}, \quad \beta(A) = \inf\{H[X] | X \in L, X \geqslant I_A\}, \tag{3.10}$$

where I_A is the indicator of set $A \in 2^\Omega$. Obviously, $\alpha \leqslant \beta$. Since H is monotone, both α and β are also monotone. Let γ be some monotone set function on 2^Ω satisfying

$$\alpha \leqslant \gamma \leqslant \beta. \tag{3.11}$$

For example, we can select $\gamma = \beta$ (or α). For any fixed $X \in L$, $X \wedge x$ is non-decreasing in x. Because of the comonotonicity among $X \wedge x_2, X \wedge x_1$, and $X \wedge x_2 - X \wedge x_1$ and the comonotonic additivity of H, $H[X \wedge x]$ is a non-decreasing function with respect to x, and has finite derivative almost everywhere. It is clear that for any $\varepsilon > 0$

$$\frac{X \wedge (t+\varepsilon) - X \wedge t}{\varepsilon} \leqslant I_{\{X(\omega)>t\}} \leqslant \frac{X \wedge t - X \wedge (t-\varepsilon)}{\varepsilon} \leqslant I_{\{X(\omega)>t-\varepsilon\}}.$$

According to the definitions of α, β and the positive homogeneity of H (see Lemma 3.3), we have

$$\begin{aligned}\frac{H[X \wedge (t+\varepsilon)] - H[X \wedge t]}{\varepsilon} &\leqslant \alpha\{\omega : X(\omega) > t\} \\ &\leqslant \gamma\{\omega : X(\omega) > t\} \leqslant \beta\{\omega : X(\omega) > t\} \\ &\leqslant \frac{H[X \wedge t] - H[X \wedge (t-\varepsilon)]}{\varepsilon} \\ &\leqslant \alpha\{\omega : X(\omega) > t-\varepsilon\} \leqslant \gamma\{\omega : X(\omega) > t-\varepsilon\}.\end{aligned}$$

Let $0 = t_0 \leqslant t_1 \leqslant \cdots \leqslant t_n = t$. It follows from

$$\gamma\{\omega : X(\omega) > t\} \leqslant \frac{H[X \wedge t] - H[X \wedge (t-\varepsilon)]}{\varepsilon} \leqslant \gamma\{\omega : X(\omega) > t-\varepsilon\}$$

that

$$\sum_1^n \gamma\{\omega : X(\omega) > t_i\}(t_i - t_{i-1}) \leqslant H[X \wedge t]$$
$$\leqslant \sum_1^n \gamma\{\omega : X(\omega) > t_{i-1}\}(t_i - t_{i-1}).$$

Since $\gamma\{\omega : X(\omega) > t\}$ is monotonic, it is integrable with respect to t. Hence, as n approaches infinity and $\max_{1 \leqslant i \leqslant n}(t_i - t_{i-1})$ approaches zero, we have

$$H[X \wedge t] = \int_0^t \gamma\{\omega : X(\omega) > x\}dx. \tag{3.12}$$

Let $t \to \infty$ and notice the continuity of H, (3.9) follows from (3.12). Theorem 2.1 is thus proved for the collection of nonnegative variables.

We now turn to the case with real-valued $X \in L$. For any fixed M (with $-M$ sufficiently large), let $X(M) = X \vee M - M$. Then $X(M) \geqslant 0$ and using the results proved for nonnegative variables,

$$\begin{aligned} H[X(M)] &= \int_0^\infty \gamma\{\omega : X \vee M - M > x\}dx \\ &= \int_M^0 \gamma\{\omega : X > x\}dx + \int_0^\infty \gamma\{\omega : X > x\}dx. \end{aligned}$$

On the other hand, since $X \vee M$ and M are comonotonic, we have

$$\begin{aligned} H[X \vee M] &= H[X(M)] + H[M] \\ &= \int_M^0 [\gamma\{\omega : X > x\} - \gamma(\Omega)]dx + \int_0^\infty \gamma\{\omega : X > x\}dx. \end{aligned}$$

Letting $M \to -\infty$ and using the continuity, we have

$$H[X] = \int_{-\infty}^0 [\gamma\{\omega : X > x\} - \gamma(\Omega)]dx + \int_0^\infty \gamma\{\omega : X > x\}dx.$$

This completes the proof of the theorem. □

Remark 3.1 *Compared with the original version of Greco Theorem (see, for example, Denneberg, 1994), Theorem 3.1 (the Modified Greco Theorem) required that H is finite for bounded risks (condition (4)). We consider such a requirement reasonable when it is applied to insurance premium calculation principle. If $1 \in L$, (4) is equivalent to a simple statement $H[1] < \infty$, which is trivial for premium calculation principles. On the other hand,*

Compared with the original proof for Greco Theorem (see Denneberg, 1994), the proof given here is much simplified.

Remark 3.2 *If the collection L consists of all variables defined on (Ω, F), for any measurable subset $A \in F$, the set function γ, defined by (3.10) and (3.11), is actually reduced to*

$$\gamma(A) = H[I_A]. \tag{3.13}$$

Under such circumstance, γ is clearly dominated by probability measure P. Furthermore, if the symmetric difference of sets A and B is negligible with respect to the probability P, then $I_A = I_B$ a.s., which implies that, by (3.13), γ takes the same values at A and B.

Remark 3.3 *Furthermore, if the collection L consists of all variables defined on (Ω, F), then the converse of the theorem holds too. To be specific, let H be defined as (3.9) and γ is a set function defined on F such that $\gamma(A) = \gamma(B)$ for any pair of sets A and B where the symmetric difference of sets A and B is negligible with respect to the probability P. Then H is monotone, comonotonically additive, continuous and finite. This fact can be proved easily as follows. First, assume $X \leqslant Y$ a.s., then there exists a negligible set in F, say N, such that $X(w) \leqslant Y(w)$ for all w in $\Omega - N$. Define X^* and Y^* as $X^* = X$ and $Y^* = Y$ if $w \in \Omega - N$ and $X^* = Y^* = 0$ otherwise. Then $X^* \leqslant Y^*$ everywhere. Since γ takes same values at any pair of sets with negligible symmetric difference,*

$$\gamma\{X > t\} = \gamma\{X^* > t\} \quad \textit{and} \quad \gamma\{Y > t\} = \gamma\{Y^* > t\}. \tag{3.14}$$

It proves that H preserves order. Second, we let X and Y be comonotonic, then, similar to the above, there exist two random variables X^* and Y^* such that X^* and Y^* are comonotonic and equations (3.14) hold. By employing Proposition 5.1 (vi) in page 64 of Denneberg (1994), the comonotonic additivity of H is implied. The remainder properties of continuity and finiteness are easy to check. This remark will be referred to later.

3.2.3 *Characterization of Distortion Premium Principles*

Theorem 2.1 says that a comonotonically additive premium principle can be represented as a Choquet integral. In this section we will study how to change a Choquet integral into a distortion integral. For simplicity and without loss of generality we just deal with collections of non-negative risks and point out that the results still hold for general case of real-valued risks.

At first we present the following theorem that reveals that, in fact, each Choquet integral has a representation that is like a distortion integral. It will motivate the way to link a Choquet integral to a distortion integral.

Theorem 3.2 *Suppose the conditions in Theorem 3.1 are satisfied. Then for any $X \in L$, there exists a bounded non-decreasing and nonnegative function g_X with $g_X(0) = 0$ such that*

$$H[X] = \int_0^\infty g_X[S_X(t)]dt. \tag{3.15}$$

Proof. Let $G_{\gamma,X}(x) = \gamma\{\omega : X(\omega) > x\}$ be the set function established in Theorem 3.1. By Lemma 3.2 there exists a non-increasing and right-continuous function $G^*_{\gamma,X}(x)$ such that $G^*_{\gamma,X}(x) = G_{\gamma,X}(x)$ almost everywhere. Then by Theorem 3.1, we have

$$H[X] = \int X d\gamma = \int_0^\infty G^*_{\gamma,X}(x)dx.$$

In order to prove the theorem, we now show that $S_X(x_1) = S_X(x_2)$ implies $G^*_{\gamma,X}(x_1) = G^*_{\gamma,X}(x_2)$. It is an equivalent statement to that there exists a map g_X from the set $\{S_X(t)|t > 0\}$ onto the set $\{G^*_{\gamma,X}(t)|t > 0\}$ such that $G^*_{\gamma,X}(x) = g_X[S_X(x)]$. Obviously, if $S_X(x_1) = S_X(x_2)$ for some $x_1 < x_2$, then $P\{\omega : X \in (x_1, x_2)\} = 0$. Let γ^* be an additive measure in (Ω, F) generated by $G^*_{\gamma,X}$, then by Lemma 3.2, $\gamma^*\{\omega : X(\omega) > x\} = G^*_{\gamma,X}(x)$ and $\int_\Omega X d\gamma = \int_\Omega X d\gamma^*$. Let

$$Z = \frac{X \wedge x_2 - X \wedge x_1}{x_2 - x_1} \in L.$$

Since $P\{\omega : X(\omega) \in (x_1, x_2)\} = 0$, it holds almost surely that

$$Z = \begin{cases} 0, & X \leqslant x_2 \\ 1, & X > x_2 \end{cases} = \begin{cases} 0, & X \leqslant x_1 \\ 1, & X > x_1 \end{cases} \quad a.s..$$

Therefore

$$H[Z] = \int Z d\gamma^* = \gamma^*\{\omega : X(\omega) > x_1\} = \gamma^*\{\omega : X(\omega) > x_2\}.$$

That is, $G^*_{\gamma,X}(x_1) = G^*_{\gamma,X}(x_2)$ is implied by $S_X(x_1) = S_X(x_2)$.

Obviously, g_X is a bounded and nonnegative function. Below we will prove that g_X is a non-decreasing function with $g_X(0) = 0$. Let $S_X(x_1) > S_X(x_2)$. Then $x_1 < x_2$, which implies $\gamma^*\{\omega : X(\omega) > x_1\} \geqslant \gamma^*\{\omega : X(\omega) > x_2\}$, i.e. $G^*_{\gamma,X}(x_1) \geqslant G^*_{\gamma,X}(x_2)$. Therefore g_X is non-decreasing. Since

$\{S_X(t) : t \geqslant 0\}$ is a subset of $[0, 1]$, we can extend the domain of definition of g_X onto $[0, 1]$ such that the extended g_X is still non-decreasing. As $G^*_{\gamma,X}(\infty) = 0$, $g_X(0) = 0$. Thus the theorem is proved. □

Notice that the subscript X of g_X means that the bounded non-decreasing and nonnegative function g_X may be related to the risk X. The remaining problem is what conditions the risk set L and the premium principle H should satisfy for g_X to be unrelated to the risk $X \in L$. In Wang et al (1997), the conditions are that (i) H is conditional state independent and (ii) the risk set L includes all Bernoulli variables. While condition (i) is necessary, the following two corollaries indicate that condition (ii) can be weakened to some extent. The first corollary shows that condition (ii) can be weakened to include only some special Bernoulli variables in certain circumstances.

Corollary 3.1 *Suppose that H is conditional state independent and the conditions in Theorem 2.1 are satisfied. If $I_{\{X>a\}} \in L$ for any $X \in L$ and $a > 0$, there exists a general distortion function g with $g(0) = 0$ such that for any $X \in L$ we have*

$$H[X] = \int_0^\infty g[S_X(t)]dt.$$

Proof. Following the proof of Theorem 3.3, it suffices to prove that for any X, Y in L and nonnegative numbers t_1 and t_2, $S_X(t_1) = S_Y(t_2)$ implies $\gamma\{\omega : X(\omega) > t_1\} = \gamma\{\omega : Y(\omega) > t_2\}$. Define two Bernoulli variables

$$U_X = I_{\{X(\omega)>t_1\}}, \qquad U_Y = I_{\{Y(\omega)>t_2\}}.$$

Both U_X and U_Y belong to L. Because $S_X(t_1) = S_Y(t_2)$, U_X and U_Y have same distribution; which implies $H[U_X] = H[U_Y]$ due to the conditional state independence. Noticing that

$$H[U_X] = \gamma\{X(\omega) > t_1\}, \qquad H[U_Y] = \gamma\{Y(\omega) > t_2\},$$

we have $\gamma\{\omega : X(\omega) > t_1\} = \gamma\{\omega : Y(\omega) > t_2\}$. The corollary is thus proved. □

The following corollary further shows that a premium principle may be a distortion principle, i.e., the distortion function is independent of individual risk, even though the risk collection contains no Bernoulli variables provided the risk collection has certain special structure.

Corollary 3.2 *Suppose that X is a fixed nonnegative risk, and*

$$L = \{X \wedge b - X \wedge a : a, b \in \bar{\mathbb{R}}^+, a \leqslant b\}$$

be all the layer risks of X. Then there exists a general distortion function g with $g(0) = 0$ such that for any $X \in L$,

$$H[X] = \int_0^\infty g[S_X(t)]dt.$$

Proof. For any fixed a and b, $a < b$, let $T = X \wedge b - X \wedge a$. It suffices to prove that

$$H[T] = \int_0^\infty g_X[S_T(t)]dt, \tag{3.16}$$

where g_X is defined as in the proof of Theorem 3.2. Since it is readily to check (3.16) by straightforward computations, the corollary is thus proved. □

Now we turn to the characterization of the distortion premium principles, i.e., necessary and sufficient conditions under which the premium $H[X]$ of a risk $X \in L$ can be represented as a distortion premium. Let $\varepsilon > 0$ and $x \geqslant 0$, and denote

$$X(x, \varepsilon) = \frac{X \wedge (x + \varepsilon) - X \wedge x}{\varepsilon}.$$

When ε approaches 0, $X(x, \varepsilon)$ converges almost everywhere and

$$\frac{d(X \wedge x)}{dx} = \lim_{\varepsilon \to 0+} \frac{X \wedge (x + \varepsilon) - X \wedge x}{\varepsilon} \tag{3.17}$$

$$= \lim_{\varepsilon \to 0+} X(x, \varepsilon) = \begin{cases} 1 & X > x \\ 0 & X \leqslant x \end{cases} = I_{\{X > x\}}. \tag{3.18}$$

Moreover,

$$\frac{dH[X \wedge x]}{dx} = \lim_{\varepsilon \to 0+} H[\frac{X \wedge (x + \varepsilon) - X \wedge x}{\varepsilon}] = \lim_{\varepsilon \to 0+} H[X(x, \varepsilon)]. \tag{3.19}$$

Theorem 3.3 *Let L be a nonempty collection of some nonnegative risks in Ω such that for any $X \in L$ and nonnegative numbers a, a_1 and a_2, $a_1 \leqslant a_2$, both aX and $X \wedge a_2 - X \wedge a_1$ also belong to L. Then a premium principle $H : L \to \bar{\mathbb{R}}^+$ is a distortion premium if and only if H satisfies monotonicity, additivity for comonotonic risks, continuity in distributions, and finiteness.*

Proof. Without loss of generality, we still only prove the theorem in the case of nonnegative risks.

For the proof of the sufficiency, it can be seen by the proof of Theorem 3.2 and Corollary 3.1 that the only thing we need to prove is that for any X, Y in L and nonnegative numbers x and y, $S_X(x) = S_Y(y)$ implies $\gamma^*\{\omega : X(\omega) > x\} = \gamma^*\{\omega : Y(\omega) > y\}$, where γ^* is an additive measure such that $H[X] = \int_0^\infty \gamma^*\{X(\omega) > t\}dt$. Obviously, both $X(x, \varepsilon)$ and $Y(y, \varepsilon)$ are included in L. Because of the additivity of the comonotonic risks, we have

$$\begin{aligned} H[X(x,\varepsilon)] &= H[\frac{X \wedge (x+\varepsilon) - X \wedge x}{\varepsilon}] \\ &= \frac{1}{\varepsilon}\{\int_0^\infty \gamma^*\{\omega : X(\omega) \wedge (x+\varepsilon) > t\}dt \\ &\quad - \int_0^\infty \gamma^*\{\omega : X(\omega) \wedge x > t\}dt\} \\ &= \frac{1}{\varepsilon}\int_x^{x+\varepsilon} \gamma^*\{\omega : X(\omega) > t\}dt. \end{aligned}$$

This implies

$$\gamma^*\{\omega : X(\omega) > x\} \geqslant H[X(x,\varepsilon)] \geqslant \gamma^*\{\omega : X(\omega) > x+\varepsilon\}.$$

Therefore, by (3.19) we have

$$\frac{dH[X \wedge t]}{dt}|_{t=x} = \lim_{\varepsilon \to 0+} H[X(x,\varepsilon)] = \gamma^*\{\omega : X(\omega) > x\}. \tag{3.20}$$

Similarly,

$$\frac{dH[Y \wedge t]}{dt}|_{t=y} = \lim_{\varepsilon \to 0+} H[Y(y,\varepsilon)] = \gamma^*\{\omega : Y(\omega) > y\}. \tag{3.21}$$

Let F_ε and G_ε denote the distributions of $X(x, \varepsilon)$ and $Y(x, \varepsilon)$ respectively. Then by (3.18), $S_X(x) = S_Y(y)$ implies $\lim_{\varepsilon \to 0+} F_\varepsilon = \lim_{\varepsilon \to 0+} G_\varepsilon$. Therefore, it follows from Condition 3 that

$$\lim_{\varepsilon \to 0+} H[x,\varepsilon] = \lim_{\varepsilon \to 0+} H[Y(y,\varepsilon)].$$

Thus $\gamma^*\{\omega : X(\omega) > t_1\} = \gamma^*\{\omega : Y(\omega) > t_2\}$ by (3.20) and (3.21). The sufficiency is then proved.

The proofs of the necessity, the monotonicity and the finiteness can be easily checked. As for the proof of additivity of comonotonic risks, see Denneberg (1994). When H is a general distortion principle, that is, $H[X] = \int_0^\infty g[S_X(t)]dt$, because general distortion function g is bounded, the continuity in distributions can be easily proved by the dominated convergence theorem. □

Remark 3.4 *We know that $H[X \wedge t]$ is a non-decreasing function of t, and $dH[X \wedge t]/dt$ is the increasing rate of $H[X \wedge t]$ when t increases. From (3.20) (or (3.21)) we can see that if H is a distortion premium principle, the increasing rate of $H[X \wedge t]$ only depends on the tail probability of X at t, i.e. $S_X(t) = P(X > t)$.*

Remark 3.5 *Alternative to the condition that L contains all Bernoulli variables, Theorem 2.3 characterizes the distortion premium principles by the continuity with respect to the probability distribution (see condition (3) in the theorem). This new characterization has the advantages of giving sufficient and necessary conditions and not imposing constraints on the risk collection, while including Bernoulli variables is only a sufficient condition.*

Remark 3.6 *Many premium calculation principles can be thought as special cases of distortion premium principles. For a detailed list, one may refer to Wang (1995) or Wu (2001). In fact, the distortion integration of a risk X is used as a way to measure risks at first in Yaari (1987). We refer to it as distortion measure of a risk. As we all known, VaR (Value at Risk) is one of the most important risk measures used in financial field in the last decades. It is also a particular distortion measure of risks. This can be easily shown as follows. Recall that for any given $\alpha \in [0, 1]$, the VaR of a risk X with parameter α is defined as*

$$VaR_\alpha(X) = inf\{x | S_X(x) < \alpha\}.$$

It is obvious that $VaR_\alpha(X) > x$ is equivalent to $S_X(x) < \alpha$. If we take the distortion function g as a two-step-up function $g(x) = 0$ if $x \in [0, \alpha]$ and $g(x)=1$ otherwise, the distortion measure of a risk X can be calculated as

$$H[X] = \int_0^\infty g[S_X(x)]\, dx = \int_{S_X(t) > \alpha} dt = VaR_\alpha(X).$$

Due to this relation, VaR will succeed the properties, such as positive homogeneity, which are possessed by distortion measures.

3.2.4 *Further Remarks on Additivity of Premium Principles*

Generally speaking, a good premium calculation principle should possess some reasonable properties among which the additivity is of special importance and has been extensively studied in the literature. By the term additivity of a premium principle H, we mean

$$H[X_1 + X_2] = H[X_1] + H[X_2]. \tag{3.22}$$

Apart from the previously discussed comonotonic additivity, there are two other types of additivities. The first, referred to as *independent additivity* and has been studied in many aspects from 1960s through 1980s, requires equation (3.22) to be satisfied for all couples of independent insurance risks X_1 and X_2. See, for example, Gerber (1979), Gerber and Goovaerts (1981), Gerber(1985), Borch (1990). The other one, *strict additivity,* says that equation (3.22) should be satisfied for all couples of X_1 and X_2. Related works can be found in, for example, Borch (1990), Venter (1991) and Albrecht (1992).

The strict additivity comes from the arbitrage-free consideration. Borch (1990) and Venter (1991) pointed out that if the strict additivity is violated, an arbitrage opportunity can be created and the rational players in the market can obtain risk free profits. Independent additivity was presented as a simplified version of strict additivity since many actuaries think that most claims caused by separate insurance contracts are mutually independent. The emerging of comonotonic additivity is due to the hedging effects between different risks. It is thought that there exists no hedging in two comonotonic risks, see for example Wang et al (1997), Dhaene and Denuit, M. (1999), so the premiums should be additive for comonotonic risks.

We here give more remarks on the additivity of premium principles. By means of the representation of comonotonic additive premium principles, the representations of strictly additive are investigated and a relationship among the three types of additivities is presented.

3.2.4.1 *Representation of Strictly Additive Premium Principles.*

The following theorem is on the representations of strictly additive premium principles as well as the countably additive premium principles.

Theorem 3.4 *Let the premium principle H on L be monotone, continuous and finite. Then H is strictly (countably) additive if and only if there* *exists a finitely (countably) additive measure γ on F, dominated by P, such that $H[X]$ is the Choquet integral of X with respect to γ for all $X \in L$.*

Proof. We prove the case of strict additivity since the case of countably additivity can be similarly checked. For the "Only if" part, as the conditions of theorem 3.1 are satisfied, there exists a set function γ on F such that for all $X \in L$, $H[X]$ is the Choquet integration of X with respect to γ. Note that for any indicator function I_A of a measurable set A in F, $H[I_A] = \gamma(A)$ by Remark 3.2. If $P(A) = 0$, then $I_A = 0$ a.s., which implies $\gamma(A) = 0$; namely, γ is dominated by P. For any sets A and B in F satisfying $A \cap B = \varnothing$, according to the strict additivity of H,

$$\gamma(A + B) = H[I_{A+B}] = H[I_A] + H[I_B] = \gamma(A) + \gamma(B).$$

So γ is a finite additive measure.

Conversely, suppose that γ is a finite additive measure and H is defined as Choquet integrations with respect to γ, i.e., $H[X] = \int X d\gamma$. Then it is easy to check that H is strictly additive since H can be thought as an integration operator defined on L with respect to the finitely additive measure γ and an integration operator with respect to a finite additive measure is linear. Notice that γ is dominated by P if and only if γ takes the same values at two sets with negligible symmetric difference when γ is finitely additive. This completes the proof. □

For countably additive H, the corresponding γ is a measure on (Ω, F), dominated by P. Since $\gamma(\Omega) = H[1] < \infty$, by Radon-Nikodym theorem, there exists an integrable nonnegative variable, written as Y, such that $\gamma(A) = \int_A Y dP$ and

$$H[X] = \int_\Omega X d\gamma = \int_\Omega XY dP = E[XY],$$

which is referred to as an *economic premium principle* by Bühlmann (1980, 1984). Moreover, if conditional state independence is imposed, then the economic premium principle H is just the expectation principle. This can be easily shown as follows. Let M be the medium of Y such that $\Pr(Y > M) = \Pr(Y < M)$, and $X_1 = I_{\{Y>M\}}$, $X_2 = I_{\{Y<M\}}$. Then X_1 and X_2 are distributed identically. From the conditional state independence, $H[X_1] = H[X_2]$. After some simple calculations, we get

$$H[X_1] = E(X_1 Y) = \int_{(M,+\infty)} y dF_Y(y) \geqslant MP(Y > M),$$

where $F_Y(y)$ is the distribution function of Y. Obviously, the equality holds if and only if $\Pr(Y > M) = 0$. Similarly,

$$H[X_2] = E(X_2Y) = \int_{[0,M)} ydF_Y(y) \leqslant MP(Y < M).$$

So $H[X_1] = H[X_2]$ if and only if $\Pr(Y = M) = 1$, which means that Y is a constant and so H is just the expectation principle.

3.2.4.2 *Relationship among Additivities.*

The relationship among the three types of additivity is shown in the following theorem. An clear fact is that strict additivity gives both independent and comonotonic additivity. The following theorem shows that the converse is also true.

Theorem 3.5 *Let H be a premium principle that satisfies the conditions of monotonicity , continuity, finiteness and conditional state independence. Then H is a strictly additive principle if and only if it is both independently additive and comonotonically additive. In fact, it follows from independent and comonotonic additivity that H is expectation principle.*

Proof. The necessity is obvious and we will prove the sufficiency only. Suppose that H is independently and comonotonically additive. By Theorem 3.3, there exists a bounded non-decreasing and nonnegative function g with $g(0) = 0$ such that

$$H[X] = \int_0^{\infty} g[S_X(x)]\,dx. \tag{3.23}$$

Let X and Y be two mutually independent Bernoulli random variables such that $P(X = 1) = 1 - P(X = 0) = p$ and $P(Y = 1) = 1 - P(Y = 0) = q$. Then $P(X + Y = 0) = (1 - p)(1 - q)$, $P(X + Y = 1) = p + q - 2pq$ and $P(X + Y = 0) = pq$. So the decumulative function of $X + Y$ is

$$S_{X+Y}(t) = P(X + Y > t) = \begin{cases} 1, & t < 0; \\ p + q - pq, & 0 \leqslant t < 1; \\ pq, & 1 \leqslant t < 2; \\ 0, & t \geqslant 2. \end{cases}$$

By equation (3.23), we have $H[X] = g(p)$, $H[Y] = g(q)$, and $H[X + Y] = g(p + q - pq) + g(pq)$. By independent additivity, $g(p) + g(q) = g(p + q -$

$pq) + g(pq)$, which gives

$$g(p) - g(pq) = g(p + q - pq) - g(q). \tag{3.24}$$

As any monotone function has finite derivatives almost everywhere with respect to Lebesgue measure, for non-decreasing g, there exists a point q_0, $0 < q_0 < 1$, such that $g'(q_0) < \infty$. We now prove that $g(x)$ has finite derivative at $x = 0$. For any given $\varepsilon > 0$, there exists a $\delta > 0$ such that when $0 < t < \delta$,

$$(g'(q_0) - \varepsilon)t < g(q_0 + t) - g(q_0) < (g'(q_0) + \varepsilon)t. \tag{3.25}$$

By (3.24),

$$g(p) - g(0_+) = \sum_{n=0}^{\infty} \left(g(pq_0^n) - g(pq_0^{n+1}\right) = \sum_{n=0}^{\infty} \left(g(pq_0^n + q_0 - pq_0^{n+1}) - g(q_0)\right).$$

Let $0 < p < \delta$. Then $0 < pq_0^n - pq_0^{n+1} = pq_0^n(1 - q_0) < \delta$ for all n. Therefore, by (3.25),

$$(g'(q_0) - \varepsilon) \sum_{n=0}^{\infty} pq_0^n(1 - q_0) < g(p) - g(0_+) < (g'(q_0) + \varepsilon) \sum_{n=0}^{\infty} pq_0^n(1 - q_0).$$

Thus

$$g'(q_0) - \varepsilon < \frac{g(p) - g(0_+)}{p} < g'(q_0) + \varepsilon \implies \lim_{p \to 0_+} \frac{g(p) - g(0_+)}{p} = g'(q_0), \tag{3.26}$$

i.e., $g(x)$ has finite derivative at $x = 0$.

Similarly, it can be proved that

$$\lim_{p \to 1_-} \frac{g(p) - g(1)}{p - 1} = g'(q_0). \tag{3.27}$$

Now equation (3.24) can be rewritten as

$$\frac{g(p + q - pq) - g(p)}{q - pq)} = \frac{1}{1 - p} \left[\frac{g(q) - g(0_+)}{q} - p \frac{g(pq) - g(0_+)}{pq} \right].$$

Let q tend to zero. By the equation (3.26), for any $p \in (0, 1)$ we have

$$g'_+(p) = g'(q_0) \tag{3.28}$$

for any $p \in (0, 1)$. Similarly, the equation (3.24) can also be rewritten as

$$\frac{g(pq) - g(p)}{pq - p} = \frac{1}{p} \left[(1 - p) \frac{g(p + q - pq) - g(1)}{(1 - p)(q - 1)} - \frac{g(q) - g(1)}{q - 1} \right].$$

Let q tend to 1. It follows from (3.27) that, for any $p \in (0,1)$

$$g'_{-}(p) = g'(q_0). \tag{3.29}$$

By the equations (3.28) and (3.29), we have $g'(p) = g'(q_0)$ for any $p \in (0,1)$. Thus, $g(x) = ax + d$, where $a = g'(q_0)$ and d are constants. Since $g(0) = 0$, $g(x) = ax$. By equation (3.23), it is proved that the premium principle H is an expectation premium principle, $H[X] = aE(X)$, which implies that H is strictly additive. The proof is complete. □

Remark 3.7 *This theorem shows that under conditional state independence, independent and comonotonic additivity imply strict additivity. But it is unknown whether the theorem remains true if there is no conditional state independence.*

3.3 Natural Sets of Distortion Premium Principles

Christofides (1998) found that for some distribution families, the proportional hazards (PH) premium principle, as a special case of distortion premium principle when the distortion is a power function, can be reduced to the well-known standard deviation (SD) premium principle. He conjectured that for a parametric distribution family with constant skewness, a PH premium principle may be equivalent to a SD principle. Young (1999) showed that Christofides' conjecture is true for location-scale families and for certain other families, but not in general. In addition, Young (1999) further stated that it remains an open problem to determine under what circumstances a distortion premium principle can be reduced to a SD premium principle.

In this section we will further discuss this problem. To be specific, for a single distortion or a set of distortions, we define a natural set as a set of distributions for which the distortion premium principle(s) can be reduced to a SD premium principle. We will show that a natural set can only be a union of location-scale families satisfying some conditions for a single distortion.

As we all know, the standard deviation premium principle is defined as

$$\pi[X] = E[X] + \lambda\sqrt{Var(X)}$$

for some $\lambda > 0$ and a distortion premium principle gives the premium

$$H_g[X] = \int_{-\infty}^{0} (g[S_X(t)] - 1)\, dt + \int_{0}^{\infty} (g[S_X(t)])\, dt,$$

where the distortion g is a non-decreasing function from $[0,1]$ onto itself. If g is a power function $g(p) = p^c$, the $g[S_X(t)]$ is referred to as a proportional hazard transformation of $S_X(t)$ and the corresponding $H_g[X]$ is called proportional hazard (PH) premium of X. For convenience, for any fixed c denote the PH premium of X by $H_c[X]$.

Let g be a fixed distortion, then it is obvious that a distortion premium principle can be reduced to a SD principle in a set, say F, of distributions, if and only if

$$\frac{H_g[X] - E[X]}{\sqrt{Var(X)}} = \frac{H_g[Y] - E[Y]}{\sqrt{Var(Y)}} \tag{3.30}$$

for any X and Y in F. We here state the formal definition of the natural set of a distortion function that is introduced by Wang (2000).

Definition 3.4 Let Ψ be the set of all distributions on (Ω, F). The natural set of a distortion g with respect to distribution $X \in \Psi$, denoted by $N_g(X)$, is defined as

$$N_g(X) = \left\{ Y : \frac{H_g[Y] - E[Y]}{\sqrt{Var(Y)}} = \frac{H_g[X] - E[X]}{\sqrt{Var(X)}}, Y \in \Psi \right\}.$$

If

$$\lambda = \lambda(X) = \frac{H_g[X] - E[X]}{\sqrt{Var(X)}},$$

we also write $N_g(\lambda)$ for $N_g(X)$.

As Young (1999) showed, a distortion premium principle can be reduced to a SD premium principle on the location-scale family $\Pi(Z) = \{X = \mu + \sigma Z : \mu \in \mathbb{R}, \sigma > 0\}$, where Z is a random variable/distribution. We call Z the underlying distribution of this location-scale family Π. In fact, every distribution in Π can be regarded as the underlying distribution of Π. Obviously, if F is a natural set, $\Pi(Z) \subseteq F$ for $Z \in F$, which means that the location-scale family with the underlying distribution being an element of the natural set F for which Christofides' conjecture is true is a subset of F.

Christofides (1998) conjectured that for a parametric family of distributions with constant skewness distortion premium principle reduces to the SD premium principle. Young (1999) shows that this conjecture is false in general. Conversely, if a distortion premium principle reduces to a SD premium principle in a parametric family of distribution, does this family have constant skewness? The answer is negative too in general, as shown in the following example.

Example 3.1 Following an example in Young (1999), let X be a random variable following a two-sided exponential distribution with parameters $\alpha = 1$, $\beta = 2.27466$ and $w = 0.1$. Its ddf and skewness are, respectively,

$$S_X(t) = \begin{cases} w + (1-w)(1-e^{\beta t}), & t < 0, \\ we^{-\alpha t}, & t \geqslant 0, \end{cases}$$

and

$$Skew(X) = \frac{E[X - E[X]]^3}{[Var(X)]^{\frac{3}{2}}} = 1.84166.$$

Let the distortion $g(p) = p^{0.5}$. Then

$$\frac{H_g[X] - E[X]}{\sqrt{Var(X)}} = 1.02386$$

Let Y have a Pareto distribution with parameters $\alpha = 43.41704$ and β. Its ddf, expectation, variance and skewness are as follows respectively:

$$S_Y(t) = \left(\frac{\beta}{1+\beta}\right)^{\alpha}, \quad E[Y] = \frac{\beta}{\alpha - 1}, \quad Var(Y) = \frac{\alpha\beta^2}{(\alpha-1)^2(\alpha-2)}$$

and

$$Skew(Y) = \frac{2(\alpha+1)\sqrt{\alpha-2}}{\sqrt{\alpha}(\alpha-3)} = 2.14677 \neq Skew(X).$$

Let the distortion be the same as above, then

$$\frac{H_g[Y] - E[Y]}{\sqrt{Var(Y)}} = \left(\frac{\alpha}{\alpha-2}\right)^{1/2} = 1.02386 = \frac{H_g[X] - E[X]}{\sqrt{Var(X)}}.$$

Hence, for the distortion $g(p) = p^{0.5}$, the distortion premium principle can be reduced to a SD premium principle for the union $\Pi_1 \cup \Pi_2$, where

$$\Pi_1 = \{\mu + \sigma X : \mu \in \mathbb{R}, \sigma > 0\} \quad \text{and} \quad \Pi_2 = \{\mu + \tau Y : \mu \in \mathbb{R}, \tau > 0\}$$

are the location-scale families with underlying distributions X and Y respectively. Thus, a distortion premium principle is reduced to a SD premium principle for a parametric family of distribution $\Pi_1 \cup \Pi_2$ whose members do not all have the same skewness.

From the preceding discussion we get the following theorem.

Theorem 3.6 *For a fixed distortion g, $N_g(X)$ is and only is the union of location-scale families: $\cup_{i\in I}\Pi_i$, where I is an index set, Π_i is a location-scale family: $\Pi_i = \{\mu_i + \sigma_i X_i : \mu_i \in \mathbb{R}, \sigma_i > 0\}$ for $i \in I$, and their underlying distributions $X_i (i \in I)$ satisfy the following condition:*

$$\frac{H_g[X_j] - E[X_j]}{\sqrt{Var(X_j)}} = \frac{H_g[X_j] - E[X_j]}{\sqrt{Var(X_j)}} \quad \textit{for} \quad i, j \in I.$$

Obviously, a fixed g may have more than one natural set, with each set corresponding to a different parameter λ. Theorem 3.6 indicates that $N_g(X)$ is the union of some location-scale families. On the other hand, if we put different distortions together, the resulting distortion collection will generate a corresponding natural set on which all the distortion premium principles with distortions in the collection are reduced to SD premium principles. Before tuning to further discussions, we need the following definition.

Definition 3.5 g is called a surjective distortion if g is a nondecreasing surjection from $[0, 1]$ onto itself. We denote the set of all distortion functions by G, the set of all two-step distortions by T, the set of all surjective distortions by S, and the set of all proportional hazard transformations (power distortions) by P. Furthermore, the natural set is and only is a location-scale family if distortion premium principle can reduce to the SD premium principle for any distortion.

Obviously, P, T and S are all subsets of G and a distortion is a surjective distortion if and only if g is a continuous distortion satisfying $g(0) = 0$ and $g(1) = 1$.

Using a two-step distortion, Wang (2000) showed that the natural set on which distortion premium principle can be reduced to a standard deviation premium principle for all distortions (or for all two-step distortions) is a location-scale family, which is stated in the theorem below..

Theorem 3.7 *Both $\bigcap_{g\in G} N_g(X)$ and $\bigcap_{g\in T} N_g(X)$ are location-scale distribution families.*

Proof. Suppose that the distortion premium principle for any distortion can reduce to the SD premium principle on the set F of distributions. Then for any $X, Y \in F$ and for any distortion g,

$$\frac{H_g[X]-E[X]}{\sqrt{Var(X)}}=\frac{H_g[Y]-E[Y]}{\sqrt{Var(Y)}}. \tag{3.31}$$

Let

$$U=\frac{H_g[X]-E[X]}{\sqrt{Var(X)}}, V=\frac{H_g[Y]-E[Y]}{\sqrt{Var(Y)}}.$$

Then by equation (3.31), because H_g is location and scale invariant, we have

$$H_g[U]=H_g[V]. \tag{3.32}$$

Denote the decumulative distribution functions of U and V by $S_U(t)$ and $S_V(t)$ respectively. Firstly, using proof by contradiction, we will show that $S_U(t)=S_V(t)$ when $t \geqslant 0$. Assume that there is a $t_0 \geqslant 0$ so that $S_U(t_0) > S_V(t_0)$. Let $\alpha = S_V(t_0)$, $0 \leqslant \alpha < 1$. There are two cases to be considered.
Case 1. $\{t : S_U(t)=\alpha\} \neq \varnothing$. Let $u_1 = \inf\{t : S_U(t) = \alpha\}$, $v_1 = \inf\{t : S_V(t)=\alpha\}$. Because the non-increasing ddf is a right continuous function, $S_U(u_1) = S_V(v_1) = \alpha$, which implies that $v_1 \leqslant t_0 < u_1$. Let the distortion

$$g(w)=\begin{cases}1, \ \alpha < w \leqslant 1;\\ 0, \ 0 \leqslant w \leqslant \alpha.\end{cases}$$

Then $H_g(U) = u_1$, and for $v_1 \in \mathbb{R}$, it can be proved that $H_g[V] = v_1$. Hence $H_g[U] \neq H_g[V]$, contradicting equation (3.32).
Case 2. $\{t : S_U(t) = \alpha\} = \varnothing$. Then there is a u_0 such that $S_U(u_0-0) \geqslant \alpha > S_U(u_0)$ and $S_U(t) > \alpha$ when $t < u_0$. Obviously, $t_0 < u_0$. Let the distortion be the same as above, then $H_g[U] = u_0$ and $H_g[V] = v_1$, which implies $H_g[U] \neq H_g[V]$, again contradicting equation (3.32).

Because a ddf is a non-increasing function, the set consisting of points at which the ddf is discontinuous is either a finite set or a countable set. Therefore, it is proved that $S_U(t) = S_V(t)$ when $t \geqslant 0$.

Now, we show $S_U(t) = S_V(t)$ when $t < 0$. Let $\tilde{U} = -U$ and $\tilde{V} = -V$. Then the decumulative distribution functions of $\tilde{U}$ and $\tilde{V}$ are $S_{\tilde{U}}(t) = 1 - S_U(-t-0)$ and $S_{\tilde{V}}(t) = 1 - S_V(-t-0)$ respectively. From equation (3.32), we have $H_g[\tilde{U}] = H_g[\tilde{V}]$. According to the above result, $S_{\tilde{U}}(t) = S_{\tilde{V}}(t)$ when $t \geqslant 0$, which implies $S_U(t-0) = S_V(t-0)$ when $t \leqslant 0$. Hence

$S_U(t) = S_V(t)$ when $t \leqslant 0$. To sum up, $S_U(t) \equiv S_V(t)$. Hence, $U = V$ almost surely. □

In fact the subscript for taking the intersection need not go through the set G of all distortions or the set T of all two-step distortions. We now prove that $\bigcap_{g\in S} N_g(X)$ is a location-scale family, and if X has continuous decumulative distribution function and convex support, then $\bigcap_{g\in P} N_g(X)$ is also a location-scale family. Before further results, we need the following two lemmas.

Lemma 3.4 *Let $S(x)$ be a decumulative distribution function of a random variable X,*

$$g(w) = \begin{cases} 0, & 0 \leqslant w \leqslant A; \\ 1, & A < w \leqslant 1 \end{cases}$$

be a two-step distortion function for $A \in (0,1)$ and $u = \inf\{t : S(t) \leqslant A\}$, then the distortion premium $H_g[X] = u$.

Proof. Since the decumulative distribution function is right continuous, $S(t) > A$ when $t < u$ and $S(t) \leqslant A$ when $t \geqslant u$. Therefore,

$$g[S(t)] = \begin{cases} 1, & t < u; \\ 0, & t \geqslant u. \end{cases}$$

If $u > 0$, we have

$$H_g[X] = \int_{-\infty}^{0} (g[S_X(t)] - 1)\,dt + \int_0^{\infty} (g[S_X(t)])\,dt = \int_0^u dt = u.$$

If $u \leqslant 0$, then

$$H_g[X] = \int_{-\infty}^{0} (g[S_X(t)] - 1)\,dt + \int_0^{\infty} (g[S_X(t)])\,dt = \int_u^0 (-1)dt = u.$$

The lemma is thus proved. □

Lemma 3.5 *(Feller, 1971, Chapter 13, Theorem 1a). Let U be a measure on $\mathbb{R}^+ = (0,\infty)$, taking finite values in bounded sets of $\mathbb{R}^+$, and*

$$\phi(\lambda) = \int_0^{\infty} e^{-\lambda x} U(dx)$$

be finite for $a < \lambda < \infty$, where $a \geqslant 0$ is known. Then U is determined by its Laplace transformation $\phi(\lambda)$.

Theorem 3.8 *$\bigcap_{g\in S} N_g(X)$ is a location-scale family.*

Proof. Denote $F = \bigcap_{g\in S} N_g(X)$ for convenience. For any surjective distortion, distortion premium principle is reduced to the SD premium principle on the set F of distributions. Thus for any $X, Y \in F$ and any surjective distortion g,

$$\frac{H_g[X] - E[X]}{\sqrt{Var(X)}} = \frac{H_g[Y] - E[Y]}{\sqrt{Var(Y)}}.$$

Further denote

$$U = \frac{H_g[X] - E[X]}{\sqrt{Var(X)}} \quad \text{and} \quad V = \frac{H_g[Y] - E[Y]}{\sqrt{Var(Y)}}.$$

Then

$$H_g[U] = H_g[V] \tag{3.33}$$

for H_g is location and scale equivalent (or linear invariant). In order to prove the theorem, it suffices to show that if equation (3.33) holds for all surjective distortions g, then U and V have a common distribution.

We temporarily denote the decumulative distribution functions of U and V by $S_U(t)$ and $S_V(t)$ respectively. We now prove $S_U(t) = S_V(t)$ for $t \geqslant 0$ by contradiction. If that's not the case, then there exists a $t_0 \geqslant 0$ such that $S_U(t_0) > S_V(t_0)$. Let $\alpha = S_V(t_0)$, $0 \leqslant \alpha \leqslant 1$, and $v = \inf\{t : S_V(t) = \alpha\}$. Select a ε such that $0 < \varepsilon < S_U(t_0) - \alpha$ and define

$$g(w) = \begin{cases} 1, & \alpha + \varepsilon < w \leqslant 1, \\ \frac{w-\alpha}{\varepsilon}, & \alpha < w \leqslant \alpha + \varepsilon, \\ 0, & 0 \leqslant w \leqslant \alpha, \end{cases}$$

$$h_1(w) = \begin{cases} 1, \alpha + \varepsilon < w \leqslant 1, \\ 0, 0 \leqslant w \leqslant \alpha + \varepsilon, \end{cases} \quad \text{and} \quad h_2(w) = \begin{cases} 1, \alpha < w \leqslant 1, \\ 0, 0 \leqslant w \leqslant \alpha. \end{cases}$$

It is easy to see that $g(w)$ is a surjective distortion and $h_1(w) \leqslant g(w) \leqslant h_2(w)$ for all $w \in [0, 1]$. Further let $u(\varepsilon) = \inf\{t : S_U(t) \leqslant \alpha + \varepsilon\}$. Then $S_U(u(\varepsilon)) \geqslant \alpha$. Since $S_U(t_0) > \alpha + \varepsilon$, we have $u(\varepsilon) > t_0$. By Lemma 3.4, we have

$$H_g[U] \geqslant H_{h_1}[U] = u(\varepsilon)$$

and

$$H_g[V] \leqslant H_{h_2}[V] = v \leqslant t_0 < u(\varepsilon).$$

Hence, $H_g[U] \neq H_g[V]$, contradicting equation (3.33).

An argument assembling what used in Theorem 3.7 yields that $S_U(t) = S_V(t)$ for $t < 0$. The theorem is thus proved. □

Theorem 3.9 *If the ddf of X is continuous and its support is a convex set, then $\bigcap_{g\in P} N_g(X)$ is a location-scale family.*

Proof. Similar to the proof in the preceding theorem, it suffices to show that if $H_g[U] = H_g[V]$ for all power distortions of the form $g(p) = p^c$, then U and V are identically distributed provided that the ddfs of both U and V are continuous and their supports are convex.

Let $g(p) = p^c$ be a power distortion. Now we represent the PH premium $H_g[X]$ in the form of a Laplace transformation of random variable X with respect to some function.

$$H_g[X] = \int_{-\infty}^{0} [(S_X(t))^c - 1]dt + \int_{-\infty}^{0} (S_X(t))^c dt = -\int_{-\infty}^{\infty} td(S_X(t))^c$$
$$= -c\int_{-\infty}^{\infty} (S_X(t))^{c-1} td S_X(t) = -c\int_{-\infty}^{\infty} (S_X(t))^c td[\ln S_X(t)].$$

Let $z = -\ln S_X(t)$. Then

$$H_g[X] = c\int_0^{\infty} S_X^{-1}(e^{-z})e^{-cz}dz,$$

which means that $H_g[X]$ is a constant multiple of the Laplace transformation of $S_X^{-1}(e^{-z})$, where $S_X^{-1}(\cdot)$ is the inverse function of $S_X(\cdot)$. Because the continuity of the ddf of X and convexity of its support, this Laplace transformation exists. Hence, according to Lemma 3.5, $H_g[U] = H_g[V]$, i.e.,

$$\int_0^{\infty} S_U^{-1}(e^{-z})e^{-cz}dz = \int_0^{\infty} S_V^{-1}(e^{-z})e^{-cz}dz \quad \text{or} \quad S_U^{-1}(e^{-z}) = S_V^{-1}(e^{-z}),$$

which implies that $S_U(t) = S_V(t)$ and so U and V are identically distributed. □

To conclude, we see that the problem of a distortion principle reducing to a SD principle in fact has nothing to do with the skewness. The key role is played by the location-scale distribution families. A PH-transformation principle is reduced to the standard deviation principle only on a natural set which is a union of location-scale families of distributions. This is merely a result of (and nothing more than) the positive linearity of distortion premium principles.

3.4 Ordering Risks by Distortion Premiums

One of the most remarkable features of modern economics is the introduction of uncertainty (risk) into the analysis of economics and the characterization of risks and uncertainties by means of random variables. The comparison between risks/uncertainties thus becomes important but intractable matters. A broadly adopted idea is to assign an equivalent deterministic measure to a risk and order risks by comparing the magnitudes of their equivalent deterministic measures. One method describing the equivalent deterministic measure of an uncertainty is the classical utility theory of Van Neumann and Morgenstern(1947), which has been playing a key role in modern econometrics. It was established based on four axioms regarding the preference of a decision-maker's attitude towards risks (i.e., ordering the random variables). Denote by $\prec$ to indicate the preference order between the risks, that is, $X \prec Y$ means that X is preferred compared with risk Y. These four axioms are stated below.

EU1. $\prec$ is reflexive, transitive and connected.

EU2. $\prec$ is continuous with respect to L_1-convergence: Let $S_X, S_Y, S_{X'}$ and $S_{Y'}$ be four decumulative distribution functions. If $X \prec Y$ and there exists an $\varepsilon > 0$ such that $\|S_X - S_{X'}\| < \varepsilon$ and $\|S_Y - S_{Y'}\| < \varepsilon$, then $X' \prec Y'$, where $\|\cdot\|$ is the L_1−norm.

EU3. $S_X(x) \leqslant S_Y(x)$ implies $X \prec Y$.

EU4. Order preservation of probability mixing: If $X \prec Y$, Z is an arbitrary risk, and for any $p \in [0,1]$ X_1 and Y_1 are two new risks with decumulative distribution functions

$$S_{X_1}(x) = pS_X(x) + (1-p)S_Z(x) \quad \text{and} \quad S_{Y_1}(x) = pS_Y(x) + (1-p)S_Z(x),$$

respectively, then $X_1 \prec Y_1$.

Based on the above four axioms, Van Neumann and Morgenstern (1947) showed that there exists a utility function u such that $X \prec Y$ if and only if the expected utilities satisfy relation $E[u(-Y)] \leqslant E[u(-X)]$, where a utility is defined as a nondecreasing function u with $u(0) = 0$. Obviously, for any real-valued random variable,

$$\begin{aligned} E[u(X)] &= \int_{-\infty}^{\infty} u(x)dF_X(x) \\ &= \int_0^{\infty} S_X(x-0)du(x+0) + \int_{-\infty}^{\infty} (S_X(x-0)-1)du(x+0), \end{aligned} \tag{3.34}$$

where $F_X(x)$ is the cumulative distribution function of X, $u(x+0)$ is the right continuous function induced by $u(x)$, and the integral $\int_0^\infty S_X(x-0)du(x+0)$ is with respect to the Lebesgue-Stiljits measure generated by $u(x+0)$. Equation (3.34) indicates that $E[u(X)]$ can be interpreted as a transformed expectation of the variable X with the Lebesgue measure being replaced by a new Lebesgue-Stiljits measure generated by $u(x+0)$.

Yaari (1987) revised the axiom system of Van Neumann and Morgenstern by replacing the decumulative distribution functions involved in EU1 through EU4 with their generalized inverse functions (quantile functions) to generate four dual axioms DU1-DU4, under which the first three remain unchanged and the duality of the fourth is rewritten as follows.

DU4. Order preservation of mixed outcomes: Let $X \prec Y$ and Z be an arbitrary risk. If for any $p \in [0,1]$, X_1 and Y_1 are two new risks with generalize inverse of decumulative distribution functions

$$S_{X_1}^{-1}(x) = pS_X^{-1}(x)+(1-p)S_Z^{-1}(x) \quad \text{and} \quad S_{Y_1}^{-1}(x) = pS_Y^{-1}(x)+(1-p)S_Z^{-1}(x),$$

respectively, then $X_1 \prec Y_1$.

Yaari (1987) also shown that DU4 is equivalent to the following one.

DU4*. If X, Y and Z are comonotonic random variables and $X \prec Y$, then for any $p \in [0,1]$,

$$pX + (1-p)Z \prec pY + (1-p)Z.$$

DU4* reflects the exact meaning of preserving the order of mixed outcomes. Yaari (1987) considered the random variables supported on $[0,1]$ and proved that under axioms EU1-EU3 and dual axiom DU4, there exists a distortion function g which assigns an equivalent deterministic measure for each risk X:

$$H_g[X] = \int_0^\infty g[S_X(t)]dt$$

such that $X \prec Y$ is equivalent to $H_g[X] \leqslant H_g[Y]$.

To sum up, once the corresponding axiom system is satisfied, each preference order corresponds to a utility/distortion function such that the comparison of the preferences between risks is equivalent to comparing the equivalent deterministic measure represented by expected utility (or distortion mean).

Furthermore, if we put a class of utility/distortion functions together, a partial order can be defined on the set of risks, indicating the consistent preference of a batch of decison-makers who have the same attitude towards risks. To be specific, suppose that D is a collection of certain utility functions. Define that X is preferred to Y and denoted by $X \prec_D Y$ if $E[u(-X)] \leqslant E[u(-Y)]$ holds for all utilities in D. The relation $\prec_D$ defined as such is a partial order. On the other hand, since a premium principle assigns a magnitude to a risk, it actually provides an equivalent deterministic measure of a risk. For example, Goovaerts et al (1982) discussed the partial ordering on a risk set generated by an Esscher principle. A distortion premium has the same form as the equivalent deterministic measure of risks under Yarri's dual theory of risk selection. In this section we in parallel address the partial ordering on a set of real-valued risks generated by a set of utility functions and distortion functions, which are referred to as *n-ordered orders* of real-valued random variables and *n-ordered dual orders* of real-valued random variables respectively.

Let $D_n = \{u(x) : \mathbb{R} \to \mathbb{R}, u(x)$ has up to the $(n-1)$th derivative, $u^{(k)}(0) \geqslant 0,\ k = 1, \ldots, n-1$ and $u^{(n-1)}(x)$ is non-decreasing$\}$ and $\tilde{D}_n = \{u(x) : \mathbb{R} \to \mathbb{R}, u(x)$ has up to the $(n-1)$th derivative, $(-1)^{k+1}u^{(k)}(0) \geqslant 0,\ k = 1, \ldots, n-1$ and $(-1)^n u^{(n-1)}(x)$ is non-decreasing$\}$.

We can use D_n and $\tilde{D}_n$ to define partial orders on a risk set and show certain equivalence between them, which is elaborated in the following subsections.

3.4.1 *n-ordered Orders of Real-valued Random Variables.*

First notice that $D_{n+1} \subset D_n$, $X \prec_{D_n} Y$ implies $X \prec_{D_{n+1}} Y$. So the order $\prec_{D_n}$is weakened when n increases in the sense that there are more risk pairs such that $E[u(X)] \leqslant E[u(Y)]$ for all $u \in D_n$. Second, since $D_1 = \{u(x) : \mathbb{R} \to \mathbb{R}, u(x)$ is non-decreasing$\}$, it is obvious that $X \prec_{D_1} Y$ implies $S_X(t) \leqslant S_Y(t)$ for all t. Third, $D_2 = \{u(x) : \mathbb{R} \to \mathbb{R}, u'(0) \geqslant 0$ and $u'(x)$ is non-decreasing$\}$ is in fact a class of all such functions that are convex and non-decreasing in $\mathbb{R}^+$.

Before defining $n-$ordered stochastic order, we introduce the following repeated integrals of cumulative/ decumulative distribution functions. Let

$$^1S_X(t) = S_X(t) \quad \text{and} \quad ^1F_X(t) = F_X(t-0) \tag{3.35}$$

and for $n = 1, 2, \cdots$, define

$$^{n+1}S_X(t) = \int_t^{\infty} {}^nS_X(u)\,du \quad \text{and} \quad ^{n+1}F_X(t) = \int_{-\infty}^{t} {}^nF_X(u)\,du. \tag{3.36}$$

Since an integral is a linear operator, a repeated integral is a linear transformation of the cumulative (decumulative) distribution function. The following lemma clearly displays the relationship between repeated integrations and high-ordered stop-loss premiums.

Lemma 3.6 *For $n = 1, 2, \cdots$,*

$$ {}^nF_X(t) = \frac{1}{(n-1)!}E[X-t]_-^{n-1}, \qquad {}^nS_X(t) = \frac{1}{(n-1)!}E[t-X]_+^{n-1}. $$

Proof. We verify the first one and the other one can be proved similarly. At first, when $n = 1$, since $(x-t)^0 = I_{(-\infty,t)}(x)$, it follows that $E(X-t)^0 = EI_{(-\infty,t)}(X) = F_X(t-0) = {}^1F_X(t)$. Suppose that the equality holds for n. Then for $n+1$,

$$ \begin{aligned} {}^{n+1}F_X(t) &= \int_{-\infty}^{t} {}^nF_X(u)\,du = \frac{1}{(n-1)!}\int_{-\infty}^{t} E[u-X]_+^{n-1}du \\ &= \frac{1}{(n-1)!}\int_{-\infty}^{t}\int_{-\infty}^{u}[u-x]^{n-1}dF_X(x)du \\ &= -\frac{1}{n!}\int_{-\infty}^{t}(x-t)^n dF_X(x) = \frac{1}{n!}E[t-X]_+^n. \end{aligned} $$

The proof is thus completed by induction. □

Definition 3.6
(i) If $E[X^k] \leqslant E[Y^k]$, $k = 1, 2, \cdots, n-1$ and ${}^nS_X(t) \leqslant {}^nS_Y(t)$ for any $t \in \mathbb{R}$, X is said to precede Y under n-ordered order (S), denoted by $X \prec_n^s Y$.
(ii) If $(-1)^{k+1}E[X^k] \leqslant (-1)^{k+1}E[Y^k]$, $k = 1, 2, \cdots, n-1$ and ${}^nF_X(t) \geqslant {}^nF_Y(t)$ for any $t \in \mathbb{R}$, X is said to precede Y under n-ordered order (F), denoted by $X \prec_n^F Y$.

The two orders defined above are generally referred to as n-ordered stochastic orders. The following theorem reveals the equivalence between orders defined by repeated integrations and by $D_n/\tilde{D}_n$.

Theorem 3.10 *Let X and Y be two real-valued random variables, then*
(1) $X \prec_{D_n} Y$ if and only if X precedes Y under n-ordered order (S), i.e., $X \prec_n^S Y$.
(2) $X \prec_{\tilde{D}_n} Y$ if and only if X precedes Y under n-ordered order (F), i.e., $X \prec_n^F Y$.

Proof. We only prove (1). (2) can be similarly checked.

The "only if" part can be easily checked by noticing that $x, x^2, \cdots, x^{n-1}$ and $(x-t)_+^{n-1}$ belong to D_n. For the "if" part, let $u(x) \in D_n$. Expanding it as the $(n-1)$th Taloy expansion,

$$u(x) = \sum_{k=0}^{n-1} \frac{u^{(k)}(0)}{k!} x^k + \frac{1}{(n-1)!} \int_0^x (x-t)^{n-1} du^{(n-1)}(t)$$
$$= \sum_{k=0}^{n-1} \frac{u^{(k)}(0)}{k!} x^k + \frac{1}{(n-1)!} \int_0^\infty (x-t)_+^{n-1} du^{(n-1)}(t),$$

we see that

$$E[u(X)] = \sum_{k=0}^{n-1} \frac{u^{(k)}(0)}{k!} EX^k + \frac{1}{(n-1)!} \int_0^\infty E(X-t)_+^{n-1} du^{(n-1)}(t).$$

Similarly,

$$E[u(Y)] = \sum_{k=0}^{n-1} \frac{u^{(k)}(0)}{k!} EY^k + \frac{1}{(n-1)!} \int_0^\infty E(Y-t)_+^{n-1} du^{(n-1)}(t).$$

By the condition $u^{(k)}(0) \geqslant 0$, $k = 1, 2, \ldots, n-1$, and Lemma 3.6,

$$E[X-t]_+^{n-1} = (n-1)!^n S_X(t) \leqslant (n-1)!^n S_Y(t) = E[Y-t]_+^{n-1}.$$

Therefore $E[u(X)] \leqslant E[u(Y)]$. □

Remark 3.8 *If $u(x) \in D_n$, then $u^{(k)}(x) \geqslant 0$ for $x \geqslant 0$, $k = 1, 2, \ldots, n-1$. Therefore, when applied to non-negative risks, the n-ordered stochastic order defined here is consistent with what is commonly defined for non-negative random variables. In the case of non-negative risks, the orders defined by repeated integrals of decumulative/cumulative distribution functions allow intuitive economic interpretations, see Goovaerts et al (1982) or Wang and Young (1998). However, it should be noted that since $x^k \in D_n$, $k = 1, 2, \ldots, n-1$, and x^k is not a non-decreasing function for even k and cannot be considered as utilities for even k, the n-ordered stochastic order for real-valued variables does not allow a clear economical interpretation. It is even more difficult to give economic interpretation for the order defined by $\tilde{D}_n$. These points will be compared with the dual orders treated in the following section.*

3.4.2 *n-ordered Dual Orders of Real-valued Random Variables.*

Let D^* be a collection of distortion functions g that have up to $(n-1)$th derivatives, satisfy $(-1)^k g^{(k)} \geqslant 0$ for $k = 1, 2, \ldots, n-1$ and have non-increasing $(-1)^{(n-1)} g^{(n-1)}$. An example of such type of functions is $g_q(p) = 1 - \left[(q-p)_+^{n-1} / q^{n-1}\right]$.

Definition 3.7 For any given two real-valued random variables X and Y, X is said to be preferred to Y in D_n^*, denoted by $X \prec_n^* Y$, if $H_g[X] \leqslant H_g[Y]$ holds for all $g \in D_n^*$.

We can define the dual repeated integrals of an inverse decumulative distribution function assembling to what we did in the last subsection, which are called *dual repeated integrals* for short. To be specific, for $q \in [0,1]$, let ${}^1S_X^{-1}(q) = S_X^{-1}(q)$ and recursively define

$$ {}^{n+1}S_X^{-1}(q) = \int_0^q {}^nS_X^{-1}(p)\, dp, n = 1, 2, \ldots. \tag{3.37}$$

In addition, similar to the moments of a random variable, we introduce the notion of dual moments of a random variable as follows.

Definition 3.8 Suppose that $g_k(p) = 1 - (1-p)^k$. Then the k-th dual moment of X is defined as

$$H_k[X] = H_{g_k}[X] = \int_0^{\infty} (1 - (1 - S_X(t))^k) dt - \int_{-\infty}^0 (1 - S_X(t))^k dt.$$

The following lemma shows that dual repeated integrals are closely related to dual moments.

Lemma 3.7

$$\begin{aligned} &{}^nS_X^{-1}(q) \\ =& \frac{1}{(n-1)!}\left[\int_0^{\infty} \left(q^{n-1} - (q - S_X(t)_+^{n-1}\right) dt - \int_{-\infty}^0 (q - S_X(t)_+^{n-1} dt\right] \end{aligned}$$

for $n \geqslant 1$, *where* $a^0 = 1$ *if* $a > 0$ *and* $a^0 = 0$ *if* $a = 0$. *In particular,*

$${}^nS_X^{-1}(1) = \frac{1}{(n-1)!} H_{n-1}[X].$$

Proof. We prove the first equality in the lemma by induction and the second is a direct result by taking $q = 1$ and Definition 3.8.

First, for $n = 1$, it is easy to verify that

$$ {}^1S_X^{-1}(q) = S_X^{-1}(q) = \int_0^\infty (1 - (1 - S_X(t))_+^0)dt - \int_{-\infty}^0 (1 - S_X(t))_+^0 dt. $$

Suppose the lemma holds for $n = k$. For $n = k + 1$,

$$ (k-1)! \quad {}^{k+1}S_X^{-1}(q) = (k-1)! \int_0^q {}^kS_X^{-1}(p)\, dp $$
$$ = \int_0^q \left(\int_0^\infty (p^{p-1} - (p - S_X(t))_+^{k-1})dt - \int_{-\infty}^0 (p - S_X(t))_+^{k-1}dt \right) dp $$
$$ = \int_0^\infty \int_0^q (p^{k-1} - (p - S_X(t))_+^{k-1})dpdt - \int_{-\infty}^0 \int_0^q (p - S_X(t))_+^{k-1}dpdt. $$

Since

$$ \int_0^q (p - S_X(t))_+^{k-1}dp = \frac{1}{k}(p - S_X(t))_+^k, $$

we obtain

$$ (k-1)! \quad {}^{k+1}S_X^{-1}(q) = (k-1)! \quad \int_0^q {}^kS_X^{-1}(p)\, dp $$
$$ = \int_0^q \left(\int_0^\infty (p^{p-1} - (p - S_X(t))_+^{k-1})dt - \int_{-\infty}^0 (p - S_X(t))_+^{k-1}dt \right) dp $$
$$ = \frac{1}{k} \left(\int_0^\infty (q^k - (q - S_X(t))_+^k)dt - \int_{-\infty}^0 (q - S_X(t))_+^k dt \right). $$

So the lemma is proved by the induction principle. □

The following theorem mimics Theorem 3.6 to exhibit the relationship between dual stochastic orders and precedences in D_n^*.

Theorem 3.11 *X precedes Y in n-ordered dual stochastic order if and only if $H_g[X] \leqslant H_g[Y]$ for all $g \in D_n^*$.*

Proof. For the "if" part, since $g_k \in D_n^*$, $k = 1, 2, \cdots, n-1$, and $g_q(p) = 1 - \left[(q-p)_+^{n-1}/q^{n-1}\right] \in D_n^*$, by Lemma 3.7 we see that $H_k[X] \leqslant H_k[Y]$ and

$$ H_{g_q}[X] = \int_0^\infty \left(1 - \frac{(q - S_X(t))_+^{n-1}}{q^{n-1}}\right) dt - \int_{-\infty}^0 \frac{(q - S_X(t))_+^{n-1}}{q^{n-1}} dt $$
$$ = \frac{1}{q^{n-1}} \left(\int_0^\infty \left(q^{n-1} - (q - S_X(t))_+^{n-1}\right) dt - \int_{-\infty}^0 (q - S_X(t))_+^{n-1}\, dt \right). $$

Consequently, ${}^nS_X^{-1}(q) \leqslant {}^nS_Y^{-1}(q)$, i.e., X precedes Y in n-ordered dual stochastic order.

For the "only if" part, let $g \in D_n^*$. The $(n-1)$th Taylor expansion of g at $q_0 = 1$ is

$$g(q) = 1 + \sum_{k=1}^{n-1} \frac{g^{(k)}(1)}{k!}(q-1)^k + \frac{1}{(n-1)!}\int_1^q (q-p)^{n-1} dg^{(n-1)}(p). \quad (3.38)$$

A simple computation shows that $g(q)$ can be rewritten as

$$g(q) = 1 + \sum_{k=1}^{n-1} \frac{(-1)^k g^{(k)}(1)}{k!}(1-q)^k - \frac{(-1)^{n-1}}{(n-1)!}\int_0^1 (p-q)_+^{n-1} dg^{(n-1)}(p). \quad (3.39)$$

By virtue of

$$1 + \sum_{k=1}^{n-1} \frac{(-1)^k g^{(k)}(1)}{k!} = \frac{(-1)^{n-1}}{(n-1)!}\int_0^1 p^{n-1} dg^{(n-1)}(p),$$

we can again represent $g(q)$ as

$$\begin{aligned} g(q) &= \sum_{k=1}^{n-1} \frac{(-1)^{k+1} g^{(k)}(1)}{k!}(1-(1-q)^k) \\ &\quad + \frac{(-1)^{n-1}}{(n-1)!}\int_0^1 (p^{n-1} - (p-q)_+^{n-1}) dg^{(n-1)}(p). \end{aligned} \quad (3.40)$$

As a result of (3.39),

$$\begin{aligned} \int_{-\infty}^0 [g[S_X(t)] - 1]dt &= -\sum_{k=1}^{n-1} \frac{(-1)^{k+1} g^{(k)}(1)}{k!}\int_{-\infty}^0 (1-S_X(t))^k dt \\ &\quad + \frac{(-1)^{n-1}}{(n-1)!}\int_{-\infty}^0 \int_0^1 (p - S_X(t))_+^{n-1} dg^{(n-1)}(p)dt. \end{aligned}$$

Similarly, (3.40) yields that

$$\begin{aligned} \int_0^\infty g[S_X(t)]dt &= \sum_{k=1}^{n-1} \frac{(-1)^{k+1} g^{(k)}(1)}{k!}\int_0^\infty (1-(1-S_X(t))^k)dt \\ &\quad + \frac{(-1)^{n-1}}{(n-1)!}\int_0^\infty \int_0^1 (p^{n-1} - (p-S_X(t))_+^{n-1}) dg^{(n-1)}(p)dt. \end{aligned}$$

Therefore, $H_g[X]$ can be computed as

$$\begin{aligned} H_g[X] &= \int_0^{\infty} g[S_X(t)]dt + \int_{-\infty}^{0} [g[S_X(t)] - 1]dt \\ &= \sum_{k=1}^{n-1} \frac{(-1)^{k+1} g^{(k)}(1)}{k!} H_k[X] + \frac{(-1)^{n-1}}{(n-1)!} \int_0^1 {}^{n}S_X^{-1}(p)\, dg^{(n-1)}(p). \end{aligned}$$

Similarly,

$$H_g[Y] = \sum_{k=1}^{n-1} \frac{(-1)^{k+1} g^{(k)}(1)}{k!} H_k[Y] + \frac{(-1)^{n-1}}{(n-1)!} \int_0^1 {}^{n}S_Y^{-1}(p)\, dg^{(n-1)}(p).$$

As $(-1)^{k+1}g^{(k)}(x) \geqslant 0$ and $(-1)^{n-1}g^{(n-1)}(x)$ is non-increasing, we get $H_g[X] \leqslant H_g[Y]$. □

Remark 3.9 *This theorem indicates that no matter the risks involved are non-negative or real-valued, the orders defined by repeated integrals of the inverse decumulative distributions allow the same economic meaning. It is significantly different from the orders defined by repeated integrals of decumulative/cumulative distributions, see Remark 3.8.*

Though the n-ordered stochastic order is defined by means of the utility functions, while the n-ordered dual stochastic order is based on distortion functions, it is interesting that these two types of orders are equivalent for $n = 1$ and $n = 2$. We state and prove them in the following theorem.

Theorem 3.12 *If X and Y are two real-valued random variables, then (1) $X \prec_1^* Y \iff X \prec_1^S Y$; and (2) $X \prec_2^* Y \iff X \prec_2^S Y$.*

Proof. (1) is trivial and we here only prove (2).

Since $H_1[X] = E[X]$, it suffices to prove that $E(X-t)_+ \leqslant E(Y-t)_+$ if and only if ${}^{2}S_X^{-1}(q) \leqslant {}^{2}S_Y^{-1}(q)$ for all $q \in [0,1]$, i.e., $\int_t^{\infty} S_X(u)du \leqslant \int_t^{\infty} S_Y(u)du$ if and only if ${}^{2}S_X^{-1}(q) \leqslant {}^{2}S_Y^{-1}(q)$ holds for all $q \in [0,1]$.

If $E(X-t)_+ \leqslant E(Y-t)_+$, then by the definition of ${}^2S_X^{-1}(q)$,

$$\begin{aligned}
{}^2S_X^{-1}(q) &= \int_0^q S_X^{-1}(p)dp = \int_{S_X^{-1}(q)}^{\infty} S_X(u)du + qS_X^{-1}(q) \\
&\leqslant \int_{S_X^{-1}(q)}^{\infty} S_Y(u)du + qS_X^{-1}(q) \\
&= \int_{S_Y^{-1}(q)}^{\infty} S_Y(u)du + qS_Y^{-1}(q) \\
&\quad + \int_{S_X^{-1}(q)}^{S_Y^{-1}(q)} S_Y(u)du + qS_X^{-1}(q) - qS_Y^{-1}(q) \\
&= {}^2S_Y^{-1}(q) + \int_{S_X^{-1}(q)}^{S_Y^{-1}(q)} (S_Y(u) - q)du. \qquad (3.41)
\end{aligned}$$

When $S_X^{-1}(q) < S_Y^{-1}(q)$, as $S_Y(u) \leqslant q$ for $u \leqslant S_Y^{-1}(q)$, we have

$$\int_{S_X^{-1}(q)}^{S_Y^{-1}(q)} (S_Y(u) - q)du \leqslant 0.$$

On the other hand, if $S_X^{-1}(q) > S_Y^{-1}(q)$, then

$$\int_{S_X^{-1}(q)}^{S_Y^{-1}(q)} (S_Y(u) - q)du = -\int_{S_Y^{-1}(q)}^{S_X^{-1}(q)} (S_Y(u) - q)du \leqslant 0$$

since $S_Y(u) \geqslant q$ for $u \geqslant S_Y^{-1}(q)$. Therefore the last integral in (3.41) is less than or equal to 0, hence by (3.41), ${}^2S_X^{-1}(q) \leqslant {}^2S_Y^{-1}(q)$. This proves the "only if" part.

Conversely, let ${}^2S_X^{-1}(q) \leqslant {}^2S_Y^{-1}(q)$. For any fixed $t \in \mathbb{R}$, let $q = S_X(t)$ and $r = S_Y(t)$. Then

$$\begin{aligned}
{}^2S_X(t) &= \int_t^{\infty} S_X(u)du = \int_0^q S_X^{-1}(p)dp - qt \leqslant \int_0^q S_Y^{-1}(p)dp - qt \\
&= \int_0^r S_Y^{-1}(p)dp - rt + \int_r^q S_Y^{-1}(p)dp + rt - qt \\
&= {}^2S_Y(t) + \int_r^q (S_Y^{-1}(p) - t)dp.
\end{aligned}$$

Note that $t \geqslant S_Y^{-1}(r)$ due to $r = S_Y(t)$. If $q > r$, then $S_Y^{-1}(p) < S_Y^{-1}(r) \leqslant t$ for $p \in (r, q)$; if $q < r$, $S_Y^{-1}(p) > t$ for $p \in (q, r)$. In either case,

$$\int_r^q (S_Y^{-1}(p) - t)dp \leqslant 0 \implies \int_t^{\infty} S_X(u)du \leqslant \int_t^{\infty} S_Y(u)du.$$

The proof is thus complete. □

3.5 Final Remarks

In this Chapter we have discussed distortion premium principles and some related topics. Apart from the characterization of a distortion premium principle, we have also examined the additivities involved in premium pricing and revealed the relationship among the three types of additivities. Furthermore, reduction of distortion premium to standard deviation principle for certain distribution families is investigated. In addition, ordering problem for real-valued risks (beyond the nonnegative risks) is addressed, which suggests that it is more reasonable to order risks in the dual theory than the original theory.

There are still some important works and developments relevant to this field which are not included in the context. For example, Dhaene et al (2002a, b), Jouini and Napp (2004), and Wang and Dhaene (1998) discussed properties of comonotonic risks from various aspects. Giorgio (2005) and Goovaerts et al (2004), among others, further explored the problem regarding risk measures. Jones and Zitikis (2003) discussed the Empirical distortion premium and Wang and Young (1998b) considered the credibility premium using distorted probability.

References

Albrecht P. (1992). Premium Calculation without Arbitrage? *Astin Bulletin*, **22**, 247-254.

Anderson G. (1996). Nonparametric Tests of Stochastic Dominance in Income Distributions, *Econometrics,* **64**, 1183-1193.

Borch K. (1960). The Safety Loading of Reinsurance, *Skandinavisk Aktuarietidskrift*, 163-184.

Borch K. (1962a). Equilibrium in A Reinsurance Market, *Econometrica*, **30**, 424-444.

Borch K. (1962b). A Contribution to the Theory of Reinsurance Markets. Skandinavisk Aktuarietidskrift, 176-189.

Borch K. (1982). Additive Insurance Premiums, *The Journal of Finance*, **37**, 1295-1298.

Borch K. (1990). Economics of insurance, Elsevier Science Publishers B. V.

Bühlmann H. (1980). An Economic Premium Principle, *Astin Bulletin*, **11**, 52-60.

Bühlmann H. (1984). The General Economic Premium Principle, Astin Bulletin, **15**, 13-21.

Christofides S. (1998). Principle for Risk in Financial Transactions, *Proceedings of the GISG/ASTIN Joblt Meeting at Glasgow*, Scotland. October, 1998, **2**, 63-109.

Crawford Ian A. (1999). Nonparametric Tests of Stochastic Dominance in Bivariate Distributions, with An Application to UK data. *Working paper*, The institute for Fiscal Studies WP 28/29.

Dhaene J, Denuit M, Goovaerts M J, Kaas R, Vyncke D. (2002a). The Concept of Comonotonicity in Actuarial Science and Finance: Theory. *Insurance: Mathematics and Economics.* **31**, 3-33.

Dhaene J, Denuit M, Goovaerts M J, Kaas R, Vyncke D. (2002b). The concept of comonotonicity in actuarial science and finance: applications. *Insurance: Mathematics and Economics.* **31**, 133-161.

Denneberg D. (1994). Non-additive Measure and Integral, *Kluwer Academic Publishers.*

Dhaene J, Denuit M. (1999). The Safest Dependence Structure among Risks. *Insurance: Mathematics and Economics*, **25**, 11-21.

Gerber H U. (1979). An Introduction to Mathematical Risk Theory, the S.S. Huebner Foundation for Insurance Education.

Gerber H U. (1985). On Additive Principles of Zero Utility, *Insurance: Mathematics and Economics*, **4**, 249-251.

Gerber H U. (1998). Utility Functions: from Risk Theory to Finance (with discussions), *North American Actuarial Journal*, **2**(3), 74-91.

Gerber H U, Goovaerts J. (1981). On the Representation of Additive Principles of Premium Calculation, *Scandinavia Actuarial Journal*, **1981**, 221-227.

Giorgio S. (2005). Measures of risk. *European Journal of Operational Research*, **163**, 5-19.

Goovaerts M J, De Vylder F, Haezendonck J. (1982). Ordering of Risks: A Review, *Insurance: Mathematics and Economics*, **1**, 131-163.

Goovaerts M J, Kaas R, Dhaene J, Tang Q. (2004). Some New Classes of Consistent Risk Measures. *Insurance: Mathematics and Economics.* **34**, 505-516.

van Heerwaarden A E, Kaas R, Goovaerts M J. (1989). Properties of the Esscher premium calculation principle. *Insurance: Mathematics and Econometrics.* **8**, 261-267.

Jones B L, Zitikis R. (2003). Empirical Estimation of Risk Measures and Related Quantiles (with discussion), *North American Actuarial Journal*, **7**(4), 44-54.

Kaas R, Van Heerwaarden A E, Goovaerts M J. (1994). Ordering of Actuarial Risks. Education series 1, CAIRE, Brussels.

Jouini E, Napp C. (2004). Conditional Comonotonicity. *Decisions in Economics and Finance*, **27**, 153-166.

Rolski T, Schnidli H, Schmidt V, Teugels J. (1999). Stochastic Processes for Insurance and Finance, John Wiley & Sons Ltd.

Schmeidler D. (1986). Integral representation without additivity, *Proceedings of the American Mathematical Society*, **97**, 255-261.

Szekli R, (1995). Stochastic Ordering and Dependence in Applied Probability. New York: Springer-Verlag.

Venter G. (1991). Premium Calculation Implications of Reinsurance without Arbitrage. *ASTIN Bulletin*, Vol. 21, No. 2, 223-230.

Wang J. (2001). A Note on Christofides' Conjecture Regarding Wang's Premium Principle. *ASTIN Bulletin*, **30** (1). 13-17.

Wang S. (1995). Insurance Pricing and Increased Limits Ratemaking by Proportional Hazards Transforms, *Insurance: Mathematics and Economics*. **17**, 43-54.

Wang S. (1996). Premium Calculation by Transforming the Layer Premium Density, *ASTIN Bulletin*, **26**, 71-92.

Wang S. (1998). An Actuarial Index of the Right-tail Risk, *North American Actuarial Journal*, **2(2)**, 88-101.

Wang S, Dhaene J. (1998). Comonotonicity, Correlation Order and Premium Principles, *Insurance:Mathematics and Economics*, **22**, 235-242.

Wang S, Young V R, Panjer H H. (1997). Axiomatic Characterization of Insurance Prices. *Insurance: Mathematics and Economics*. **21**, 173-183.

Wang S, Young V R. (1998a). Ordering Risks: Expected Utility Theory versus Yaari's Dual Theory of Risk, *Insurance: Mathematics and Economics*. **22**, 145-161.

Wang S, Young V R. (1998b). Risk-Adjusted Credibility Premiums Using Distorted Probabilities. *Scandinavian Actuarial Journal*, **1998**(2), 143-165.

Wu X. (2001a). Premium Calculation Principles and Some Related Subjects. *Dissertation for Ph.D.*, East China Normal University, 2001.

Wu X. (2001b). The Natural Sets of Wang's Premium Principle, *ASTIN*

Bulletin, **31**(1), 139-145.

Wu X. (2003). The Stochastic Order and Dual Stochastic Order of Real-Valued Random Variables, *Chines Journal of Applied Statistics and Probability*, **19**(1), 71-78.

Wu X, Wang J. (2003). On Characterization of Distortion Premium Principle, *ASTIN Bulletin*, **33**(1), 1-10.

Yaari M E. (1987). The Dual Theory of Choice under Risk, *Economics*, **55**, 95-115.

Young V R. (1999a). Optimal Insurance under Distortion Premium Principle, *Insurance:Mathematics and Economics*, **25**, 109-122.

Young V R. (1999b). Discussion of Christofides' Conjecture Regarding Distortion Premium Principle. *ASTIN Bulletin* **29**, 191-195.

Chapter 4

Fuzzy Comprehensive Evaluation and Fuzzy Information Processing for Risks

4.1 Introduction

Throughout human history, unexpected economic losses have occurred. Such losses would continue to occur whether or not a system of insurance had ever been devised. Through the operation of an insurance system, losses can be predicted before they occur. The predictability of losses is central to an insurance system's operations. Because an insurance system allows losses to be predicted, it allows the costs of such losses to be financed and redistributed in advance.

Thus, the capability to predict and evaluate losses is usually regarded as the insurer's unique property and an important part of core competence. When a famous insurance expert, Danny Chung, referred to the insurers' losses caused by 911 event, he said that in order to make insurance companies thrive again, the insurers should return to the basics: studying risks seriously, and evaluating risks scientifically (See Shang et al. (2003)).

Traditionally the insurers use statistics to evaluate and analyze risks. It is an effective method, especially when a large quantity of survey data can be collected. In recent years some other methods are introduced, such as the application of fuzzy mathematics and the so called 'hybrid technique' (See Huang and Shi (2002), Shang, Lu, Xu and Chen (2001)). When statistical data is relatively insufficient and we have to deal with the "small sample problem", these new methods perform well.

This chapter will illustrate the application of fuzzy mathematics in evaluating and analyzing risks. Fuzzy comprehensive evaluation and fuzzy information processing (including information distribution and information diffusion) play an important role in it. Other applications of fuzzy mathematics in insurance will be introduced in Chapter 5.

4.2 Fuzzy Comprehensive Evaluation for Risks

4.2.1 *Basic Concepts and Process*

The insurers often need to evaluate various risks, such as mortality risk in life insurance, risks of certain diseases in health insurance, risks of traffic accidents in auto insurance, etc. Usually there is more than one factor that initiates the risk. When we evaluate the risk, we have to consider multiple risk factors and make a comprehensive decision, a process called comprehensive evaluation. When referred to fuzzy factors, we call it fuzzy comprehensive evaluation.

The main steps of fuzzy comprehensive evaluation are as follows (See Zhang, Lu and Zhu (1991) for details).

4.2.1.1 *Construct Factor Set*

A factor set U is an ordinary set of various factors that influence the results of evaluation, $U = \{u_1, u_2, \cdots, u_m\}$ where $u_i (i = 1, 2, \cdots, m)$ stands for each factor, which can be fuzzy or not. The relationship between u_i and U is either $u_i \in U$ or $u_i \notin U$, only one of which must be satisfied.

4.2.1.2 *Construct Weight Set*

Generally speaking, the importances of different factors are different. We set a weight $a_i (i = 1, 2, \cdots, m)$ for each u_i to reflect its importance. The set $A = \{a_1, a_2, \cdots, a_m\}$ is called a factor weight set or weight set in short.

Usually $a_i (i = 1, 2, \cdots, m)$ have unitary and non-negative properties:

$$\sum_{i=1}^{m} a_i = 1, \quad a_i \geqslant 0, \quad i = 1, 2, \cdots, m. \tag{4.1}$$

Since a_i can be considered as the membership grade of importance, the weight set is a fuzzy subset on the factor set and can be expressed as $A = \frac{a_1}{u_1} + \frac{a_2}{u_2} + \cdots + \frac{a_m}{u_m}$.

4.2.1.3 *Construct Evaluation Set*

The various possible results of final evaluation for an object of study consist of an evaluation set $V : V = \{v_1, v_2, \cdots, v_n\}$, where $v_i (i = 1, 2, \cdots, n)$ denotes each possible final evaluation result. The purpose of fuzzy comprehensive evaluation is to find out the best evaluation result based on all influence factors.

4.2.1.4 *Single Factor Fuzzy Evaluation*

When we evaluate the membership grade for an object of study based on one factor, we call it single factor fuzzy evaluation.

Suppose the evaluation is based on the i-th factor u_i. The membership grade to the j-th element v_j of the evaluation set is r_{ij}. The evaluation result for the i-th factor u_i is the fuzzy set $R_i = \frac{r_{i1}}{v_1} + \frac{r_{i2}}{v_2} + \cdots + \frac{r_{in}}{v_n}$, called single factor evaluation set. In fact R_i is also a fuzzy subset of evaluation set V, denoted by $R_i = (r_{i1}, r_{i2}, \cdots, r_{in})$.

In this way, we get a series of single factor evaluation set as follows:

$$\begin{aligned} R_1 &= (r_{11}, r_{12}, \cdots, r_{1n}), \\ R_2 &= (r_{21}, r_{22}, \cdots, r_{2n}), \\ &\cdots\cdots\cdots\cdots \\ R_{mn} &= (r_{m1}, r_{m2}, \cdots, r_{mn}). \end{aligned} \tag{4.2}$$

Let single factor evaluation set R_i be the row of R, which is called single factor evaluation matrix, then

$$R = \begin{pmatrix} r_{11} & r_{12} & \cdots & r_{1n} \\ r_{21} & r_{22} & \cdots & r_{2n} \\ \cdots & \cdots & \cdots & \cdots \\ r_{m1} & r_{m2} & \cdots & r_{mn} \end{pmatrix}. \tag{4.3}$$

4.2.1.5 *Fuzzy Comprehensive Evaluation*

Now let's consider the fuzzy comprehensive evaluation based on all factors.

From single factor evaluation matrix R, the i-th row reflects the influence of the i-th factor to each element of evaluation set and the j-th column reflects the influence of the each factor to the j-th element of evaluation set. Therefore the sum $\tilde{R}_j = \sum_{i=1}^{m} r_{ij} \quad (j = 1, 2, \cdots, n)$ may be regarded as the total influence of all factors to the j-th element. However, $\tilde{R}_j$ doesn't take the importance of various factors into account. To reflect the comprehensive influence of all factors, we may multiply r_{ij} with the weight $a_i (i = 1, 2, \cdots, m)$. Thus we obtain the fuzzy comprehensive evaluation as follows:

$$B = \begin{pmatrix} a_1 \; a_2 \; \cdots \; a_m \end{pmatrix} \circ \begin{pmatrix} r_{11} & r_{12} & \cdots & r_{1n} \\ r_{21} & r_{22} & \cdots & r_{2n} \\ \cdots & \cdots & \cdots & \cdots \\ r_{m1} & r_{m2} & \cdots & r_{mn} \end{pmatrix} = \begin{pmatrix} b_1 \; b_2 \; \cdots \; b_n \end{pmatrix}. \tag{4.4}$$

Where $\circ$ is a fuzzy operator that can be explained in various ways and B is fuzzy comprehensive evaluation set.

4.2.2 *An Example of Risk Evaluation*

In this section we use fuzzy comprehensive evaluation to evaluate the risk of suffering from diseases related to better living conditions.

In recent years, the prevalence rates of certain diseases related to better living conditions have gone up in China. It is meaningful to collect information on the prevalence rates of diseases and to find out the relationship between prevalence rates and risk factors of these diseases for medical research, health insurance and life insurance. During 1997-1998, a survey on hypertension, coronary heart disease, diabetes mellitus and hyperlipidemia was carried out in a community in Shanghai. Based on the data surveyed from 18749 adults, we studied how risk factors such as age, family history, Body Mass Index (BMI), influence the prevalence rate of these diseases. For the sake of conciseness, we will focus on the analysis of hypertension. The analysis methods for other diseases are similar.

4.2.2.1 *Determination of Main Risk Factors*

There are many risk factors initiating hypertension included in the above-mentioned survey. To find the chief ones among these factors, we make analysis of variance on the influence of some risk factors, such as age, family history, BMI, smoking history and drinking history, using survey data.

The steps of analysis are as follows:

Divide every factor into several levels. For example, making ten years a level and we get seven levels for age. Another example is to divide smoking history into three levels, which are free from smoking, smoking amount less than 54,750 cigarettes till the investigation and amount above 54,750 cigarettes, etc.

Divide all the 18,749 adults into 5 groups according to the residential district one belongs to. Then make single-factor repeated-trials analysis of variance on every factor's influence on the prevalence rate of hypertension.

That is, for every factor we mentioned before, we make five experiments according to the five districts, which are restricted by the different levels divided before. And the observed values we obtain are the prevalence rates of hypertension.

Based on the observed values, we make analysis of variance using software S-PLUS. The result shows that age, family history and BMI greatly impact the prevalence rate of hypertension. In contrast, the influence of drinking history and smoking history are not as remarkable. So it is clear that age, family history and BMI may be regarded as three main risk factors influencing the prevalence rate of hypertension.

Since that the relationship between age and BMI might affect the result of risk evaluation, we divide the whole group into three subgroups: the youth group (aged 15∼34), the middle-aged group (aged 35∼54), and the elderly group (older than 55). Thus we regard age and BMI as independent factors in every subgroup.

The discussion below is aimed at each subgroup mentioned above, meanwhile males and females are analyzed separately as well.

4.2.2.2 *Evaluation of the Risk*

Now let us consider the following problem: if we know the levels of the three main risk factors for a certain resident or for a certain group of residents, how can we evaluate the risk of suffering from hypertension (including mild and serious)?

The evaluation goes as follows:

The concept of illness fuzzy set

Generally speaking, we can divide the severity scale of an illness into free from the illness, mild and serious. Because the boundaries among the three scales are not clear, it is better to illustrate them with fuzzy sets.

Definition 4.1 Illness fuzzy set $V' = (v_0', v_1', v_2')$ is a kind of measure on the prevalence situation or risk for a certain disease of a certain group of residents. It is a fuzzy set, regarding evaluation set $V = (v_0, v_1, v_2)$ as its universal field, which fits $\sum_{i=0}^{2} v_i' = 1$, where v_0,v_1,v_2 stand for free from illness, mild illness and serious illness respectively, and v_0', v_1', v_2' stand for their membership grade accordingly.

Illness fuzzy set with fixed level of a certain risk factor

First consider a group of residents formed by fixing a certain level of a certain risk factor. For example, with BMI ranging from 21 to 23,or all young females with no family history of hypertension, etc.

We aim to determine the illness fuzzy sets for all such groups (for every level of every appointed risk factor) and use these fuzzy sets to evaluate the risk of each person or each group.

Thus the survey data are used to determine each membership grade of such group's illness fuzzy set. If the total number of residents of this group is big enough, the statistical frequency in every circumstance during the survey approximately replaces the membership grade directly. But, if the total number of residents or the number of residents suffered from hypertension is relatively small, then this method is unfavorable, for it can't reflect the true situation. We will use information distribution method and information diffusion method to discuss this situation later in this chapter.

Multi-factor fuzzy comprehensive evaluation

In medical science and health insurance, it is often needed to evaluate the risk of hypertension of a group with a fixed level of any of the three risk factors. To do this, we establish multi-factor fuzzy comprehensive evaluation. The method goes as follows:

First, fix the level of every risk factor and calculate the respective illness fuzzy set $R_1 = (R_{10}, R_{11}, R_{12}), R_2 = (R_{20}, R_{21}, R_{22}), R_3 = (R_{30}, R_{31}, R_{32})$, with method mentioned before, and give a note as below:

$$R = \begin{pmatrix} R_1 \\ R_2 \\ R_3 \end{pmatrix} . \tag{4.5}$$

Then, perform comprehensive evaluation.

Note the weights that each risk factor initiates the prevalence rate as W_1, W_2 and W_3. The selection of the weights will be discussed later.

Thus the result of comprehensive evaluation goes as follows:

$$B = (W_1, W_2, W_3) \circ R = W \circ R = (B_0, B_1, B_2) . \tag{4.6}$$

Here the operator "$\circ$" is viewed as a generalized matrix multiplication, namely

$$B = W \circ R = \left(\sum_{i=1}^{3} W_i * R_{i0}, \sum_{i=1}^{3} W_i * R_{i1}, \sum_{i=1}^{3} W_i * R_{i2} \right) . \tag{4.7}$$

Where $*$ stands for ordinary multiplication, $\sum$ stands for generalized addition which means $x \oplus y = \min(1, x + y)$.

Fuzzy set B gained through this way is called the risk evaluation fuzzy set or risk vector of that group.

Determination of weights w_1, w_2 and w_3

There are two ways of determining the weights w_i. One comes from one's experience or the opinions of several medical experts, which is quite simple but relatively arbitrary. Another way is to try to solve the inverse-problem of comprehensive evaluation. (See [4] and [5])

In this chapter, optimization technique is used to get the weights on the basis of the latter method. It goes as follows:

Select a number of representative groups (we select 9 groups in this chapter). For each group, the method of calculating statistical frequency is used to get the comprehensive evaluation vector $B = (B_0, B_1, B_2)$, and therefore we get w_1, w_2,w_3(which fits $w_i \geqslant 0$ and $\sum w_i = 1$) by solving the inverse problem of $W \circ R = B$.

In fact, it is almost impossible to get the exact solution of this equation. In practice, w is obtained by seeking a vector w which enables $A = W \circ R$ and B get most closely under the meaning of Hamming approaching degree of fuzzy sets. This means one try to get the solution that makes $\sigma_H(A, B) = 1 - \frac{1}{n} \sum\limits_{i=1}^{n} |u_A(x_i) - u_B(x_i)|$ reach its maximum using optimization method.

At last, we take the mean $\bar{w}_1, \bar{w}_2$,$\bar{w}_3$ of the nine solutions achieved from each group as the weight we actually use.

4.2.2.3 *Applications*

Suppose we get an illness fuzzy set corresponding to a certain disease for a certain group, then we can calculate some characteristic values of that group and apply them into medical science and insurance or some other areas. For this purpose, we first establish the definition of characteristic mapping of fuzzy set.

Definition 4.2 Let A be the universal field, $\tilde{A} = \{all\ fuzzy\ sets\ defined\ on\ A\}$, set $C \subseteq R^n$, mapping $\tilde{g} : \tilde{A} \to C$ is called a "characteristic mapping of fuzzy set" if and only if it can show characteristic of the problem discussed.

Example: Given a certain group, suppose the risk evaluation fuzzy set of hypertension is $B = (B_0, B_1, B_2)$. Further, according to the statistics data offered by hospitals, the average annual examination and treatment expenses of hypertension are p_0, p_1 and p_2,which are associated with free from hypertension, mild and serious respectively.

The average annual hospitalization periods (days) are H_0, H_1 and H_2 respectively. And let $\tilde{A} = \{all\ illness\ fuzzy\ sets\}$, then

$$\left(B_0', B_1', B_2'\right) \to \left(B_0', B_1', B_2'\right) \circ \begin{pmatrix} P_0 \ H_0 \\ P_1 \ H_1 \\ P_2 \ H_2 \end{pmatrix} = \left(\bar{P} \ \bar{H}\right) \tag{4.8}$$

is a characteristic mapping of fuzzy set from $\tilde{A}$ to R^2, where $\bar{P}$ and $\bar{H}$ are viewed respectively as the expected examination and treatment expenses and hospitalization period (days) of hypertension of that group within a year.

Now, we make a further assumption that there exists a medical insurance product being aimed at hypertension. The standard annual premium of a relatively large group G, such as males age 35~44, is M. Then consider a sub group G_A composed of members of G, for example, males aged 35~44 with BMI values between 21 and 23 and without family history. Suppose the risk evaluation fuzzy set of G and G_A be known as $\left(B_0', B_1', B_2'\right)$ and $\left(B_0'', B_1'', B_2''\right)$ respectively.

On the basis of the characteristic mapping of fuzzy set given in the example, the expected examination and treatment expenses of G and G_A would be obtained, which are $\bar{p}$ and $\bar{p}_A$ respectively.

Then, $\bar{p}_A/\bar{p}$ is viewed as the adjusted coefficient of net premium corresponding to subgroup G_A.

4.3 Fuzzy Information Distribution in Risk Evaluation and Analysis

4.3.1 *Concept of Fuzzy Information Distribution*

When we use the fuzzy comprehensive evaluation method to evaluate the risk of certain diseases in Section 4.2, the membership grade for the illness fuzzy set is mostly obtained by calculating the statistical frequency. For example, there are a great number of records falling into the interval [22, 24] of Body Mass Index (BMI) when we consider the influence of risk factors on certain diseases, so the membership grade for the illness fuzzy set obtained by calculating the statistical frequency is reasonable. However, in the case of BMI=25, a small sample which only contains 31 records for the young people is incomplete data, where the information we obtained may be regarded as the so-called mass-body fuzzy information. It is difficult to use statistical methods to calculate membership grade in this case. Huang Chongfu and Liu Zunrong. have discussed the processing of small sample problems, including Information Distribution Method and Information Diffusion Method. (Huang and Shi (2002)) Here we use these methods to calculate membership grade when dealing with the small sample. First we introduce some definitions:

Definition 4.3 Let $W = \{w_1, w_2, \cdots, w_m\}$ be a given sample observed from an experiment and $U = \{u_1, u_2, \cdots, u_n\}$ be a discrete universal field of W for monitoring. A mapping from $U \times W$ to [0, 1] $\mu : U \times W \to [0,1]$ is called an information distribution of W on U if it satisfies:

(a) $\forall w \in W$, if $\exists u \in U$, which satisfies $u = w$ then $\mu(u,w) = 1$;

(b) For $w \in W, \forall u', u'' \in U$, if $\|u' - w\| \leqslant \|u'' - w\|$, then $\mu(u', w) \geqslant \mu(u'', w)$, i.e., μ is decreasing when $\|u - w\|$ is increasing;

(c) $\sum\limits_{i=1}^{n} \mu(u_i, w_j) = 1,\ \ j = 1, 2, \cdots, m.$

Definition 4.4 The vector, which is made up of the quantities of information gains by each sample point w_j contributing to each controlling point u_i in U in some fashion μ, is called information row vector of sample point w_j. denoted by $q_{ij} = \mu(u_i, w_j)$. The image of fuzzy transformation, a fuzzy set whose universal field is evaluation set, is called risk vector in this chapter.

Definition 4.5 $Q_i = \sum\limits_{j=1}^{m} q_{ij}$ is called the information gross provided by W from controlling point u_i, and $Q = (Q_1, Q_2, \cdots, Q_n)$ is called original information distribution matrix for W on U, in short, information distribution matrix.

Definition 4.6 Let e_0 denote the error obtained by normal method and e_N denote the error by new method then $\rho = \frac{e_0 - e_N}{e_0} \times 100\%$ is called the reducible deviation by new method.

4.3.2 *Information Distribution Method*

Let us use an example to show how IDM(Information Distribution Method) is applied to the determination of the membership grade for the illness fuzzy set. We want to calculate the value of membership grade 2(serious illness) for all the illness fuzzy sets with fixed BMI level.

As mention above, in the case of large sample problem, the membership grade for the illness fuzzy set obtained by calculating the statistical frequency method is reasonable. Hence, we regard it as a standard. As an illustration, we draw randomly 700 out of 6658 records surveyed in Section 4.2 and regard the statistic result from 6658 records as a standard. For the influence of risk factor BMI on serious illness of hypertension, a comparison of the result from 6658 and from 700 by using statistic method is shown below in Figure 4.1.

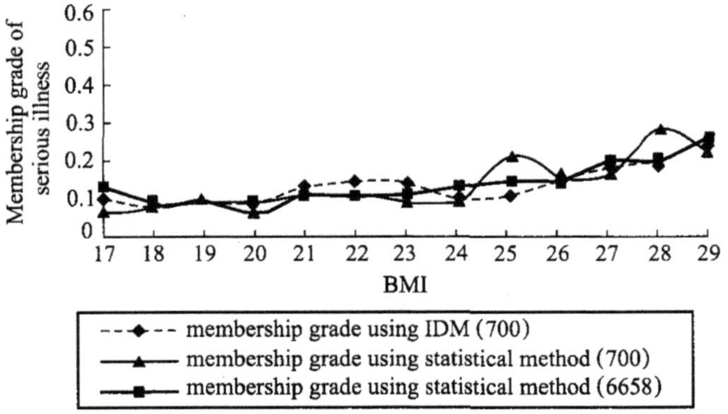

Fig. 4.1 Comparision

It is found that the statistic curve of 700 encircling the one of 6658 fluctuates up and down for fewer records falling into each interval of BMI. As a result, the average relative error is 19.56%. If we solve the same problem for the above 700 records by using IDM, what is the result?

At first, let us denote the universal field of BMI by $\{b\,|b \in [17,30]\}$ and of risk of hypertension by $V = \{v_0, v_1, v_2\} = \{free\ from\ hypertension,\ mild,\ serious\}$. Implementation of the IDM can be processed according to the following steps:

Determine controlling points: Having divided the universal field into 13 grades with equal spacing, we select mid point of each interval as controlling point. i.e. $B = \{b_1, b_2, \cdots, b_{13}\} = \{17.5, 18.5, \cdots, 29.5\}$;

Construct information distribution matrix Q: Q constructed from B and V is used to save up the information of 700 original data points. The detail of construction is as follows:

Each record includes two segments b (the value of BMI) and v (v_0 or v_1 or v_2), and b could contributes its information to one or two adjacent controlling points subject to the condition that total amount of information here is conducted in linear form. i.e.

$$\mu(b_i, b) = \begin{cases} 1 - \dfrac{|b - b_i|}{\Delta}, & |b - b_i| \leqslant \Delta, \\ 0, & |b - b_i| > \Delta, \end{cases} \tag{4.9}$$

where $i = 1, 2, \cdots, 13$ and denote spacing by Δ.

As an illustration, considering a record with $b = 22.9$ and $v_i = v_1$. When contributing its information to Q, only controlling points $b_6 = 22.5$ and $b_7 = 23.5$ get the share. Therefore

$$\begin{aligned} q_{6,1} &= 1 - \frac{|b - b_6|}{\Delta} = 1 - \frac{|22.9 - 22.5|}{1} = 0.6, \\ q_{7,1} &= 1 - \frac{|b - b_7|}{\Delta} = 1 - \frac{|22.9 - 23.5|}{1} = 0.4. \end{aligned} \tag{4.10}$$

After 700 data have been treated with this process and information gains at each controlling point have been summed up, an information distribution matrix Q will turn out which is shown in Table 4.1.

Table 4.1 Information Distribution Matrix Q

BMI	Risk vector on Hypertension		
	v_0	v_1	v_2
b_1=17.5 (17~18)	9.65	1.92	1.20
b_2=18.5 (18~19)	14.41	1.44	1.28
b_3=19.5 (19~20)	29.77	4.56	3.76
b_4=20.5 (20~21)	50.96	12.72	4.11
b_5=21.5 (21~22)	73.81	13.12	11.08
b_6=22.5 (22~23)	84.01	20.56	14.00
b_7=23.5 (23~24)	69.83	21.21	8.61
b_8=24.5 (24~25)	54.71	22.28	9.26
b_9=24.5 (25~26)	37.87	12.19	9.36
b_{10}=26.5 (26~27)	21.44	14.42	8.20
b_{11}=27.5 (27~28)	18.16	6.94	6.04
b_{12}=28.5 (28~29)	6.99	3.87	3.63
b_{13}=29.5 (29~30)	3.79	3.26	1.47

Establish the fuzzy relationship matrix $\tilde{R}$. Each element in $\tilde{R}$ can be determined by normalizing each element of information map Q. i.e. $r_{ij} = \frac{Q_{ij}}{\sum\limits_{i=1}^{13}\sum\limits_{j=0}^{2} Q_{ij}}$ $(i = 1, 2, \cdots, 13; j = 0, 1, 2)$.

Risk evaluation with single factor. Given the magnitude for BMI, we can calculate the membership grade for the illness fuzzy set by using fuzzy transformation $\tilde{V}_0 = B_0 \odot \tilde{R}$, where $\odot$ stands for fuzzy operator $M(\bullet, \oplus)$. For example, given an old people with BMI=29, whose information row vector should be $B_0 = \{0,0,0,0,0,0,0,0,0,0,0,0.5,0.5\}$, so his/her risk vector is $\tilde{V}_0 = B_0 \odot \tilde{R} = 0.058/v_0 + 0.032/v_1 + 0.030/v_2$. For defuzzification, it is normalized and the illness fuzzy set with BMI=29(still denote $\tilde{V}_0$) is $\tilde{V}_0 = 0.483/v_0 + 0.267/v_1 + 0.250/v_2$.

Finally, we compare the result from large sample (6658) statistic with the above result from small sample (700) obtained by IDM (see Figure 4.1), and find that their curves are almost consistent. The relative error by IDM is 12% and the reducible deviation is 38.65%. It is shown that the IDM is a better method when dealing with small sample.

4.3.3 *Improving IDM*

In Figure 4.1, the length of each interval of BMI is set to 1, so we assign 1 to Δ in BMI accordingly. The primary concern when distributing information is how to choose appropriate distribution functions. Here we try to choose a non-linear distribution function independent of the condition $\mu_1(u_1, v) + \mu_2(u_2, v) = 1$ as follows:

$$\mu(b_i, b) = \begin{cases} 1 - \dfrac{|b - b_i|^\lambda}{\Delta^\lambda}, & |b - b_i| \leqslant \Delta, \quad \lambda > 0, \\ 0, & |b - b_i| > \Delta, \end{cases} \tag{4.11}$$

and compare it with the original one. As to the controlling point, let θ be the shift from original controlling points, that is, we move the controlling points $|\theta|$ units from their original location. When $\theta < 0$, move to left; and $\theta > 0$, move to right. Under the condition $0 \leqslant \lambda \leqslant 3, -1 \leqslant \theta \leqslant 1$, we use Matlab and apply the linear search algorithm to minimize the object function $f(\lambda, \theta)$ in the model where $f(\lambda, \theta)$ represents the difference between the results obtained by small sample and large sample. The final result is as follows:

$$\min\{f(\lambda, \theta) \,|0 \leqslant \lambda \leqslant 3, -1 \leqslant \theta \leqslant 1\} = 0.0196,$$

where $\hat{\lambda} = 2.45, \hat{\theta} = 0.26$. Then we apply this result as an appropriate distribution function to the 700 sample set, and make comparisons with the result from the large sample statistics. The results are comparable. The average relative error e_N is only 9.5% and reducible deviation ρ is 51.43%.

The comparisons are made between different fuzzy operators $\odot$ used in the fuzzy transformation $\tilde{V}_0 = B_0 \odot \tilde{R}$. $\odot$ is set to be $M(\wedge, \vee)$, $M(\bullet, \vee)$, $M(\wedge, \oplus)$ and $M(\bullet, \oplus)$ respectively and the best one we find is $M(\bullet, \oplus)$.

4.3.4 *Applications*

Verified by the above computational results from IDM, we again turn to Section 4.2 and make further division of two important factors initiating hypertension, the age and BMI. People of the same sex and the same age belong to the same group. By ages ranging from 15∼84, we get 140 groups. After BMI are divided by age interval 15∼35, 35∼40, 40∼45, 45∼50, 50∼55, 55∼60, 60∼65, 65∼70, and 70∼84 (to prevent the affluence of age on statistic of BMI, see Section 4.2), people from the above age interval, of the same BMI and the same sex, are grouped together. The illness fuzzy set for family history is from statistics in Section 4.2. Using the weights in Section 4.2, we then make comprehensive evaluations to derive risk evaluation fuzzy sets of different group of people according to sex, age, BMI and family history.

For example, the risk evaluation fuzzy set of the female group aged 30, and BMI=25, having no family history is calculated as follows:

For female group, aged 30, the single risk evaluation fuzzy set is (0.991, 0.009, 0);

For female group, BMI=25, the single risk evaluation fuzzy set is (0.975, 0.025, 0);

For female group, having no family history, the single risk evaluation fuzzy set is (0.9936, 0.0064, 0);

Then comprehensive evaluation is made and the final result is

$$\begin{aligned}&\begin{pmatrix}0.1883 \; 0.1565 \; 0.6552\end{pmatrix} \odot \begin{pmatrix}0.991 & 0.009 & 0\\ 0.975 & 0.025 & 0\\ 0.9936 & 0.0064 & 0\end{pmatrix}\\ &= \begin{pmatrix}0.9902 \; 0.0098 \; 0\end{pmatrix}.\end{aligned} \tag{4.12}$$

In the same way, the evaluation fuzzy set of the male group, aged 53, BMI=23, having family history is

$$\begin{aligned}&\begin{pmatrix}0.1883 \; 0.1565 \; 0.6552\end{pmatrix} \odot \begin{pmatrix}0.827 & 0.141 & 0.032\\ 0.822 & 0.161 & 0.017\\ 0.0615 & 0.8092 & 0.0893\end{pmatrix}\\ &= \begin{pmatrix}0.3247 \; 0.5819 \; 0.0672\end{pmatrix}.\end{aligned} \tag{4.13}$$

4.4 Information Diffusion and Its Application to Risk Analysis

In Section 4.3 we use Information Distribution Method to deal with the small sample and get some favorable result. IDM is one method of Fuzzy Information Processing. However it also has its disadvantages. For example, in 1-dimension case, one piece of information is only distributed to two controlling points nearby. When the length Δ of each interval of BMI is too small, many controlling points will have no impact of information which may lead to an incorrect result. When Δ is too large, the precision in calculation will decrease.

In this section, we will introduce another method of Fuzzy Information Processing — Information Diffusion Method and apply it to risk analysis of coronary heart disease.

4.4.1 *Mechanism of Information Diffusion*

For an incomplete sample W, we may consider each point w_j of this sample as a "representative" of all points in its neighborhood, that is, each point w_j not only provides the information on itself, but also contains some information for points around it. Thus, all points in its neighborhood share the information provided by w_j. The closer the point is to w_j, the more information it shares. The process of sharing the information of w_j is called Information Diffusion Process.

Definition 4.7 Let W be a sample and V be a basic universal field. Information diffusion is defined as a map $\mu : W \times V \to [0,1]$ satisfying:

(a) $\forall w_j \in W$, if v_j is the observational value of w_j, then $\mu(w_j, v_j) = \sup_{v\in V} \mu(w_j, v)$;

(b) $\forall w_j \in W$, $\mu(w_j, v)$ decreases with $\|w_j - v\|$ increasing;

(c) $\forall w_j \in W$, $\int_v \mu(w, v)dv = 1$, $\int_v$ is replaced by $\sum\limits_v$ in discrete case..

Definition 4.8 The range of diffusion is defined as the Euclidean distance R. The diffusion is limited (unlimited) if R is finite (infinite).

In the chapter, the information diffusion we deal with is unlimited; therefore the method introduced in this chapter is called Unlimited Information Diffusion Method (UIDM). According to the viewpoint that any sample point will provide information to all points in its neighborhood, a diffusion model is constructed and the derivation of the information diffusion function is in a way similar to that in molecular diffusion and heat conduction. Let us first consider a 2D case as follows.

Let information density function (IDF) $\rho(x, y, t)$ be the information density at the point (x, y) and the moment t.

Initially $\rho\,|_{t=0} = \rho(x, y, 0) = \delta(x, y)$, where $\delta(x, y) = \begin{cases} \infty, & \text{at}(0,0), \\ 0, & \text{otherwise}, \end{cases}$ and $\int_{-\infty}^{\infty}\int_{-\infty}^{\infty} \delta(x, y) = 1$.

Now consider information diffusion in the x-y plane.

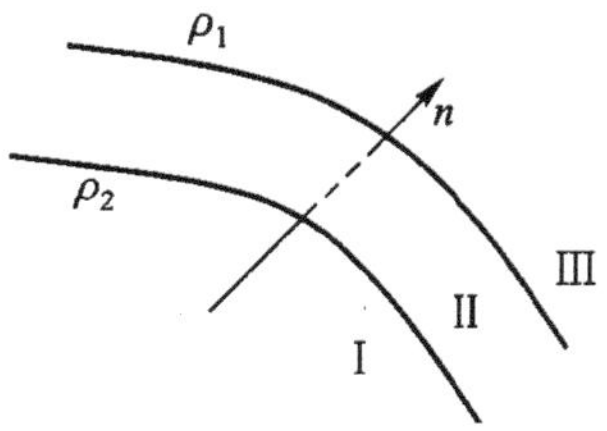

Fig. 4.2 Sketch map of information diffusion

Figure 4.2 shows information diffusion through a region with length Δl and width Δn. During a time interval Δt the amount of information ΔI that flows form region I (with information density $\rho_2 > \rho_1$) to region III (with information density ρ_1) is $\Delta I = -k\frac{\rho_1 - \rho_2}{\Delta n}\Delta l \Delta t$, where $k > 0$ is the information conduction coefficient, and $\frac{\rho_1 - \rho_2}{\Delta n}$ is the gradient of information density. The minus sign shows that information flows from the high-density region to the low-density region. For an area Ω with boundary Γ, the amount of information accumulated in time interval $[t_1, t_2]$ is

$$I = \int_{t_1}^{t_2} \left\{ \int_{\Gamma} k \frac{\partial \rho}{\partial n} dl \right\} dt = \int_{t_1}^{t_2} \left\{ \iint\limits_{\Omega} k \left(\frac{\partial^2 \rho}{\partial x^2} + \frac{\partial^2 \rho}{\partial y^2} \right) dx dy \right\} dt. \quad (4.14)$$

Where n is the normal direction of the boundary Γ.

The amount of information accumulated in area Ω can also be expressed as

$$I = \iint\limits_{\Omega} c[\rho(x, y, t_2) - \rho(x, y, t_1)] dx dy = \iint\limits_{\Omega} \int_{t_1}^{t_2} c \frac{\partial \rho}{\partial t} dt dx dy. \quad (4.15)$$

So

$$\int_{t_1}^{t_2}\left\{\iint\limits_{\Omega} k\left(\frac{\partial^2\rho}{\partial x^2}+\frac{\partial^2\rho}{\partial y^2}\right)dxdy\right\}dt=\iint\limits_{\Omega}\int_{t_1}^{t_2} c\frac{\partial\rho}{\partial t}dtdxdy. \tag{4.16}$$

Since t_1, t_2 and Ω are arbitrary, we have $k(\frac{\partial^2\rho}{\partial x^2}+\frac{\partial^2\rho}{\partial y^2})=c\frac{\partial\rho}{\partial t}$.

With the initial condition, the following Cauchy problem is deduced $\begin{cases}\frac{\partial\rho}{\partial t}=a^2(\frac{\partial^2\rho}{\partial x^2}+\frac{\partial^2\rho}{\partial y^2})\\ t=0:\rho=\delta(x,y)\end{cases}$ with solution $\rho(x,y,t)=\frac{1}{4a^2\pi t}e^{-\frac{x^2+y^2}{4a^2t}}$.

If the source of information is at point (x_0, y_0), then $\rho(x,y,t)$ takes the form $\frac{1}{4a^2\pi t}e^{-\frac{(x-x_0)^2+(y-y_0)^2}{4a^2t}}$. Therefore, the information diffusion function (See Figure 4.3) may be chosen as $e^{-\frac{(x-x_0)^2+(y-y_0)^2}{\lambda}}$ where the parameter λ is the parameter to be decided.

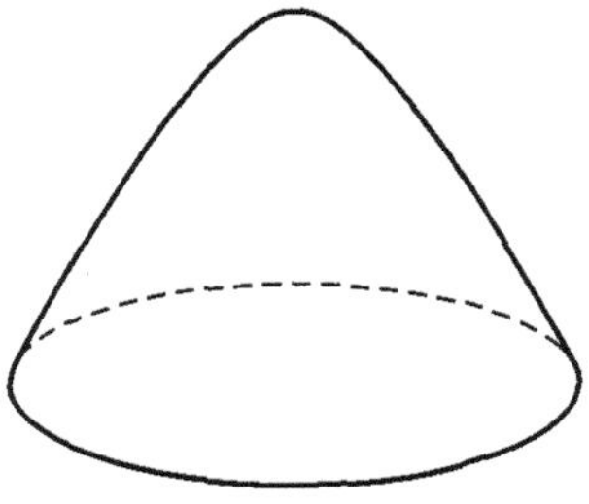

Fig. 4.3 Sketch map of information diffusion function (bell shape)

In 1D case, the information diffusion function may be chosen as $e^{-\frac{(x-x_0)^2}{\lambda}}$. To choose information diffusion function in this way may not satisfy the property (c) of Definition 4.7, but it will not affect the result of the calculation in this chapter.

4.4.2 *An Example of Application — 1D Problem*

Now we use Information Diffusion Method to analyze risk of coronary heart disease. During a survey on coronary heart disease in Shanghai, we obtained more than 10,000 residents' records, which indicated whether they suffered from coronary heart disease and related risk factors. The major risk factors are age and Body Mass Index (BMI). We apply these records to analysis of the relationships between prevalence rate of coronary heart disease (PRD) and risk factors including age and BMI. Let's focus on relationship between PRD and age first. This is a 1-D problem.

4.4.2.1 *Large Sample*

First select 16,650 records for residents aged from 33 to 78. (Let agelevel = age/3, then agelevel $\in [11, 26)$). The interval [11,26) may be divided into 15 sub-intervals. In each subinterval $[a, b)$, if there are x residents suffering from CHD and y healthy residents, then according to the statistical approach, $r = x/(x + y)$ may be regarded as the PRD at controlling point $v = (a + b)/2$. Figure 4.4 shows the obtained $r - v$ curve. Since the sample size is large, this result may be regarded as a standard one, with which the results for small samples are compared.

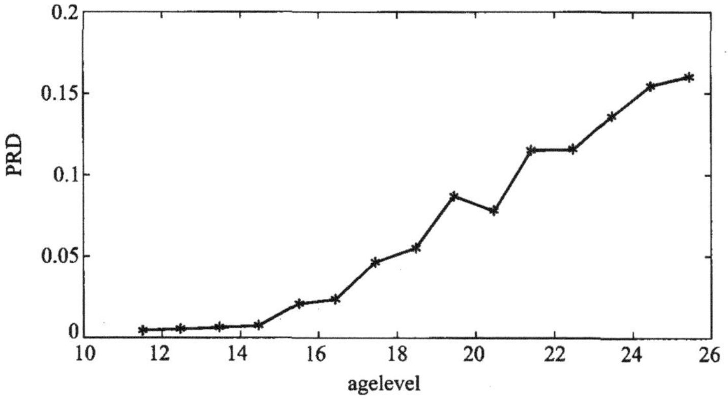

Fig. 4.4 $r - v$ curve for large sample

4.4.2.2 *Small Sample — Statistical Approach*

Now randomly choose 105 records from the 16,650 records. There are seven records in each subinterval on average. Therefore, we call these records a small sample. The statistical approach is still employed, and a new $r - v$ curve is obtained. Figure 4.5 shows that the curve of the small sample fluctuates wildly. It deviates largely from the overall trend that the PRD increases with age.

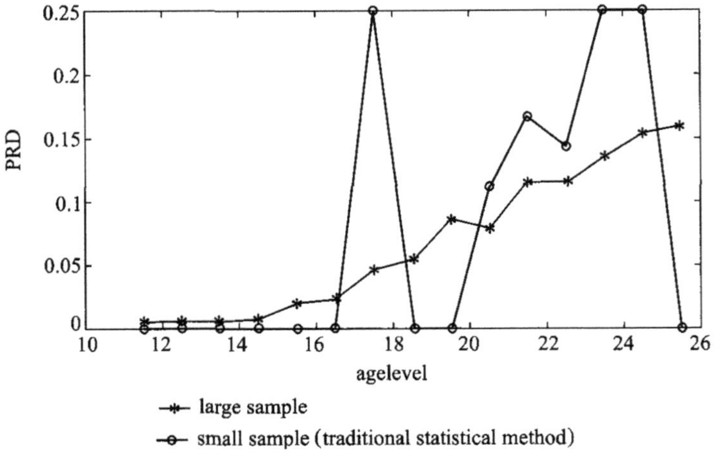

Fig. 4.5 Comparison of $r-v$ curves (large and small samples)

4.4.2.3 *Small Sample — UIDM*

To approve the treatment of small sample problems, the UIDM is employed. Compared with the probability density function of normal distribution, we set λ to have the value of 2. Choose IDF as $\mu_1(w_n, v) = e^{-\frac{|w_n - v|^2}{2}}$ and diffuse the information carried by sample points to the whole field. The information for the controlling points may be written as

$$\begin{aligned} {}^{ILL}\mu_1(v) &= \sum_{ILL} \mu_1(w_n, v), \\ {}^{HEAL}\mu_1(v) &= \sum_{HEAL} \mu_1(w_n, v), \qquad \forall v \in V. \end{aligned} \tag{4.17}$$

Where ILL and HEAL denote the sufferers and healthy people, respectively. Now we have the function for PRD as follows:

$$r_1(v) = \frac{{}^{ILL}\mu_1(v)}{({}^{ILL}\mu_1(v) + {}^{HEAL}\mu_1(v))}. \tag{4.18}$$

The comparison of three $r-v$ curves given in Figure 4.6 shows that the UIDM is more effective than the traditional statistical method while dealing with small samples.

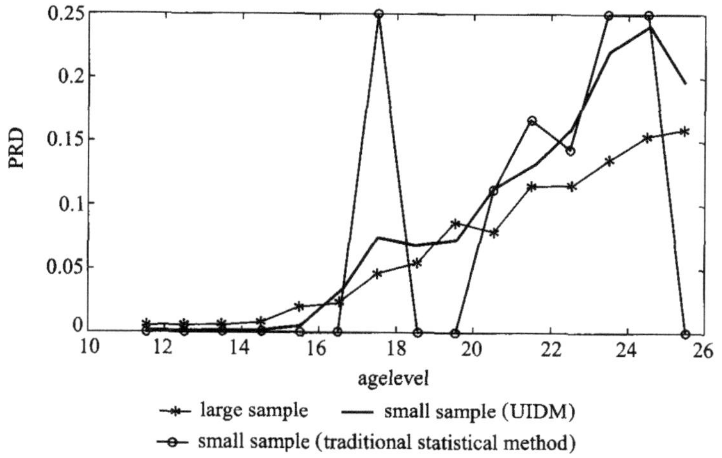

Fig. 4.6 Comparison of three $r - v$ curves

4.4.3 *An Example of Application — 2D Problem*

In this section, the relationship between PRD and two risk factors (age, BMI) is considered. The comparison of different methods for this 2D problem is in a way similar to that in 1D case.

4.4.3.1 *Large Sample*

As the large sample, 13,005 records with agelevel $\in [11, 26)$ and BMI $\in [20, 26)$ are chosen. Applying the statistical method to these data, the obtained $r - (v^{(1)}, v^{(2)})$ surface is shown in the Figure 4.7. Although this surface is not very smooth, the PRD still increase with age and BMI on the whole, and the surface is used as a standard with which the PRD surface for the small sample is compared.

4.4.3.2 *Small Sample — Statistical Approach*

To form a small sample, 630 records are randomly chosen from the 13,005 records. The average amount of the records in each subfield is seven. A new $r - (v^{(1)}, v^{(2)})$ surface is constructed by applying the statistical method to this small sample. Figure 4.8 shows that this PRD surface fluctuates abnormally.

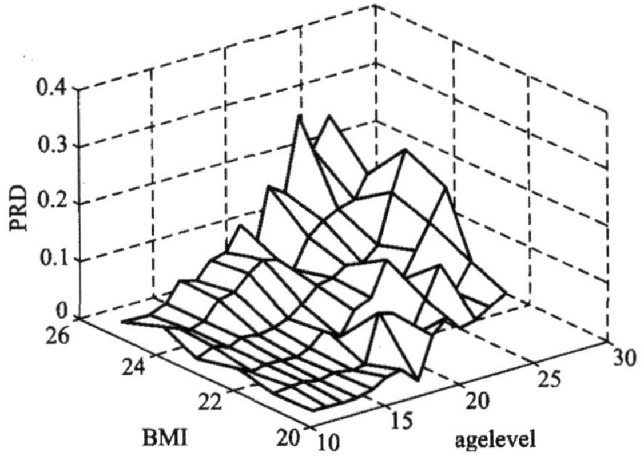

Fig. 4.7 PRD surface of large sample (traditional statistical method)

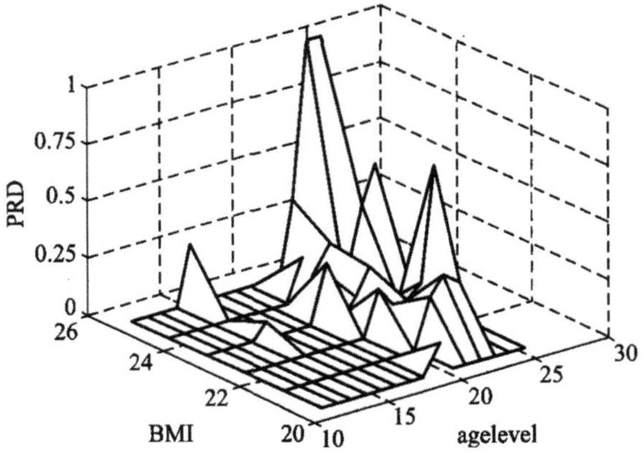

Fig. 4.8 PPRD surface of small sample (traditional statistical method)

4.4.3.3 *Small Sample — UIDM*

Now turn to UIDM for this 2D small sample problem. We choose IDF as

$$\mu_2(w_n, v) = e^{-\frac{\left|w_n^{(1)} - v^{(1)}\right|^2 + \left|w_n^{(2)} - v^{(2)}\right|^2}{2}} \tag{4.19}$$

to take into account two risk factors: agelevel and BMI. With this IDF, the information for controlling points may be written as

$$\begin{aligned} {}^{ILL}\mu_2(v) &= \sum_{ILL} \mu_2(w_n, v), \\ {}^{HEAL}\mu_2(v) &= \sum_{HEAL} \mu_2(w_n, v), \qquad \forall v \in V. \end{aligned} \tag{4.20}$$

Where ILL and HEAL denote the sufferers and healthy people, respectively. Therefore the two-dimension PRD is $r_1(v) = \frac{{}^{ILL}\mu_1(v)}{({}^{ILL}\mu_1(v) + {}^{HEAL}\mu_1(v))}$ and the PRD surface is shown in Figure 4.9.

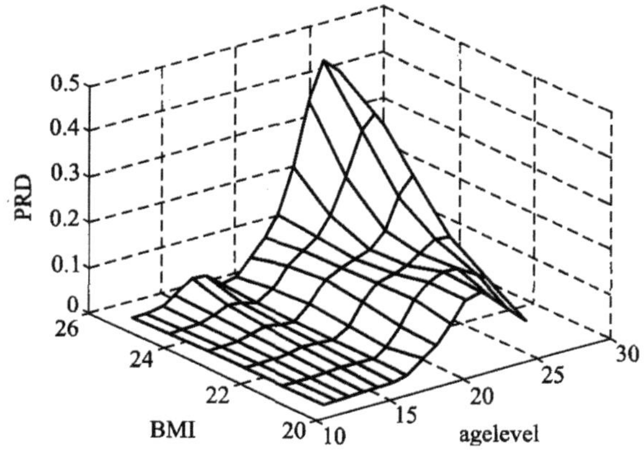

Fig. 4.9 PRD surface of small sample (UIDM)

4.4.4 *Optimized Information Diffusion Method (OIDM)*

In Section 4.4.2 and Section 4.4.3, the parameter λ was chosen as $\lambda = 2$. This arbitrariness in determining the parameter λ may be eliminated by introducing the optimization criteria for information diffusion (See Shang, Lu and Shen (2000), Shang, Wu, Lu and Shen (2001) and Shang, Lu and Jin (2003).).

For example, when there exists a large sample in the problem under consideration or a similar problem, the optimization criterion of parameter λ can be chosen so that the closer the results of the small sample is to results of the large sample, the better the parameter λ is (See Shang, Lu and Shen (2000)). However, there is no such large sample in most cases and the application of this method is limited. Another optimization criterion is to require that the curve of the result to have the minimum fluctuation

(See Shang, Wu, Lu and Shen (2001)). This is because we think that the function of object variable (e.g. PRD) to risk factors should not have big fluctuation. This criterion, however, should be used in combination with other optimization criteria.

We still cite the problem of prevalence rate of coronary heart disease as an example and set up the optimization criteria and models.

4.4.4.1 *OIDM in 1D Case*

In Section 4.4.2.3, we used UIDM to process the 1D small sample (only contains 105 records). The Information Diffusion Function used is $e^{-\frac{|w_n - v|^2}{2}}$. Now let IDF $= e^{-\frac{|w_n - v|^2}{\lambda}}$, where λ is determined by the optimization model later. The model involves two criteria:

- **Minimum Fluctuation Criterion**

The fluctuation of PRD curve should be minimal under the choice of parameter λ.

Another aspect worthy of attention is that any treated result should be the reflection of the original sample to a certain extent. Hence the second criterion is presented as follows:

- **Limited Departure Criterion**

There should not be great disparity between result produced from OIDM and the original small sample.

Assume that the diffused PRD from the bell-shaped IDF is $p^\lambda(v)$. Analogous to the curvature of curve, Fluctuation Index $F(\lambda) = \int\limits_{11}^{26} \left(\frac{\partial^2 p^\lambda}{\partial v^2}\right)^2 dv$ is defined to measure the fluctuation of PRD curve.

To implement the Limited Departure Criterion, we first set up the observed cumulative distribution. Again regard the midpoint of the subinterval as the representative of that subinterval. Then $OH_i = \sum\limits_{j=1}^{i} SH_j^o, i = 1, 2, \cdots, 15$ could be deemed as the cumulative number of healthy persons in c_i, where SH_j^o is the observed number of healthy persons in $\Omega_j = [c_j - \frac{d}{2}, c_j + \frac{d}{2})$ in the given sample, d is the length of the subinterval.

Fit the data (c_i, OH_i) by suitable method (such as polynomial curve fitting, spline fitting, etc.) the resultant curve is recorded as $FH(c)$, which is the standard that the diffused results would be compared to. Correspondingly, the diffused cumulative distribution is $DH^{\lambda}(c) = \sum_{j=1}^{i} SH_j^d(\lambda), c \in \Omega, i = 1, 2, \cdots, 15$.

Then Departure Measure for number of healthy residents is calculated as $T^h(\lambda) = \frac{\int |FH(c)-DH^{\lambda}(c)|dc}{\int FH(c)dc}$. The Departure Measure of number of CHD patients is treated in the same way, $T^s(\lambda) = \frac{\int |FS(c)-DS^{\lambda}(c)|dc}{\int FS(c)dc}$.

The optimization model is

$$\begin{aligned} &\min F(\lambda), \\ &\text{s.t. } T^h(\lambda) < \theta_h, \quad T^s(\lambda) < \theta_s, \quad \lambda \in (0, 20). \end{aligned} \tag{4.21}$$

Where θ_h, θ_s are departure indices and the selection of them rely on the reliability of sample.

Cubic polynomial is employed to fit the observed distribution in this paper. The fitted distribution curves for the numbers of healthy-residents and CHD patients are obtained as

$$FH(c) = 0.0189c^3 - 1.3961c^2 + 38.0832c - 275.6892, \tag{4.22}$$

where $11 < c < 26$,

$$FS(c) = \begin{cases} 0, & 11 \leqslant c \leqslant 16.5, \\ -0.0122c^3 + 0.8051c^2 - 16.7219c + 112.0764, & 16.5 < c < 26. \end{cases} \tag{4.23}$$

Set $\theta_h = 0.05, \theta_s = 0.1$. Monte Carlo optimization method provides the original value of this model. With the help of Matlab, the optimal parameter is found out to be $\lambda = 7.2853$.

Figure 4.10 demonstrates the PRD produced by different methods. Both UIDM ($\lambda = 2$) and OIDM solve the small sample problem quite well. OIDM exhibits a smoother and more accurate result than UIDM.

To show the advantage of the optimization model set up in this paper which is abbreviated to model A, another optimization model, model B, is also examined.

Model B: $\begin{aligned} &\min F(\lambda), \\ &\text{s.t. } \lambda \in (0, 20). \end{aligned}$

The resultant optimal parameter is $\lambda^b = 19.9878$. Correspondingly, $F(\lambda^b) = 8.4626 \times 10^{-5}$. The outcome of model A is denoted as λ^a and $F(\lambda^a) = 3.5673 \times 10^{-4}$. It seems that model B is more effective than model A with lower Fluctuation Index. But the Departure Measures tell a different story. $\theta_h(\lambda^a) = 0.0500, \theta_s(\lambda^a) = 0.0899, \theta_h(\lambda^b) = 0.0809$ and

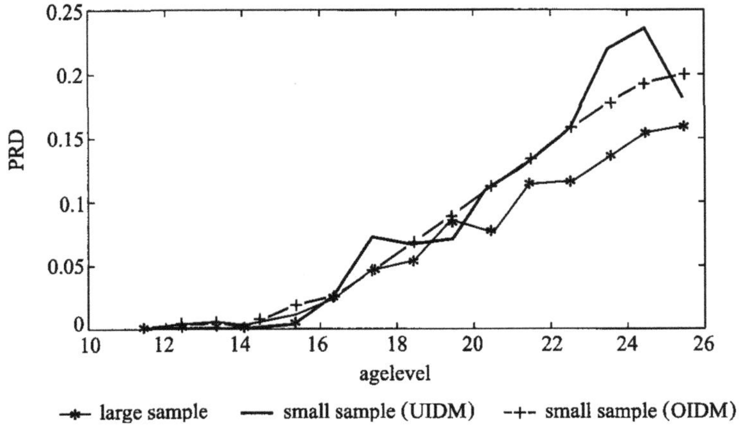

Fig. 4.10 Comparison between 1D PRDs

$\theta_s(\lambda^b) = 0.1499$. Therefore, although PRD curve with λ^b fluctuates less in comparison to that withλ^a, it experiences greater departure.

4.4.4.2 *OIDM in 2D Case*

In Section 4.4.3, UIDM ($\lambda = 2$) is applied to a 2D small sample problem in order to find the relationship between PRD surface of CHD and two risk factors – age and BMI.

Now OIDM is applied to the same problem. Bell-shaped Information Diffusion Function is chosen as $e^{-\frac{|w_n^{(1)} - v^{(1)}|^2}{\lambda_1} - \frac{|w_n^{(2)} - v^{(2)}|^2}{\lambda_2}}$. The process to find out the optimized parameter $\lambda = [\lambda_1, \lambda_2]$ is analogous to that in 1D case.

Construct fluctuation Index as:

$$F(\lambda) = \int_a^b \int_c^d \left(\left(\frac{\partial^2 p^\lambda}{\partial {v^{(1)}}^2} \right) + \left(\frac{\partial^2 p^\lambda}{\partial {v^{(2)}}^2} \right) \right) dv^{(1)} dv^{(2)}. \tag{4.24}$$

The triangle-based cubic interpolation is used to fit the sample surface. Set $\theta_h = 0.3, \theta_s = 0.2$ and $\lambda_i \in (0, 20), i = 1, 2$.

The solution of 2D optimization model is $[\lambda_1, \lambda_2] = [6.8064, 3.8395]$.

Obviously, OIDM also exhibits a smoother and more accurate result than UIDM in 2D case (see Figure 4.11).

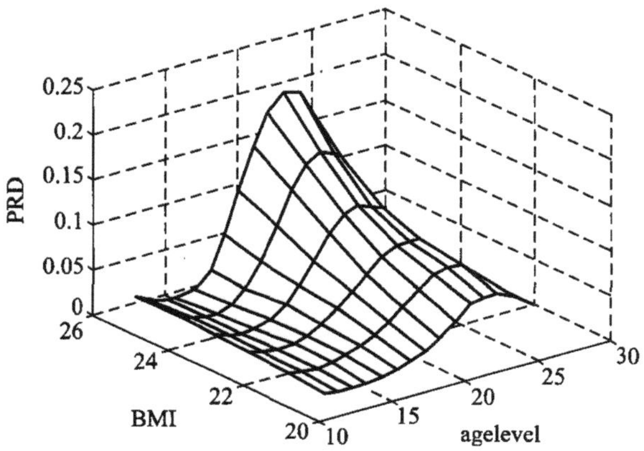

Fig. 4.11 2D OIDM PRD surface

4.5 Conclusion

In this chapter we use fuzzy comprehensive evaluation and fuzzy information processing to evaluate and analyze the risk of certain diseases, but these fuzzy techniques are also useful in dealing with other problems. Another thing worthy of our attention is that we have successfully combined fuzzy technique with other deterministic and statistical methods. This approach is called 'Hybrid' technique (See Shang, Lu, Xu and Chen (2001)) and has been applied to insurance industry and achieved positive results in recent years (See Cummins and Derig (1997)).

References

Cummins J D, Derig R A. (1997). Fuzzy financial pricing of property-liability insurance, *North American Actuarial Journal*, **1**, 21-40.

Huang C F, Shi Y. (2002). *Towards Efficient Fuzzy Information Processing*, Physica-Verlage.

Li A D. (1986). *Foundation and Applications of Fuzzy Mathematics*, Xinjiang People's Press.

Shang H J, et al. (2003). *Population, Disease, Insurance*, Fudan University Press.

Shang H J, Lu Y C, Xu X M, Chen Q. (2001). The 'Hybrid' Technique for Risk Analysis of Some Diseases, *Chinese Annuals of Mathematics*, **22**(4), Ser. B 475-484.

Shang H J, Lu Y C, Shen Y. (2000). A 2-D Information Limited Diffusion Method with Optimum Parameters, *Proceedings of the NAFIPS-2000 Conference*, Atlanta, USA.

Shang H J, Wu X Y, Lu Y C, Shen Y. (2001). The Choice of Information Diffusion Function with Optimum Parameters, *Proceedings of Joint 9th IFSA World Congress and 20th NAFIPS International Conference*, Vancouver, Canada.

Shang H J, Lu Y C, Jin P. (2003). Higher Dimensional Information Diffusion and Its Application, *Proceedings of the NAFIPS-2003 Conference*, Chicago, USA.

Zhang S W, Lu Y C, Zhu W X. (1991). *Fuzzy Mathematics and Its Applications*, Tongji University Press.

Chapter 5

Application of Fuzzy Mathematics to Actuarial Science

5.1 Introduction

Fuzzy sets were introduced in 1965, when Lotfi A. Zadeh published his historic article 'Fuzzy Sets', where he described the concept of a fuzzy set and some basic principles of fuzzy set theory (FST).

The first application of FST to insurance and actuarial problems is due to De Wit (1982). Some eight years later, fuzzy sets were rediscovered by Lemaire (1990), where the examples presented cover such areas as underwriting, reinsurance and financial mathematics. Ostasziewski (1993) presented a review of possible applications of FST in actuarial science in areas such as the economics of risk, the time value of money, individual models, collective models and risk classification. Cummins and Derrig (1993, 1997), Derrig and Ostaszewski (1994, 1995) and Young (1996) have applied the fuzzy approach in non-life insurance context. Buehlmann and Berliner (1992), Berliner and Buehlmann (1993) have developed the theory of fuzzy 'zooming' of cash flows, while Babad and Berliner (1994, 1995) have used a slightly different approach towards the uncertainty-the Intervals of Possibilities. Other areas of applications have included asset allocation (Guo and Huang, 1996), underwriting and marketing (Hellman, 1995: Young, 1993), the matching of assets and liabilities (Chang and Wang, 1995).

In recent years more and more articles and books about the theory and applications of FST have been published all over the world. In this chapter, the following sections are presented the basic definitions and principles of FST and the fuzzy tools and techniques that have been applied to actuarial and insurance problems. Section 5.3 gives the basic definitions, methods and principles, which represent in Insurance Game. Some factors of strategy sets in insurance game are fuzzy factors and its utilities cannot be estimated exactly. The applied example is also given which is on the condition of complete information static game to get Nash equilibrium. Section 5.4 deals with the notion of fuzzy multi-objective groups decision and its uses in the life insurance. Section 5.5 looks at fuzzy cluster method and gives examples of the applications about the risk of complications for some diseases. Regression Forecasting Model of risk with Fuzzy factors is explained in Section 5.6 and applications is presented.

5.2 Some Basic Notions of Fuzzy Set Theory

Definition 5.1 Definition of a fuzzy set: Given a universe of discourse U, a fuzzy set A in it is defined by

$$\mu_A : U \to M.$$

μ_A is called the membership function of A and for each element x of U, gives the degree of membership of x in A, M is an ordered set, normally is taken to be the unit interval, $M = [0, 1]$. The definition is a generalization of the characteristic function of an ordinary set, where the characteristic function χ of a set A is

$$\chi(x) = \begin{cases} 0, & \text{if } x \notin A, \\ 1, & \text{if } x \in A. \end{cases}$$

The two extreme values 0 and 1 represent, respectively, the lowest and highest degree of membership. The degree of membership could be interpreted as the "truth value" of a statement such as "x is a member of A".

Definition 5.2 The α-cut of a fuzzy set A: The α-cut of a fuzzy set A is the crisp set A_α defined as

$$A_\alpha = \{x \in U : \mu_A(x) \geqslant \alpha\}.$$

It could be thought of as an error interval whose truth value is α, i.e. there is a $\alpha\%$ belief that a particular element is in the set. For example a 0.90-cut of A contains all elements that are at least 90% in the set,and a 1-cut contains the elements that are for certain in the set. In the decision making process, the fuzzy decision, represented by a fuzzy set is replaced by an appropriate α-cut, and the so defined crisp set gives the set of optimal decisions. The α-level in a fuzzy set A is $A_\alpha = \{x \in U : \mu_A(x) = \alpha\}$ and $A_\alpha = \bigcup\limits_{k \geqslant \alpha} A_k$.

Definition 5.3 A normal fuzzy set A: A fuzzy set A is normal if there is an $x \in U : \mu_A(x) = 1$; if it is not and $m = \sup \mu_A(x), x \in U$, then the new set $A' = A/m$, with $\mu_A(x) = \mu_A(x)/m$ is normal.

Definition 5.4 A convex fuzzy set: $A \subset R$ is convex if for $c \in [0, 1]$ and for any x and y

$$\mu_A(cx + (1 - c)y) \geqslant \min(\mu_A(x), \mu_A(y)).$$

Definition 5.5 The union: The union of fuzzy sets A and B is the fuzzy set $A \cup B$ with membership function

$$\mu_{A\cup B}(x) = \max(\mu_A(x), \mu_B(x)), \quad x \in U.$$

Definition 5.6 The intersection: The intersection of A and B is $A \cap B$ with membership function

$$\mu_{A\cap B}(x) = \min(\mu_A(x), \mu_B(x)), \quad x \in U.$$

Definition 5.7 The complement: The complement-A of a fuzzy set A is defined as

$$\mu_{-A}(x) = 1 - \mu_A(x).$$

Definition 5.8 Relation: A fuzzy relation, R, in the product space $X \times Y = \{(x, y) | x \in X, y \in Y\}$ with each ordered pair (x, y) a grade of membership $\mu_R(x, y)$ in R. More generally, an n-ary fuzzy relation in a product space $X = X_1 \times X_2 \times \cdots \times X_n$ is a fuzzy set in X characterized by n-variate membership function $\mu_R(x_1, x_2, \cdots, x_n), x_n \in X_i, i = 1, 2, \cdots, n$.

Definition 5.9 Composition of relation: If R_1 and R_2 are two fuzzy relations in X^2, then by the composition of $R_1$and R_2 is meant a fuzzy relation in X^2 which is denoted by $R_1 \circ R_2$ and is defined by

$$\mu_{R_1 \circ R_2}(x, y) = \sup_v \min[R_1(x, v), R_2(v, y)],$$

where the supremum is taken overall v in X.

Definition 5.10 Fuzzy sets induced by mappings: Let f: $X \to Y$ be a mapping from X to Y,with the image of x under f denoted by $y = f(x)$. Let A be a fuzzy set in X. Then the mapping f induces a fuzzy set B in

Y whose membership function is given by $\mu_B(y) = \sup_{x \in f^{-1}(y)} \mu_A(x)$ where $f^{-1}(y)$ denotes the set of points in X which are mapped by f into y.

5.3 Application of FST in Life Insurance Game

5.3.1 *Background*

With the mature of China's capital market and the reform of social secure system, life insurance is playing an increasingly important role in people's daily life. China, as a rising and broad insurance market, is attracting more and more attention of insurance companies all over the world. Generally the insurance companies in Shanghai can be divided into two types: Sino-funded, which is characterized by its early entrance into the market comparatively strong social background and larger market share. We nickname it the aboriginal. The opponent, whom we call the newcomer, is foreign-funded company with the characters of more advanced management technology and fund. The two parties are restricted not only by fund, staff, system support and policy but also by the capacity of the market. They set various management aims according to their development stages, which will directly affect the company's decision-making on exploiting new insurance product. Moreover, confined by the capacity of the market, an insurance product of one company will inevitably affect and be affected its counterpart of any other company. Therefore, only if full consideration of the bilateral effects, they will reach the equilibrium by developing products of various orientations.

Generally, a company is inclined to take competition into consideration in its process of new product exploitation. Seeing that not yet a model has been set up in this field, we are now trying building one that predicts the utility of the company by looking into the effects of operating factors. Due to the fuzziness of these factors and the utility, we turn to Fuzzy Mathematics to solve the problem. Here we have built a game model, which is more scientific and feasible.

5.3.2 *Some Relative Concepts and Theorems*

Definition 5.11 Judgement Number of Importance: we define ${}_ie_{jk}$ as Judgement Number of Importance to indicate the comparison between the importance of f_j to $S_i \in S$ and that of f_k. The relation between linguistic operator of importance and Judgement Number of Importance is listed below.

Table 5.1

Importance	same	somewhat	more or less
Judgement Number	1	2	3
Importance	notable	obvious	quite
Judgement Number	4	5	6
Importance	very much	extraordinary	extreme
Judgement Number	7	8	9

Definition 5.12 Judgement Matrix of Importance:
Assembling all ${}_ie_{jk}$ from each two factors of F with conditions:
(1) ${}_ie_{jk} > 0$,
(2) ${}_ie_{jk} = 1/{}_ie_{kj}$,
(3) $j = k$, ${}_ie_{jj} = {}_ie_{kk} = 1$,
we get

$$ {}_iE = \begin{bmatrix} {}_ie_{11} & {}_ie_{12} & \cdots & {}_ie_{1k} \\ {}_ie_{21} & {}_ie_{22} & \cdots & {}_ie_{2k} \\ \cdots & \cdots & \cdots & \cdots \\ {}_ie_{k1} & {}_ie_{k2} & \cdots & {}_ie_{kk} \end{bmatrix}_{k\times k} \qquad (i = 1, 2, \cdots, m) $$

as the Judgement Matrix of Importance of factor set F to strategy S_i.

Definition 5.13 Completely Consistent Judgement Matrix Of Importance ${}_iE$, if its element satisfies ${}_ie_{jl} \cdot {}_ie_{lk} = {}_ie_{jk}$.

Definition 5.14 Matrix of the Grade of Membership about Importance: we set

$$ A = \begin{bmatrix} \alpha_{11} & \alpha_{12} & \cdots & \alpha_{1k} \\ \alpha_{21} & \alpha_{22} & \cdots & \alpha_{2k} \\ \cdots & \cdots & \cdots & \cdots \\ \alpha_{m1} & \alpha_{m2} & \cdots & \alpha_{mk} \end{bmatrix}_{m\times k} $$

as the Matrix of the Grade of Membership about Importance of factor set F to strategy set $\widetilde{S}$. where $\alpha_{ij} = \frac{a_{ij}}{\sum_{j=1}^{k} a_{ij}}$, $a_{ij} = \sqrt[k]{{}_ie_{j1} * \cdots * {}_ie_{jk}}(i = 1, 2, \cdots, m, j = 1, 2, \cdots, k)$. Therefore a_{ij} indicates to what degree does the factor f_j associate with strategy S_i, affect the utility of X, i.e. the weight.

Definition 5.15 Judgement Number of Superiority: we define ${}_ih_{jk}$ as Judgement Number of Superiority to indicate whether factor f_i make the utility of X advantageous or disadvantageous when participant Y change its strategy from $\widetilde{S}_j$ to $\widetilde{S}_k$. The relation between linguistic operator of superiority and Judgement Number of Superiority is listed below.

Table 5.2

Superiority	same	somewhat	more or less
Judgement Number	1	2	3
Superiority	notable	obvious	quite
Judgement Number	4	5	6
Superiority	very much	extraordinary	extreme
Judgement Number	7	8	9

Definition 5.16 Judgement Matrix of Superiority: assembling all ${}_ih_{jk}$ from each two strategies of $\widetilde{S}$ with conditions:
(1) ${}_ih_{jk} > 0$,
(2) ${}_ih_{jk} = 1/{}_ih_{kj}$,
(3) $j = k$, ${}_ih_{jj} = {}_ih_{kk} = 1$,
we get

$$
{}_iH = \begin{bmatrix} {}_ih_{11} & {}_ih_{12} & \cdots & {}_ih_{1n} \\ {}_ih_{21} & {}_ih_{22} & \cdots & {}_ih_{2n} \\ \cdots & \cdots & \cdots & \cdots \\ {}_ih_{n1} & {}_ih_{n2} & \cdots & {}_ih_{nn} \end{bmatrix}_{n\times n} \qquad (i = 1, 2, \cdots, n)
$$

as the Judgement Matrix of Superiority of strategy set $\widetilde{S}$ to factor f_i.

Definition 5.17 Completely Consistent Judgement Matrix of superiority ${}_iH$, if its element satisfies ${}_ih_{jl} \cdot {}_ih_{lk} = {}_ih_{jk}$.

Definition 5.18 Matrix of the Grade of Membership about superiority: we set

$$
R = \begin{bmatrix} r_{11} & r_{12} & \cdots & r_{1n} \\ r_{21} & r_{22} & \cdots & r_{2n} \\ \cdots & \cdots & \cdots & \cdots \\ r_{k1} & r_{k2} & \cdots & r_{kn} \end{bmatrix}_{k\times n}
$$

as the Matrix of the Grade of Membership about Superiority of factor set F to strategy set $\widetilde{S}$. where $r_{ij} = \sqrt[n]{{}_ih_{j1} * \cdots *_i h_{jn}}$ $(i = 1, 2, \cdots, k, j =$

$1, 2, \cdots, n$). It is clear that r_{ij} means to what degree does the factor f_i, associated with strategy $\widetilde{S}_j$, affect the utility of X.

Definition 5.19 According to the operation $(\bullet, \oplus)$, we signify utility matrix with $P = A \bullet R = (u_{ij})_{m*n}$, regard $u_{ij} = \sum_{t=1}^{k} \alpha_{it} r_{tj}$ as the utility of X when it chooses strategy S_i, meanwhile Y selects strategy $\widetilde{S}_j$.

We regard every element in $\alpha_i = (\alpha_{i1}, \alpha_{i2}, \cdots, \alpha_{ii})$ as the weight of X, and consider superiority $r_{1j}, r_{2j}, \cdots, r_{kj}$ of factor $f_1, \cdots, f_k$ when Y selects strategy $\widetilde{S}_j$, so we can denote the expectation of utility with $u_{ij} = \sum_{t=1}^{k} \alpha_{it} r_{tj}$.

Theorem 5.1 *If Judgement Matrix is completely consistent, its maximum eigenvalue is equal to the dimension of the matrix.*

Because it is hard to satisfy the complete consistence in daily practice, we use general consistence, inspection index is $c_m = \frac{\lambda_{\max} - m}{(m-1)R_m}$, R_m is random consistence index (please refer to the graph below), therefore the judgement matrix will become satisfactorily consistent when $c_m \leqslant 0.1$, otherwise we need adjust the judgement number until $c_m \leqslant 0.1$.

Table 5.3

m	1	2	3	4	5
R_m	0.00	0.00	0.52	0.89	1.12
m	6	7	8	9	10
R_m	1.26	1.36	1.41	1.46	1.49
m	11	12	13	14	
R_m	1.52	1.54	1.56	1.58	

As is defined above, we can acquire A as the Matrix of the Grade of Membership about Importance of X and R as the Matrix of the Grade of Membership about Superiority of X. Similarly we can obtain B as the Matrix of the Grade of Membership about Importance of Y and $\widetilde{R}$ as the Matrix of the Grade of Membership about Superiority of Y. we can get the utility matrix of X and Y with $P = A \bullet R = (u_{ij})_{m*n}$, $\widetilde{P} = B \bullet \widetilde{R} = (\widetilde{u}_{ij})_{n*m}$, and it is from P and the transit matrix of $\widetilde{P}$ we can construct utility pair matrix $G = ((u_{ij}, \widetilde{u}_{ji}))_{m*n}$, i.e.

$$\begin{bmatrix} (u_{11}, \widetilde{u}_{11}) & \cdots & (u_{1j}, \widetilde{u}_{j1}) & \cdots & (u_{1n}, \widetilde{u}_{n1}) \\ \cdots & \cdots & \cdots & \cdots & \cdots \\ (u_{i1}, \widetilde{u}_{1i}) & \cdots & (u_{ij}, \widetilde{u}_{ji}) & \cdots & (u_{in}, \widetilde{u}_{ni}) \\ \cdots & \cdots & \cdots & \cdots & \cdots \\ (u_{m1}, \widetilde{u}_{1m}) & \cdots & (u_{mj}, \widetilde{u}_{jm}) & \cdots & (u_{mn}, \widetilde{u}_{nm}) \end{bmatrix}.$$

5.3.3 *Model of Game*

Definition 5.20 Nash equilibrium: Let u_{ij} be the utility of X when X selects strategy S_i, while Y selects strategy $\widetilde{S}_j$. Let $\widetilde{u}_{ji}$ be utility of Y when X chooses strategy S_j, while Y chooses strategy $\widetilde{S}_i$. If strategies S_i and $\widetilde{S}_h$ satisfy $u_{th} \geqslant u_{ih}$, $i \neq t$, $S_i, S_t \in S$ and $\widetilde{u}_{th} \geqslant \widetilde{u}_{tj}, j \neq h, \widetilde{S}_j, \widetilde{S}_h \in \widetilde{S}$. Then the strategy combination of S_i and $\widetilde{S}_h$ is called Nash equilibrium.

Sometimes, the Nash equilibrium defined by definition 10 does not exist. At this time what the participants concern is the expected utility. If the probability of Y to select strategy $\widetilde{S}_j, \widetilde{p}_j \geqslant 0 (j = 1, 2, \cdots, n, \sum\limits_{j=1}^{n} \widetilde{p}_j = 1)$ is known, then the expected utility of participant X is $v_i = \sum\limits_{j=1}^{n} \widetilde{p}_j u_{ij}, i = 1, 2, \cdots, m$ when X selects strategy S_i. For the same sake, if the probability of X to select strategy S_i, $p_i \geqslant 0$ $(i = 1, 2, \cdots, m, \sum\limits_{i=1}^{m} p_i = 1)$ is known, then the expected utility of Y is $v_j = \sum\limits_{i=1}^{m} p_i \widetilde{u}_{ji}, j = 1, 2, \cdots, n$, when Y selects strategy $\widetilde{S}_j$. In above cases, $p = (p_1, p_2, \cdots, p_m)$ and $\widetilde{p} = (\widetilde{p}_1, \widetilde{p}_2, \cdots, \widetilde{p}_n)$ is called the "mixed strategy" of X and Y respectively.

Definition 5.21 Mixed-Strategy Nash equilibrium: let p and $\widetilde{p}$ be the mixed strategy of X and Y respectively, M and $\widetilde{M}$ be the spaces of their mixed-strategy. If mixed-strategy p^* and $\widetilde{p}^*$ satisfy

$$v(p^*, \widetilde{p}^*) \geqslant v(p, \widetilde{p}^*), \quad p, \widetilde{p}^* \in M,$$

and

$$\widetilde{v}(p^*, \widetilde{p}^*) \geqslant \widetilde{v}(p, \widetilde{p}^*), \quad \widetilde{p}, \widetilde{p}^* \in \widetilde{M},$$

then mixed-strategy combination $(p^*, \widetilde{p}^*)$ is called a Mixed-Strategy Nash equilibrium.

In regard to finite game, we have the conclusion as follows:

Theorem 5.2 *To every finite game, there exist a pure or Mixed-Strategy Nash equilibrium at least.*

5.3.4 *The Example of Application*

5.3.4.1 *The Example*

In 2000, as two pop kinds of insurance products in Shanghai market, the Unit-Linked product and the Par product are paid more and more attention to by many companies and are considered whether to exploit as main product. Here we build a model which involves two companies (suppose there are only two companies), the aboriginal and the newcomer, to start a game.

S and $\widetilde{S}$ are the strategy sets of the aboriginal and the newcomer. Let $S = \widetilde{S} = \{S_1, S_2\}$. S_1 stands for the strategy to exploit the Unit-Linked product while S_2, stands for the strategy to exploit the Par product. We also let $F = \{f_1, \cdots, f_7\}$ as the aboriginal's factor set, whose elements $f_1, \cdots, f_7$ denote yield, market share, financial stability, competition, return of investment, administration level and system support, while $\widetilde{F} = \{\widetilde{f_1}, \cdots, \widetilde{f_9}\}$ as the newcomer's factor set, whose elements $\widetilde{f_1}, \cdots, \widetilde{f_9}$ are the nine factors such as yield, market share, financial stability, fame of trademark, the risk of eluding policies, competition, return of investment, administration level and system support.

(1) First let us consider from the side of the aboriginal. As far as the Unit-Linked product is concerned, the Judgement Matrix of Importance is

$$
{}_1E = \begin{bmatrix}
1 & 5 & 2 & 4 & 2 & 1/5 & 1/6 \\
1/5 & 1 & 1/6 & 1/2 & 1/5 & 1/8 & 1/9 \\
1/2 & 6 & 1 & 5 & 1/2 & 1/4 & 1/5 \\
1/4 & 2 & 1/5 & 1 & 1/4 & 1/8 & 1/9 \\
1/2 & 5 & 2 & 4 & 1 & 1/4 & 1/5 \\
5 & 8 & 4 & 8 & 4 & 1 & 1/2 \\
6 & 9 & 5 & 9 & 5 & 2 & 1
\end{bmatrix}_{7\times 7}.
$$

Since ${}_1E$ is not completely consistent, we consider whether the matrix is generally consistent. After calculate $c_m = \frac{\lambda_{\max} - m}{(m-1)R_m}$ according to Theorem 5.1 ($\lambda_{\max}$, the maximum eigenvalue of ${}_1E$ equals 7.5 and $m = 7, R_m = 1.36$), we find $c_m = 0.06127 < 0.1$ which means the consistence of ${}_1E$ is satisfied enough namely it is generally consistent.

Similarly, as far as the Par product is concerned, the Judgement Matrix of Importance is

$$
{}_2E = \begin{bmatrix} 1 & 4 & 2 & 3 & 2 & 1/5 & 1/5 \\ 1/4 & 1 & 1/4 & 1/3 & 1/3 & 1/7 & 1/6 \\ 1/2 & 4 & 1 & 3 & 1/4 & 1/3 & 1/3 \\ 1/3 & 3 & 1/3 & 1 & 1/4 & 1/4 & 1/3 \\ 1/2 & 3 & 4 & 4 & 1 & 1/3 & 1/2 \\ 5 & 7 & 3 & 4 & 3 & 1 & 1 \\ 5 & 6 & 3 & 3 & 2 & 1/2 & 1 \end{bmatrix}_{7\times 7} .
$$

${}_2E$ is still not completely consistent, so we have to consider whether the matrix is generally consistent. After calculate $c_m = \frac{\lambda_{\max} - m}{(m-1)R_m}$ according to Theorem 5.1 ($\lambda_{\max}$, the maximum eigenvalue of ${}_2E$ equals 7.64 and $m = 7, R_m = 1.36$), we find $c_m = 0.07843 < 0.1$ which means the consistence of ${}_2E$ is satisfied enough namely it is generally consistent.

Then we can get A as the Matrix of the Grade of Membership about Importance of factor set F to strategy set S,

$$
A = \begin{bmatrix} 0.1057 & 0.0221 & 0.0799 & 0.0295 & 0.0919 & 0.2820 & 0.3889 \\ 0.1238 & 0.0325 & 0.0873 & 0.0554 & 0.1374 & 0.3127 & 0.2509 \end{bmatrix} .
$$

Next, let us analyze the influence of $\tilde{S}$ on the superiority of each factor in F which means the newcomer's action is considered.

$$
{}_1H = \begin{bmatrix} 1 & 3 \\ 1/3 & 1 \end{bmatrix}, \quad {}_2H = \begin{bmatrix} 1 & 2 \\ 1/2 & 1 \end{bmatrix}, \quad {}_3H = \begin{bmatrix} 1 & 1 \\ 1 & 1 \end{bmatrix}, \quad {}_4H = \begin{bmatrix} 1 & 1/3 \\ 3 & 1 \end{bmatrix},
$$

$$
{}_5H = \begin{bmatrix} 1 & 1/3 \\ 3 & 1 \end{bmatrix}, \quad {}_6H = \begin{bmatrix} 1 & 1/2 \\ 2 & 1 \end{bmatrix}, \quad {}_7H = \begin{bmatrix} 1 & 1/2 \\ 2 & 1 \end{bmatrix}.
$$

Obviously, the matrixes above are all completely consistent, and then the Matrix of the Grade of Membership about Superiority is easy to get. We notate it as

$$
R = \begin{bmatrix} 1.7321 & 0.5774 \\ 1.4142 & 0.7071 \\ 1 & 1 \\ 0.5774 & 1.7321 \\ 1.4142 & 0.7071 \\ 0.7071 & 1.4142 \\ 0.7071 & 1.4142 \end{bmatrix}_{7\times 2} .
$$

Finally we acquire the utility matrix P of the aboriginal,

$$P = A \bullet R = \begin{bmatrix} 0.9156 & 1.221 \\ 0.9725 & 1.1719 \end{bmatrix}.$$

(2) Second let us consider from the side of the newcomer.

As far as the Unit-Linked product is concerned, the Judgement Matrix of Importance is

$$_1E = \begin{bmatrix} 1 & 1/6 & 1/3 & 1/7 & 2 & 1/5 & 1/3 & 1/5 & 1/5 \\ 6 & 1 & 4 & 1/2 & 5 & 2 & 4 & 2 & 2 \\ 3 & 1/4 & 1 & 1/5 & 2 & 1/3 & 1/2 & 1/2 & 1/3 \\ 7 & 2 & 5 & 1 & 7 & 3 & 4 & 2 & 2 \\ 1/2 & 1/5 & 1/2 & 1/7 & 1 & 1/5 & 1/4 & 1/4 & 1/3 \\ 5 & 1/2 & 3 & 1/3 & 5 & 1 & 3 & 2 & 3 \\ 3 & 1/4 & 2 & 1/4 & 4 & 1/3 & 1 & 1/3 & 1/3 \\ 5 & 1/2 & 2 & 1/2 & 4 & 1/2 & 3 & 1 & 1/2 \\ 5 & 1/2 & 3 & 1/2 & 3 & 1/3 & 3 & 2 & 1 \end{bmatrix}_{9\times 9}.$$

Since $_1E$ is not completely consistent, we consider whether the matrix is generally consistent. After calculate $c_m = \frac{\lambda_{\max} - m}{(m-1)R_m}$ according to Theorem 5.1 ($\lambda_{\max}$, the maximum eigenvalue of $_1E$ equals 9.5229 and $m = 9, R_m = 1.46$), we find $c_m = 0.04477 < 0.1$ which means the consistence of $_1E$ is satisfied enough namely it is generally consistent.

Similarly, as far as the Par product is concerned, the Judgement Matrix of Importance is

$$_2E = \begin{bmatrix} 1 & 1/6 & 1/3 & 1/6 & 2 & 1/4 & 1/3 & 1/4 & 1/4 \\ 6 & 1 & 4 & 1/2 & 4 & 2 & 3 & 3 & 2 \\ 3 & 1/4 & 1 & 1/4 & 2 & 1/3 & 1/2 & 1/3 & 1/2 \\ 6 & 2 & 4 & 1 & 7 & 3 & 4 & 2 & 2 \\ 1/2 & 1/4 & 1/2 & 1/7 & 1 & 1/5 & 1/4 & 1/4 & 1/3 \\ 4 & 1/2 & 3 & 1/3 & 5 & 1 & 2 & 2 & 3 \\ 3 & 1/3 & 2 & 1/4 & 4 & 1/2 & 1 & 1/2 & 1/3 \\ 4 & 1/3 & 3 & 1/2 & 4 & 1/2 & 2 & 1 & 2 \\ 4 & 1/2 & 2 & 1/2 & 3 & 1/3 & 3 & 1/2 & 1 \end{bmatrix}_{9\times 9}.$$

$_2E$ is still not completely consistent, so we have to consider whether the matrix is generally consistent. After calculate $c_m = \frac{\lambda_{\max} - m}{(m-1)R_m}$ according to Theorem 5.1 ($\lambda_{\max}$, the maximum eigenvalue of $_2E$ equals 9.5139 and $m = 9, R_m = 1.46$), we find $c_m = 0.04400 < 0.1$ which means the consistence of $_2E$ is satisfied enough namely it is generally consistent.

Then we can get B as the Matrix of the Grade of Membership about Importance of factor set $\tilde{F}$ to strategy set $\tilde{S}$.

$$B = \begin{bmatrix} 0.0276 & 0.1960 & 0.0497 & 0.2589 & 0.0266 & 0.1544 & 0.0614 & 0.1058 & 0.1196 \\ 0.0423 & 0.1965 & 0.0517 & 0.2518 & 0.0276 & 0.1461 & 0.0703 & 0.1168 & 0.0969 \end{bmatrix}.$$

Next, let us analyze the influence on each factor's superiority in $\widetilde{F}$ to $\widetilde{S}$, when the aboriginal's action is considered.

$${}_1H = \begin{bmatrix} 1 & 1/2 \\ 2 & 1 \end{bmatrix}, \quad {}_2H = \begin{bmatrix} 1 & 1/2 \\ 2 & 1 \end{bmatrix}, \quad {}_3H = \begin{bmatrix} 1 & 1 \\ 1 & 1 \end{bmatrix},$$

$${}_4H = \begin{bmatrix} 1 & 1/3 \\ 3 & 1 \end{bmatrix}, \quad {}_5H = \begin{bmatrix} 1 & 2 \\ 1/2 & 1 \end{bmatrix}, \quad {}_6H = \begin{bmatrix} 1 & 1/3 \\ 3 & 1 \end{bmatrix},$$

$${}_7H = \begin{bmatrix} 1 & 1/2 \\ 2 & 1 \end{bmatrix}, \quad {}_8H = \begin{bmatrix} 1 & 4 \\ 1/4 & 1 \end{bmatrix}, \quad {}_9H = \begin{bmatrix} 1 & 2 \\ 1/2 & 1 \end{bmatrix}.$$

Obviously, the matrixes above are all completely consistent, and then the Matrix of the Grade of Membership about Superiority is easy to get. We notate it as

$$\tilde{R} = \begin{bmatrix} 0.7071 & 1.4142 \\ 0.7071 & 1.4142 \\ 1 & 1 \\ 0.5774 & 1.7321 \\ 1.4142 & 0.7071 \\ 0.5774 & 1.7321 \\ 0.7071 & 1.4142 \\ 2 & 0.5 \\ 1.4142 & 0.7071 \end{bmatrix}_{9\times 2}.$$

Finally we acquire the utility matrix $\widetilde{P}$ of the newcomer,

$$\widetilde{P} = B \bullet \widetilde{R} = \begin{bmatrix} 0.9082 & 1.3249 \\ 0.7450 & 1.3245 \end{bmatrix}.$$

(3) To construct the utility pair matrix G, we combine P (the utility matrix of the aboriginal) and the transit of $\widetilde{P}$(the utility matrix of the newcomer),

$$G = \begin{bmatrix} (0.9156, 0.9802) & (1.2210, 0.7450) \\ (0.9725, 1.3249) & (1.1719, 1.3245) \end{bmatrix}.$$

By use of the knowledge of complete information static game, the above one has a Nash equilibrium at the "left-down" corner of matrix G, that is (0.9725,1.3249). That is to say, to balance both utilities the aboriginal should exploit the Par product and the newcomer should exploit the Unit-Linked product.

5.3.4.2 *Conclusion*

In regard of the insurance company's utility, this section provide the administrator a relatively scientific decision-making method-game which means the two participants determine their product exploitation orientation on condition of limited resource after full consideration of the utilities of both sides. Since the indefinite feature of many factors, the common method of utility determining is not suitable any more, so we use fuzzy mathematics and optimization theory to solve this problem. Due to the limitation of the article, we only consider the simplest case-the complete information static game. So we can expand this idea to the incomplete information dynamic game in practical application.

5.4 Decision-Making Method Applied in Life Insurance Companies

5.4.1 *Background*

Many world-famous insurance companies start their business affairs in Chinese insurance market,which is wide and potential, since China entered into WTO. Whether state owned insurance companies or foreign ones, they all try to develop their business in this big market. There are two problems that they must face with:

1. To exploit which type of insurance product.

Pure safeguard,pure investment, both safeguard and investment(where the effect of safeguard is more notable), both safeguard and investment(where the effect of investment is more notable).

2. To invest which kind of project?

For example of investment projects, for simple they are denoted by D1, D2, D3, D4 respectively. The supervisors of the insurance company, not only need to consider which type of most popular investment project can be developed, but also they need to consider which type the company wants to develop. After balancing both of them, they can then decide which type should be developed ultimately. By all appearances, "What type project can be developed" is based on current impersonal condition, considering all factors synthetically and then decide if the company has the ability to develop such life insurance investment type. Because the policymaker decides it passively according to the current impersonal condition, we define this method of decision as Passive Decision. That is, we do the two-stage fuzzy comprehensive valuation to the above four categories according to all the impersonal condition. But "what project type want to be developed" is based on the life insurance company's short-term or metaphase operational goals. This method of decision is initiative, so we define this kind of decision as Initiative Decision. It is sure that such important decision should be co-determined by several supervisors during practical decision, so this is a matter of multi-object fuzzy group decision. Of course, it's the most perfect to consider both of the impersonality condition and the goals. If we do so, we can get the synthetic decision. All of this problems are involved the decision-making in the supervisors of the insurance company. We usually employ the concepts and techniques of probability theory and, more particularly, the tools provided by decision theory, control theory and information theory. What are involved in this section are decision-making in fuzzy environment, so we use FST to deal with these problems.

5.4.2 *The Passive Decision—Two-stage Fuzzy Comprehensive Valuation*

This mathematics model is defined by two-stage fuzzy comprehensive valuation with five primary factors, and each includes several sun-factors.See figure 5.1 for detail:

Now we introduce the procedure of passive decision:

1. Classifying the primary factors and sub-factors, from the fig 5.1 we can know: $U = \{u_1, u_2, u_3, u_4, u_5\}$, $u_i = \{u_{i1}, u_{i2}, \cdots, u_{in}\}$ where $i = 1, 2, 3, 4, 5, \cdots, n$ for different i, i and n needn't to be equal.

2. Setting up the set of weight: the set of weighted primary factors is denoted by ${}_kA = \{a_1, a_2, a_3, a_4, a_5\}, k = 1, 2, 3, 4$, that is, the kth kind of product D_k has the set of weighted primary factors ${}_kA$; the set of weighted sub-factors is denoted by ${}_kA_i = \{{}_ka_{i1}, \cdots, {}_ka_{in}\}$, $k = 1, 2, 3, 4$; $i = 1, 2, \cdots, 5$, that is, ${}_ka_{ij}$ is the jth sub-factor's weight of the product D_k's i^{th} primary factor for product D_k. These weights can be determined by the way of specialist valuation popularly in the world.

3. Setting up the set of valuation: $V = \{v_1, v_2, v_3, v_4\}, v_1, v_2, v_3$ and v_4

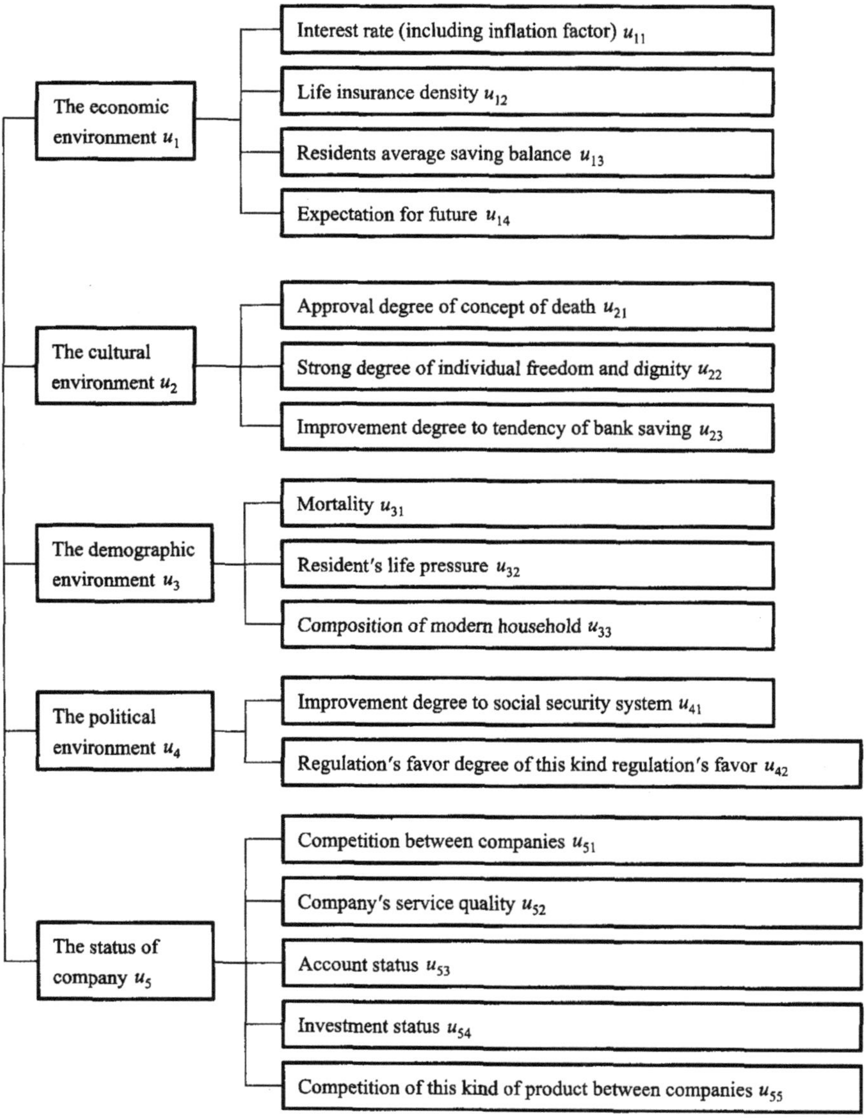

Fig. 5.1

respectively represent "good", "fair good", "common", "not good".

4. One-stage fuzzy comprehensive valuation: with the market statistic data we can know ${}_kR_i$ $(i = 1, 2, \cdots, 5; k = 1, \cdots, 4)$—the matrix of D_k's single factor comprehensive valuation, the respective set of one-stage fuzzy

comprehensive valuation is ${}_kB_i =_k A_i \bullet_k R_i$ $(i = 1, 2, \cdots, 5; k = 1, \cdots, 4)$.

5. Two-stage fuzzy comprehensive valuation: the matrix of one-stage fuzzy comprehensive valuation is the matrix of single factor of two-stage fuzzy comprehensive valuation. So we can get ${}_kR = ({}_kB_1, {}_kB_2, \cdots, {}_kB_5)^T$, and the product D_k's set of two-stage fuzzy comprehensive valuation is ${}_kB' = {}_kA \bullet {}_kR$ $(k = 1, 2, 3, 4)$. After normalization it is denoted by ${}_kB = \{r_{k1}, r_{k2}, r_{k3}, r_{k4}\}$,$r_{k1}, r_{k2}, r_{k3}$ and r_{k4} respectively represent the degree of "good", "fairly good", "common", "not good" of D_k.

5.4.3 *The Initiative Decision—Multi-object Fuzzy Group Decision*

Normally, Life insurance company's operating targets are: stable finance, increasing market share, expanding social affluence, improving investment return, reducing managing overhead and decreasing claim ratio, etc.

Obviously, some aspects are contrary, for example, dangling for stable finance means reducing the risk, while this is always accompanied by the cost of reducing revenue and effecting the market share of insurance company. For the supervisors of the insurance company, not everybody's operating goal is the same because of different duty and salary. How to handle this?

Since these objects are fuzzy, we apply the way of multi-object fuzzy group decision to analyze them. According to every decision-maker's preference, we can get the group's preference, then we sort a group of programs on the basis of the group's preference to get the most popular program. Now we concern the objective set: $B = \{b_1, b_2, b_3, b_4, b_5, b_6\}$, where b_1, b_2, b_3, b_4, b_5 and b_6 represents finance stabilization, the increase of market share, the enlargement of social effect, the improvement of investment return, the decrease of managing overhead and the decrease of the claim ration. The set of programs is denoted by $D = \{D_1, D_2, D_3, D_4\}$, where D_1, D_2, D_3, D_4's meaning is same as the meaning in the passive decision.

Let us consider some concepts at first.

Definition 5.22 The decision-maker M_i $(i = 1, 2, \cdots, m)$ contrasts b_j's importance with b_k's importance, where b_j and b_k are factors of object set $(j = 1, 2, \cdots, 6)$. The contrast scale is denoted by ${}_ie_{jk}$, which is denoted as the judgement number of importance. Generally the relation between tone operator of importance and the judgement number of importance is:

Table 5.4

Superiority	same	somewhat	more or less
Judgement Number	1	2	3
Superiority	notable	obvious	quite
Judgement Number	4	5	6
Superiority	very much	extraordinary	extreme
Judgement Number	7	8	9

Definition 5.23 We define the 6×6 square matrix:

$$
{}_iE = \begin{bmatrix} {}_ie_{11} & {}_ie_{12} & \cdots & {}_ie_{16} \\ {}_ie_{21} & {}_ie_{22} & \cdots & {}_ie_{26} \\ \cdots & \cdots & \cdots & \cdots \\ {}_ie_{61} & {}_ie_{62} & \cdots & {}_ie_{66} \end{bmatrix}_{6\times 6},
$$

if it satisfies:
(1) ${}_ie_{jk} > 0$,
(2) ${}_ie_{jk} = 1/{}_ie_{kj}$,
(3) $j = k$, ${}_ie_{jj} = {}_ie_{kk} = 1$,
then ${}_iE$ denotes duality contrast judgement matrix of importance which is decided by the decision-maker M_i.

Definition 5.24 When the factors of matrix ${}_iE$ satisfy the character of transmitting: ${}_ie_{jl} \cdot {}_ie_{lk} = {}_ie_{jk}$, ${}_iE$ is defined as fully unanimous judgement matrix of importance.

Definition 5.25 If $\alpha_i = (\alpha_{i1}, \alpha_{i2}, \cdots, \alpha_{i6})$ $(i = 1, 2, \cdots, m)$ is the membership vector of relative importance, which is determined by the decision-maker M_i $(i = 1, 2, \cdots, m)$, where $\alpha_{ij} = \frac{a_{ij}}{\sum\limits_{j=1}^{6} a_{ij}}$, $a_{ij} = \sqrt[6]{{}_ie_{j1} \cdot \cdots \cdot {}_i e_{j6}}$, $i = 1, 2, \cdots, m$, $j = 1, 2, \cdots, 6$, and $\cdot$ is the multiplication operator.

Then the matrix

$$
A = \begin{bmatrix} \alpha_{11} & \alpha_{12} & \cdots & \alpha_{16} \\ \alpha_{21} & \alpha_{22} & \cdots & \alpha_{26} \\ \cdots & \cdots & \cdots & \cdots \\ \alpha_{m1} & \alpha_{m2} & \cdots & \alpha_{m6} \end{bmatrix}_{m\times 6}
$$

is the decision group's membership matrix of the object set's relative importance.

Definition 5.26 We contrast the superiority of object b_i between program D_k and program D_j. Its contrast scale ${}_ih_{jk}$ is defined by the judgement number of superiority. Generally the relation between tone operator of superiority and the judgement number of superiority is:

Table 5.5

Superiority	same	somewhat	more or less
Judgement Number	1	2	3
Superiority	notable	obvious	quite
Judgement Number	4	5	6
Superiority	very much	extraordinary	extreme
Judgement Number	7	8	9

Definition 5.27 We define the 4×4 square matrix:

$$ {}_iH = \begin{bmatrix} {}_ih_{11} & {}_ih_{12} & \cdots & {}_ih_{14} \\ {}_ih_{21} & {}_ih_{22} & \cdots & {}_ih_{24} \\ \cdots & \cdots & \cdots & \cdots \\ {}_ih_{41} & {}_ih_{42} & \cdots & {}_ih_{46} \end{bmatrix}_{4\times 4}, $$

if it satisfies
(1) ${}_ih_{jk} > 0$,
(2) ${}_ih_{jk}=1/{}_ih_{kj}$,
(3) $j = k, {}_ih_{jj} = {}_ih_{kk} = 1$,
then we regard the matrix ${}_iH$ as duality contrast judgement matrix of object b_i's superiority.

Definition 5.28 When the factors of matrix ${}_iH$ satisfy the character of transmitting: ${}_ih_{jl} \cdot {}_ih_{lk} = {}_ih_{jk}$, the matrix ${}_iH$ is defined as fully unanimous judgement matrix of superiority.

Definition 5.29 We denote $r_j = (r_{1j}, r_{2j}, \cdots, r_{6j})^T$ $(j = 1, 2, \cdots, 4)$ as the membership vector of program D_j's relative superiority, where $r_{ij} = \frac{b_{ij}}{\sum\limits_{j=1}^{4} b_{ij}}$, $b_{ij} = \sqrt[4]{{}_ih_{j1} \cdot \cdots \cdot {}_i h_{j4}}$, $i = 1, 2, \cdots, 6$, $j = 1, 2, \cdots, 4$, $\cdot$ is the multiplication operator.

Then the matrix

$$ R = \begin{bmatrix} r_{11} & r_{12} & \cdots & r_{14} \\ r_{21} & r_{22} & \cdots & r_{24} \\ \cdots & \cdots & \cdots & \cdots \\ r_{61} & r_{62} & \cdots & r_{64} \end{bmatrix}_{6\times 4} $$

is defined by the membership matrix of the program set D's relative superiority.

Definition 5.30 With the operator($\bullet$), we say that $V = A \bullet R$ is the decision group's matrix of program set's valuation, where v_{ij} is the decision-maker M_i's valuation of the program D_j.

Theorem 5.3 *When the judgement matrix satisfies fully unanimity, its maximum characteristic root is equal to the matrix's dimension.*

Because it's difficult to satisfy the fully unanimity, in practice we often consider acceptably approximate unanimity. The test index is $c_m = \frac{\lambda_{\max} - m}{(m-1)R_m}$, *where* R_m *is a random unanimity index(we can know* $R_6 = 1.26$, $R_4 = 0.89$ *from the bibliography(3)). So the judgement matrix is considered to satisfy the unanimity when* $c_m \leqslant 0.1$. *If* $c_m > 0.1$, *we should adjust the judgement number until* $c_m \leqslant 0.1$.

Theorem 5.4 $G = (1)_{m\times 4}$ *shows the matrix of superiority program.* $V = (v_{ij})_{m\times 4}$ *show the decision group's matrix of program set's valuation. Then the factor* $1\text{-}v_{ij}$ *of the matrix* $G\text{-}V{=}(1 - v_{ij})_{m\times 4}$ *is the distance between the program* D_j *chose by decision-maker* M_i *with the superior program* ($i = 1, 2, \cdots, m; j = 1, 2, 3, 4$).

Theorem 5.5 u_{ij} *shows the program* D_j*'s membership degree of "superiority" at the point of* M_i*'s view. Then we can get the sum of* D_j*'s square of weighted distance to superiority and square of weighted distance to inferiority in the group decision:*

$$F(u_{1j}, u_{2j}, \cdots, u_{mj}) = \sum_{i=1}^{m} [u_{ij}{}^2(1 - v_{ij})^2 + (1 - u_{ij})^2 v_{ij}{}^2],$$

if $u_{1j} = 1/[1 + (1 - v_{1j})^2/v_{1j}{}^2], u_{2j} = 1/[1 + (1 - v_{2j})^2/v_{2j}{}^2], \cdots, u_{mj} = 1/[1 + (1 - v_{mj})^2/v_{mj}{}^2]$, *F will be minimal.*

Now we see the procedure of the initiative decision on six objects.

First, each decision-maker judges the degree of importance between two objects according to his experience and knowledge, then determines the duality contrast judgement matrix of importance. After the unanimity test and adjustment if requisite, we can get the normalized vector of membership degree of relative importance between two objects for each decision-maker. At last we will know the matrix A—the decision group's matrix of membership degree of object set B's relative importance.

Second, contrast every object's superiority among all programs to get set D's duality contrast judgement matrix of its superiority. After the unanimity test and adjustment if requisite, we can get the normalized vector of membership degree to relative superiority, then know the matrix R—the object set B's matrix of membership degree of program set D's relative superiority.

Third, we can obtain the decision group's valuation matrix of program set D on the basis of $V = A \bullet R$.

Fourth, from Definition 30 and Theorem 5.5 u_{ij} can be calculated, where $i = 1, 2, \cdots, m$, $j = 1, 2, 3, 4$. That is, the decision-maker M_i should choose the program which corresponds to $\max\{u_{i1}, u_{i2}, u_{i3}, u_{i4}\}$, where $i = 1, 2, \cdots, m$.

Fifth, among the decision group everyone's position, responsibility and decision risk are different. And their influence in the group's decision can not be equal. So we determine the weight of every decision-maker and denote them by $\omega_1, \omega_2, \cdots, \omega_m$, where $\omega_i > 0$, $i = 1, 2, \cdots, m$, and $\Sigma\omega_i = 1$.

Sixth, define the characteristic function

$$\lambda_{ij}(M_i, D_j) = \begin{cases} 1, & \text{if } M_i \text{ choose } D_j, \\ 0, & \text{if } M_i \text{ doesn't choose } D_j, \end{cases}$$

where $i = 1, 2, \cdots, m$; $j = 1, 2, 3, 4$.

The group's decision on program is the program that responds $\text{Max}\{\sum_{i=1}^{m} \lambda_{i1}\omega_i, \sum_{i=1}^{m} \lambda_{i2}\omega_i, \cdots, \sum_{i=1}^{m} \lambda_{i4}\omega_i\}$.

5.4.4 *Synthetic Decision*

How to form the synthetic decision from the passive decision and initiative decision? Concerning the operation ability, we mainly use following ways:

1. The way of sort

In the passive decision we have gotten every program's fuzzy set of general valuation ${}_kB=(r_{k1}, r_{k2}, r_{k3}, r_{k4})$, $k = 1, 2, 3, 4$. Now we use $S_k = r_{k1} + r_{k2}$ to represent the degree of "good" or "fairly good" of the kth kind of investment projects. Then we sort S_k from large to small, K_k shows the sorting serial number of D_k, where $k = 1, 2, 3, 4$. Under impersonal condition, smaller the serial number is, more popular the corresponding investment projects is. In the initiative decision, we sort $\sum_{i=1}^{m} \lambda_{ik}\omega_i$ from large to small, where $k = 1, 2, 3, 4$. K' represents the sorting serial number of D_k, that is, we sort the degree that every program satisfies most decision-makers' object. Smaller the serial number is, more satisfactory this kind of investment project is. According to the decision principle—the decision not only can be made under the present impersonal condition, but also satisfies the company's goals. We make $T = \min\{K_1 + K'_1, K_2 + K'_2, K_3 + K'_3, K_4 + K'_4\}$, which corresponding program D_k is our synthetic decision—to develop the k_{th} kind of life insurance investment project.

2. The way of Borda number

The program set D is regard as the domain. And L_i $(i = 1, 2, 3)$ is a linear order about the factors of D. L_1 and L_2 are the linear orders about the factors of D in the passive decision, that is, we sort the four kinds by membership degree of "good" and "fairly good" from large to small and correspondingly regard the orders as L_1 and L_2 in accordance with $B = ({}_1B,{}_2B,{}_3B,{}_4B)^T$—the normalized matrix of two-stage fuzzy comprehensive valuation. And L_3 is the linear order about the factors of D in the initiative decision. We sort $\sum_{i=1}^{m} \lambda_{i1}\omega_i, \sum_{i=1}^{m} \lambda_{i2}\omega_i, \sum_{i=1}^{m} \lambda_{i3}\omega_i, \sum_{i=1}^{m} \lambda_{i4}\omega_i$ from large to small. So lager the sorting serial number is, more superiority the corresponding program is. For $d \in D$, $B_i(d)$ represents the number of factors which are behind d in the linear order L_i. $B(d) = \sum_{i=1}^{m} B_i(d)$, then $B(d)$ is named as Borda number. Four programs are sorted by the corresponding Borda number from large to small, so the program which Borda number is the largest is the best one of synthetic decision.

5.5 The Risk Analysis of Complications for Some Diseases

5.5.1 *Background*

With the development of economy and the improvement of living conditions, the prevalence rate of certain diseases related to better living conditions (generally including hypertension, coronary heart disease, diabetes, hyperlipemia, obesity) are tending to raise. In order to prevent and control these diseases more effectively, we recently conducted a survey on the incidence of these diseases and relevant factors in a community of Shanghai. In chapter 4, some research have been done. (1) Have to evaluate the prevalence risk for a certain disease with some risk factors, (2) determine the distribution of prevalence rates for some diseases. This section is the further research on the following two subjects. Firstly, the risk of complications. It means which diseases tend to occur together among the five diseases mentioned above. The method of fuzzy cluster, which is superior to statistics method, is used in this section. Secondly, the "Illness

Degree". It is a new concept mentioned in this section. It reflects systematically the ratio of patient and the servility among a certain group of people, while the traditional concept "prevalence rate" only describes the ratio of patient. This section also focuses on the complications commonly seen—Hypertension and Coronary heart disease and studies the relationship between the "illness degree" of these two diseases. We would like to introduce their methods and steps by a application example.

5.5.2 *The Risk of Complications*

5.5.2.1 *Determining the Variable*

Complications are very common in these five diseases. They affect each other and sometimes lead to happen mutually. During the treatment, we should consider them systematically. So the study on the complications is very meaningful for the treatment and prevention of diseases.

Which diseases are easy to occur together and how much is the possibility of complications among the five diseases? Fuzzy cluster method is used to solve this problem based on the data obtained from the survey. Fuzzy cluster has two advantages in this study. Firstly if we define the severity by three states, including 0,1,2, i.e. free from illness, mild illness, and serious illness. We can find non-crisp boundaries among these states. Secondly, the fuzzy cluster is dynamic way, we can realize our objective by controlling relevant value. Here we treat the five diseases as five variables, and use the cluster method to classify them. A five-dimension variable $(Y_1, \cdots, Y_5)$ is used to describe a sample's state, where Y_1 is Hypertension, Y_2 is Coronary heart disease, etc. Each Y_i has three states. The relevant number reflects merely the order, not their quantity. Hence the variable is qualitative.

5.5.2.2 *Define the Similar Matrix R*

"Related coefficient" is usually used to measure the similarity of qualitative variable. It not only describes linear relationship of variables, but also shows nonlinear relationship of them. Suppose qualitative variable X has possible states in total: $x_1, \cdots, x_r$; Y has the state: $y_1, \cdots, y_c$. n_{ij} is the sample number where $x = x_i$, and $y = y_j$. And we can use the following table to describe variable X and Y.

Table 5.6

	y_1	y_2	$\cdots$	y_c	$\sum$
x_1	n_{11}	n_{12}	$\cdots$	n_{1c}	n_1
x_2	n_{21}	n_{22}	$\cdots$	n_{2c}	n_2
$\cdots$	$\cdots$	$\cdots$	$\cdots$	$\cdots$	$\cdots$
x_r	n_{r1}	n_{r2}	$\cdots$	n_{rc}	n_r
$\sum$	$n_{.1}$	$n_{.2}$	$\cdots$	$n_{.c}$	n

Coefficient $\hat{\gamma}$ can measure the related degree of variable X and Y.

$$\hat{\gamma} = \frac{C-D}{C+D},$$

where $C = \sum\limits_{i<k}\sum\limits_{j<l} n_{ij}n_{kl}$, $D = \sum\limits_{i<k}\sum\limits_{j>l} n_{ij}n_{kl}$. Here $-1 \leqslant \hat{\gamma} \leqslant 1$ and $\hat{\gamma}$ is symmetrical to X and Y. Because in this paper the disease as a variable is qualitative, "related coefficient" ($\hat{\gamma}$) is suit for measuring arbitrarily the similarity of two diseases. The bigger of the value $\hat{\gamma}$, the more similar of the two diseases and the higher of the possibility of complications. But $\hat{\gamma}$ is the measurement in the sense of statistics, we need the value with the fuzzy concept, that is membership μ. We define $\mu = 0$ when $-1 \leqslant \hat{\gamma} \leqslant 0$; It means variable X and Y are negative correlated and the two diseases don't occur at the same time. Under the other condition, that is $0 \leqslant \hat{\gamma} \leqslant 1$, we have $\mu = \hat{\gamma}$. The disease variable has three states, so a table of 3×3 is used to describe the relationship of any two diseases.

Table 5.7 The relationship of hypertension and coronary heart disease

		Coronary heart disease			
		0	1	2	sum
hypertension	0	15437	133	35	15605
	1	1841	248	51	5140
	2	360	409	230	999
	sum	17368	790	316	18744

With the method and formula mentioned above, we can get related coefficient between hypertension and Coronary heart disease: $\hat{\gamma} = 0.93593$. Similarly, we can also get the related coefficient of other complications.

Hereby we got the element r_{ij} of fuzzy similar matrix R from $\hat{\gamma}$, here $i, j = 1, \cdots, 5$, and they respectively correspond to hypertension, Coronary heart disease and so on. We define $r_{ii} = 1$ because surely a disease occurs

Table 5.8 Related coefficient of arbitrary two diseases

Disease	$\hat{\gamma}$
Hypertension and coronary heart disease	0.93593
Hypertension and diabeteson	0.55177
Hypertension and hyperlipemia	0.65110
Hypertension and obesity	0.46971
Coronary heart disease and diabeteson	0.59779
Coronary heart disease and hyperlipemia	0.78078
Coronary heart disease and obesity	0.43876
Diabetes and hyperlipemia	0.82823
Diabetes and obesity	0.34879
Hyperlipemia and obesity	0.53137

together with itself.

So the similar matrix R is

$$R = \begin{bmatrix} 1 & 0.93593 & 0.55177 & 0.65110 & 0.46971 \\ & 1 & 0.59779 & 0.78078 & 0.43876 \\ & & 1 & 0.82823 & 0.34879 \\ & & & 1 & 0.53137 \\ & & & & 1 \end{bmatrix}.$$

Here R is symmetrical, so only half of the elements are listed. Matrix R is self-reversal and symmetrical, but not transitive. We must transform it into a fuzzy equivalent matrix and then analyze with fuzzy clustering.

5.5.2.3 *The Transitive Closure t(R)*

The traditional method to get equivalent matrix is to construct transitive closure $t(R)$ with square method. Specifically the process is: $R^2 \Rightarrow R^4 \Rightarrow \cdots \Rightarrow R^{2^n}$, when $R^{2^n} = R^{2^{n+1}}$, R^{2^n} is the transitive closure $t(R)$ we want. Here $R^2 = R * R$ and $* = (\vee, \wedge)$. The above-mentioned method is widely used. In this application example, we got

$$R^4 = R^8 = \begin{bmatrix} 1 & 0.93593 & 0.78078 & 0.78078 & 0.53137 \\ & 1 & 0.78078 & 0.78078 & 0.53137 \\ & & 1 & 0.82823 & 0.53137 \\ & & & 1 & 0.53137 \\ & & & & 1 \end{bmatrix} = t(R).$$

Then we do fuzzy clustering on $t(R)$ and have the following results:

If $\lambda > 0.93593$, then $\{Y_1\}, \{Y_2\}, \{Y_3\}, \{Y_4\}, \{Y_5\}$;

If $0.93593 \geqslant \lambda > 0.82823$, then $\{Y_1, Y_2\}, \{Y_3\}, \{Y_4\}, \{Y_5\}$;

If $0.82823 \geqslant \lambda > 0.78078$, then $\{Y_1, Y_2\}, \{Y_3, Y_4\}, \{Y_5\}$;
If $0.78708 \geqslant \lambda > 0.53137$, then $\{Y_1, Y_2, Y_3, Y_4\}, \{Y_5\}$;
If $0.53137 \geqslant \lambda > 0$, then $\{Y_1, Y_2, Y_3, Y_4, Y_5\}$.

5.5.2.4 *Optimum Fuzzy Equivalent Matrix* $R_{\min}$

The transitive closure $t(R)$ is derived from a series of non-identical transformation. Perhaps the classification by $t(R)$ does not match the reality. So another way of solving such problem is to look for a fuzzy equivalent matrix which has minimum "distance" to R.

Let matrix Y be perturbation matrix of R, $(R+Y)$ becomes fuzzy equivalent matrix when and only when $(R+Y)^2 = R+Y$. Let $R+Y = X$, then the equality above is turned into $X^2 = X$. Objective Function:

$$F(x) = 1/2 \parallel R - X \parallel_F^2 = \sum_{i=1}^{n-1} \sum_{j=i+1}^{n} (x_{ij} - r_{ij})^2.$$

The problem is transformed into getting a solution X^* of $X^2 = X$ and which minimize F. We get

$$X = \begin{bmatrix} 1 & 0.93593 & 0.64521 & 0.64521 & 0.44716 \\ & 1 & 0.64521 & 0.64521 & 0.44716 \\ & & 1 & 0.82823 & 0.44716 \\ & & & 1 & 0.44716 \\ & & & & 1 \end{bmatrix},$$

which is the optimum fuzzy equivalent matrix $R_{\min}$.

Then we do clustering on the fuzzy equivalent matrix $R_{\min}$ and have the following results:
If $\lambda > 0.93593$, then $\{Y_1\}, \{Y_2\}, \{Y_3\}, \{Y_4\}, \{Y_5\}$;
If $0.93593 \geqslant \lambda > 0.82823$, then $\{Y_1, Y_2\}, \{Y_3\}, \{Y_4\}, \{Y_5\}$;
If $0.82823 \geqslant \lambda > 0.64521$, then $\{Y_1, Y_2\}, \{Y_3, Y_4\}, \{Y_5\}$;
If $0.64521 \geqslant \lambda > 0.44716$, then $\{Y_1, Y_2, Y_3, Y_4\}, \{Y_5\}$;
If $0.44716 \geqslant \lambda > 0$, then $\{Y_1, Y_2, Y_3, Y_4, Y_5\}$.

5.5.2.5 *Some Results*

From the conclusion of the classification, we can see that Hypertension and Coronary heart disease are mostly probably to occur together and Diabetes and Hyperlipemia are the second. The four diseases are higher correlated with each other. Obesity is relatively less correlated with the other four diseases. The conclusions are identical with medical proof.

If ignoring the value of λ, we can obtain the same result from $t(R)$ and $R_{\min}$, which indicates that in this study of these complications both of the two methods are practicable and can testily and verify each other.

5.5.3 *The Illness Degree of Diseases*

5.5.3.1 *Basic Concept and Method*

People often use "prevalence rate" to measure the ratio of the people suffering from some diseases among a certain group, which means the percentage of sufferers in that group. Only two states, health and illness, are considered in this concept. But we know there is a transitional state of "sub-healthy" between healthy and suffering from a disease for many chronic diseases. Once getting sick, there is also a process that the disease changes from mild illness to serious illness. So we introduce a new concept definition, Illness Degree. It is defined as a continuous variable $\xi \in [0, 1]$ which measures the severity. $\xi = 0$ means a person or a certain group is healthy concerning a disease, while $\xi = 1$ means he/she or all members of this group are very suffering from this disease. As for other circumstances, a number between 0 and 1 can be used to describe the severity.

An evaluation vector can be obtained as the result of a comprehensive fuzzy evaluation. However,in practice, a certain one-dimensional magnitude (i.e. a number) is often to be expected to describe the risk level of a disease. Hence, we introduce the risk characteristic number.

Definition 5.31 A risk characteristic number E is a weighted combination of all the components of an evaluation vector $(b_1, b_2, \cdots, b_n)$ obtained from a comprehensive fuzzy evaluation,namely $E = \sum_{i=1}^{n} W_i b_i$ Where the weights $w_1, w_2, \cdots, w_n$ are defined according to the nature of the problem.

For instance, vector(b_1, b_2, b_3, b_4) is the evaluation vector of a hypertension risk. Let the average annual medical expenses of patients suffering from mild, moderate,serious hypertension and free from hypertension are respectively taken for the weight w_1, w_2, w_3, w_4, then E can be viewed as the expected annual medical expenses of the person valued. In this case, the first characteristic number can be used to calculate the medical insurance premium.

5.5.3.2 ξ_h: *Illness Degree of Hypertension(IDOH)*

With the definition above-mentioned, ξ_h should indicate the degree or probability of a person suffering from hypertension. For an individual, it is a complex medical problem to find the value of ξ_h. We will not discuss it in this section. But for a group of people with a certain scale, we can make full use of the surveyed data and statistic method to get the value of ξ_h. Let us look back on the concept of "risk characteristic number" E. Here we define

$$\xi = \frac{\text{the actual } E \text{ of a certain group}}{\text{the likely maximum } E \text{ of a certain group}}.$$

So ξ_h is a ratio of a group's actual E and the group's likely maximum E. Let w_i be annual medical expense with the severity degree i, therefore ξ_h means the ratio of the actual medical expense and the cost if all people in the group are seriously ill. So we name ξ_h the illness degree in the sense of medical expense. We can study the value of ξ_h for different groups with diverse age and gender characteristic. The following table is the details.

Table 5.9 The age and gender distribution of ξ_h measured by medical expense

age	ξ_h(male)	ξ_h(female)	ξ_h
$15 \sim 19$	0.003	0.000	0.002
$20 \sim 24$	0.010	0.003	0.007
$25 \sim 29$	0.004	0.005	0.004
$30 \sim 34$	0.014	0.007	0.011
$35 \sim 39$	0.022	0.022	0.022
$40 \sim 44$	0.033	0.037	0.035
$45 \sim 49$	0.059	0.075	0.066
$50 \sim 54$	0.091	0.124	0.105
$55 \sim 59$	0.144	0.179	0.161
$60 \sim 64$	0.162	0.191	0.176
$65 \sim 69$	0.227	0.223	0.225
$70 \sim 74$	0.266	0.252	0.260
$75 \sim 79$	0.256	0.239	0.247
$80 \sim \infty$	0.157	0.154	0.155

From the table above, we suggest that ξ_h is rising with the increase of age. When the age is less than 40, ξ_h rises slowly, while the age is beyond 40, it rises rapidly. And at the scope of $70 \sim 74$, ξ_h reaches the maximum, then it decreases step by step. Therefore it tells us that once people are beyond

40-year-old, the medical expense is rising significantly. And it reminds us at the same time that we should be cautious of hypertension since our young age.

5.5.3.3 ξ_c: *Illness Degree of Coronary Heart Disease (IDOC)*

The definition and calculation method of ξ_c is similar with ξ_h. It also measures the value in the meaning of medical expense. The following table is the ξ_c with different age and gender distribution.

Table 5.10 The age and gender distribution of ξ_c

age	ξ_c(male)	ξ_c(female)	ξ_c
$15 \sim 19$	0	0	0
$20 \sim 24$	0.004	0.003	0.004
$25 \sim 29$	0	0	0
$30 \sim 34$	0.004	0.003	0.004
$35 \sim 39$	0.002	0.003	0.003
$40 \sim 44$	0.002	0.009	0.005
$45 \sim 49$	0.008	0.016	0.011
$50 \sim 54$	0.018	0.029	0.022
$55 \sim 59$	0.037	0.053	0.045
$60 \sim 64$	0.045	0.077	0.061
$65 \sim 69$	0.072	0.085	0.079
$70 \sim 74$	0.095	0.128	0.111
$75 \sim 79$	0.1	0.097	0.099
$80 \sim \infty$	0.071	0.072	0.071

From the table above, it shows ξ_c is positively correlated with age. From 45 on, in its age it increases faster, and between the scope of $70 \sim 74$, ξ_c reaches the maximum and then goes down.

5.5.3.4 *The Relationship between Hypertension and Coronary Heart Disease*

The conclusion derived from the fuzzy clustering suggests the possibility of complication of Hypertension and Coronary heart disease is the biggest one. But the clustering can only explain the probability of complications. We still don't know what's the exact relationship of two diseases once the complications set in. So here we study it further with illness degree, which is a further and complementary step for the former research. We dotted $\xi_h = \xi_h(T)$ and $\xi_c = \xi_c(T)$, here T represents age, in a chart ξ_h-ξ_c.

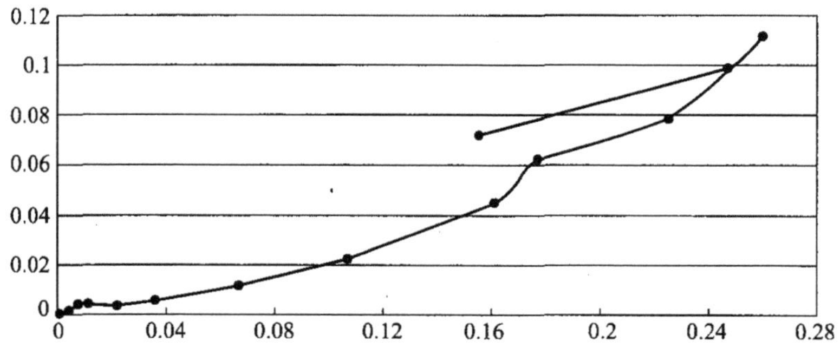

Fig. 5.2 the relationship of ξ_h and ξ_c

The chart shows the relationship between ξ_h and ξ_c, although which is in the form of parameter equation. Strictly speaking, ξ_c isn't a single-valued function on ξ_h. But in the chart, it is almost near the single-valued function except for the very old age. So we try to use a function to fit it. Firstly we use the linear fitting.

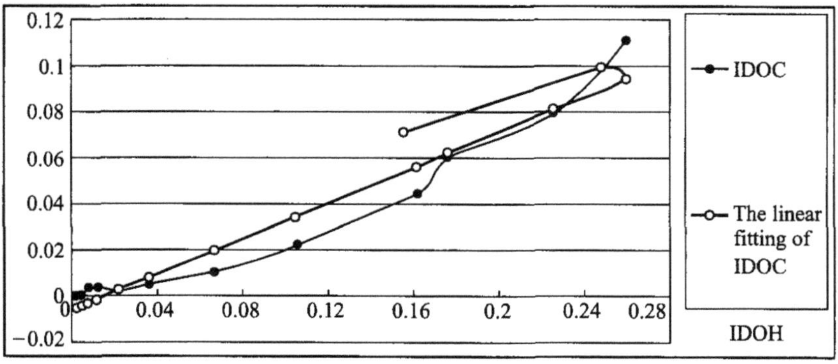

Fig. 5.3 the linear fitting of ξ_c

F-test, $190.95 > F(1,10) = 10$ ($\alpha = 0.01$), shows under $\alpha = 0.01$ ξ_h and ξ_c are linearly correlated. But we can judge from the chart that the absolute error is large. The result of regression indicates the linear fitting is not the best way. Therefore we try a polynomial fitting.

F-test, $822.66 > F(2,9) = 8.02$ ($\alpha = 0.01$). It indicates under the condition $\alpha = 0.01$ the polynomial relationship between ξ_h and ξ_c is significant.

Comparing the result of the linear and the polynomial fitting, we get a conclusion that the latter method is better than the former, in respect of

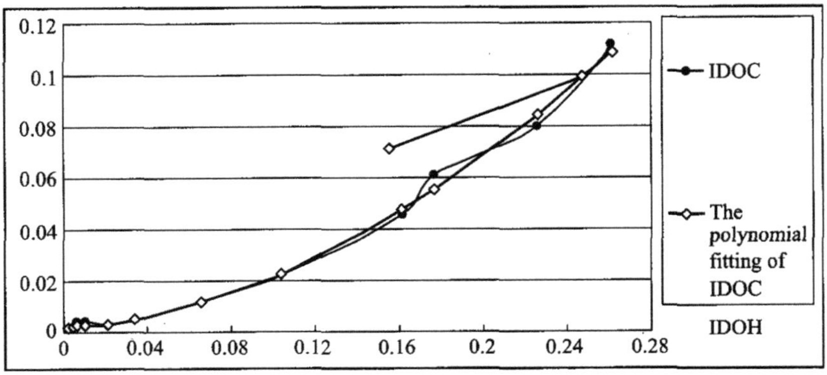

Fig. 5.4 the polynomial fitting of ξ_c

absolute error or relative error, except for several points.

5.5.3.5 *The Application to Insurance*

While calculating the risk characteristic number, this section uses w_i as the medical expense for the severity state i. Consequently the illness degree is the one in term of the medical expense. The bigger the value, the higher the average annual medical expenses for a group of people. Obviously, the calculation of illness degree is helpful to the underwriting in medical insurance (especially to locate the highly risky people).

For example, there is a 10-year-term medical insurance for hypertension. If the insured buys the policy at the age of 15, the insurer's responsibility will end when the insured grows to 25. At that time, his risk can be quantified by the average value of the hypertension illness degree during these ages, which is 0.0045((0.002+0.007)/2). If the insurance begins at his age of 18, the risk value is 0.0102. It can be calculated in the same way for other cases. Risk level is determined according to these values. Thereby the standard of loading will be decided.

As for those guarantee slips insuring several diseases, we can add up the risk value, then compare them and evaluate the risk level, and finally determine the standard of loading.

The illness degree mentioned here is calculated in terms of medical expense. Actually illness degree in other sense can also be constructed. For example, taking w_i as the expected left life span under the condition of the Severity State i, then $E = \sum_{i=1}^{n} W_i b_i$ represents the expected left life span

Table 5.11 The comparison of the linear and polynomial fitting

age	ξ_h	ξ_c	Value		Absolute error		Relative error	
			linear fitting	polynomial fitting	linear fitting	polynomial fitting	linear fitting	polynomial fitting
$15 \sim 19$	0.002	0	−0.005	0.001	0.005	0.001	***	***
$20 \sim 24$	0.007	0.004	−0.003	0.002	0.007	0.002	1.8608	0.5368
$25 \sim 29$	0.004	0	−0.004	0.001	0.004	0.001	***	***
$30 \sim 34$	0.011	0.004	−0.002	0.002	0.005	0.002	1.397	0.47129
$35 \sim 39$	0.022	0.003	0.003	0.003	0.000	0.001	0.0102	0.221553
$40 \sim 44$	0.035	0.005	0.008	0.005	0.003	0.000	0.5278	0.04346
$45 \sim 49$	0.066	0.011	0.020	0.012	0.008	0.000	0.73595	0.029912
$50 \sim 54$	0.105	0.022	0.035	0.023	0.012	0.001	0.55132	0.041528
$55 \sim 59$	0.161	0.045	0.056	0.047	0.011	0.002	0.2491	0.042411
$60 \sim 64$	0.176	0.061	0.062	0.055	0.001	0.006	0.02219	0.09898
$65 \sim 69$	0.225	0.079	0.081	0.084	0.002	0.005	0.02509	0.06493
$70 \sim 74$	0.26	0.111	0.094	0.109	0.016	0.002	0.1487	0.01799
$75 \sim 79$	0.247	0.099	0.099	0.099	0.000	0.000	0	0
$80 \sim \infty$	0.155	0.071	0.071	0.071	0.000	0.000	0	0

Note: Since $\xi_c = 0$, the relative error is expressed by *** Based on the analysis above we know that there exists polynomial relationship between ξ_h and ξ_c, and the bigger ξ_h is, the bigger ξ_c is.

for the whole group of people. With proper changes, the illness degree in the sense of "risk of death" is available too. This can be used in the underwriting prance of life insurance.

The concept of "illness degree" introduced in this section is useful not only for diseases related to better living conditions. For other diseases, such a concept can also be introduced only if there are statistic data concerned.

5.6 Regression Forecasting Model with Fuzzy Factors

5.6.1 *Background*

More and more attention is paid to the prevalence risk analysis of some diseases in medical science and medical insurance. The popular method of this analysis is trying to find the relationship between the possibility of suffering from the disease (with the severity scale) and some related risk factors so that it could help people to forecast the prevalence risk of single person or a group of residents. Statistical method has always been used to solve this problem in the past years. For instance, on the basis of survey data of a certain disease, regression method is used to establish a mathematical model for the relationship between prevalence rate and some risk factors, which is called forecasting model.

But, in real world, among the risk factors, there exist some fuzzy ones with noncrisp boundaries which influence the prevalence of some diseases. Thus if we combined statistical method with fuzzy technique, better results might be obtained.

In this section, we try to establish a forecasting model of hypertension based on the survey data on hypertension and its related factors in a community of Shanghai. The method used is regression with fuzzy factors. It is exactly a kind of hybrid technique combining statistical method with fuzzy techniques and some examples will be used to show we do get the better result.

5.6.2 *Regression Forecasting Model with Crisp Factors*

It is well known that there are many risk factors influencing hypertension, among them, fatness is a very important one. Body Mass Index(BMI), recommended by WHO, is a measurement of one's fatness, whose formula is as follows:

$$BMI = weight(kilogram)/[height(meter)]^2.$$

If investigation is made among a group which is large enough, we approximately assume the prevalence rate of hypertension(denoted as y)and BMI(denoted as x)satisfy the linear relationship as follows:

$$y = \beta_0 + \beta_1 x,$$

where β_0, β_1 can be determined by least square method.

Among the more than 17,450 adults under investigation on hypertension in a certain community of Shanghai, there are 4,789 middle-aged males. Using the total number of persons and the number of people suffered from hypertension accordingly, we can get prevalence rate respectively to every BMI as follows:

Table 5.12

BMI	16	17	18	19	20	21	22
PROH	0.0667	0.0789	0.0155	0.0273	0.0278	0.0548	0.0651
BMI	23	24	25	26	27	28	
PROH	0.1068	0.1532	0.1528	0.1911	0.2676	0.3428	

Where PROH stands for prevalence rate of hypertension.

By calculating β_0 and β_1, we obtain linear regression model $y = -0.3624 + 0.02189x$, where x range from 16 to 28 (i.e. $16 < x < 28$).

5.6.3 *Regression Forecasting Model with Crisp Factors and Fuzzy Factors*

Till now, we just have considered the relationship between the prevalence rate and the level of fatness. But there are still some other factors, such as family history, smoking history and drinking history which influence hypertension. Because these factors and their influence to hypertension have some non-crisp characteristics, it is more favorable to handle these factors with fuzzy mathematical method.

We will inspect how to evaluate these "fuzzy factors" initiating hypertension's risk below, but let us first review some concepts and methods advanced in Chapter 4, which go briefly as follows:

5.6.3.1 *Some Concepts, Methods and an Application Example*

The concept of illness fuzzy set

Generally speaking, we can divide the severity scale of people's suffering from an illness into free from the illness, mild, moderate and serious. Because the boundaries among the four scales are not crisp, it is better to illustrate them with fuzzy sets.

Definition 5.32 Illness fuzzy set $V' = (v'_1, v'_2, v'_3, v'_4)$ is a kind of measure on the prevalence situation or risk for a certain disease of a certain group of residents. It is a fuzzy set, regarding evaluation set $V = (v_1, v_2, v_3, v_4)$ as its universal field, which fits $\sum_{i=1}^{4} v'_i = 1$, where v_1, v_2, v_3, v_4 stand for free from illness, mild illness, moderate illness and serious illness respectively, and v'_1, v'_2, v'_3, v'_4 stand for their membership grade accordingly.

Illness fuzzy set with fixed level of certain risk factor

We can divide every factor among the three fuzzy risk factors mentioned above into certain different "levels". For instance, divide family history into two levels, which are no family history and with family history, denoted as level 1 and level 2 respectively. Divide smoking history into three level, which are free from smoking, smoking amount less than 54,750 cigarettes till the investigation and above 54,750 cigarettes, we denote them respectively as level 1, level 2 and level 3. Divide drinking history into three levels, which are free from drinking, drinking amount of alcohol less than 130 kilograms and above 130 kilograms, denoted as level 1, level 2 and level 3, respectively.

We can determine the illness fuzzy set for a group of residents formed by fixing a certain risk factor, with the survey data.

For example: Consider persons with BMI value 21 and having no family history: the number of data involved is 811, where 791, 16, 4, 0 are the persons number of free from hypertension, mild, moderate and serious respectively. Then the occurring frequencies of each severity level are respectively 0.9753, 0.0197, 0.0049 and 0. Then we approximately regard these occurring frequencies (0.9953, 0.0197, 0.0049, 0) as the illness fuzzy set of hypertension of these residents.

Fuzzy Comprehensive Evaluation

In medical science and medical insurance, it is often necessary to evaluate the risk of hypertension of a whole group, which means performing fuzzy comprehensive evaluation on a whole group is needed. And the method to do this is called fuzzy comprehension evaluation. To fulfill this, we establish double-level fuzzy comprehensive evaluation.

The method goes as follows:

First, perform single-level fuzzy evaluation, fix the level of every risk factor and calculate the respective illness fuzzy sets with the method mentioned above. For instance, we can obtain $(R'_{11}, R'_{12}, R'_{13}, R'_{14})$ for the group of people having no family history, and $(R''_{11}, R''_{12}, R''_{13}, R''_{14})$ for the group of people having family history, and therefore obtain an evaluation matrix

$$R_1 = \begin{pmatrix} R'_{11} & R'_{12} & R'_{13} & R'_{14} \\ R''_{11} & R''_{12} & R''_{13} & R''_{14} \end{pmatrix}$$

for family history. Similarly, we can obtain R_2 for smoking history, R_3 for drinking history.

Note the weights that each risk factor initiates hypertension as a vector A, where A=(0.64 0.24 0.12). And the weight set of different level of each risk factor are selected as below:

$$\begin{aligned} A_1 &= (0.08 \quad 0.92), \\ A_2 &= (0.3 \quad 0.3 \quad 0.4), \\ A_3 &= (0.3 \quad 0.3 \quad 0.4), \\ B_i &= A_i \cdot R_i. \end{aligned}$$

Here, the weight sets come from the opinion of some experts. Thus we obtain the following table:

Table of weights' distribution

$$\begin{cases} 0.64 \quad \mathit{family} \quad \mathit{history} \begin{cases} 0.08 & \mathit{level}\ 1 \\ 0.92 & \mathit{level}\ 2 \end{cases} \\ 0.24 \quad \mathit{smoking} \quad \mathit{history} \begin{cases} 0.30 & \mathit{level}\ 1 \\ 0.30 & \mathit{level}\ 2 \\ 0.40 & \mathit{level}\ 3 \end{cases} \\ 0.12 \quad \mathit{drinking} \quad \mathit{history} \begin{cases} 0.30 & \mathit{level}\ 1 \\ 0.30 & \mathit{level}\ 2 \\ 0.40 & \mathit{level}\ 3 \end{cases} \end{cases}.$$

Third, perform double-level comprehensive evaluation. Let $R = \begin{bmatrix} B_1 \\ B_2 \\ B_3 \end{bmatrix}$.

The results are as follows:

$$B = A \cdot R = (0.64\ 0.24\ 0.12) \cdot R = (b_1, b_2, b_3, b_4).$$

Then, we normalize this fuzzy set B and get a set, for the sake of convenience, we still denote it as B, i.e. $B = (b'_1, b'_2, b'_3, b'_4)$, where $\sum b'_i = 1$.

Here, B is a fuzzy set with evaluation set $V = \{free, mild, moderate, serious\}$ as universal field.

5.6.3.2 *Regression Forecasting Model with Crisp Factors and Fuzzy Factors*

In section 5.6.2, we have established a linear regression model with no fuzzy factors, which means the relationship between prevalence rate y and BMI value x is equation $y = \beta_0 + \beta_1 x$.

Now we take fuzzy factors into account and modify the equation above into $y = \beta_0 + \beta_1 x + \beta_2 E$, where E represents the revised quantity of the equation initiated by fuzzy factors mentioned above, we call it fuzzy factor influence expectation. The value of E is related to x.

Consider a group of residents with fixed x value. Using the fuzzy comprehensive evaluation method mentioned above, we can determine its risk evaluation fuzzy set (also called risk vector) B.

We try to get E from B for a certain x value. Obviously, if the first two components of B are relatively large, which means the possibility of free from disease or mild illness is relatively large, then the prevalence risk will be below the average level, and it makes y value a decreasing tendency. So the E has a tendency of smaller than 0. On the contrary, if the last two components of B are relatively large, the prevalence risk will be above the average level. Then there is a tendency of the increasing of y value, which means E will be greater than 0.

To describe this phenomenon quantitatively, we introduce a concept of influence coefficient vector of evaluation set. It goes as below:

Definition 5.33 Influence coefficients vector of evaluation set is a column vector

$$\begin{bmatrix} h(\nu_1) \\ h(\nu_2) \\ \vdots \\ h(\nu_n) \end{bmatrix}.$$

Where h is a map from evaluation set $\{v_1, v_2, \cdots, v_n\}$ to closed interval $[-a, a]$, $(a > 0)$ with $\sum h(v_i) = 0$.

Once the map h be determined, the influence coefficient vector would be determined as well. Then we can determine fuzzy factor influence expectation as below:

$$E = (b'_1, b'_2, \cdots, b'_n)\begin{bmatrix} h(\nu_1) \\ h(\nu_2) \\ \vdots \\ h(\nu_n) \end{bmatrix} = \sum h(v_i) \cdot b'_i.$$

Now, we get a fuzzy factor influence expectation in a certain sample group with fixed value of BMI. Repeat steps above in other sample groups, we get a sequence of influence expectation:

$$E_1, E_2, \cdots, E_N,$$

where N is the number of sample groups.

Therefore, we use least square method again to estimate the coefficients of equation

$$y = \beta_0 + \beta_1 x + \beta_2 E.$$

And we verify the regression equation with the traditional statistical method, which is called F-examination.

5.6.4 *Example and Comparison of Two Kinds of Regression Model*

Let us look at the following example.

Suppose we consider a male, middle-aged group in the above-mentioned survey. We have already obtained normalized fuzzy set B. Our purpose now is to get the fuzzy factor influence expectation E in every sample group with fixed BMI value.

For the problem of prevalence risk, we select an influence coefficient vector of evaluation set as follows:

When BMI$\leqslant$ 19:

$$\begin{bmatrix} h(free) \\ h(mild) \\ h(moderate) \\ h(serious) \end{bmatrix} = \begin{bmatrix} -1 \\ -1/3 \\ 1/3 \\ 1 \end{bmatrix}.$$

When 20$\leqslant$BMI$\leqslant$24:

$$\begin{bmatrix} h(free) \\ h(mild) \\ h(moderate) \\ h(serious) \end{bmatrix} = \begin{bmatrix} -3/2 \\ -5/12 \\ 5/12 \\ 3/2 \end{bmatrix}.$$

When BMI$\geqslant$24:

$$\begin{bmatrix} h(free) \\ h(mild) \\ h(moderate) \\ h(serious) \end{bmatrix} = \begin{bmatrix} -2 \\ -1/2 \\ 1/2 \\ 2 \end{bmatrix}.$$

Obviously, h is a map from evaluation set V to closed interval $[-2, 2]$ with $\sum h[v_i] = 0$.

Then we get fuzzy factor influence expectation E as below :

$$E = \begin{cases} (b_4 - b_1) + \frac{1}{3}(b_3 - b_2), & \text{when BMI} \leqslant 19, \\ \frac{3}{2}b_4 - b_1) + \frac{5}{12}(b_3 - b_2), & \text{when } 20 \leqslant \text{BMI} \leqslant 24, \\ 2(b_4 - b_1) + \frac{1}{2}(b_3 - b_2), & \text{when BMI} > 24. \end{cases}$$

Submit the components of risk vector B of each BMI into the formula above, then the fuzzy factor influence expectation of fuzzy factors connected with hypertension's prevalence risk under each BMI considered will be obtained.

Through calculation, we know the forecasting model should be :

$$y = -0.0996 + 0.0274X + 0.7299E,$$

where, y stands for hypertension's prevalence rate, X stands for BMI, and E stands for fuzzy factor influence expectation.

Now, we make comparisons of the two forecasting models.

Table 5.13 and 5.14 show that:

(1) Model with fuzzy factors has better forecasting precision than another one.

Table 5.13 Comparisons of forecasting precision

BMI	Actual prevalence rate y_i	Regression model		Regression model	
		forecasting error $\widehat{y_i}$	forecasting value $\Sigma_i = \widehat{y_i} - y_i$	forecasting error $\widehat{y_i}$	forecasting value $\Sigma_i = \widehat{y_i} - y_i$
16	0.0666	−0.012	−0.079	0.025	−0.042
17	0.0789	0.010	−0.069	0.069	−0.010
18	0.0154	0.032	0.017	0.021	0.006
19	0.0273	0.054	0.027	0.049	0.022
20	0.0278	0.076	0.048	0.059	0.031525
21	0.0548	0.097	0.042	0.071	0.016
22	0.0651	0.119	0.054	0.037	0.051255
23	0.1068	0.141	0.034	0.134	0.027
24	0.1532	0.163	0.010	0.150	−0.003
25	0.1528	0.185	0.032	0.146	−0.007
26	0.1911	0.207	0.016	0.253	0.062
27	0.2676	0.229	−0.039	0.265	0.032436
28	0.3428	0.251	−0.092	0.283	−0.060
Sample standard error S		/	0.051255	/	0.0324239

Table 5.14 Comparisons of S_e and F value

Regression model with no fuzzy factors	0.031525	30.3359
Regression model with fuzzy factors	0.012607612	42.15118311

(2) Standard error S_e declines from 0.031525 to 0.012608, which indicates the later model has better forecasting result.

(3) F value rises from 30.3358 to 42.15118311, which indicates the validity of the regression-forecasting model improves greatly.

5.6.5 *Conclusion*

A. Regression forecasting model with fuzzy factors given in this section is obtained by a hybrid technique combining fuzzy technique with statistical methon. Better results are achieved in analysis of prevalence risk by using this model, which shows bright developing prospects of hybrid technique.

B. The method advanced in this section can be applied can be applied into not only the prevalence risk forecasting of hypertension bur also the analysis of prevalence risk of other diseases. Furthermore, it can also be applied into other risk analysis and management problem of some kinds as well.

C. The regression model $y = \pounds_0 + \pounds_1 x + \pounds_2 E$ shown in this section is a kind of simplest situation. It can be popularized to the situation of multi-variable and multi-layer fuzzy factors. In that case, the model will be:

$$\begin{aligned} y_i = \pounds_0 + \pounds_1 x_{1i} + \pounds_2 x_{2i} + \cdots + \pounds_k x_{ki} + \pounds_{k+1} E_{1i} \\ + \pounds_{k+2} E_{2i} + \cdots + \pounds_{k+m} E_{mi}, \quad i = 1, 2, \cdots, N, \end{aligned}$$

where, y_i are goals being forecasted, $x_{1i}, x_{2i}, \cdots, x_{ki}$ are k crisp factors, $E_{1i}, E_{2i}, \cdots, E_{mi}$ stand respectively for m fuzzy factors, and E_{si} ($s = 1, 2, \cdots, m$) stands for respectively for the fuzzy influence expectation of the s-th fuzzy factor in the i-th sample group.

References

Zhang W Y. (1996). Game Theory and Information Economics, *Shanghai Publish House*, 1996.

Chen S Y. (1944). The Theory and Application of System Fuzzy Decision, *Dalian Science and Engineering University Press*, 1944.

Xie K X, et al. (1998). Optimization Method, *Tianjing University Press*, 1998.

Zhang S W, Lu Y C, Zhu W X. (1991). Application of Fuzzy Mathematics, *Tongji University Press*, 1991.

Lu Y C, Guan Z Y, Gen H. (2000). Fuzzy Decision Applied to Life Insurance, *Fuzzy Sets and Mathematics*, 2000, **14**.

Shang H J, Lu Y C, Wang X W. (1998). Fuzzy Risk Evaluation for Diseases Related to Better Living Conditions and Premium-rate Calculations for a Health Insurance Product, *The second Annual Conference Proceedings of APRIA, Singapore*, 1998.

Gu H M, et al. (1994). Applied Statistical Method, *Jinan University Press*, 1994.

Huang T C, Lu Y C. (1994). Linear Regression Forecasting Model With Fuzzy Factors, *Fuzzy System and Mathematics (supplement)*, 1994.

Zheng Z K, et al. (1998). Statistical Analysis Of Obesity, *Proceedings of the Annual Conference of China Statistical Society*, 1998.

Shang H J, Yu Y N, Li Y. (1998). The Age Distributions of Prevalence Rates and Incidence Rates for Some Diseases and Their Applications to Insurance, 2th *Annual Conference of APRIA*, 1998.

Shang H J, Lu Y C, Wang X W. (1998). Fuzzy Risk Evaluation for Diseases Related to Better Living Conditions and Premium-rate Calculations for a Health Insurance Product, 2th *Annual Conference of APRIA*, 1998.

Shang H J, Lu Y C, Chen Q, Xu X M. (1999). Risk Analysis and Evaluation of Some Diseases(I,II), 18th *International Conference of NAFIPS*, 1999.

Zhou G Y, Xia L X. (1993). The Analysis and Application of Non-quantitative Data, *Science Press*, 1993.

Zhu J Y. (1987). Several Key Problem Applying Fuzzy Clustering, *Fuzzy System and Mathematics*, 1987, **1**, 1.

Fu G Y. (1987). A Method to Find the Solution of Optimum Fuzzy Equivalent Matrix, *Fuzzy System and Mathematics*, 1987, **11**, 2.

Chapter 6

Some Applications of Financial Economics to Insurance

6.1 Introduction

In actuarial science the basic idea to deal with the valuation of insurance and pension is to determine the "expected discounted value " or the "actuarial present value" of the future cash flows, such as the death benefit, survival benefit or surrender benefit of the policies. If we consider a traditional insurance policy, in which both of the survival benefit and death benefit are given, but the insurer does not know when they should pay the death benefit and what the probability that they should pay the survival benefit is. In this case there is only one random factor that is the future life of the insured. Thus, when we calculate the actuarial present value (i.e., discounted expected value), we only calculate the expectation with respect to this random factor $T(x)$ i.e., the future life of aged x. It is easy to compute the actuarial present value by the knowledge of traditional actuarial mathematics in this case. But if we consider a unit-linked policy in which both of the survival benefit and death benefit depend on the market value of the investing account, then it turns out to be a stochastic process, and it is hard to get its valuation by means of traditional actuarial mathematics, especially when surrender or early retirement are allowed before the maturity date. Furthermore, because of the uncertainty of the economy or the health situation of the person, it should be considered that the future salary of a member of pension plan is not determinate in advance. Thus, if the death and survival benefit of a pension plan depend on the salary of the member at that time, the valuation of pension plan cannot also be obtained by the traditional actuarial science. Especially, when the survival benefit or the death benefit depend on a kind of historical average of the salary, the valuation of the pension plan is much more complicated.

It is well known that the finance and insurance industries have much in common. The different tools that these industries provide to their customers for managing financially insurable risks essentially rely on the same two fundamental concepts: risk pooling and risk transfer. The problem of finding a fair value of a derivative and the problem of finding the present value of liabilities of insurer are remarkably similar each other, i.e., they are all to calculate the present value of the future cash flows. In recent years an increasing interest has been revealed in applying financial pricing techniques to the fair valuation of insurance liabilities; see for example, Shimko (1992a, 1992b), Penjer et al. (1998), Babble & Marrill (1999), Grosen & Jørgeson (2000) and Shen (2002). In fact, the valuation of a unit-linked insurance without surrender option is similar to the pricing of European Option. On the other hand, the valuation of a unit-linked insurance with surrender option is similar to the pricing of American option. Actually, the method of pricing of Asia option can be used to determine the valuation of the pension plan when the both of death and survival benefit depend on the average salary.

This chapter is concerned with the study of applications of financial economics to actuarial mathematics, especially to insurance and pension plan. Two approaches in financial economics are introduced. One approach is a combination of financial economics, actuarial mathematics, partial differential equation (P.D.E.) and numerical analysis. Several P.D.E. models are derived using actuarial mathematics and the basic principle in financial economics. The another one is the generalized expected discounted value approach (G.E.D.V.). From the point view of actuarial science there are two kinds of models: one kind is for the insurance and the other kind is for the pension plan. However, these two kinds of models do not have big differences from the point view of mathematics. Thus, in this chapter we will focus on the models for the insurance. Several models are derived for the dynamics of liability of a policy which can be used for the valuation of insurance policies with a variety of benefit structures. Also some analytic solutions are obtained by solving the corresponding PDE and GEDV approach.

The major part of the material in this chapter is the recent research work by the author and her formal graduate students. See for example, Friedman & Shen (2002), Shen & Xu(2005), Pan, Mao & Liu(2000), Wang & Xu(2002), Yu & Li (2003), Liu, Long & Wang(2004), Huo(2005) and Wei(2005). However, only part of these research work are described in this chapter in detail because of limitations of the space. This chapter is organized as follows. The general framework for the liability of unit-linked insurance policy will be established in Section 6.2. Three general frameworks have been introduced: the first one is the P.D.E. approach for the valuation of the liability of unit-linked policy without surrender; the second one is the P.D.E. approach for the valuation of the liability of unit-linked policy with surrender option; and the third is the generalized expected discounted value approach. Section 6.3 is devoted to the valuation of first kind of unit-linked insurance without surrender option, using P.D.E. approach. Section 6.4 is focused on the valuation of the second kind unit-linked policy without surrender options, using P.D.E. approach and G.E.D.V. approach. The fair valuation of second kind unit-linked policy with surrender option is discussed in Section 6.5.

6.2 General Framework of the Valuation of Unit-linked Insurance Policy

In this section we first give the general mathematical model for liability of a unit-linked insurance policy, in which both survival and death benefit depend on the market value of the investing account. This section consists of three parts. The first part covers the mathematical model for the valuation of a unit-linked insurance policy without surrender option. The second part consider a model for the policy with surrender option. In Section 6.2.3 generalized expected discounted value approach is given. The main notation and assumptions in this section are the following:

(i) T—policy term,
t—the time passes since policy issued, $0 \leqslant t \leqslant T$,
x_0—the age of the insured when the policy issued.

(ii) $r(t)$—risk free interest rate,
$\mu(t) = \mu_d(t + x_0)$—mortality force function of aged $x_0 + t$.
The life insurance policy can be modelled as a continuous-time Markov model. Wolthuis (1994) provides the specification of a continuous-time Markov model in actuarial life insurance mathematics. We consider the states of active (a), dead (d), and withdrawn or surrender (s). The transition intensities from active membership to the dead or surrender states are denoted by $\mu_d(t + x_0)$ and $\mu_s(t+x_0)$, respectively. These are referred to as forces of decrement in traditional actuarial terminology.

(iii) A_t—the market value of the investing account at time t and evolves according to the following stochastic differential equation:

$$dA_t = \alpha(t, A_t)dt + \sigma(t, A_t)dW_t, \tag{6.1}$$

where $\alpha(t, A_t)$ is the growing rate and $\sigma(t, A_t)$ is the stochastic volatility rate, both of them depend on time t and assent value A_t; W_t is the standard Brownian motion defined on the filtered probability space $(\Omega, \mathcal{F}, \mathcal{P})$ on interval $[0, T]$. By financial calculus (see Baxter & Rennie(1996)), under some assumption (6.1) can be adjusted to

$$dA_t = \theta(t, A_t)dt + \sigma(t, A_t)dW_t^Q, \tag{6.2}$$

where Q is a risk-neutral probability measure equivalent to $\mathcal{P}$, and W_t^Q is a standard Brownian motion under Q.

(iv) The responsibilities of the insurer in the policy term are:

Survival benefit: If the insured still survives at the maturity date T, then he/she will be paid $S(T, A_T)$ by insurer at that time, where $S(T, A_T)$ is called survival benefit, and it depends on the market value of the investing account at time T and the policy term T.

Death benefit: If the insured dies at time t, $0 < t < T$, then he/she will be paid $b(t, A_t)$ by the insurer at the time t which also depends on the market value of A at time t, and the policy is terminated.

(v) $v(t, A)$—the insurance liability, i.e., the value of policy.

6.2.1 *Differential Equation Models for the Valuation of Policies without Surrender Option*

First we derive a partial differential equation model for the liability of policy, in which the surrender is not allowed. There are several approaches to derive the partial differential equation model for $v(t, A)$ in financial economics with one being from martingale which is often used in financial mathematics and with the other being from the balance law in financial economics. In this chapter we adopt the latter approach, i.e., we use the balance principle in financial economics and the stochastic calculus to get the PDE model directly, which is also a basic approach in applied partial differential equation. Basic balance principle in financial economics (see Shimko (1992)) is the following:

Basic Balance Principle: *In a risk-neutral economy, the expected capital gain (ECG) add the expected cash flows (ECF) to get total return(TR), and the total return should be the risk free interest return:*

$$TR = ECG + ECF. \tag{6.3}$$

If we consider $v(t, A)$ during time period $[t, t + dt]$, then $ECG = E^Q[dv]$, $TR = r(t)vdt$. If the insured dies during this period, then the insured should pay the benefit $b(t, A)$ but the policy is terminated immediately. Noticing that $\mu_d(x_0 + t) = \mu(t)$ is the transition intensity from active to dead, by traditional actuarial mathematics (refer to Shimko(1992) and Bowers etc (1997)) the expected sum at risk for death should be $\mu(t)(b(t, A) - v(t, A))dt$. In other words, $ECF = \mu(t)(b(t, A) - v(t, A))dt$. Thus it turns out from (6.3) that

$$E^Q[dv] = r(t)vdt - \mu(t)(b(t, A) - v)dt. \tag{6.4}$$

On the other hand, from *Itô's* lemma (refer to Baxter & Rennie(1996)) we get:

$$dv = (\frac{\partial v}{\partial t} + \theta(t, A)\frac{\partial v}{\partial A} + \frac{1}{2}\sigma^2(t, A)\frac{\partial^2 v}{\partial A^2})dt + \sigma(t, A)\frac{\partial v}{\partial A}dW_t^Q. \tag{6.5}$$

Taking the mean under Q on the both sides of (6.5) and noticing that $E^Q[dW_t^Q] = 0$, we obtain the following partial differential equation for $v(t, A)$:

$$\frac{\partial v}{\partial t} + \theta(t, A)\frac{\partial v}{\partial A} + \frac{1}{2}\sigma^2(t, A)\frac{\partial^2 v}{\partial A^2} - (r(t) + \mu(t))v + \mu(t)b(t, A) = 0. \tag{6.6}$$

The survival payment determines the final condition:

$$t = T : v = S(T, A). \tag{6.7}$$

Hence, the general PDE model of the unit-linked policies without surrender option is the following:

$$\begin{cases} \frac{\partial v}{\partial t} + \theta(t,A)\frac{\partial v}{\partial A} + \frac{1}{2}\sigma^2(t,A)\frac{\partial^2 v}{\partial A^2} - (r(t)+\mu(t))v + \mu(t)b(t,A) = 0, \\ t = T : v = S(T,A). \end{cases} \tag{6.8}$$

Remark 6.1 *It is easy to see that when surrender is allowed and the surrender benefit is just the value of policy at the surrender time, then the P.D.E. model for that policy is just the same as (6.8).*

In this case the expected sum at risk should be $\mu(t)(b(t,A)-v)dt+\mu_s(t)(v-v)dt = \mu(t)(b(t,A)-v)$.

Remark 6.2 *If surrender is allowed, the force of surrender μ_s is known and the surrender benefit is given by $h(t,A)$, then similar to the derivation of (6.8), the PDE model on $v(t,A)$ is the following:*

$$\begin{cases} \frac{\partial v}{\partial t} + \theta(t,A)\frac{\partial v}{\partial A} + \frac{1}{2}\sigma^2(t,A)\frac{\partial^2 v}{\partial A^2} - r(t)v \\ \quad +\mu(t)(b(t,A)-v) + \mu_s(t)(h(t,A)-v) = 0, \\ t = T : v = S(T,A). \end{cases} \tag{6.9}$$

Remark 6.3 *In a special case that $\sigma(t,A)$ in (6.2), the stochastic volatility of the market value of investing account, is zero, it turns out that*

$$dA_t = \theta(t,A_t)dt. \tag{6.10}$$

Thus, the P.D.E model of $v(t,A)$ is reduced to the following partial differential equation of first order:

$$\begin{cases} \frac{\partial v}{\partial t} + \theta(t,A)\frac{\partial v}{\partial A} - (r(t)+\mu(t))v + \mu(t)b(t,A) = 0, \\ t = T : v = S(T,A). \end{cases} \tag{6.11}$$

6.2.2 *P.D.E. Model for the Valuation of Policies with Surrender Option*

Now we consider the valuation of policies with surrender option but the force of surrender is not given in advance. It is analogous to the American options that the valuation of policies with surrender option is much more complicated. Since now we have to determine not only the value of the policy, but also the optimal time to surrender. This is a free boundary problem. It is impossible to get the analytical solution to the free boundary problem and we must recur to the numerical method.

Concerning the surrender, we make the following assumptions:

(S1). The surrender benefit at time t is given by $h(t, A)$.
(S2). The insured chooses to surrender at time t *if and only if* the surrender benefit $h(t, A)$ is not less than the value of the policy $v(t, A)$.

By the arbitrage-free principle and assumption (S2), the following inequalities hold in the (t, A) plane (refer to Friedman & Shen (2001) and Wilmott, et al., (1993)):

$$\begin{cases} \frac{\partial v}{\partial t} + rA\frac{\partial v}{\partial A} + \frac{1}{2}\sigma^2 A^2 \frac{\partial^2 v}{\partial A^2} - (r(t) + \mu(t))v + \mu(t)kA \leqslant 0, \\ v(t, A) \geqslant h(t, A). \end{cases} \tag{6.12}$$

If we denote by Γ the boundary of the set $\{v(t, A) > h(t, A)\}$ in the (t, A) plane, then the optimal time to surrender is the time t when the path $t \mapsto (t, A_t)$ hits Γ. The boundary $\Gamma : A = A_f(t)$ is called a *free boundary*, and determination of Γ is an important aspect in the study of the value of policy $v(t, A)$. On the free boundary $\Gamma : A = A_f(t)$, we need to impose two additional conditions (refer to Friedman (1982) and Wilmott, Dewynne & Howison (1993)):

$$on \quad A = A_f(t) : v(t, A) = h(t, A), \tag{6.13}$$

$$\frac{\partial v}{\partial A}(t, A_f) = \frac{\partial h}{\partial A}(t, A_f). \tag{6.14}$$

For all time t, the A axis can be divided into disjoint regions: the surrender region and the non-surrender region. It turns out that (6.12) can be decomposed into two cases. In the surrender region the following is satisfied:

$$\begin{cases} \frac{\partial v}{\partial t} + r(t)A\frac{\partial v}{\partial A} + \frac{1}{2}\sigma^2 A^2 \frac{\partial^2 v}{\partial A^2} - (r(t) + \mu(t))v + \mu(t)kA < 0, \\ v(t, A) = h(t, A), \end{cases} \tag{6.15}$$

while in the non-surrender region,

$$\begin{cases} \frac{\partial v}{\partial t} + r(t)A\frac{\partial v}{\partial A} + \frac{1}{2}\sigma^2 A^2 \frac{\partial^2 v}{\partial A^2} - (r(t) + \mu(t))v + \mu(t)kA = 0. \\ v(t, A) > h(t, A). \end{cases} \tag{6.16}$$

Thus, the corresponding PDE model for the valuation of policy with surrender options in non-surrender region is:

$$\begin{cases} \frac{\partial v}{\partial t} + r(t)A\frac{\partial v}{\partial A} + \frac{1}{2}\sigma^2 A^2 \frac{\partial^2 v}{\partial A^2} - (r(t) + \mu(t))v + \mu k A = 0, \\ at\ \ t = T: \ \ v(T, A) = S(T, A), \\ \text{on } \ A = A_f(t): \ v(t, A_f) = h(t, A_f), \\ \frac{\partial v}{\partial A}(t, A_f) = \frac{\partial h}{\partial A}(t, A_f), \end{cases} \tag{6.17}$$

where A_f is unknown and it should be determined along with the solution $v(t, A)$.

6.2.3 *Generalized Expected Discounted Value Approach*

The traditional actuarial approach to the valuation of a policy is to determine "discounted expected values" of future cash flows, which includes survival benefit and death benefit payed by the insurer. If we consider a traditional life insurance, in which both of the survival benefit and death benefit are given, but the insurer does not know when they should pay the death benefit and what about the probability that they should pay the survival benefit. In this case there is only one random factor that is the future life of the insured. Thus, when we calculate the actuarial present value (i.e., discounted expected value), we only calculate the expectation with respect to this random factor $T(x)$ (the future life of aged x). But if we consider a unit-linked policy, in which both of the survival and death benefit related to two stochastic factors: one is the stochastic market value of the investing account and the other is the future life of the insured. In this case the traditional expected present value has been extended to an "generalized expected discounted value" approach (Babbel & Merrill (1998)) where expectation of the discounted future cash flows are taken with respect to not only the future life $T(x)$ but also the "risk-netural" probability measure $\{\mathcal{Q}\}$.

In actuarial mathematics, as shown in Bowers et al (1997) , the age-at-death is a random variable. Consider the case of a death benefit. Let X be the age-at-death random variable. Then the survivorship function is given by the following:

$$s(x) = 1 - F_X(x), \tag{6.18}$$

where $F_X(x)$ is the distribution function of X. The force of mortality, or hazard rate, is defined as

$$\mu_d(x) = -\frac{s'(x)}{s(x)}. \tag{6.19}$$

We also have

$$s(x) = \exp\left(-\int_0^x \mu_d(\tau)d\tau\right). \tag{6.20}$$

Now consider the random variable $T(x_0)$, the future life time of a life aged x_0. We have

$$\Pr(T(x_0) > t|T(x_0) > t_0) = \frac{s(x_0+t)/s(x_0)}{s(x_0+t_0)/s(x_0)} = \exp\left(-\int_{t_0}^t \mu_d(x_0+\tau)d\tau\right). \tag{6.21}$$

Thus, the conditional probability distribution function of $T(x_0)$ is

$$F_{T(x_0)|T(x_0)>t_0}(t) = 1 - \frac{s(x_0+t)/s(x_0)}{s(x_0+t_0)/s(x_0)} = 1 - \exp\left(-\int_{t_0}^t \mu_d(x_0+\tau)d\tau\right) \tag{6.22}$$

and the conditional probability density function is

$$f_{T(x_0)|T(x_0)>t_0}(t) = \mu_d(x_0+t)\exp\left(-\int_{t_0}^t \mu_d(x_0+\tau)d\tau\right). \tag{6.23}$$

We now assume that the random variable $T(x_0)$ and the stochastic process A_t are independent.

Using the martingale idea and the double expectation theorem, we have

$$\begin{aligned} v(t, A_t) &= E^Q[E[\text{discounted future cash flows}|T(x_0) > t, A_t]] \\ &= E^Q[E^{T(x_0)|T(x_0)>t}[\text{discounted future cash flows}|A_t]]. \end{aligned} \tag{6.24}$$

This is the basic formula of G.E.D.V. approach. We will use it to get the liability of unit-linked policy later on.

Remark 6.4 *If A_t is determinate, i.e., the volatility term $\sigma(t, A_t)$ is zero, then the liability of the policy can be obtained as the actuarial present value of future cash flows by the traditional actuarial mathematics as follows:*

$$\begin{aligned} v(t, A_t) &= E[\textit{discounted future cash flows}|T(x_0) > t] \\ &= E^{T(x_0)|T(x_0)>t}[\textit{ discounted future cash flows}]. \end{aligned} \tag{6.25}$$

It is obvious that (6.24) is an extension of (6.25).

6.3 Fair Valuation of First Kind of Unit-linked Policy

Based on the general framework stated in the previous section, we consider the fair valuation of several kinds of unit-linked policies in the subsequent sections. In this section we first consider a unit-linked policy by specifying the assumptions (iii) and(iv) in section 6.2 as follows:

(iii') The asset A_t can be traded in a arbitrage-free market and its market value of the investing account is Geometrical Brownian Motion, i.e.,

$$dA_t = \alpha(t)A_t dt + \sigma A_t dW_t, \quad A_0 \text{ is given,} \tag{6.26}$$

where σ is a constant. Then after risk-adjusted (refer to Baxter & Rennie (1996)),

$$dA_t = r(t)A_t dt + \sigma A_t dW_t^Q, \tag{6.27}$$

where $r(t)$ is the risk free interest rate.

(iv') The policy will be terminated at the expiring date T, i.e.,

$$S(T, A) = 0. \tag{6.28}$$

The death benefit is the maximum between the market value of the investing account A_t and the fixed benefit B

$$b(t, A_t) = \max\{A_t, B\}. \tag{6.29}$$

Then the general model of (6.8) becomes

$$\begin{cases} \dfrac{\partial v}{\partial t} + r(t)A\dfrac{\partial v}{\partial A} + \dfrac{1}{2}\sigma^2 A^2 \dfrac{\partial^2 v}{\partial A^2} - (r(t) + \mu(t))v + \mu(t)\max(A, B) = 0, \\ t = T : v(T, A) = 0. \end{cases} \tag{6.30}$$

6.3.1 *The Case $\sigma(t, A) = 0$*

To compare the P.D.E. approach and the traditional actuarial mathematics, we first consider the special case where market value of the investing account A_t is determinate, i.e., the volatility σ is zero. Then (6.27) becomes

$$dA_t = r(t)A_t dt. \tag{6.31}$$

Its solution is:

$$A_t = A_0 e^{\int_0^t r(t)dt}. \tag{6.32}$$

Two methods which have been introduced so far to get the financial fair value of this policy are: 1) Reduce the P.D.E. model (6.30) to the partial differential equation of first order, then solve it. 2) Use the traditional actuarial mathematics to calculate the actuarial present value.

Under the present situation the P.D.E. of first order model for this policy is the following:

$$\begin{cases} \dfrac{\partial v}{\partial t} + r(t)A\dfrac{\partial v}{\partial A} + -(r(t) + \mu(t))v + \mu(t)\max(A, B) = 0, \\ t = T : v(T, A) = 0. \end{cases} \tag{6.33}$$

To solve (6.33), it is enough to solve the following ordinary differential equation:

$$\begin{cases} \dfrac{dv(t, A(t))}{dt} = (r(t) + \mu(t))v - \mu(t)\max(A(t), B), \quad 0 < t < T, \\ t = T : v(T, A(T)) = 0. \end{cases} \tag{6.34}$$

It is easy to get the solution to (6.34) as follows.

$$v(t) = \int_t^T \max\{A(\tau), B\}\mu(\tau)e^{-\int_t^\tau (r(s) + \mu(s))ds} d\tau. \tag{6.35}$$

In contrast, we now use traditional actuarial mathematics to get the valuation of the above policy. By Remark 6.3 in Subsection 6.2.3, we have

$$\begin{aligned} v(t, A) &= E[\text{discounted future death benefit} | T(x_0) > t] \\ &= E^{T(x_0)|T(x_0)>t}[\max\{A(T(x_0)), B\}e^{-\int_t^{T(x_0)} r(\tau)d\tau}] \\ &= \int_t^T \max\{A(\tau), B\}\mu(\tau)e^{-\int_t^\tau (r(s) + \mu(s))ds} d\tau. \end{aligned} \tag{6.36}$$

Which is just the same as (6.35). But later on we will find that P.D.E. approach is more sophisticate than the traditional actuarial mathematics especially when we deal with more complicated policy, such as the policy with surrender option and so on.

6.3.2 The Case $\sigma(t, A) \neq 0$

To get the fair value of policy described above when $\sigma \neq 0$, we have to solve P.D.E. (6.30) directly. By Duhamel's principle (refer to Gu & Li etc. (1987)), we have

Lemma 6.1 *If $W(t, A : \tau)$ satisfies*

$$\begin{cases} \dfrac{\partial W}{\partial t} + r(t)A\dfrac{\partial W}{\partial A} + \dfrac{1}{2}\sigma^2 A^2 \dfrac{\partial^2 W}{\partial A^2} - (r(t) + \mu(t))W = 0, \\ t = \tau : \quad W(t, A; \tau) = \max\{A, B\}\mu(\tau). \end{cases} \tag{6.37}$$

Then

$$v(t, A) = \int_t^T W(t, A; \tau)d\tau \tag{6.38}$$

is the solution to (6.30).

To solve (6.37), in a similar way to the paper by Black & Scholes (1973), we introduce the following transforms for both independent and dependent variables.

$$\begin{cases} \widetilde{W} = We^{\int_t^\tau (r(s) + \mu(s))ds}, \\ \widetilde{A} = Ae^{\int_t^\tau r(s)ds - \frac{1}{2}\sigma^2(\tau - t)}, \\ \widetilde{t} = \frac{1}{2}\sigma^2(\tau - t). \end{cases} \tag{6.39}$$

Then (6.37) becomes

$$\begin{cases} \dfrac{\partial \widetilde{W}}{\partial \widetilde{t}} = \widetilde{A}\dfrac{\partial \widetilde{W}}{\partial \widetilde{t}} + \widetilde{A}^2 \dfrac{\partial^2 \widetilde{W}}{\partial \widetilde{A}^2}, \\ \widetilde{t} = 0 : \quad \widetilde{W}(\widetilde{t}, \widetilde{A}; \tau) = \max(\widetilde{A}, B)\mu(\tau). \end{cases} \tag{6.40}$$

Furthermore, we introduce

$$\widetilde{A} = e^y. \tag{6.41}$$

Thus,

$$\begin{cases} \dfrac{\partial \widetilde{W}}{\partial \widetilde{t}} = \dfrac{\partial^2 \widetilde{W}}{\partial y^2}, \\ \widetilde{t} = 0, \quad \widetilde{W}(\widetilde{t}, y; \tau) = \max(e^y, B)\mu(\tau). \end{cases} \tag{6.42}$$

By the Poisson formula for the solution to the Cauchy problem of the heat equation (refer to Gu and Li etc. (1987)) we get the solution to (6.42):

$$\widetilde{W}(\widetilde{t},y;\tau)=\frac{\mu(\tau)}{2\sqrt{\pi\widetilde{t}}}\int_{-\infty}^{+\infty}\max(e^{\xi},B)e^{-\frac{(y-\xi)^2}{4\widetilde{t}}}d\xi. \tag{6.43}$$

Thus,

$$\widetilde{W}(\widetilde{t},\widetilde{A};\tau)=\frac{\mu(\tau)}{2\sqrt{\pi\widetilde{t}}}\int_{0}^{+\infty}\frac{\max(\widetilde{\xi},B)}{\widetilde{\xi}}e^{-\frac{(\ln\widetilde{A}-\ln\widetilde{\xi})^2}{4\widetilde{t}}}d\widetilde{\xi}. \tag{6.44}$$

Finally, we get

$$\begin{aligned}
&W(t,A;\tau)\\
&=\frac{e^{-\int_t^\tau(r(s)+\mu(s))ds}\mu(\tau)}{\sigma\sqrt{2\pi(\tau-t)}}\cdot\\
&\quad\int_0^{+\infty}\frac{\max(\widetilde{\xi},B)}{\widetilde{\xi}}e^{-\frac{\left(\ln A+\int_t^\tau r(s)ds-\frac{1}{2}\sigma^2(\tau-t)-\ln\widetilde{\xi}\right)^2}{2\sigma^2(\tau-t)}}d\widetilde{\xi}\\
&=\frac{e^{-\int_t^\tau(r(s)+\mu(s))ds}\mu(\tau)}{\sigma\sqrt{2\pi(\tau-t)}}\cdot\\
&\quad\int_{-\infty}^{+\infty}\max(e^x,B)e^{-\frac{\left(\ln A+\int_t^\tau r(s)ds-\frac{1}{2}\sigma^2(\tau-t)-x\right)^2}{2\sigma^2(\tau-t)}}dx\\
&=e^{-\int_t^\tau(r(s)+\mu(s))ds}\mu(\tau)\cdot\\
&\quad\left(\int_{\ln B}^{+\infty}\frac{e^{x-\frac{\left(\ln A+\int_t^\tau r(s)ds-\frac{1}{2}\sigma^2(\tau-t)-x\right)^2}{2\sigma^2(\tau-t)}}}{\sigma\sqrt{2\pi(\tau-t)}}dx\right.\\
&\quad\left.+\frac{B}{\sigma\sqrt{2\pi(\tau-t)}}\int_{-\infty}^{\ln B}e^{-\frac{\left(\ln A+\int_t^\tau r(s)ds-\frac{1}{2}\sigma^2(\tau-t)-x\right)^2}{2\sigma^2(\tau-t)}}dx\right)
\end{aligned}$$

$$= e^{-\int_t^\tau (r(s)+\mu(s))ds}\mu(\tau)\cdot$$
$$\left(\frac{Ae^{\int_t^\tau r(s)ds}}{\sigma\sqrt{2\pi(\tau-t)}}\int_{\ln B}^{+\infty} e^{-\frac{\left(\ln A+\int_t^\tau r(s)ds+\frac{1}{2}\sigma^2(\tau-t)-x\right)^2}{2\sigma^2(\tau-t)}}dx\right.$$
$$\left.+\frac{B}{\sigma\sqrt{2\pi(\tau-t)}}\int_{-\infty}^{\ln B} e^{-\frac{\left(\ln A+\int_t^\tau r(s)ds-\frac{1}{2}\sigma^2(\tau-t)-x\right)^2}{2\sigma^2(\tau-t)}}dx\right)$$
$$= e^{-\int_t^\tau (r(s)+\mu(s))ds}\mu(\tau)\left(Ae^{\int_t^\tau r(s)ds}\Phi(d_1)+B(1-\Phi(d_2))\right), \tag{6.45}$$

where the function Φ is the cumulative distribution function for a standard normal random variable given by

$$\Phi(x) = \frac{1}{\sqrt{2\pi}}\int_{-\infty}^{x} e^{-\frac{\xi^2}{2}}d\xi, \tag{6.46}$$

and

$$d_1 = \frac{\ln\frac{A}{B}+\int_t^\tau r(s)ds+\frac{1}{2}\sigma^2(\tau-t)}{\sigma\sqrt{(\tau-t)}}, \tag{6.47}$$

$$d_2 = \frac{\ln\frac{A}{B}+\int_t^\tau r(s)ds-\frac{1}{2}\sigma^2(\tau-t)}{\sigma\sqrt{(\tau-t)}} = d_1-\sigma\sqrt{\tau-t}. \tag{6.48}$$

Thus, by Lemma 6.1, the solution to (6.30) is:

$$v(t,A) = \int_t^T W(t,A;\tau)d\tau. \tag{6.49}$$

6.4 Fair Valuation of Second Kind of Unit-linked Policy without Surrender Option

In this section we derive the fair valuation for the second kind of unit-linked policy by two approaches: one approach is to solve P.D.E., and the other is given by generalized expected discounted value (G.E.D.V) approach.

First we specify the assumptions (ii), (iii) and (iv) by (ii)", (iii)" and (iv)", respectively:

(ii") Both of $r(t)$ and $\mu(t) = \mu_d(t + x_0)$ are assumed to be constants $r(t) = r$ and $\mu(t) = \mu$ for the sake of simplicity.

(iii") The asset A_t can be traded in a arbitrage-free market and its market value of the investing account is a Geometrical Brownian Motion, i.e.,

$$dA_t = \alpha A_t dt + \sigma A_t dW_t, \quad A_0 \quad \text{is given,} \tag{6.50}$$

where both α and σ are constants. Then after risk-adjusted (refer to Baxter & Rennie (1996)),

$$dA_t = rA_t dt + \sigma A_t dW_t^Q, \tag{6.51}$$

where r is the risk free interest rate.
It is well known that the solution to (6.51) is given by

$$A_t = A_0 e^{(r-\frac{1}{2}\sigma^2)t+\sigma W_t^Q}. \tag{6.52}$$

(iv") The Survival benefit has interest rate guarantee, i.e.,

$$S(T, A_T) = \max(A_T, \ Ge^{r_G T}), \tag{6.53}$$

where G is a constant and r_G is the guaranteed interest rate with $r_G < r$.
The death benefit is proportional to the market value of the investing account:

$$b(t, A_t) = kA_t, \tag{6.54}$$

where k is a constant, $0 < k < 1$.

6.4.1 *P.D.E. Approach*

Under the above assumptions, the partial differential equation (6.8) becomes:

$$\begin{cases} \dfrac{\partial v}{\partial t} + rA\dfrac{\partial v}{\partial A} + \dfrac{1}{2}\sigma^2 A^2 \dfrac{\partial^2 v}{\partial A^2} - (r+\mu)v + \mu k A = 0, \\ t = T : v = \max\{A, \ Ge^{r_G T}\}. \end{cases} \tag{6.55}$$

In this subsection we use slightly different approach from those used in the previous section to find the solution of this model (6.55). To this end, we first consider the situation $A = 0$.

From (6.52) it turns out that if there is a time t_0 such that $A_{t_0} = 0$, then $A_t \equiv 0$ for $t \geqslant 0$. In this special case, equation (6.55) becomes an ordinary differential equation:

$$\begin{cases} \dfrac{dv(t,0)}{dt} - (r+\mu)v(t,0) = 0, \\ t = T : v(t,0) = Ge^{r_G T}. \end{cases} \tag{6.56}$$

Thus, it is easy to get the solution:

$$v(t,0) = Ge^{r_G T}e^{-(r+\mu)(T-t)} \tag{6.57}$$

Finding the analytic solution of the PED model (6.55) consists of two steps:

First step:

Define

$$u(t,A) = v(t,A) - H(t), \tag{6.58}$$

where $H(t) = Ge^{r_G T}e^{-(r+\mu)(T-t)}$.

Then $u(t,A)$ satisfies the following equation:

$$\begin{cases} \dfrac{\partial u}{\partial t} + rA\dfrac{\partial u}{\partial A} + \dfrac{1}{2}\sigma^2 A^2 \dfrac{\partial^2 u}{\partial A^2} - (r+\mu)u + \mu k A = 0, \\ t = T : u(T,A) = \max\{A - Ge^{r_G T}, 0\}. \end{cases} \tag{6.59}$$

By the additive principle for the linear equation, the solution to equation (6.59) can be decomposed into $u = u_1 + u_2$, where u_1 and u_2 satisfy the following, respectively:

$$\begin{cases} \dfrac{\partial u_1}{\partial t} + rA\dfrac{\partial u_1}{\partial A} + \dfrac{1}{2}\sigma^2 A^2 \dfrac{\partial^2 u_1}{\partial A^2} - (r+\mu)u_1 = 0, \\ t = T : u_1(T,A) = \max(A - Ge^{r_G T}, 0), \end{cases} \tag{6.60}$$

$$\begin{cases} \dfrac{\partial u_2}{\partial t} + rA\dfrac{\partial u_2}{\partial A} + \dfrac{1}{2}\sigma^2 A^2 \dfrac{\partial^2 u_2}{\partial A^2} - (r+\mu)u_2 + \mu k A = 0, \\ t = T : u_2(T,A) = 0. \end{cases} \tag{6.61}$$

Second step:

Now we first solve (6.60). In a similar way to that in Section 6.3, we introduce the following transforms for both independent and dependent variables to simplify equation (6.60)

$$\begin{cases} \widetilde{u_1} = u_1 e^{(r+\mu)(T-t)}, \\ \widetilde{A} = A e^{(r-\frac{1}{2}\sigma^2)(T-t)}, \\ \tau = \dfrac{1}{2}\sigma^2 (T-t). \end{cases} \tag{6.62}$$

Then $\widetilde{u_1}$ satisfies

$$\begin{cases} \dfrac{\partial \widetilde{u_1}}{\partial \tau} = \widetilde{A}\dfrac{\partial \widetilde{u_1}}{\partial \widetilde{A}} + \widetilde{A}^2 \dfrac{\partial^2 \widetilde{u_1}}{\partial \widetilde{A}^2}, \quad 0 < \widetilde{A} < \infty, \\ \tau = 0: \quad \widetilde{u_1}(0, \widetilde{A}) = \max(\widetilde{A} - Ge^{r_G T}, 0). \end{cases} \tag{6.63}$$

Furthermore, we introduce

$$\widetilde{A} = e^y. \tag{6.64}$$

Thus,

$$\begin{cases} \dfrac{\partial \widetilde{u_1}}{\partial \tau} = \dfrac{\partial^2 \widetilde{u_1}}{\partial \widetilde{y}^2}, \quad -\infty < y < +\infty, \\ \tau = 0: \quad \widetilde{u_1} = \max\{e^y - Ge^{r_G T}, 0\}. \end{cases} \tag{6.65}$$

Using the Poisson formula for the solution to the Cauchy problem of the heat equation (refer to Gu & Li etc. (1987)), we can get the solution to equation (6.65):

$$\begin{aligned} \widetilde{u_1}(\tau, y) &= \frac{1}{2\sqrt{\pi\tau}} \int_{-\infty}^{+\infty} \max\{e^z - Ge^{r_G T}, 0\} e^{-\frac{(y-z)^2}{4\tau}} dz \\ &= \frac{1}{2\sqrt{\pi\tau}} \int_{\ln G + r_G T}^{+\infty} (e^z - Ge^{r_G T}) e^{-\frac{(y-z)^2}{4\tau}} dz \\ &= \frac{e^{y+\tau}}{2\sqrt{\pi\tau}} \int_{\ln G + r_G T}^{+\infty} e^{-\frac{(z-(y+2\tau))^2}{4\tau}} dz - \frac{Ge^{r_G T}}{2\sqrt{\pi\tau}} \int_{\ln G + r_G T}^{+\infty} e^{-\frac{(z-y)^2}{4\tau}} dz, \end{aligned}$$

i.e.,

$$\widetilde{u_1}(\tau, y) = e^{y+\tau}\Phi\left(\frac{y + 2\tau - \ln G - r_G T}{\sqrt{2\tau}}\right) - Ge^{r_G T}\Phi\left(\frac{y - \ln G - r_G T}{\sqrt{2\tau}}\right), \tag{6.66}$$

in which the function Φ is the cumulative distribution function for a standard normal random variable, given by

$$\Phi(x) = \frac{1}{\sqrt{2\pi}} \int_{-\infty}^{x} e^{-\frac{\xi^2}{2}} d\xi.$$

The solution to (6.60) can be obtained by substituting the transform reversely into (6.66):

$$u_1(t, A) = Ae^{-\mu(T-t)}\Phi(d_3) - Ge^{r_G T-(r+\mu)(T-t)}\Phi(d_4), \tag{6.67}$$

where

$$d_3 = \frac{\ln\frac{A}{G} - r_G T + (r + \frac{1}{2}\sigma^2)(T-t)}{\sqrt{\sigma^2(T-t)}}, \quad d_4 = d_3 - \sqrt{\sigma^2(T-t)}. \tag{6.68}$$

By the uniqueness of solution to (6.61) (see Gu & Li etc., (1987)), we look for $u_2(t, A)$ as follows:

$$u_2(t, A) = Au_3(t). \tag{6.69}$$

Thus u_3 satisfies the following ordinary differential equation:

$$\begin{cases} \frac{du_3(t)}{dt} - \mu u_3 + \mu k = 0, & 0 < t < T, \\ t = T: \quad u_3(T) = 0 \end{cases} \tag{6.70}$$

Thus, it is easy to get

$$u_3(t) = k\left(1 - e^{-\mu(T-t)}\right). \tag{6.71}$$

Then

$$u_2(t, A) = kA\left(1 - e^{-\mu(T-t)}\right). \tag{6.72}$$

Combining (6.58), (6.67) and (6.72), we finally get the fair valuation of this unit-link policy:

$$\begin{aligned} v(t, A) &= u_1(t, A) + u_2(t, A) + H(t) \\ &= Ae^{-\mu(T-t)}\Phi(d_3) + Ge^{r_G T-(r+\mu)(T-t)}(1 - \Phi(d_4)) \\ &\quad + kA(1 - e^{-\mu(T-t)}), \end{aligned} \tag{6.73}$$

where d_3, d_4 are defined by (6.68).

6.4.2 G.E.D.V. Approach

In this subsection, we use the Generalized Expected Discounted Value Approach to get the financial fair value for the liability of the unit-linked life insurance policy previously described in this section.

By (6.22) and (6.23), the conditional probability distribution function of $T(x)$ and the conditional probability density function are

$$F_{T(x_0)|T(x_0)>t_0}(t) = 1 - \frac{s(x_0+t)/s(x_0)}{s(x_0+t_0)/s(x_0)} = 1 - \exp\left(-\int_{t_0}^{t} \mu_d(x_0+\tau)d\tau\right), \tag{6.74}$$

$$f_{T(x_0)|T(x_0)>t_0}(t) = \mu_d(x_0+t)\exp\left(-\int_{t_0}^{t} \mu_d(x_0+\tau)d\tau\right), \tag{6.75}$$

respectively. Similarly to (6.52), we have

$$A_s = A_t e^{(r-\frac{1}{2}\sigma^2)(s-t)+\sigma(W_s^Q - W_t^Q)}, \quad \forall s > t. \tag{6.76}$$

Let

$$Y = \sigma(W_s^Q - W_t^Q) - \frac{\sigma^2}{2}(s-t), \tag{6.77}$$

$$Z = \sigma(W_T^Q - W_t^Q) - \frac{\sigma^2}{2}(T-t). \tag{6.78}$$

Then both Y and Z are normal distributions under probability measure Q. Their mean and variance are

$$\begin{aligned} E[Y] &= -\frac{\sigma^2}{2}(s-t), \\ E[Z] &= -\frac{\sigma^2}{2}(T-t), \\ Var(Y) &= \sigma^2(s-t), \\ Var(Z) &= \sigma^2(T-t). \end{aligned} \tag{6.79}$$

Then

$$\begin{aligned} A_s &= A_t e^{Y+r(s-t)}, \\ A_T &= A_t e^{Z+r(T-t)}. \end{aligned} \tag{6.80}$$

From the results in Section 6.2.3, we get

$$\begin{aligned}
&v(t, A_t)\\
&= E^Q[E[\text{discounted future cash flows}|T(x_0) > t, A_t]\\
&= E^Q[E^{T(x_0)|T(x_0)>t}[\text{discounted future cash flows}|A_t]]\\
&= E^Q[E^{T(x_0)|T(x_0)>t}[\max\{Ge^{r_G T}, A_T\}e^{-r(T-t)} + kA_{T(x_0)}e^{-r(T(x_0)-t)}]|A_t]\\
&= E^Q[E^{T(x_0)|T(x_0)>t}[\max\{Ge^{r_G T}, A_t e^{Z+r(T-t)}\}e^{-r(T-t)}\\
&\qquad +kA_t e^{Y+r(T(x_0)-t)}e^{-r(T(x_0)-t)}]|A_t]\\
&= I_1 + I_2, \qquad (6.81)
\end{aligned}$$

where

$$\begin{aligned}
I_1 &= E^Q[E^{T(x_0)|T(x_0)>t}[\max\{Ge^{r_G T}, A_t e^{Z+r(T-t)}\}e^{-r(T-t)}|A_t]],\\
I_2 &= E^Q[E^{T(x_0)|T(x_0)>t}[kA_t e^{Y+r(T(x_0)-t)}e^{-r(T(x_0)-t)}]|A_t]. \qquad (6.82)
\end{aligned}$$

Now we compute I_1 and I_2, respectively.

$$\begin{aligned}
I_1 &= E^Q[E^{T(x_0)|T(x_0)>t}[\max\{Ge^{r_G T}, A_t e^{Z+r(T-t)}\}e^{-r(T-t)}|A_t]]\\
&= \frac{1}{\sqrt{2\pi\sigma^2(T-t)}}\cdot\\
&\quad \int_{-\infty}^{\infty} \max\{Ge^{r_G T-r(T-t)}, A_t e^z\}e^{-\mu(T-t)}e^{-\frac{(z+\sigma^2(T-t)/2)^2}{2\sigma^2(T-t)}}dz\\
&= \frac{Ge^{r_G T-(r+\mu)(T-t)}}{\sqrt{2\pi\sigma^2(T-t)}}\int_{-\infty}^{\ln\frac{G}{A_t}+r_G T-r(T-t)} e^{-\frac{(z+\sigma^2(T-t)/2)^2}{2\sigma^2(T-t)}}dz\\
&+ \frac{A_t e^{-\mu(T-t)}}{\sqrt{2\pi\sigma^2(T-t)}}\int_{\ln\frac{G}{A_t}+r_G T-r(T-t)}^{+\infty} e^z e^{-\frac{(z+\sigma^2(T-t)/2)^2}{2\sigma^2(T-t)}}dz\\
&= \frac{Ge^{r_G T-(r+\mu)(T-t)}}{\sqrt{2\pi\sigma^2(T-t)}}\int_{-\infty}^{\frac{\ln\frac{G}{A_t}+r_G T-r(T-t)+\frac{1}{2}\sigma^2(T-t)}{\sqrt{\sigma^2(T-t)}}} e^{-\frac{x^2}{2}}dx\\
&+ \frac{A_t e^{-\mu(T-t)}}{\sqrt{2\pi\sigma^2(T-t)}}\int_{\frac{\ln\frac{G}{A_t}+r_G T-r(T-t)-\frac{1}{2}\sigma^2(T-t)}{\sqrt{\sigma^2(T-t)}}}^{+\infty} e^{-\frac{x^2}{2}}dx\\
&= Ge^{r_G T-(r+\mu)(T-t)}\left(1-\Phi\left(\frac{\ln\frac{A_t}{G}-(r-\frac{1}{2}\sigma^2)(T-t)-r_G T}{\sqrt{\sigma^2(T-t)}}\right)\right)\\
&+ A_t e^{-\mu(T-t)}\Phi\left(\left(\frac{\ln\frac{A_t}{G}+(r+\frac{1}{2}\sigma^2)(T-t)-r_G T}{\sqrt{\sigma^2(T-t)}}\right)\right). \qquad (6.83)
\end{aligned}$$

To calculate I_2, noticing that Y defined in (6.77) is the normal distribution under the probability measure Q, we get

$$E[e^Y] = \frac{1}{\sqrt{2\pi\sigma^2(s-t)}} \int_{-\infty}^{\infty} e^y e^{-\frac{(y+\sigma^2(s-t)/2)^2}{2\sigma^2(s-t)}} dy = 1. \tag{6.84}$$

Then we have

$$\begin{aligned} I_2 &= E^Q[E^{T(x_0)|T(x_0>t}[kA_t e^{Y+r(T(x_0)-t)} e^{-r(T(x_0)-t)}]|A_t] \\ &= E^{T(x_0)|T(x_0)>t}[kA_t E^Q[e^Y]] \\ &= \int_t^T kA_t \mu e^{-\mu(s-t)} ds \\ &= kA_t(1-e^{-\mu(T-t)}). \end{aligned} \tag{6.85}$$

Combining (6.81) with (6.83) and (6.85), we obtain the final result as follows,

$$\begin{aligned} v(t, A_t) = {} & A_t e^{-\mu(T-t)}\Phi(d_3) + Ge^{r_G T-(r+\mu)(T-t)}(1-\Phi(d_4)) \\ & + kA_t(1-e^{-\mu(T-t)}), \end{aligned} \tag{6.86}$$

where d_3 and d_4 are defined in (6.68). It is the same results as (6.73).

6.5 Fair Valuation of Second Kind of Unit-linked Policy with Surrender Option

Now we consider the valuation of policies with surrender option. Analogous to the American options, the valuation of policies with surrender option is much more complicated. Since we now have to determine not only the value of the policy, but also the optimal time to surrender. This is a free boundary problem. It is impossible to get the analytical solution to free boundary problem and we must recur to the numerical method. In Section 6.5.1 we first discuss the impact of the parameters, which appears in the model(6.55), on existence and behavior of the free boundaries, i.e., the surrender possibility. Then Section 6.5.2 is focused on the local analysis of the surrender near the expiring date. Section 6.5.3 is devoted to the integral equation on $v(t, A)$. Two approaches have been introduced to get the numerical solution for the value of policy and the free boundary in Section 6.5.4: one is to reduce the free boundary problem to the linear complementary problem, then use SOR method to get the numerical solution, and the other is to solve the integral equation derived in Section 6.5.3 by the numerical method.

In this Section the notation and assumptions on the model are the same as that in Section 6.4, that is, the following assumptions still hold:

(ii") Both of $r(t)$ and $\mu(t) = \mu_d(t + x_0)$ are assumed to be constants for the sake of simplicity.

(iii") The asset A_t can be traded in a arbitrage-free market and its market value of the investing account is a Geometrical Brownian Motion, i.e.,

$$dA_t = \alpha A_t dt + \sigma A_t dW_t, \quad A_0 \text{ is given,} \tag{6.87}$$

where both α and σ are constants. Then after risk-adjusted (refer to Baxter & Rennie (1996)),

$$dA_t = rA_t dt + \sigma A_t dW_t^Q, \tag{6.88}$$

where r is the risk free interest rate.

(iv") The Survival benefit has interest rate guarantee, i.e.,

$$S(T, A_T) = \max(A_T,\ Ge^{r_G T}), \tag{6.89}$$

where G is a constant and r_G is the guaranteed interest rate, $r_G < r$.

The death benefit is proportional to the market value of the investing account,

$$b(t, A_t) = kA_t, \tag{6.90}$$

where k is a constant, $0 < k < 1$.

Concerning the surrender, we make the following assumptions:
(S1'). The surrender benefit at time t is given by the following:

$$h(t, A) = \max\left(\frac{t - T_0}{T - T_0}\max(A,\ Ge^{r_G t}),\ 0\right), \tag{6.91}$$

i.e., surrender is not allowed from $t = 0$ to $t = T_0$, and it is allowed from $t = T_0$ to T with the deducted benefit which is the larger of two quantities: (a) the market value of A at time t, and (b) the value of account with interest rate guarantees.

(S2). The insured chooses to surrender at time t if and only if the surrender benefit $h(t, A)$ is not less than the value of the policy $v(t, A)$. Now the P.D.E. model is as follows: In the surrender region the following is satisfied:

$$\begin{cases} \dfrac{\partial v}{\partial t} + rA\dfrac{\partial v}{\partial A} + \dfrac{1}{2}\sigma^2 A^2 \dfrac{\partial^2 v}{\partial A^2} - (r+\mu)v + \mu k A < 0, \\ v(t,A) = h(t,A) = \max\left(\frac{t-T_0}{T-T_0}\max(A,\ Ge^{r_G t}),\ 0\right), \end{cases} \tag{6.92}$$

while in the non-surrender region,

$$\begin{cases} \dfrac{\partial v}{\partial t} + rA\dfrac{\partial v}{\partial A} + \dfrac{1}{2}\sigma^2 A^2 \dfrac{\partial^2 v}{\partial A^2} - (r+\mu)v + \mu k A = 0. \\ v(t,A) > h(t,A) = \max\left(\frac{t-T_0}{T-T_0}\max(A,\ Ge^{r_G t}),\ 0\right). \end{cases} \tag{6.93}$$

Thus, the corresponding PDE model for the valuation of policy with surrender options in non-surrender region is:

$$\begin{cases} \dfrac{\partial v}{\partial t} + rA\dfrac{\partial v}{\partial A} + \dfrac{1}{2}\sigma^2 A^2 \dfrac{\partial^2 v}{\partial A^2} - (r+\mu)v + \mu k A = 0, \\ at\ \ t = T: \quad v(T,A) = \max(Ge^{r_G T}, A), \\ \text{on } A = A_f(t): \ \ v(t,A_f) = h(t,A_f) = \max\left(\frac{t-T_0}{T-T_0}\max(A_f, G^{r_G t}), 0\right), \\ \dfrac{\partial v}{\partial A}(t,A_f) = \dfrac{\partial h}{\partial A}(t,A_f), \end{cases} \tag{6.94}$$

where A_f is unknown and it should be determined along with the solution $v(t, A)$.

6.5.1 Analysis of Parameters

There are some parameters in the model (6.92) and (6.93) such as r, r_G, G, T, T_0, μ, σ, k, etc, which will definitely have impact on existence and behavior of the free boundaries i.e., the possibility of surrender, and the value of the policy. This will be discussed in this subsection by theoretical analysis. Here we always assume that

$$\frac{1}{T-T_0} - (r - r_G) > 0. \tag{6.95}$$

Suppose that the free boundary $A = A_f$ does exist in the time period $[T_0, T]$, i.e., the surrender region exists and the inequality in (6.92) is satisfied. Then if we substitute $v(t, A) = h(t, A)$ into the inequality in (6.92), we can deduce the necessary condition for existence of the free boundaries.

Hereinafter we will divide the plane (t, A) into two areas: $\{(t, A)|Ge^{r_G t} < A\}$ and $\{t, A)|Ge^{r_G t} > A\}$ to discuss the necessary condition for existence of the free boundaries.

(Region 1) In the region of $\{(t, A)|Ge^{r_G t} < A\}$, the value of the policy is $v(t, A) = h(t, A) = \dfrac{t - T_0}{T - T_0}A$. Substituting it into the inequality in (6.92) we have

$$\frac{A}{T - T_0}(1 - \mu(t - T_0)) + \mu k A < 0. \tag{6.96}$$

Because A is always positive, (6.96) implies that

$$t > T_0 + \frac{1}{\mu} + k(T - T_0), \tag{6.97}$$

Owing to $t \leqslant T$, we must have

$$\mu > \frac{1}{(1 - k)(T - T_0)}. \tag{6.98}$$

The above analysis shows that if surrender exists in the region of $\{(t, A)|Ge^{r_G t} < A\}$, then the parameters must satisfy the inequality (6.98), and the free boundary exists only in the period of $(T_0 + \dfrac{1}{\mu} + k(T - T_0),\ T]$.

(Region 2) While in the region of $\{(t, A)|Ge^{r_G t} > A\}$, the value of the policy is $v(t, A) = h(t, A) = \dfrac{t - T_0}{T - T_0}Ge^{r_G t}$. Substituting it into the inequality in (6.92), we obtain that

$$\frac{Ge^{r_G t}}{T - T_0}(1 - (r + \mu - r_G)(t - T_0)) + \mu k A < 0. \tag{6.99}$$

Since both A and $Ge^{r_G t}$ are positive, the inequality (6.99) is equivalent to the following two inequalities:

$$1 - (r + \mu - r_G)(t - T_0) < 0, \tag{6.100}$$

and

$$A < \frac{Ge^{r_G t}}{\mu k(T - T_0)}((r + \mu - r_G)(t - T_0) - 1). \tag{6.101}$$

Because $t < T$, (6.100) implies that

$$\mu > \frac{1}{T - T_0} - (r - r_G). \tag{6.102}$$

For (6.101), there are two possibilities:

- $\dfrac{(r + \mu - r_G)(T - T_0) - 1}{\mu k(T - T_0)} \geqslant 1,$
- $\dfrac{(r + \mu - r_G)(T - T_0) - 1}{\mu k(T - T_0)} < 1.$

Then it is easy to see that in both cases there exists an area in which both inequalities (6.101) and $Ge^{r_G t} > A$ are satisfied. The above analysis shows that if surrender exists in the region of $\{(t, A)|Ge^{r_G t} > A\}$, the parameters must satisfy (6.102), and the free boundary exists only within the time period $(T_0 + \dfrac{1}{r + \mu - r_G}, T]$.

Now we can summarize the result as follows.

(Case 1) When $0 < \mu < \dfrac{1}{T - T_0} - (r - r_G)$, neither (6.98), nor (6.102) are satisfied. Therefore, the insured will not choose surrender before maturity date.

(Case 2) When $\dfrac{1}{T - T_0} - (r - r_G) < \mu < \dfrac{1}{(1 - k)(T - T_0)}$, (6.98) is not satisfied, but (6.102) is satisfied. Therefore, there is probably only one free boundary, i.e., the insured will choose surrender in the region $\{(t, A)|Ge^{r_G t} > A\}$ within the time period $(T_0 + \dfrac{1}{r + \mu - r_G}, T]$. On the other hand, there is no free boundary in region $\{(t, A)|Ge^{r_G t} < A\}$. This means that no insured will choose surrender in this area.

(Case 3) When $\mu > \dfrac{1}{(1 - k)(T - T_0)}$, both inequalities (6.98) and (6.102) are satisfied. Therefore, there are probably two free boundaries such that one of these is in the area $\{(t, A)|Ge^{r_G t} > A\}$ within the time period $(T_0 + \dfrac{1}{r + \mu - r_G}, T]$, and the other is in the area $\{(t, A)|Ge^{r_G t} < A\}$ within the time period $(T_0 + \dfrac{1}{\mu} + k(T - T_0), T]$.

What we discussed above are the necessary conditions on when there exist free boundaries. In fact, they are also the sufficient conditions as well. In other words, if the above conditions are satisfied, then there must exist free boundaries. This fact can be proved by the variational principle and other PDE tools (see Friedman (1982)). In Friedman & Shen (2001) a similar problem has been studied in detail.

6.5.2 *Local Analysis of Free Boundary near the Expiry Date*

In this subsection we make further discussion on the free boundary under the assumption $\frac{1}{T-T_0}-(r-r_G)<\mu<\frac{1}{(1-k)(T-T_0)}$. From the results (in Case 2) in previous subsection we know that in this case there is probably only one free boundary, i.e., the insured will choose surrender in the region $\{(t,A)|Ge^{r_Gt}>A\}$ within the time period $(T_0+\frac{1}{r+\mu-r_G}, T]$. On the other hand, there is no free boundary in region $\{(t,A)|Ge^{r_Gt}<A\}$. This means that no insured will choose surrender in this area. In what follows, we consider the local analysis of free boundary near the expiry date in detail in the region $\{(t,A)|0<t<T, Ge^{r_Gt}>A\}$. Now model (6.94) becomes

$$\begin{cases}\frac{\partial v}{\partial t}+rA\frac{\partial v}{\partial A}+\frac{1}{2}\sigma^2A^2\frac{\partial^2 v}{\partial A^2}-(r+\mu)v+\mu kA=0,\\ t=T:\ \ v(T,A)=Ge^{r_GT},\\ on\ \ A=A_f(t):\ v(t,A_f)=\frac{t-T_0}{T-T_0}Ge^{r_Gt},\\ \frac{\partial v}{\partial A}(t,A_f)=0.\end{cases} \tag{6.103}$$

To simplify (6.103), we introduce the following transformations:

$$\begin{cases}t=T-\frac{2\tau}{\sigma^2},\\ A=Ge^{r_Gt}e^x,\\ v=Ge^{r_Gt}\left(\frac{t-T_0}{T-T_0}+w(\tau,x)\right).\end{cases} \tag{6.104}$$

After these transformations, region $\{(t,A)|0<t<T, Ge^{r_Gt}>A\}$ in (t,A) plane becomes the region $\{(\tau,x)|0<\tau<\frac{1}{2}\sigma^2T,\ -\infty<x<0\}$ in (τ,x) plane. The free boundary $A=A_f(t)$ in (t,A) plane becomes $x=x_f(\tau)$ in (τ,x) plane. Region $\{(\tau,x)|0<\tau<\frac{1}{2}\sigma^2T,\ -\infty<x<0\}$

consists of two parts: one is the surrender region and the other is the non-surrender region.

Corresponding PDE model for $w(\tau, x)$ in the non-surrender region is:

$$\begin{cases} \dfrac{\partial w}{\partial \tau} = \dfrac{\partial^2 w}{\partial x^2} + \left(\dfrac{2r}{\sigma^2} - 1\right)\dfrac{\partial w}{\partial x} - \dfrac{2(r+\mu-r_G)}{\sigma^2} w + H(\tau, x), \quad -\infty < x < 0, \\ \tau = 0, \quad w(0, x) = 0, \\ \text{on } x = x_f(\tau): \; w(\tau, x_f(\tau)) = 0, \\ \dfrac{\partial w}{\partial x}(\tau, x_f(\tau)) = 0, \end{cases} \tag{6.105}$$

where

$$H(\tau, x) = \frac{2\mu k e^x}{\sigma^2} - \frac{2(r+\mu-r_G)\left(T - T_0 - \frac{2\tau}{\sigma^2}\right) - 1}{\sigma^2 (T - T_0)}. \tag{6.106}$$

Furthermore, the constraint on $v(t, A)$

$$v(t, A) \geqslant h(t, A) \tag{6.107}$$

becomes the constraint on $w(\tau, x)$

$$w(\tau, x) \geqslant 0, \;\; \forall (\tau, x) \in \{(\tau, x) | 0 < \tau < \frac{1}{2}\sigma^2, \; -\infty < x < 0\}. \tag{6.108}$$

Now (6.92) and (6.93) become as follows: while in the non-surrender area in $\{(\tau, x) | 0 < \tau < \frac{1}{2}\sigma^2 T, \;\; -\infty < x < 0\}$

$$\begin{cases} \dfrac{\partial w}{\partial \tau} = \dfrac{\partial^2 w}{\partial x^2} + \left(\dfrac{2r}{\sigma^2} - 1\right)\dfrac{\partial w}{\partial x} - \dfrac{2(r+\mu-r_G)}{\sigma^2} w + H(\tau, x), \\ w(\tau, x) > 0, \end{cases} \tag{6.109}$$

while in the surrender region

$$\begin{cases} \dfrac{\partial w}{\partial \tau} > \dfrac{\partial^2 w}{\partial x^2} + \left(\dfrac{2r}{\sigma^2} - 1\right)\dfrac{\partial w}{\partial x} - \dfrac{2(r+\mu-r_G)}{\sigma^2} w + H(\tau, x), \\ w(\tau, x) = 0. \end{cases} \tag{6.110}$$

Assume that the solution is smooth enough, then by (6.105), (6.109) and (6.110) we have

$$\begin{cases} \dfrac{\partial w}{\partial \tau}(0, x) = H(0, x), \quad -\infty < x < 0, \\ w(0, x) = 0, \quad -\infty < x < 0, \\ w(\tau, x) > 0, \quad 0 < \tau < \frac{1}{2}\sigma^2 T, \quad -\infty < x < 0, \end{cases} \tag{6.111}$$

in the non-surrender region and while in the surrender region

$$\begin{cases} \frac{\partial w}{\partial \tau}(0,x) > H(0,x), & -\infty < x < 0, \\ w(\tau,x) = 0, \quad 0 < \tau < \frac{1}{2}\sigma^2 T, & -\infty < x < 0. \end{cases} \tag{6.112}$$

The behavior of function $H(\tau, x)$ play very important role on existence of the free boundary. First we consider the behavior of $H(0, x)$. It is clear that $H(0, x)$ is a monotone increasing function of x. Let

$$x_0 = \ln \frac{(r + \mu - r_G)(T - T_0) - 1}{\mu k(T - T_0)}, \tag{6.113}$$

which is the solution to $H(0, x) = 0$. Now we consider the location of the free boundary near $t = T$ in the following two cases: Case 2' and Case 2", respectively.

(Case 2') If the parameters satisfy

$$\frac{(r + \mu - r_G)(T - T_0) - 1}{\mu k(T - T_0)} < 1, \tag{6.114}$$

then $x_0 < 0$, and when $x < x_0$, $H(0, x) < 0$, while $x_0 < x < 0$, $H(0, x) > 0$. In what follows we prove that in this case, x_0 is the starting point of the free boundary $x = x_f(\tau)$ at time $t = 0$ in (τ, x) plane. We have $H(0, x) < 0$, $\forall x < 0$. If insured does not surrender, then (6.111) holds. Thus, when $\tau \to 0^+$, $w(\tau, x) < 0$, which contradicts the constrain (6.108) $w(\tau, x) \geqslant 0$. Thus, $\{(0, x)|x < x_0\}$ is in the surrender region. Because of $H(0, x) > 0$, $\forall x > x_0$, and $\frac{\partial w}{\partial \tau} \geqslant H(0, x)$, we conclude that when $\tau \to 0^+$, $w(\tau, x) > 0$. From the above analysis we conclude that x_0 is starting point of the free boundary $x = x_f(t)$ at time $t = 0$ in (τ, x) plane, i.e.,

$$x_f(0^+) = x_0.$$

It turns out that in (t, A) plane the location of free boundary $A = A_f(t)$ near time $t = T$ is given by the following:

$$A_f(T^-) = Ge^{r_G T} \frac{(r + \mu - r_G)(T - T_0) - 1}{\mu k(T - T_0)}.$$

(Case 2") If the parameters satisfy

$$\frac{(r + \mu - r_G)(T - T_0) - 1}{\mu k(T - T_0)} \geqslant 1, \tag{6.115}$$

then $x_0 \geqslant 0$. First we prove that in this case $\{(0,x)|x < 0\}$ is in the surrender region, that is

$$\frac{\partial w}{\partial \tau}(0,x) > H(0,x) \quad \text{for} \quad x < 0. \tag{6.116}$$

If the above is not true, then there exists some $\bar{x} < 0$ such that,

$$\frac{\partial w}{\partial \tau}(0,\bar{x}) = H(0,\bar{x}) < 0.$$

It turns out that when $\tau \to 0^+$, $w(\tau,x) < 0$ which contradict (6.108). Thus (6.116) holds, i.e., the insured has to surrender in this area. Thus, $x_f(0^+) \geqslant 0$, in (τ,x) plane, i.e., $A_f(T^-) \geqslant Ge^{r_G T}$ in (t,A) plane. But in Case(2) the surrender can happen only in the area $\{(t,A)|Ge^{r_G t} \geqslant A\}$. Thus, we have

$$A_f(T^-) = Ge^{r_G T}. \tag{6.117}$$

Combining Case 2' with Case 2", we have

$$A_f(T^-) = \min\left(\frac{(r+\mu-r_G)(T-T_0)-1}{\mu k(T-T_0)}Ge^{r_G T}, Ge^{r_G T}\right). \tag{6.118}$$

In Section 6.5.4.2, we will combine the integral equation of $v(t,A)$ derived in the next subsection with the location of the free boundary near the expiry date (6.118) to get free boundary numerically.

6.5.3 *Integral Equation on $v(t,A)$*

In this subsection we derive the integral equation for the liability of policy $v(t,A)$ under the assumption

$$\frac{1}{T-T_0} - (r-r_G) < \mu < \frac{1}{(1-k)(T-T_0)}.$$

From the analysis in Subsection 6.5.2 (Case 2), we conclude that the free boundary exists only in the area $\{(t,A)|Ge^{r_G t} \geqslant A\} \bigcap \{(t,A)|A < \dfrac{(r+\mu-r_G)(T-T_0)-1}{\mu k(T-T_0)}Ge^{r_G t}\}$.

When $A < A_f(t)$, $v(t,A) = h(t,A) = \dfrac{t-T_0}{T-T_0} G e^{r_G t}$. Thus,

$$
\begin{cases}
\dfrac{\partial v}{\partial t} + rA\dfrac{\partial v}{\partial A} + \dfrac{1}{2}\sigma^2 A^2 \dfrac{\partial^2 v}{\partial A^2} - (r+\mu)v \\
\quad = \begin{cases} -\mu k A, & A > A_f, \\ \dfrac{1-(r+\mu-r_G)(t-T_0)}{T-T_0} G e^{r_G t}, & A \leqslant A_f, \end{cases} \\
t = T: \quad v(T,A) = \max(Ge^{r_G T}, A).
\end{cases}
\tag{6.119}
$$

We can write the solution of this partial differential equation as the sum of three terms:

$$
v(t,A) = v_1(t,A) + v_2(t,A) + v_3(t,A) = \widetilde{v}(t,A) + v_3(t,A), \tag{6.120}
$$

where v_1 satisfy

$$
\begin{cases}
\dfrac{\partial v_1}{\partial t} + rA\dfrac{\partial v_1}{\partial A} + \dfrac{1}{2}\sigma^2 A^2 \dfrac{\partial^2 v_1}{\partial A^2} - (r+\mu)v_1 = 0, \\
t = T: \quad v_1(T,A) = \max\{Ge^{r_G T}, A\},
\end{cases}
\tag{6.121}
$$

and v_2 is the solution to the following problem:

$$
\begin{cases}
\dfrac{\partial v_2}{\partial t} + rA\dfrac{\partial v_2}{\partial A} + \dfrac{1}{2}\sigma^2 A^2 \dfrac{\partial^2 v_2}{\partial A^2} - (r+\mu)v_2 = -\mu k A, \\
t = T: \quad v_2(T,A) = 0.
\end{cases}
\tag{6.122}
$$

From Section 6.4 we know that the solution to (6.120) and (6.122) are given by the following:

$$
v_1(t,A) = Ae^{-\mu(T-t)}\Phi(d_3) + Ge^{r_G T - (r+\mu)(T-t)}\Phi(-d_4), \tag{6.123}
$$

$$
v_2(t,A) = kA(1 - e^{-\mu(T-t)}). \tag{6.124}
$$

Thus $v_1 + v_2$ is the value of policy without the surrender. It turns out that v_3 should be the solution to the following problem:

$$
\begin{cases}
\dfrac{\partial v_3}{\partial t} + rA\dfrac{\partial v_3}{\partial A} + \dfrac{1}{2}\sigma^2 A^2 \dfrac{\partial^2 v_3}{\partial A^2} - (r+\mu)v_3 = f(t,A), \\
t = T: \quad v_3(T,A) = 0
\end{cases}
\tag{6.125}
$$

where

$$
f(t,A) = \begin{cases} 0, & A > A_f(t), \\ \mu k A + \dfrac{1-(r+\mu-r_G)(t-T_0)}{T-T_0} G e^{r_G t}, & A \leqslant A_f(t). \end{cases}
\tag{6.126}
$$

To solve (6.125), we use the Duhamel principle stated in Section 3:

Lemma 6.2 *Suppose $w(t, A; \tau)$ is the solution to the following problem:*

$$\begin{cases} \dfrac{\partial w}{\partial t} + rA\dfrac{\partial w}{\partial A} + \dfrac{1}{2}\sigma^2 A^2 \dfrac{\partial^2 w}{\partial A^2} - (r+\mu)w = 0, \\ t = \tau : w(\tau, A) = -f(\tau, A), \end{cases} \tag{6.127}$$

then the solution to (6.125) and (6.126) is

$$v_3(t, A) = \int_t^T w(t, A; \tau)d\tau. \tag{6.128}$$

It is easy to see that the solution to problem (6.127) is

$$w(t, A; \tau) = \frac{1}{2\sqrt{\pi\xi}} e^{-(r+\mu)(\tau-t)} \int_{-\infty}^{+\infty} \left(-f(\tau, e^z) e^{-\frac{(y-z)^2}{4\xi}} \right) dz, \tag{6.129}$$

where $\xi = \frac{1}{2}\sigma^2(\tau - t)$, $y = \ln A + (r - \frac{1}{2}\sigma^2)(\tau - t)$. By the definition of $f(t, A)$ in (6.126) and in a similar way to the derivation in Section 6.4.1, we have

$$\begin{aligned} & w(t, A; \tau) \\ = & \frac{1}{2\sqrt{\pi\xi}} e^{-(r+\mu)(\tau-t)} \int_{-\infty}^{\ln A_f(\tau)} \left(-f(\tau, e^z) e^{-\frac{(y-z)^2}{4\xi}} \right) dz \\ = & \frac{1}{2\sqrt{\pi\xi}} e^{-(r+\mu)(\tau-t)} \cdot \\ & \left(-\frac{1-(r+\mu-r_G)(\tau-T_0)}{T-T_0} G e^{r_G \tau} \int_{-\infty}^{\ln A_f(\tau)} e^{-\frac{(y-z)^2}{4\xi}} dz \right. \\ & \left. - \int_{-\infty}^{\ln A_f(\tau)} (\mu k e^z e^{-\frac{(y-z)^2}{4\xi}}) dz \right) \\ = & -\frac{1-(r+\mu-r_G)(\tau-T_0)}{T-T_0} e^{-(r+\mu)(\tau-t)} G e^{r_G \tau} \Phi(d_5) \\ & -\mu k A^{-\mu(\tau-t)} \Phi(d_6) \\ = & g(A, A_f(\tau), t, \tau), \end{aligned} \tag{6.130}$$

where

$$d_5 = \frac{\ln(\frac{A_f(\tau)}{A}) - (r - \frac{1}{2}\sigma^2)(\tau - t)}{\sqrt{\sigma^2(\tau - t)}},$$

$$d_6 = \frac{\ln \frac{A_f(\tau)}{A} - (r + \frac{1}{2}\sigma^2)(\tau - t)}{\sqrt{\sigma^2(\tau - t)}}.$$

Finally, we get the integral equation for the value of policy with surrender as follows:

$$v(t, A) = \widetilde{v}(t, A) + \int_t^T g(A, A_f(\tau), t, \tau)d\tau, \tag{6.131}$$

where $\widetilde{v}(t, A) = v_1(t, A) + v_2(t, A)$ is defined as before. From (6.131) and the assumptions on the coefficient, we can draw two conclusions. The first one is that $f(t, A)$ is non-positive, hence, $v_3(t, A)$ is non-negative. Thus the value of policy with surrender is large than or equal to the value of policy without surrender. The second conclusion is that from (6.131) it is impossible to get the analytic solution for the value of policy with surrender. In the next subsection we give the numerical results for this integral equation.

6.5.4 *Numerical Results*

In this subsection two numerical approaches to get the fair valuation of a policy with surrender option are derived. One approach is that we first reduce the "free boundary problem" to a "linear complementary problem"; then we use the finite difference method based on Subsection 6.2.2. and Subsection 6.5.1. The other approach is to solve the integral equation (6.131) numerically.

6.5.4.1 *Linear Complementary Problem and Projected SOR Method*

Similarly to that in Section 6.4.1, we first make the following transformations to simplify (6.94):

$$\begin{cases} \widetilde{v} = ve^{(r+\mu)(T-t)}, \\ y = \ln A + (r - \frac{1}{2}\sigma^2)(T - t), \\ \tau = \dfrac{1}{2}\sigma^2(T - t). \end{cases} \tag{6.132}$$

Let

$$\widetilde{f}(\tau, y) = \frac{\mu k}{\frac{1}{2}\sigma^2} e^{y + \tau + \frac{2\mu\tau}{\sigma^2}}, \tag{6.133}$$

and

$$g(\tau, y)$$
$$= \max\left[\left(1 - \frac{2\tau}{\sigma^2(T - T_0)}\right)\max\left(e^{y+\tau+\frac{2\mu\tau}{\sigma^2}}, Ge^{r_G T + \frac{2\tau(r+\mu-r_G)}{\sigma^2}}\right), 0\right]. \tag{6.134}$$

The original free boundary problem (6.94) can be reduced to the following:

$$\begin{cases} \dfrac{\partial\widetilde{v}}{\partial\tau} = \dfrac{\partial^2\widetilde{v}}{\partial y^2} + \widetilde{f}(\tau, y), \\ \tau = 0: \quad \widetilde{v}(0, y) = g(0, y), \\ y = y_f: \quad \widetilde{v}(\tau, y) = g(\tau, y), \\ \dfrac{\partial\widetilde{v}}{\partial y}(\tau, y) = \dfrac{\partial g}{\partial y}(\tau, y). \end{cases} \tag{6.135}$$

Thus (6.92) and (6.93) are reduced to:

$$\begin{cases} \dfrac{\partial\widetilde{v}}{\partial\tau} - \dfrac{\partial^2\widetilde{v}}{\partial y^2} - \widetilde{f}(\tau, y) \geqslant 0, \\ \widetilde{v}(\tau, y) \geqslant g(\tau, y). \end{cases} \tag{6.136}$$

There are two cases for (6.136) to consider.

- When $\widetilde{v}(\tau, y) = g(\tau, y)$, the insured chooses to surrender and $\widetilde{v}(\tau, y)$ satisfies:

$$\frac{\partial\widetilde{v}}{\partial\tau} - \frac{\partial^2\widetilde{v}}{\partial y^2} - \widetilde{f}(\tau, y) > 0; \tag{6.137}$$

- When $\widetilde{v}(\tau, y) > g(\tau, y)$, the insured will hold his/her policy and $\widetilde{v}(\tau, y)$ satisfies:

$$\frac{\partial\widetilde{v}}{\partial\tau} - \frac{\partial^2\widetilde{v}}{\partial y^2} - \widetilde{f}(\tau, y) = 0. \tag{6.138}$$

Then the free boundary problem can be written as the following linear complementary problem:

$$\begin{cases} (\dfrac{\partial\widetilde{v}}{\partial\tau} - \dfrac{\partial^2\widetilde{v}}{\partial y^2} - \widetilde{f}(\tau, y))(\widetilde{v}(\tau, y) - g(\tau, y)) = 0, \\ \dfrac{\partial\widetilde{v}}{\partial\tau} - \dfrac{\partial^2\widetilde{v}}{\partial y^2} - \widetilde{f}(\tau, y) \geqslant 0, \quad \widetilde{v}(\tau, y) \geqslant g(\tau, y), \\ \widetilde{v}(0, y) = g(0, y). \end{cases} \tag{6.139}$$

The optimal time of surrender for τ is the time τ as the path $\tau \mapsto (\tau,\, y_\tau)$ hits $\widetilde{\Gamma}$, where $\widetilde{\Gamma}$ is the boundary of the set $\{\widetilde{v}(\tau,y) > g(\tau,y)\}$ in the (τ,y) plane, i.e., $\widetilde{\Gamma}$ is the free boundary of (6.135). It is remarkable to see that free boundaries do not appear in problem (6.139).

Finite difference method is a tool for obtaining numerical solutions to partial differential equations and linear complementary problems. It is very powerful and flexible and, if applied correctly, is capable of generating accurate solutions. We now apply this method to the linear complementary problem. The idea underlying finite difference method is to replace the partial derivatives occurring in partial differential equations by approximation based on Taylor series expansion of functions near the points of interest. First we divide the y-axis into equally spaced nodes with a distance δy apart, and derive the τ-axis into equally spaced nodes with a distance $\delta\tau$ apart. This divides the (τ, y) plane into a mesh, where the mesh points have the form $(m\delta\tau,\, n\delta y)$. We then concern only with the values of $\widetilde{v}(\tau,y)$ at the mesh points $(m\delta\tau,\, n\delta y)$.

We write $\widetilde{v}_n^m = \widetilde{v}(m\delta\tau, n\delta y)$, $\widetilde{f}_n^m = \widetilde{f}(m\delta\tau, n\delta y)$, $g_n^m = g(m\delta\tau, n\delta y)$ and consider the numerical analysis on a bounded domain: $0 \leqslant m \leqslant M,\ N^- \leqslant n \leqslant N^+$, where $M = \dfrac{\frac{1}{2}\sigma^2 T}{\delta\tau}$ and N^-, N^+ are enough negative and positive numbers, respectively. Here we consider the Crank-Nicolson finite difference scheme which is essentially an average of the implicit and explicit methods to approximate the partial derivatives (refer to Lu & Gu et al. (1988)):

$$\frac{\partial\widetilde{v}}{\partial\tau}(\tau+\frac{\delta\tau}{2},y) = \frac{\widetilde{v}_n^{m+1}-\widetilde{v}_n^m}{\delta\tau} + O((\delta\tau)^2), \tag{6.140}$$

$$\begin{aligned}&\frac{\partial^2\widetilde{v}}{\partial y^2}(\tau+\frac{\delta\tau}{2},y)\\ &= \frac{1}{2}(\frac{\widetilde{v}_{n+1}^{m+1}-2\widetilde{v}_n^{m+1}+\widetilde{v}_{n-1}^{m+1}}{(\delta y)^2}) + \frac{1}{2}(\frac{\widetilde{v}_{n+1}^{m}-2\widetilde{v}_n^{m}+\widetilde{v}_{n-1}^{m}}{(\delta y)^2}) + O((\delta y)^2).\end{aligned} \tag{6.141}$$

Ignoring terms $O((\delta\tau)^2)$ and $O((\delta y)^2)$, the inequality $\dfrac{\partial\widetilde{v}}{\partial\tau} - \dfrac{\partial^2\widetilde{v}}{\partial y^2} - \widetilde{f}(\tau,y) \geqslant 0$ is approximated by

$$\widetilde{v}_n^{m+1} - \frac{1}{2}\alpha(\widetilde{v}_{n+1}^{m+1} - 2\widetilde{v}_n^{m+1} + \widetilde{v}_{n-1}^{m+1}) \geqslant \widetilde{v}_n^m + \frac{1}{2}\alpha(\widetilde{v}_{n+1}^{m} - 2\widetilde{v}_n^{m} + \widetilde{v}_{n-1}^{m}) + \delta\tau\cdot\widetilde{f}_n^m, \tag{6.142}$$

where α is given by $\alpha = \dfrac{\delta\tau}{(\delta y)^2}$. It's known that the Crank-Nicolson finite difference method is stable for $\alpha > 0$.

If we define Z_n^m by

$$Z_n^m = \widetilde{v}_n^m + \frac{1}{2}\alpha(\widetilde{v}_{n+1}^m - 2\widetilde{v}_n^m + \widetilde{v}_{n-1}^m) + \delta\tau \cdot \widetilde{f}_n^m,$$

then (6.142) becomes

$$\widetilde{v}_n^{m+1} - \frac{1}{2}\alpha(\widetilde{v}_{n+1}^{m+1} - 2\widetilde{v}_n^{m+1} + \widetilde{v}_{n-1}^{m+1}) \geqslant Z_n^m. \tag{6.143}$$

The condition $\widetilde{v}(\tau, y) - g(\tau, y) \geqslant 0$ is approximated by

$$\widetilde{v}_n^m - g_n^m \geqslant 0, \tag{6.144}$$

and the boundary condition and initial condition are approximated by:

$$\widetilde{v}_{N^-}^m = g_{N^-}^m, \quad \widetilde{v}_{N^+}^m = g_{N^+}^m, \quad \widetilde{v}_n^0 = g_n^0. \tag{6.145}$$

Let $\widetilde{\mathbf{v}}^{\mathbf{m}}$ and $\mathbf{g}^{\mathbf{m}}$ denote the vectors as follows:

$$\widetilde{\mathbf{v}}^{\mathbf{m}} = \begin{pmatrix} \widetilde{v}_{N^-+1}^m \\ \vdots \\ \widetilde{v}_{N^+-1}^m \end{pmatrix}, \quad \mathbf{g}^{\mathbf{m}} = \begin{pmatrix} g_{N^-+1}^m \\ \vdots \\ g_{N^+-1}^m \end{pmatrix}, \tag{6.146}$$

and let the vector $\mathbf{b}^{\mathbf{m}}$ and the matrix $\mathbf{M}$ be given by:

$$\mathbf{b}^{\mathbf{m}} = \begin{pmatrix} Z_{N^-+1}^m \\ \vdots \\ Z_0^m \\ \vdots \\ Z_{N^+-1}^m \end{pmatrix} + \frac{1}{2}\alpha \begin{pmatrix} g_{N^-}^{m+1} \\ 0 \\ \vdots \\ 0 \\ g_{N^+}^{m+1} \end{pmatrix}, \tag{6.147}$$

$$\mathbf{M} = \begin{pmatrix} 1+\alpha & -\frac{1}{2}\alpha & 0 & \cdots & 0 \\ -\frac{1}{2}\alpha & 1+\alpha & -\frac{1}{2}\alpha & & \vdots \\ 0 & -\frac{1}{2}\alpha & \ddots & \ddots & 0 \\ \vdots & & \ddots & \ddots & -\frac{1}{2}\alpha \\ 0 & \cdots & & -\frac{1}{2}\alpha & 1+\alpha \end{pmatrix}. \tag{6.148}$$

Then we can rewrite our approximation (6.143)–(6.145) in the vector-matrix form:

$$\begin{cases} (\mathbf{M}\widetilde{\mathbf{v}}^{\mathbf{m+1}} - \mathbf{b}^{\mathbf{m}})(\widetilde{\mathbf{v}}^{\mathbf{m+1}} - \mathbf{g}^{\mathbf{m+1}}) = 0, \\ \mathbf{M}\widetilde{\mathbf{v}}^{\mathbf{m+1}} - \mathbf{b}^{\mathbf{m}} \geqslant 0, \quad \widetilde{\mathbf{v}}^{\mathbf{m+1}} - \mathbf{g}^{\mathbf{m+1}} \geqslant 0. \end{cases} \tag{6.149}$$

From (6.149) we can see that the vector $\mathbf{b}^{\mathbf{m}}$ contains the information at the time-step $m\delta\tau$ and it can be used to determine the value of $\widetilde{\mathbf{v}}$ at the time-step $(m+1)\delta\tau$. At each time-step $m\delta\tau$ we can calculate the value of the vectors $\mathbf{g}^{\mathbf{m}}$ and $\mathbf{b}^{\mathbf{m}}$ from the values of $\widetilde{\mathbf{v}}^{\mathbf{m}}$ which has already been obtained in the previous steps. In this way we need only to solve the problem (6.149). This problem can be solved by using **Projected SOR method.**

Projected SOR Method

If we solve the problem $\mathbf{M}\widetilde{\mathbf{v}}^{\mathbf{m+1}} = \mathbf{b}^{\mathbf{m}}$ by SOR method, the iterative formulas are (refer to Cao (1996)):

$$\begin{cases} y_n^{m+1,j+1} = \dfrac{1}{1+\alpha}(b_n^m + \dfrac{1}{2}\alpha(\widetilde{v}_{n-1}^{m+1,j+1} + \widetilde{v}_{n+1}^{m+1,j})), \\ \widetilde{v}_n^{m+1,j+1} = \widetilde{v}_n^{m+1,j} + \omega(y_n^{m+1,j+1} - \widetilde{v}_n^{m+1,j}). \end{cases} \tag{6.150}$$

where $\widetilde{v}_n^{m,j}$ is the j-th iteration at the m-th time-step and $\omega > 1$ is the over-correction or over-relaxation parameter.

To satisfy the constraint $\widetilde{\mathbf{v}}^{\mathbf{m+1}} \geqslant \mathbf{g}^{\mathbf{m+1}}$, we simply modify the iterative formula as follows:

$$y_n^{m+1,j+1} = \frac{1}{1+\alpha}(b_n^m + \frac{1}{2}\alpha(\widetilde{v}_{n-1}^{m+1,j+1} + \widetilde{v}_{n+1}^{m+1,j})), \tag{6.151}$$

$$\widetilde{v}_n^{m+1,j+1} = \max\{\widetilde{v}_n^{m+1,j} + \omega(y_n^{m+1,j+1} - \widetilde{v}_n^{m+1,j}),\ g_n^{m+1}\}. \tag{6.152}$$

Thus the projected SOR method is to iterate (on j) between equations (6.151) and (6.152) until the difference $\| \ \widetilde{\mathbf{v}}^{\mathbf{m+1,j+1}} - \widetilde{\mathbf{v}}^{\mathbf{m+1,j}} \ \|$ is small enough. Thus in this way we obtain the numerical solution of the vector problem (6.149).

The Time-stepping Algorithm

Let

$$\widetilde{\mathbf{v}}^{\mathbf{m+1,j}} = \begin{pmatrix} \widetilde{v}_{N^-+1}^{m+1,j} \\ \vdots \\ \widetilde{v}_{N^+-1}^{m+1,j} \end{pmatrix}.$$

Then at the time-step $m+1$, we start with the initial guess $\widetilde{\mathbf{v}}^{\mathbf{m+1,0}}$ to generate $\widetilde{\mathbf{v}}^{\mathbf{m+1,j+1}}$ by using the projected SOR method. When $j \to \infty$, $\widetilde{\mathbf{v}}^{\mathbf{m+1,j}} \to \widetilde{\mathbf{v}}^{\mathbf{m+1}}$. Then the algorithmic steps are as follows:

(1) Given $\widetilde{\mathbf{v}}^{\mathbf{m}}$, calculate the vector $\mathbf{b}^{\mathbf{m}}$ and $\mathbf{g}^{\mathbf{m}}$, using the formula (6.147) and (6.146), respectively;
(2) start with the initial guess $\widetilde{\mathbf{v}}^{\mathbf{m+1,0}} = \max\{\widetilde{\mathbf{v}}^{\mathbf{m}}, \mathbf{g}^{\mathbf{m}}\}$;
(3) first generate $y_n^{m+1,j+1}$ by (6.151) in the increasing n-order, then generate $\widetilde{v}_n^{m+1,j+1}$ by (6.152);
(4) test whether $\| \widetilde{\mathbf{v}}^{\mathbf{m+1,j+1}} - \widetilde{\mathbf{v}}^{\mathbf{m+1,j}} \|$ is smaller than a parameter chosen in advance or not. If it is, then go to the step (5); otherwise, go to the step (3) and continue to iterate;
(5) when $\widetilde{\mathbf{v}}^{\mathbf{m+1,j}}$ has converged to a required level, put $\widetilde{\mathbf{v}}^{\mathbf{m+1}} = \widetilde{\mathbf{v}}^{\mathbf{m+1,j}}$;
(6) return to step (1) to calculate the value of $\widetilde{\mathbf{v}}$ at the next time-step till completed.

In the subsection 6.5.1, we have theoretically analyzed the impact of the parameter appearing in the equation on surrender. In this subsection we analyze the result obtained by the numerical method. We have derived before that the value of the policy satisfies:

$$\begin{cases} \dfrac{\partial v}{\partial t} + rA\dfrac{\partial v}{\partial A} + \dfrac{1}{2}\sigma^2 A^2 \dfrac{\partial^2 v}{\partial A^2} - (r+\mu)v + \mu k A \leqslant 0, \\ v(t,A) \geqslant h(t,A). \end{cases} \tag{6.153}$$

As discussed in Subsection 6.2.2, one of the most difficult parts of the free boundary problem (6.94) is that we do not know where the free boundaries are. However, by converting it to a linear complementary problem, in which the free boundary does not appear, we are still able to solve the problem by the finite difference method without knowing the exact position of the free boundary (refer to Wilmott, Dewynne & Howison (1993)).

Now the main numerical results are listed.

Suppose that $\sigma = 0.4,\ r = 0.05,\ r_G = 0.02,\ k = 0.4,\ T = 30,\ T_0 = 10,\ G = 500$. Then

$$\frac{1}{T-T_0} - (r - r_G) = 0.02, \quad \frac{1}{(1-k)(T-T_0)} = 0.083.$$

Now we give the results obtained by Projected SOR and compare them with the results in subsection 6.5.1:

(Case 1) Let $\mu = 0.01$. This is the Case 1 in subsection 6.5.1. The numerical solution for the value of the policy at time $t = 0$ is shown in Table 6.1, in which A_0 represents the value of the investing account at time 0, v_n represents the value of the policy at time $t = 0$ without surrender options, and v_s represents the value of the policy with surrender options. From the Table 6.1 we can see that v_s is consistent with v_n for any A_0. This means that there is no sense to surrender before maturity date under this situation, i.e., there is no free boundary in the PDE model.

Table 6.1

A_0	v_s	v_n
8.16617	152.93275	152.93275
14.87973	155.79686	155.79686
27.11264	161.99510	161.99510
49.40245	175.04304	175.04304
90.01713	201.74086	201.74086
164.02191	254.91702	254.91702
298.86740	358.33418	358.33418
544.57191	555.50110	555.50110
992.27472	925.60690	925.60690

(Case 2) Let $\mu = 0.04$. This is the Case 2 in Subsection 6.5.1. The numerical solution for the value of the policy at time $t = 0$ is shown in Table 6.2a. It is obvious from Table 6.2a that v_s is larger than v_n. This means that a free boundary does exist under this situation. Furthermore, It is shown by the numerical solution that the free boundary exists when A is relatively small. At every time t, A-axis is divided into two parts: $A < A_f(t)$ and $A > A_f(t)$. The former is the surrender region, the latter is the non-surrender region. The location of the free boundary $A = A_f(t)$ is also obtained by the numerical results (refer to Table 6.2b).

Table 6.2a

A_0	v_s	v_n
8.16617	67.98093	67.98086
14.87973	70.65974	70.65960
27.11264	75.98586	75.98560
49.40245	86.48497	86.48453
90.01713	106.93309	106.93242
164.02191	146.22221	146.22126
298.86740	220.71727	220.71602
544.57191	360.31765	360.31612
992.27472	619.45079	619.44907

Table 6.2b

t	$A = A_f(t)$
24.3	23.83130
24.6	58.09038
24.9	77.71125
25.2	103.85935
25.5	139.07314
26.4	182.72824
27.3	240.08667
28.2	315.44994
29.1	414.46975

(Case 3) Let $\mu = 0.1$. This is the Case 3. From the theoretical analysis it follows that there may exist two free boundaries. In the area $\{(t, A)|Ge^{r_G t} > A\}$ the time period for the free boundary is $(T_0 + \frac{1}{r + \mu - r_G}, T]$ and in the area $\{(t, A)|Ge^{r_G t} < A\}$ the time period for the free boundary is $(T_0 + \frac{1}{\mu} + k(T - T_0), T]$. The numerical solution is shown in Table 6.3a :

Table 6.3a

A_0	v_s	v_n
8.16617	22.21863	22.21861
14.87973	24.75637	24.75633
27.11264	29.52458	29.52450
49.40245	38.48160	38.48146
90.01713	55.25990	55.25964
164.02191	86.54346	86.54304
298.86740	144.55790	144.55727
544.57191	251.58630	251.58543
992.27472	448.18384	448.18275

From Table 6.3a we can see that v_s is still larger than v_n which means that the free boundary exists. By the numerical results, we can also deduce that there are two free boundaries, i.e. the insured will surrender before maturity date, not only when A is relatively small, but also when A is large enough. Namely, A is divided into three parts, $A < A_f^1(t)$, $A_f^1(t) < A < A_f^2(t)$ and $A > A_f^2(t)$. $A < A_f^1(t)$ and $A > A_f^2(t)$ are the surrender region and $A_f^1(t) < A < A_f^2(t)$ is the non-surrender region. The location of the free boundaries can also be seen from the numerical results (refer to Table 6.3b and Table 6.3c).

Table 6.3b

t	$A = A_f^1(t)$
21.6	211.02994
22.5	277.27228
24.6	351.42629
26.7	445.41214
29.1	559.47565

Table 6.3c

t	$A = A_f^2(t)$
28.2	4693.81048
28.5	2552.93766
28.8	2530.06431
29.1	2507.39589
29.4	1840.88185

Comparing the numerical results with the theoretical analysis, we can see that these results by two approaches are quite consistent. Actually, these phenomena that the possibility of surrender increases as μ becomes larger and larger can also be easily understood from the point of view of actuarial mathematics.

6.5.4.2 *Solving Integral Equation (6.131)*

In what follows, we introduce a new approach by means of solving the integral equation (6.131) to get the free boundary.

It turns out from (6.131) and (6.103) that when $A = A_f(t)$,

$$\frac{t - T_0}{T - T_0} G e^{r_G t} = \widetilde{v}(t, A_f(t)) + \int_t^T g(A_f(t), A_f(\tau), t, \tau) d\tau. \tag{6.154}$$

From (6.118), we know the location of the free boundary at the expire date $A_f(T)$. Let

$$t_0 = T, \quad t_1 = T - \delta t, \quad t_2 = T - 2\delta t, \quad \cdots. \tag{6.155}$$

To get $A_f(t_1)$ we use the following approximation:

$$\begin{aligned}&\frac{t_1 - T_0}{T - T_0} G e^{r_G t_1}\\ &= \widetilde{v}(t_1, A_f(t_1)) + \frac{\delta t}{2}(g(A_f(t_1), A_f(T^-), t_1, T) + g(A_f(t_1), A_f(t_1), t_1, t_1).\end{aligned}$$

The above is an algebra equation of $A_f(t_1)$, it is easy to get the solution. Then we can use the similar way to get $A_f(t_2), A_f(t_3), \cdots, A_f(t_{n-1})$. To get $A_f(t_n)$ we use the approximation again as follows:

$$\begin{aligned}
&\frac{t_n - T_0}{T - T_0} G e^{r_G t} \\
&= \widetilde{v}(t_n, A_f(t_n)) + \frac{\delta t}{2}(g(A_f(t_n), A_T^-, t_n, T) + 2g(A_f(t_n), A_f(t_1), t_n, t_1) + \cdots \\
&+ 2g(A_f(t_n), A_f(t_{n-1}), t_n, t_{n-1}) + g(A_f(t_n), A_f(t_n), t_n, t_n)). \qquad (6.156)
\end{aligned}$$

In this way we can get the whole free boundary.

Now we give some numerical results. Suppose $\mu = 0.19$, $\tau = 0.4$, $r_G = 0.1$, $k = 0.9$, $T = 30$, $T_0 = 20, G = 500$, $\delta t = 0.05$. Then

$$\frac{1}{T - T_0} - (r - r_G) < \mu < \frac{1}{(1-k)(T - T_0)}, \qquad (6.157)$$

and

$$\frac{(r + \mu - r_G)(T - T_0) - 1}{\mu k (T - T_0)} < 1, \qquad (6.158)$$

$$A_f(T^-) = \frac{(r + \mu - r_G)(T - T_0) - 1}{\mu k (T - T_0)} G e^{r_G T} = 8222.15. \qquad (6.159)$$

By the method we expressed above we get the free boundary $A = A_f(t)$ (curve L1 in Fig.6.1):

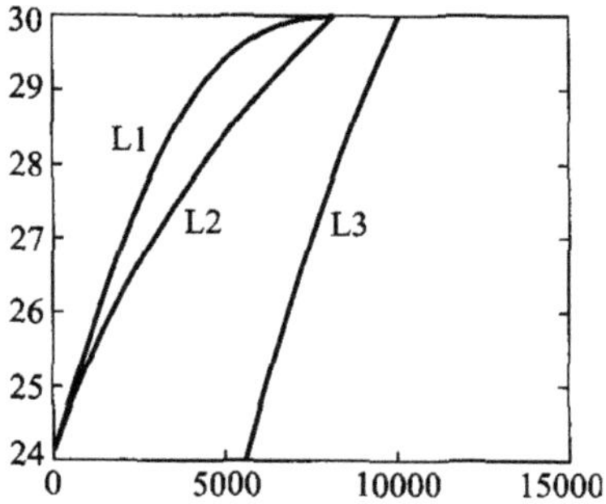

Fig. 6.1 Free boundary when $\frac{(r + \mu - r_G)(T - T_0) - 1}{\mu k (T - T_0)} < 1$.

In Fig 6.1, the vertical axis is time t-axis, and the horizontal axis is A-axis, curve L2 is $A = \frac{(r + \mu - r_G)(T - T_0) - 1}{\mu k (T - T_0)} G e^{r_G t}$, and curve L3 is

$A = Ge^{r_G t}$.

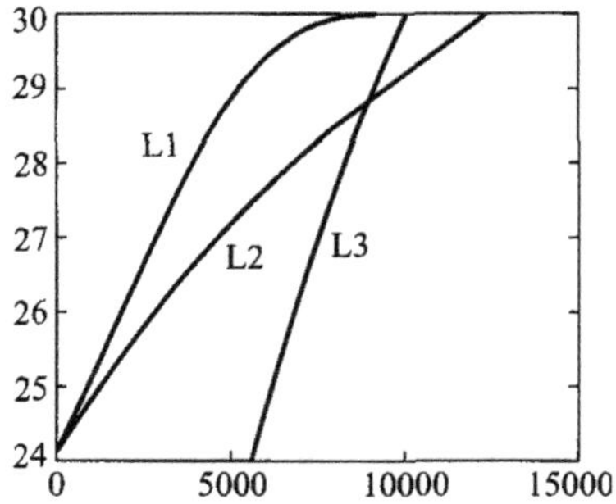

Fig. 6.2 Free boundary when $\frac{(r+\mu-r_G)(T-T_0)-1}{\mu k(T-T_0)} \geqslant 1$.

In Fig 6.2 we choose $k = 0.06$ and the other parameters remain the same as the above. This is Case 2"

$$\frac{(r+\mu-r_G)(T-T_0)-1}{\mu k(T-T_0)} \geqslant 1, \tag{6.160}$$

$$A_f(T^-) = Ge^{r_G T} = 10042.77. \tag{6.161}$$

Curve L1 in Fig 6.2 is the free boundary, and curve L2 and L3 are the same as that in Fig 6.1.

References

Baxter M, Rennie A. (1996). Financial Calculus. Cambridge Univ. Press, Cambridge.

Bowers N L, Gerber H U, Hickman J C, Jones D A, Nesbitt C J. (1997). Actuarial Mathematics, 2nd edition, Society of Actuaries, Itasca, Illinois.

Babbel D, Merrill C. (1998). Economic Valuation Models for Insurers, *North American Actuarial Jounrnal*, **2**, No.3, 1-17.

Black F, Scholes M. (1973). The pricing of options and corperate Liability, *Journal of Political Economy,* **81**, 3, 637-654.

Cao Z H. (1996). Numerical Linear Algebra, Fudan Univ. Press, Shanghai.

Friedman A. (1982). Variational Principles and Free-Boundary Problems, Wiley-Interscience Publication, John Wiley & Sons, New York.

Friedman A, Shen W. (2002). A variational Inequality Approach to Finantial Valuatiopn of Retirement Benefits Based on Saraly, *Finance and Stochastics,* **6**, 273-302.

Grosen A, Jørgensen P L. (2000). Fair valuation of life insurance liabilities: The impact of interest rate guarantees, surrender options, and bonus policies. *Insurance: Mathematics and Economics,* **26**, 37-57.

Gu C H, Li D Q, et al. (1987). Equations of Mathematical Physics, Shanghai Science and Technology Press, Shanghai.

Huo K. (2005). The Futher Discussion of Some New Unit-linked Policies, to appear in *Journal of Fudan University (Natural Science)*, **44**, 3.

Liu Y Q, Long W L, Wang C. (2004). Two Pricing Models of Equity-Linked Policy that Can Be Transformed to Traditional Policy, *Journal of Fudan University (Natural Science)*, **43**, 3, 329-335.

Lu J P, Gu L Z, et al. (1998). Finite-difference Method of Partial Differential Equations, Higher Education Press, Beijing.

Panjer H H. (1998). Financial Economics with Applications to Investment, Insurance and Pensions, The Actuarial Foundation, Schaumburg, Illinois.

Pan S L, Mao D, Liu W Y. (2000). Two Pricing Models of Pension Based on Salary, *Journal of Fudan University (Natural Science)*, **39**,5, 477-481.

Shimko D C. (1992a). Finance in Continuous Time: A Primer, Kolb Publishing Company, Miami, Florida.

Shimko D C. (1992b). The valuation of multiple claim insurance contracts. *Journal of financial and quantitative analysis,* **27**, 2, 229-246.

Shen W X. (2002). Some results on applications of financial economics to pensions and life insurance, Series Contemporary Applied Mathematics (3): Actuarioal Science – Theory and Practice, 253-260, Higher Education Press, Beijing.

Shen W X, Xu H P. (2005). The Valuation of Unit-linked Policies with or without Surrender Options, *Insurance: Mathyematics an Economics* **36** 79-92.

Wang Y M, Xu H P. (2002). Two Pricing Models of Equity-Linked Policies, *Journal of Fudan University (Nature Science)*, **41**, 5, 530-534.

Wei G S. (2005). New Methods to Solve Free Boundary, to appear in*Journal of Fudan University (Natural Science)*, **44**, 3.

Wilmott P, Dewynne J, Howison S. (1993). Option Pricing: Mathematical Models and Computation, Oxford Financial Press, Oxford.

Wolthuis H. (1994). Life Insurance Mathematics: The Markovian Model, Caire Education Series2, Caire, Brussels.

Yu H Y, Li H. (2002). Pricing Analysis of Unit-linked Insurance Product with Surrender Nature, *Journal of Fudan University (Nature Science)* **42** 2, 178-182.

Chapter 7

Exploring on the Risk Profile of China Insurance for Setting Appropriate Solvency Capital Requirement

7.1 Introduction

It seems easy to understand the concept of insurer's solvency and its supervision rules. As an insurer's solvency condition is a dynamic concept and the existed systems of solvency supervision are evolving all the time, the assessment and supervision of insurer's solvency condition is not as easy as it looks like. It has always been a central concern for insurance regulators, policyholders, rating agencies, financial analysts, investors, as well as insurers.

The nature of insurance business determines the need of strict regulation on insurer's promises to policyholders for indemnifying their insured losses. The government and insurance regulators are authorized by laws to protect policyholders' interests and are authorized to charge taxes and regulatory fees from premiums paid by policyholders.

It is also the nature of insurance business that the regulator is not able to guarantee every insurer on the market keeping solvent. But it is expected by the public and insurance customers that the number and the size of insolvent insurers would be controlled on a reasonable and acceptable level under a well-built regulatory system which prudentially controls solvency risk.

An insurer is facing various types of risk during its business process, and each risk may damage the insurer's solvency condition to some extent. There are different classifications of insurer's risks according to the purposes of risk identification and assessment.

Regulators have been making efforts in building effective systems to control insurer's solvency risks. For instance with the priority system (*CARRMEL*) in The Risk-Focused Surveillance Framework of the NAIC

(2004), it tries to control solvency risks through several aspects of *Capital adequacy*; *Asset management*; *Reinsurance*; *Reserves*; *Management competency*; *Earnings* and *Liquidity.* In the Basel II system by the Bank for International Settlements (2003), it is proposed to control financial institution's risk through three pillars: *minimum capital requirement* in Pillar I; *qualitative risk management and supervisory process requirement* in Pillar II and *disclosure requirement* in Pillar III.

Among all the ways in controlling and supervising insurer's solvency risks, capital requirement or capital adequacy for each insurer is a core and basic regulatory tool. The regulator may set a minimum level of required capital for an insurer, and then compare it to the insurer's actual capital and surplus.

This comparison tells the insurer's capital adequacy and then the corresponding regulatory actions may be taken according to the levels of the capital adequacy. This principle could be intuitively and comparatively described by the following example of a speculative currency exchange system in some investment banks.

In such a system, an investor may deposit US$ 2,000 into an investment bank, then he or she will have the right to buy or to sell up to US\$2,000$\times$50 = US$ 100,000 amount of other currency, using the extended fund provided by this investment bank. To avoid losing money from the customer's buying or selling activities, the bank has to design a "solvency supervising system" to save its fund provided to this customer. This system must have two main functions. First, it will monitor and check the balance of the customer's account in real time; second, it has an early warning and a selling-out signal of balance benchmark. Once the balance of the customer's account is below the benchmark, the bank will immediately sell out the foreign currency in the account to keep the balance above the bank's fund.

Similarly, capital requirement of a solvency supervision model in any legislative is to build such a system that has similar two main functions:

(1) Assessing and monitoring the balance of an insurer's actual capital and surplus;

(2) Setting a benchmark or minimum level of capital for early warning and for stopping insurer's business.

To build the first function of assessing an insurer's surplus, it goes both on the valuations of asset and liability sides respectively. The valuations are based on prudential principles/rules usually prescribed by statutory accounting principles for asset values and by actuarial standards for liability values.

To set an appropriate minimum level of capital requirement for an insurer to carry on its business, there has been a generally accepted principle that the calculation of the minimum level should be based on the risks the insurer assumes.

For an emerging insurance market like China, the appropriateness of the minimum level of capital for insurers will have significant effect on the development of insurance industry. A too high level of required capital will largely increase the capital cost for insurers and will reduce the efficiency of the market, particularly in the period of low investment returns on capital market. On the other hand, a too low level will lose the early warning function of the supervision system to those nearly insolvent insurers and may put their policyholders in dangerous situations.

This study will provide an analysis on the risk construction of insurers on China market, for the purpose of setting appropriate minimum capital requirement. It keeps a comparative prospective on the calculations of actual capital and the risk-based minimum capital, as well as the comparison between the required capital approach and other solvency control approaches to insurers' solvency risk.

7.2 Toward a Risk-oriented Approach of Solvency Supervision System for China Insurers

As a full member of International Association of Insurance Supervisors (IAIS), the China Insurance Regulatory Commission (CIRC) has agreed to follow with the IAIS' Insurance Core Principles formally issued on October 2003. In fact, the commissioner of CIRC emphasized the similar principle of insurance supervision and risk control in his speech on the IAIS annual conference held in Jordan on 7 October 2004. CIRC will host the 2006 annual conference of IAIS in Beijing and may further confirm the consistency between Chinese regulatory principles and the IAIS'.

Also in his speech at the 2005 annual conference of China insurance, CIRC commissioner announced the five measures for controlling solvency risks. These include (1) internal control; (2) solvency capital requirement; (3) on site inspection; (4) investment control; and (5) guarantee fund mechanism. CIRC has been making significant progresses on these five aspects since CIRC established in 1998.

7.2.1 *Internal Control*

In the second year of its formation, CIRC issued the Internal Control Directive for Insurance Companies (CIRC [No.131, 1999]) which prescribed the main components of building internal control system for insurers. Although the directive is mainly based on the Guidance Principles of Internal Control for Financial Enterprises issued by the People's Bank of China in 1997, it clearly demonstrates that CIRC has right understanding on insurers' risk control and has established a fundamental preparation to start up. In fact, CIRC is currently to draft the Guidance Principle of Insurance Corporate Governance and to revise the previous version of the internal control directive to be more consistent to risk profile of China insurance, according the commissioner's speech on the 2005 annual conference.

Regarding to insurance corporate governance and risk management, CIRC also issued the Qualification Rules for Senior Managers of Insurance Companies (CIRC [No.2, 2002]) and further revised it (CIRC [No.2, 2003]) in 23 July 2003.

Comparing to the Internal Control for Insurance Undertakings Paper, issued by the Committee of European Insurance and Occupational Pension Fund Supervisors (Madrid Working Group, 2003), and to the Insurance Core Principle 10: Internal Control by IAIS (2003), CIRC's work may be not so integrated but still significant in considering its history and resources.

7.2.2 *Solvency Capital Requirement*

Capital requirements for insurers are divided into two thresholds. The first requirement sets for new insurers to start insurance business on the market. The second is for existing insurers carrying on and expanding their business.

A. Capital requirement for new insurers

China used to set very high capital requirement for insurance business license application. Both the Provisional Insurance Regulation by the People's Bank of China (PBOC) on July 1996 and the Administration of Insurance Companies by the China Insurance Regulatory Commission (CIRC [No.2, 2000]) required RMB 500 millions for new companies to write business over the whole country or RMB 200 millions to write regional business. Another RMB 50 millions should be added for an extra branch from the fourth branch for whole country company and from the third branch for regional company. This requirement had been a very heavy load for new insurers preparing for their business, particularly for foreign insurers on

China market. The main reason is that the basic annual interest rate has been dropping from 10.98% in 1993 to the current 1.98%. The investment return of insurance capital has been also falling down in recent years, 4.3%, 3.14% and 2.68% respectively in years 2001 to 2003.

Considering the low investment return and capital efficiency of insurance companies on China market, CIRC reduced its capital requirement in the revised version of the Administration of Insurance Companies (CIRC 2004) which requires paid-up capital RMB 200 millions for a business license and RMB 50 millions for an extra branch.

B. Capital requirement for existed insurers

It is not as easy as setting minimum capital requirement for issuing new business licenses. For those existing insurers which have been expanding their business with high growth rate (exceeding the annual growth rate of 30%) for many years, it has always been a hard and difficult decision for regulator to make.

Short of technical expertise and practical experiences, Chinese insurance regulator had to borrow capital standards from the other regulatory regimes as a starting point for this hard decision.

In the Chapter 7 of the Provisional Insurance Regulation (PBOC, 1996), minimum capital requirements were set based on a very much simple version of "asset-liability matching" principle for both life and P & C insurers:

Table 7.1 Minimum Capital requirement in Provisional Insurance Regulation (PBOC, 1996)

P & C Insurers		Life insurers	
Minimum capital	Net premium in previous year (P)	Minimum capital	Admitted liability value (L)
$100m$	$\leqslant 200m$	$100m$	$\leqslant 300m$
$\max\{100m, (1/3)P\}$	$200m \sim 3,000m$	$\max\{100m, (1/4)L\}$	$300m \sim 1,000m$
$\max\{1,000m, (1/4)P\}$	$> 3,000m$	$\max\{250m, (1/6)L\}$	$1,000m \sim 3,000m$
		$\max\{500m, (1/8)L\}$	$> 3,000m$

In the Administration of Insurance Companies (CIRC [No.2, 2000]), CIRC simply used the EU solvency directives (the Council Directive 73/239/EEC for P&C insurers and the Council Directive 79/267/EEC for life insurers) for calculating minimum capital requirement. CIRC formally issued the Administration for Solvency Margin and Regulatory Indices

(CIRC[No.1, 2003]) on 24 March 2003, which did not update the minimum capital standards as EU did in the Council Directive 2002/13/EC and the Council Directive 2002/127/EC.

Since the implementation of the CIRC[No.1, 2003], insurers on China market have practiced submitting Solvency Report for 3 years and have collected 4 year's successive solvency data of all the companies writing business on the market. It is the high time for regulators and expertise to judge the current standards and to design and develop more practical and sounded models of capital requirement based on the observed consequences of practicing solvency reports. It is also the main concern of this paper.

7.2.3 *On Site Inspection*

As an emerging market, the insurance regulation in China has long been focusing on business conducts of insurers. As a consequence, on site inspection has been playing a major role for insurance supervisors to check if the insurers comply with the established regulations and rules. CIRC has also developed the Manual of On-site Inspection for Life Insurers in 2004, and a similar Manual for P&C Insurers is coming soon.

7.2.4 *Investment Control*

Investment risk control for insurance companies has always been a central topic for insurance regulation. During the period of 1980—1995, before the Insurance Law was issued, the insurance business of the People's Insurance Company of China (1980), China Pacific (1986), Ping-an Insurance (1988), AIA Shanghai Branch (1992) and Tokyo Marin Shanghai Branch (1993) was under the Provisional Insurance Administration Rules by the State Council of China issued in 1985. As a temporary insurance regulation, it was short of detailed rules and restrictions on the use of insurance capital. The insurers enjoyed relatively flexibility and freedom for investing on various assets. This also resulted in non-performing assets for those companies.

Since the enactment of the China Insurance Law (1995), investment of insurance capital was suddenly and strictly restricted in bank savings and government bonds. This period was followed by a slow and long process of releasing the investment restrictions in the later years.

On October 1999, CIRC issued "Provisional Administration Rules for Insurance Companies Investing in Security Funds" (CIRC[1999], No.206) which allows a certain percent of insurers' capital invested in security funds.

The percentage restriction was further extended in following years.

On February 2004, the State Council of China issued "Several opinions for promoting further opening up, reform and stable development of China capital market". It followed by CIRC and CSRC joint issued the "Provisional Regulations on Administration of Stock Investment of Insurance Institutional Investors" (CIRC [2004, No.12]) which allows a certain percent of insurers' capital invested in stock exchange.

7.2.5 *Guarantee Fund*

When the Financial & Accounting Principles for Insurance was issued by the Ministry of Finance of China (No.8, 1999) , it required that each insurance company should set 1% of its net premium for property, casualty and other short term business up to 6% of total asset value. But the insurance guarantee fund was regarded as long term reserve kept by the insurers until year 2005. On March 12 of 2005, CIRC asked in CIRC[No.26, 2005] that all insurance companies must submit their prepared guarantee funds into the two separate bank accounts for the guarantee funds by life insurers and non-life insurers at the China Industrial & Commercial Bank by the end of year 2005.

It has not been clear about whether CIRC can completely collect the fund from insurers, particularly from large insurers. It must be a hard job.

Obviously, CIRC is working towards the consistency to IAIS' Insurance Core Principles and the three pillar principles of risk management in Basel II. However, the right principles and methodologies can only be effective based on the clear understanding, identifying and assessment of risk construction of insurers and insurance industry of China. It is much harder to explore the risks damaging insurers' solvency than to explore the principles and models used in other regimes.

7.3 Risk Construction of Chinese Insurers

7.3.1 *Risk Concepts*

The concept of risk itself has been so dynamic and uncertain that it provides academics and theorists much space to describe, to define, to debate and then to publish. But the general agreement is that risk is consisted of two components, *loss* and *uncertainty.*

People from different areas may further define what the term of loss means to their purposes. The most popular way is to define *loss* as the deviation between a person's expectation and the actual result.

For the term of *uncertainty*, it seems less controversial in using probability to measure it although the discussion on subjective or objective explanation of probability has been carrying on for centuries among mathematicians.

Hence, we simply agree that risk is consisted of two un-separated components, *loss* and *uncertainty*. If the loss can be identified and quantitatively described by accounting rules or other ways, the risk we are to explore may be described like a random variable and our ideal target is to study for its probability distribution. Since the probability distribution provides complete information that may not be available in practice, what we can usually do is to get some partial but important information such as its mean value, variance and so on about this distribution.

For our purpose of risk studies, we may have to identify all kinds of risks facing an insurer and to investigate co-relations among these risks and the overall risk of the insurer. We also need to study these risks on the industry level and then to investigate the deviations of each index between an individual insurer and the industry.

We will focus our study target on China insurance market, and explore the possible answers to the following questions:

- What are the risks an insurer is facing with?
- What risks are more significant than others in damaging insurer's solvency?
- What kinds of risks can be quantitatively assessed and what are not?

Based on the above investigations, we may further explore the possible answers to the following questions:

- What risks of an insurer should be controlled by setting up capital requirement and what may only be controlled by other ways of risk management?
- How can the co-relation among risk categories be assessed and be used to encourage insurer spread risks?

7.3.2 *Identification of Methodologies*

On emerging market like China, both practitioners and regulators of insurance are under great pressure in building a business operation and management system and an effective regulatory system. They tend to learn experience and knowledge from insurance developed markets. As a consequence, the applicability and fitness of international best practices to domestic market has always been a controversial issue among all interest related parties. There is hardly any clear conclusion on the issue because the market is so dynamic and the risk is evolving so fast every day. On the other hand, the investigations exploring the risk construction of insurers and China insurance industry are valuable contributions to the market.

Risk study is never an easy work, particular referring to that of China insurance. Before we can reach any inductive conclusions to the above questions, we have to judge our study methodologies and understand what possibly conclusions they could provide, based on our available resources.

7.3.2.1 *Normative Studies: International Comparisons and Case Analysis*

The nature of the insurance business determines and constitutes the common structure of risk for insurance. There have been sufficient studies on this topic and have been summarized into textbooks for students and professionals. As an illustration, the risk construction for life and non-life insurers may be intuitively described in Figure-1 and Figure-2.

Figure 1-2 provides a basic structure of insurer's risk construction referring to what risks an insurer is facing. As to the question of what risks are more significant than others, comparative studies between American market, European market and others, along with some case studies, may provide more educative evidences. The following study reports are good examples for this purpose.

- Massey's Report (2001): Insurance Company Failure: the reasons why insurance companies fail.
- Sharma Report (2002): Prudential supervision of insurance undertakings, The Conference of Insurance Supervisory Services of the Member States of the European Union.
- The HIH Royal Commission of Australia (2003): Failure of HIH, Vol. I & II.
- Ronnie Baird etc. (2001), Report of the Financial Services Authority on the review of the Regulation of the Equitable Life Assurance Society from 1 January 1999 to 8 December 2000, which Her Majesty 's Government is submitting as Evidence to the Inquiry Conducted by Lord Penrose.
- The serial failures of Japanese insurers 1997—2002.
- Risk disclosures for the IPOs of China Life Insurance Company, People's Insurance Company of China (PICC), Ping-an Insurance of China.

It also provides a list of insurer's risks as a starting point for further investigation on risks of insurers on China market.

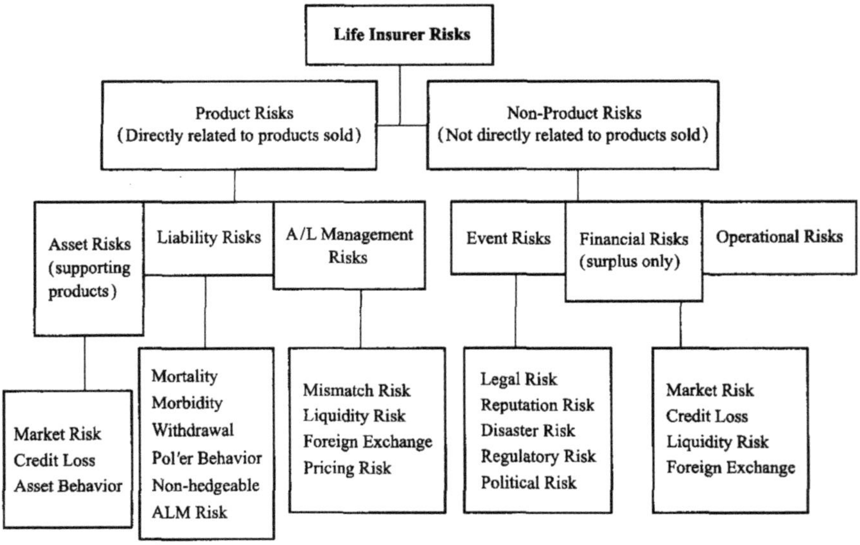

Fig. 7.1 Risk construction of life insurer.

7.3.2.2 *Statistical Analysis*

Insurers writing business on China market are requested to submit audited financial reports (going concern basis) and audited solvency reports (breaking up basis) to CIRC annually and non-audited report quarterly. These reports provide a substantial database for doing statistical analysis on the risks listed through international comparative studies. From year 2004, CIRC has been trying to do a intensive analysis and to summarize a survey about financial condition and solvency of overall industry and some selected individual companies based on their submitted annual and seasonal reports.

The statistical analysis on financial ratios, along with the international comparisons, may provide good views on quantitative risks of insurers. The auditors' managerial opinions attached with financial and solvency reports also provide suggestive views on qualitative risks of insurers.

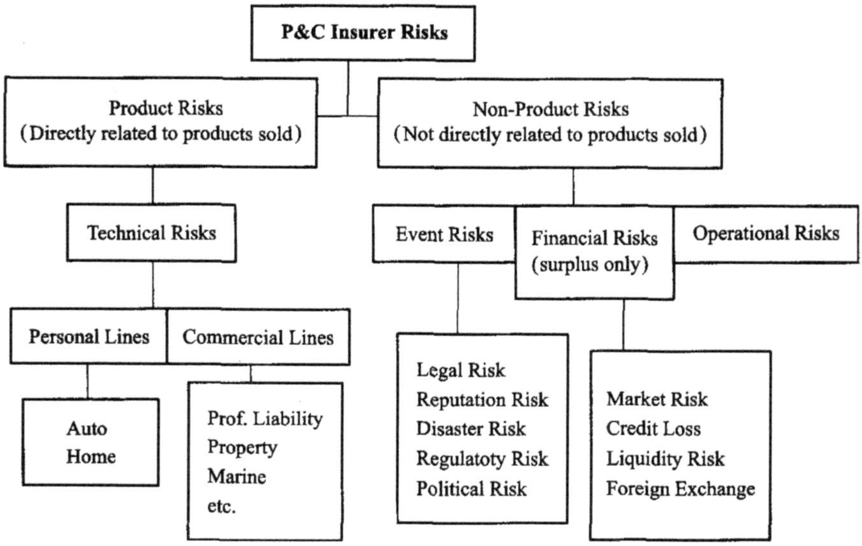

Fig. 7.2 Risk construction of P & C insurer.

7.3.2.3 *Field Study and Cases Analysis on China Insurers*

Statistical and financial analysis can definitely provide substantial evidences for identifying risks of insurers on China market. However, financial and solvency reports submitted by insurers are only summarized data that may not be sufficient to identify and assess some specific risks of insurers. For example of high receivable premium risk, it has long been heard that this is a serious issue for P & C insurers in China. However, it looks not so serious a issue according to financial reports. For the top three P & C insurers (simply named as Company A, Company B and Company C), the reported rates of receivable premium in years 2002 and 2003 are as follows:

Table 7.2 Receivable premium of the 3 large P&C companies (CIRC Statistics 2004)

Company	Rate of receivable premium (%) 2002	2003
A	3.93	4.07
B	1.11	1.77
C	6.55	6.16

The number looks pretty low if compared to same index of some small companies on the market. For instance of a foreign branch of P&C company, the receivable premium rates were 19% and 26% respectively in years 2002 and 2003. The three big companies have more than 90% of the market share. The very low rates of receivable premium may contain a big risk if the figures from their solvency reports are with big foams.

To further investigate the issue, field study and case analysis on some major business lines and in some branches of these companies are necessary. Study groups consisting of supervisors, industry people and academics have been organized by CIRC for various specific study issues. Except for receivable premium, other issues include commission rate, policy renewal rate, and so on. These studies help to build a clear profile of risks.

7.3.2.4 *Combined Approach*

There are many methods we can choose to identify and assess risks. Individual method may be used for individual and specific risk. But for our final target of setting minimum capital requirement to control solvency risk, individual approach may not be able to capture the dynamic and comprehensive profile of insurers' risks and the assessment. Instead, we have to combine the above methods together for our purpose. Our currently working approach may be simply summarized in four steps:

Step 1: study on other people's works (international best practices) like those listed examples in (1), and then summarise a list of various risks damaging insurer's solvency.

Step 2: compared to China market and based on finance and solvency reports and other available data of insurers, use statistical analysis on some significant risks such as reserving risk and other risk indicators.

Step 3: field studies by study group or individuals are carried out for further identifying specific risks selected after step 2.

Step 4: parallel to step 3, case studies on individual issues are recommended to our graduate students as summer and winter vacation assignments. Most of them provide good work after spending days in the local insurance branches in their hometowns.

7.3.3 *Keeping Up an Overall and Historical View on the Evolution of Risk Profile of China Insurance*

Considering the dynamic nature of risk, it is necessary to have a clear picture of the evolving process of risks facing insurers. It is actually a vertical and historical view of risk construction of China insurance, and it may greatly enhance the effect in understanding the risks through other horizontal views in the above approaches.

Investigators taking this prospective may build this picture of risk profile with their own views. What important is that the evidences used to support their views should be concrete and substantial. In the following, we divide China insurance into three periods and then highlight the main characteristics in each period, along with possible and necessary supportive evidences. For the length of text, however, we present a brief summary here only.

7.3.3.1 *Period 1: 1980 — 1995*

China was experimenting the state-owned commercial insurance in this period without a formal issued Insurance Act. The People's Insurance Company of China was a state-owned, writing composite business from 1980 and almost without any market competition, although China Pacific and Ping-an insurance were formed with state owned capital in 1986 and 1988 respectively. The AIA Shanghai Branch and Tokyo Marine Shanghai Branch were introduced as windows to look at foreign insurance in year 1992 and 1993.

The typical problem in this period is the non-performing asset produced by wrong investment strategy and mismanagement. This is parallel to the similar issue of the four big state-owned commercial banks of China. As to the risks involved, it may mean the influence on the operations in later years and later periods. The heavy amount of non-performing assets was separated from China P&C Insurance Company and China Life Insurance Company by the state-owned group companies for the purpose of their IPOs in Hong Kong and New York stock exchange.

For example of China P&C Insurance Company, by its IPO disclosure document, the stock company was separated from the holding company from the valuation date of 30 September 2002. The holding company still retained net asset value of RMB 3,749 million, most of assets were actually non-performing. The stock company was separated with the net value of RMB 10.271 billions of new business related assets. The comparison of these two numbers may, in some sense, tell the ratio of non-performing assets.

7.3.3.2 *Period 2: 1995 — End of 2003*

The enactment of the Insurance Law (1995) greatly promoted the concept and principles of commercial insurance in China. The gradually opening up of insurance market and particularly the WTO agreement signed on November 1999 steered up the fast growing of insurance business. The average annual growth rate during this period is over 30%.

Comparing to growth of asset size, the growth of capital to support the assets was relatively slow. According to a report by Standard & Poor published in 2003, China insurance was short of capital of RMB 15 to 20 billions for life insurance and RMB 5 to 10 billions for P&C insurance by end of year 2002.

Under the Insurance Law (1995) and CIRC's Administration of Insurance Companies (2002), the regulation was relatively very strict. Products pricing, clauses and application procedures are completely controlled by the regulator. The investment of insurance fund was also strictly restricted mainly on bank deposits and bonds.

Before 1999, most life insurers sold annuity and other life products with fixed interest rate as follows:

Table 7.3 Sources: China Insurance Annual Statistics, 2000

Year	1988	1997	1998	1999
Fixed rate for Life products	8.8%	7.5%–8.8%	6.5%–5%	2.5%

Those guaranteed rates were made referring to the basic interest rate that time, but the rates kept dropping since then, as the recorded table shown below:

Table 7.4 Annual interest rate adjusted (Source: China Finance Annual Statistics 2002)

Adjusted date	05/01/96	08/23/96	10/23/97	07/01/98	12/07/98	06/09/99	02/21/02
rate(%)	7.47	5.67	5.22	4.77	3.78	2.25	1.98

As a consequence, huge amount of interest gap losses was reported from life insurance industry. According to the speech of the CIRC commissioner at the 2003 Annual conference of China Insurance, the loss was about RMB 50 billion by the end year 2002. This number would be increasing in the following years as the long-term nature of those products sold.

For an individual example of China Life, it disclosed this in the IPO document (pp. 179-180) as follows:

Owners' equity of our predecessor, China Life Insurance (Group) Company, was a deficit of RMB 176,353 million (US$21,305 million) as of June 30, 2003 and a deficit of RMB 175,463 million (US$21,197 million) as of December 31, 2002. The net losses incurred by our predecessor were RMB 714 million (US$86 million) for the six months ended June 30, 2003 and RMB 6,990 million, RMB 3,295 million and RMB 2,250 million (US$272 million) for 2000, 2001 and 2002, respectively. These losses were attributable to losses incurred by our predecessor on policies retained by CLIC in the restructuring, which has offset the profitability of the policies transferred to us. On a pro forma basis after giving effect to the restructuring, our net profit was RMB 3,128 million (US$378 million) for the six months ended June 30, 2003 and RMB 4,524 million (US$547 million) in 2002.

7.3.3.3 *Period 3: 2004 — Near Future*

It seems that China insurance has been entering a hard period by the end of year 2004. The overall picture looks like a very thin sandwich: the insurance is in the middle of two weak sides of underwriting and investment profits. This picture might be influenced by the following elements.

On underwriting side, the deregulation of product pricing and premium rating started from motor insurance from year 2003 (e.g. CIRC[No.87, 2002]) which released the highly controlled premium rating in such a short preparation period (experimented in Guangdong province in 2002). Experience has shown that sudden deregulation of pricing and premium rating would stimulate price competition and add cost to insurers at least in a few years. Another reason contributing to insurers cost is the sudden entry of new insurers in a short period. The following events joint together may composes a typical story referring to the issue.

In July 2004, for instance, CIRC issued 18 new business licenses (8 life, 7 P&C and 3 Health). One direct consequence is that those new insurers were hiring senior managers and technical professionals from other insurers with much higher payments.

November 2004, Pacific-Aetna Life Insurance held a special press conference in Shanghai and criticized and accused Citiinsurance of malicious competition. The later was just licensed to prepare writing life insurance business in China and then had just successfully hired a group of experienced managers and professionals from the Pacific-Aetna Life Insurance

Company, including the general manager of marketing, general manager and most technicians of the IT department and others from Pacific-Aetna Life Insurance. This unusual movement seriously damaged the business of Pacific-Aetna Life Insurance.

In China Pacific P & C, a sister company of Pacific-Aetna Life Insurance, the assistant general manager and immediate past general manager of Motor Insurance Department, the general manager of product development, the responsible actuary and others left China Pacific P&C successively within half year of that period.

Insurance experience shows that if the business keeps stable growing like P &C business in recent years, the added cost may be covered for some time by the advantages of non strict accounting and actuarial standards. If the business growth shows a relatively sudden slow, the cost and loss will significantly show high. For example of life insurance of China, the premium increased only 7.2% percent from year 2003 to 2004 but the payment and expenses showed significant increases.

Table 7.5 Between premium and payments (CIRC Statistics 2003—2004, RMB 0000 from CIRC web)

	Premium	Payment	Expenses (with P&C)
2003	30,109,911.83	3,646,954.43	3,612,183.63
2004	32,282,490.91	4,369,177.19	4,358,195.90
Increase rate	7.2%	19.8%	20.6%

On investment side, the suddenly added capital by the IPO and other strategic investors was huge. The three companies financed capital by IPO at Hong Kong and New York was about US$ 5 billions, for instance. However, the interest rate and investment have been keeping low and the regulation and management on foreign currency capital has not been clearly made. In year 2004, the investment return of China insurance industry has been the worst ever since. Although the industry average rate has not reported so far, the investment return in the first half year 2004 was in the P&C industry 0.02%, China Life 2.7% and Ping-an insurance 3.2%.

It seems that the current return of investment is unbearable by insurers for long.

7.3.4 *Risk Characteristics and Proposed Principles for Solvency Capital Requirement*

7.3.4.1 *Main Characteristics of Risk Profile*

Based on the analysis in Sections 3 and 4, we conclude a dynamic and evolving risk profile of China insurance. This profile may be described with two main characteristics of the three historical periods and the "three worlds map" of market structure.

A. Three historical periods of risk evolvement

With the classification of the three periods, it helps to look forward the risk of China insurance, with well understanding of its logical links in the past. In the current period, the most significant risks are investment risk for life insurers mainly, underwriting risks caused by premium rating deregulation for non-life insurers mainly, and regulatory risk (even risk) for the whole industry.

B. The "three worlds map"

The first world companies include the market dominant insurers of China Life Insurance Company on life side and the China P & C Insurance Company on non-life side (China Reinsurance Company and other reinsurance companies are not considered in this report).

The second world companies include two medium size insurers of Ping-an Insurance and China Pacific Insurance groups.

The third world companies consist of other small, new and developing companies.

Simply, China insurance market consists of three companies (worlds): large, medium and small ones. These three groups of companies are currently facing different significance of risk and challenges, which are jointly forming the special characteristic of risk profile of China insurance.

The "three worlds map" of risk profile is also a big challenge for insurance regulator in setting up solvency supervision standards including minimum capital requirement.

a. The first world companies have been released from capital shortage since their IPOs in Hong Kong and New York. Instead, they are facing with the serious challenge of capital return and efficiency. As compensation, both companies have been emphasizing underwriting profit and management quality. Except for investment, they are facing less risk than others.

b. The second world companies are relatively similar to the market dominant companies on the issue of capital return and efficiency, with much less effect on size. Not only on size of market share, they are also in the middle of both the advantages and disadvantages on the issues of corporate governance, internal control and management, business underwriting and capital investment. Jointly considering with investment risk, they are facing least risk than the first and the third world companies.

c. The third world companies are either just entering the market or expanding their market shares taking the opportunity that the first and the second world began to concern business profit and the regulator began to deregulate premium and product clauses. Most new companies are injected with private capital and the owners may be with very successful experience on capital investment but are with little insurance knowledge. Except for historical burden like non-performing asset and interest gap loss, the third world companies have hardly any advantages to compete to the above two worlds companies. They may have to pay more acquisition cost to get business than the other two worlds companies. Overall, they are facing more significant risk than the above two world companies.

The two main characteristics jointly show that China insurance has been entering a high-risk period, both on investment, on underwriting and on corporate governance, as well as on insurance regulation. If the regulator misunderstands the true risk profile of China insurance and makes wrong regulatory decisions, significant risks may be expanded and new risks may be accumulated in a short period.

7.3.4.2 *Guiding Principles for Setting Capital Requirement*

For purpose of controlling solvency risk and its supervision policies referring to the current and evolving risk profile of China insurance, we may emphasis on the following two points:

(i) Referring to the three pillar principle of risk management and comparing to the risk profile between China insurance and other matured markets, China may need to build a risk management system with the same emphasis on each pillar of risk management, not only depends on capital requirement and not expects to require all three world companies with one set of simple standards.

(ii) Although capital requirement is a core component of solvency risk control system, it is an evolving process consistent to the evolving risk profile of China insurance. It should avoid sudden changes of requirement rules like the change in the Provisional Insurance Regulation (PBOC 1996) and in the Administration of Insurance Companies (CIRC [No.2, 2000]).

It should avoid unpractical expectation for charging insurer with capital requirement on every risk and with one building model.

We suggest the regulator to start from improving the current minimum solvency margin model and to cover more significant quantitative risks step by step. Meanwhile, the regulator may develop risk management guidelines and encourage insurers to build their internal risk management systems to reduce their statutory capital requirement and to increase capital investment freedom.

References

Basel Committee on Banking Supervision: The New Basel Capital Accord, July 2003.

National Association of Insurance Commissioners (NAIC): Risk-Focused Surveillance Framework, June 2004.

International Association of Insurance Supervisors (IAIS, 2003): Insurance Core Principles and Methodology.

Committee of European Insurance and Occupational Pensions Supervisors (CEIOPS, 2003): Internal Control for Insurance Undertakings, by the Madrid Working Group.

China Insurance Regulatory Commission (CIRC): Collection of Insurance Regulation & Rules 2000—2004.

Asian Development Bank (2003): People's Republic of China Strengthening the Insurance Industry Regulatory and Supervising System.

Massey's Report (2001): Insurance Company Failure: the reasons why insurance companies fail, by A.M. Best

Sharma Report (2002): Prudential supervision of insurance undertakings, The Conference of Insurance Supervisory Services of the Member States of the European Union.

The HIH Royal Commission of Australia (2003): Failure of HIH, Vol. I & II.

Ronnie B, et al. (2001). Report of the Financial Services Authority on the review of the Regulation of the Equitable Life Assurance Society from 1 January 1999 to 8 December 2000, which Her Majesty's Government is submitting as Evidence to the Inquiry Conducted by Lord Penrose.

Index

www.ingramcontent.com/pod-product-compliance
Ingram Content Group UK Ltd.
Pitfield, Milton Keynes, MK11 3LW, UK
UKHW020358150926
8624IPUK00004B/219

9 789812 565051